Living and Working in

Germany

A Survival Handbook

Edited by
Dan Finlay

SURVIVAL BOOKS • LONDON • ENGLAND

First published 2000
Second Edition 2003

Survival Books Limited, 1st Floor,
60 St James's Street, London SW1A 1ZN, United Kingdom
☎ +44 (0)20-7493 4244, 🖷 +44 (0)20-7491 0605
✉ info@survivalbooks.net
💻 www.survivalbooks.net
To order books, please refer to page 472.

British Library Cataloguing in Publication Data.
A CIP record for this book is available
from the British Library.
ISBN 1 901130 57 6

Printed and bound in Finland by WS Bookwell Ltd

ACKNOWLEDGEMENTS

My sincere thanks to all those who contributed to the successful publication of the second edition of this book, in particular Kathryn Dingle of Deutsche Bahn, Dr. Friedrich Lampe, Jürgen Ebert of the Postbank, and Joe and Kerry Laredo (revising, proof-reading and desktop publishing). Also a special mention to the many people who assisted with the first edition – written by Nick Daws – including Bev Laflamme, Iva Pearlstein, Norman and Su Griffiths, Ralph Lohmann, Alf B. Meier and Roberta Beach Jacobson. I must also express thanks to the many people who took the trouble to read and comment on the draft versions, including Dave Thomas, Anita and Joerg Epple, and Karen Verheul. Also a special thank you to Jim Watson for the superb cover, illustrations, cartoons and maps.

OTHER TITLES BY SURVIVAL BOOKS

Living and Working Series

Abroad; America; Australia;
Britain; Canada; France;
the Gulf States & Saudi Arabia;
Holland, Belgium &
Luxembourg; Ireland; Italy;
London; New Zealand; Spain;
Switzerland

Buying a Home Series

Abroad; Britain; Florida;
France; Greece & Cyprus;
Ireland; Italy;
Portugal; Spain

Other Titles

The Alien's Guide to Britain;
The Alien's Guide to France;
The Best Places to Live
in France;
The Best Places to Live
in Spain;
How to Avoid Holiday &
Travel Disasters;
Retiring Abroad;
Rioja and its Wines;
The Wines of Spain

Order forms are on page 472.

What Readers & Reviewers

When you buy a model plane for your child, a video recorder, or some new computer gizmo, you get with it a leaflet or booklet pleading 'Read Me First', or bearing large friendly letters or bold type saying 'IMPORTANT – follow the instructions carefully'. This book should be similarly supplied to all those entering France with anything more durable than a 5-day return ticket. It is worth reading even if you are just visiting briefly, or if you have lived here for years and feel totally knowledgeable and secure. But if you need to find out how France works then it is indispensable. Native French people probably have a less thorough understanding of how their country functions. – Where it is most essential, the book is most up to the minute.

LIVING FRANCE

Rarely has a 'survival guide' contained such useful advice. This book dispels doubts for first-time travellers, yet is also useful for seasoned globetrotters – In a word, if you're planning to move to the USA or go there for a long-term stay, then buy this book both for general reading and as a ready-reference.

AMERICAN CITIZENS ABROAD

It is everything you always wanted to ask but didn't for fear of the contemptuous put down – The best English-language guide – Its pages are stuffed with practical information on everyday subjects and are designed to complement the traditional guidebook.

SWISS NEWS

A complete revelation to me – I found it both enlightening and interesting, not to mention amusing.

CAROLE CLARK

Let's say it at once. David Hampshire's *Living and Working in France* is the best handbook ever produced for visitors and foreign residents in this country; indeed, my discussion with locals showed that it has much to teach even those born and bred in l'Hexagone. – It is Hampshire's meticulous detail which lifts his work way beyond the range of other books with similar titles. Often you think of a supplementary question and search for the answer in vain. With Hampshire this is rarely the case. – He writes with great clarity (and gives French equivalents of all key terms), a touch of humour and a ready eye for the odd (and often illuminating) fact. – This book is absolutely indispensable.

THE RIVIERA REPORTER

A mine of information – I may have avoided some embarrassments and frights if I had read it prior to my first Swiss encounters – Deserves an honoured place on any newcomer's bookshelf.

ENGLISH TEACHERS ASSOCIATION, SWITZERLAND

HAVE SAID ABOUT SURVIVAL BOOKS

What a great work, wealth of useful information, well-balanced wording and accuracy in details. My compliments!

THOMAS MÜLLER

This handbook has all the practical information one needs to set up home in the UK – The sheer volume of information is almost daunting – Highly recommended for anyone moving to the UK.

AMERICAN CITIZENS ABROAD

A very good book which has answered so many questions and even some I hadn't thought of – I would certainly recommend it.

BRIAN FAIRMAN

We would like to congratulate you on this work: it is really super! We hand it out to our expatriates and they read it with great interest and pleasure.

ICI (SWITZERLAND) AG

Covers just about all the things you want to know on the subject – In answer to the desert island question about the one how-to book on France, this book would be it – Almost 500 pages of solid accurate reading – This book is about enjoyment as much as survival.

THE RECORDER

It's so funny – I love it and definitely need a copy of my own – Thanks very much for having written such a humorous and helpful book.

HEIDI GUILIANI

A must for all foreigners coming to Switzerland.

ANTOINETTE O'DONOGHUE

A comprehensive guide to all things French, written in a highly readable and amusing style, for anyone planning to live, work or retire in France.

THE TIMES

A concise, thorough account of the DOs and DON'Ts for a foreigner in Switzerland – Crammed with useful information and lightened with humorous quips which make the facts more readable.

AMERICAN CITIZENS ABROAD

Covers every conceivable question that may be asked concerning everyday life – I know of no other book that could take the place of this one.

FRANCE IN PRINT

Hats off to *Living and Working in Switzerland*!

RONNIE ALMEIDA

CONTENTS

12. HEALTH   267

13. INSURANCE 283

14. FINANCE 303

15. LEISURE 331

18. ODDS & ENDS 397

19. THE GERMANS 421

20. MOVING OR LEAVING GERMANY 429

APPENDICES 435

INDEX 463

ORDER FORMS 472

IMPORTANT NOTE

Germany is a diverse country with many faces, a variety of ethnic groups, religions and customs, and continuously changing rules, regulations (particularly regarding business, social security and taxes), interest rates and prices. A change of government in Germany can have far-reaching effects on many important aspects of life. **I cannot recommend too strongly that you check with an official and reliable source (not always the same) before making any major decisions, or taking an irreversible course of action. However, don't believe everything you're told or read – even, dare I say it, herein!**

Useful addresses and references to other sources of information have been included in all chapters and in **Appendices A to C** to help you obtain further information and verify details with official sources. Important points have been emphasised, **in bold print**, some of which it would be expensive, or even dangerous, to disregard. **Ignore them at your peril or cost.** Unless specifically stated, the reference to any company, organisation or product in this book doesn't constitute an endorsement or recommendation.

EDITOR'S NOTES

- Frequent references are made in this book to the European Union (EU), which comprises Austria, Belgium, Denmark, Finland, France, Germany, Greece, Ireland, Italy, Luxembourg, the Netherlands, Portugal, Spain, Sweden and the United Kingdom, and the European Economic Area (EEA), which includes the EU countries plus Iceland, Liechtenstein and Norway.

- Times are shown using am for before noon and pm for after noon (see also **Time Difference** on page 417).

- Prices should be taken as estimates only, though they were mostly correct at the time of publication. Unless otherwise stated, all prices quoted usually include VAT (*Mehrwertsteuer/MwSt* or *Umsatzsteuer/USt*) at 7 or 16 per cent.

- His/he/him also means her/she/her (please forgive me ladies). This is done to make life easier for both the reader and (in particular) the author, and isn't intended to be sexist.

- The German translation of many key words and phrases is shown in brackets in *italics*.

- All references to Frankfurt are to Frankfurt-am-Main and not Frankfurt-an-der-Oder.

- Warnings and important points are shown in **bold** type.

- The following symbols are used in this book: ☎ (telephone), 🖨 (fax), 💻 (Internet) and ✉ (e-mail).

- Lists of **Useful Addresses**, **Further Reading** and **Useful Websites** are contained in **Appendices A** to **C** respectively.

- For those unfamiliar with the metric system of weights and measures, imperial conversion tables are included in **Appendix D**.

- A map of Germany showing the states (*Länder*) is included in **Appendix E**.

INTRODUCTION

Whether you're already living or working in Germany or just thinking about it – this is **THE BOOK** for you. Forget about all those glossy guidebooks, excellent though they are for tourists; this amazing book was written particularly with you in mind and is worth its weight in *Geld*. *Living and Working in Germany* is designed to meet the needs of anyone wishing to know the essentials of German life, including immigrants, temporary workers, businessmen, students, retirees, long-stay tourists, holiday home owners and even extra-terrestrials. However long your intended stay in Germany, you will find the information contained in this book invaluable.

General information isn't difficult to find in Germany (provided you speak German) and a multitude of books are published on every conceivable subject. However, reliable and up-to-date information in English specifically intended for foreigners living and working in Germany isn't so easy to find, least of all in one volume. Our aim in publishing this book was to help fill this void and provide the comprehensive **practical** information necessary for a relatively trouble-free life.

You may have visited Germany as a tourist, but living and working there's a different matter altogether. Adjusting to a different environment and culture and making a home in any foreign country can be a traumatic and stressful experience, and Germany is no exception. You need to adapt to new customs and traditions and discover the German way of doing things – for example, finding a home, paying bills and obtaining insurance. For most foreigners in Germany, overcoming the everyday obstacles of life has previously been a case of pot luck. **But no more!** With a copy of *Living and Working in Germany* to hand you will have a wealth of information at your fingertips. Information derived from a variety of sources, both official and unofficial, not least the hard-won personal experiences of the editor, his family, friends, colleagues and acquaintances.

Living and Working in Germany is a comprehensive handbook on a wide range of everyday subjects and represents the most up-to-date source of general information available to foreigners in Germany. It isn't, however, simply a monologue of dry facts and figures, but a practical and entertaining look at life in Germany.

Adapting to life in a new country is a continuous process and, although this book will help reduce your beginner's phase and minimise the frustrations, it doesn't contain all the answers (most of us don't even know the right questions to ask!). What it will do is help you make informed decisions and calculated judgements, instead of uneducated guesses and costly mistakes. **Most important, it will help save you time, trouble and money, and repay your investment many times over.**

Although you may find some of the information a bit daunting, don't be discouraged. Most problems occur only once and fade into insignificance after a short time (as you face the next half a dozen!). The majority of foreigners in Germany would agree that, all things considered, they enjoy living there. A period spent in Germany is a wonderful way to enrich your life, broaden your horizons and hopefully please your bank manager. I trust that this book will help you to avoid the pitfalls of life in Germany and smooth your way to a happy and rewarding future in your new home.

Viel Glück!

1.

FINDING A JOB

German workers enjoy some of the highest salaries in the world, with generous benefits and job protection mandated by the state. Finding a job in Germany, however, is anything but plain sailing, as the high unemployment figures (currently 11.3 per cent) suggest. However, if you're well qualified and experienced, and have lots of perseverance and at least some luck, you will find that openings in various sectors do exist. At the bottom end of the scale are jobs that most Germans aren't willing to do (being unemployed in Germany is often a considerably more comfortable proposition than being fully employed on a low wage in Britain or the US), although the number of foreigners willing to do them has increased. If you're a national of a European Union (EU) country, you will (at least theoretically) be on an equal footing with the locals in the job hunt. Americans and other nationalities without the automatic right to work in Germany must meet visa and work permit requirements (see **Chapter 3**) in order for a prospective employer to justify hiring them in preference to an EU national.

Employment Prospects

To find employment in Germany takes special qualifications or experience in a field or profession where demand matches or exceeds supply. Unless you're intending to seek out a job in the upper echelons of a multi-national organisation, one which has connections with an English-speaking country, certain scientific or academic areas in which English is the *lingua franca*, or in a sector such as IT in which demand greatly exceeds supply, it's essential to have at least a good working knowledge of German. Fluency is always highly desirable. Most Germans study English in school and, although only a small proportion are fluent, enough are sufficiently competent to make a native command of English less of an automatic advantage in the job market unless you have complementary skills or experience.

The free public education system is geared toward producing highly skilled workers through on-the-job training and apprenticeship programmes as well as a large academic elite. By the time a young German has earned his qualifications, he has considerable first-hand experience of the profession or trade he's entering. Surprisingly, however, there are still some areas where training programmes haven't kept up with demand and, if you have experience in one of these, your prospects of finding a job may be good, even with no German initially.

Information technology (IT) is the principal area of demand. The Government stated its readiness in August 2000 to issue up to 20,000 'green cards' to foreign experts, enabling them to work for five years in the country, but so far only 5,000 have been taken up, mostly by young products of India's thrusting and rapidly expanding IT sector, who usually have no prior knowledge of German. In fact, the Bundesverband der Deutschen Industrie (BDI), the German employers' organisation, has stated that the number of foreigners required with qualifications in this and related fields is more like 150,000 and has been lobbying the government to permit more immigrants to meet the demand. The government, nervous about popular reaction to encouraging more immigration at a time of severe unemployment, however economically advantageous has rather fallen between two stools. The green cards are therefore hedged with conditions, one of which is that those who obtain them may not bring their families with them, which explains why the take-up has been low. However, given that market forces usually prevail in the long term, it's likely that Germany will be forced to offer green cards under less restrictive conditions in the future.

Other areas where there's currently a shortage of qualified staff, especially engineers, are the automobile, chemical and machine tool industries.

Although most opportunities are in western Germany, resolute job seekers with much-needed management and organisational skills, and the patience to effect lasting change, may find opportunities in eastern areas.

In order to find a job in Germany, it's important to have a positive reason for living and working there – being fed up with your boss or your job isn't the best motive for moving there. It helps if you can show that you have friends or family in the area, or to experience of living or working abroad. Having a genuineinterest in German culture or specific aspects of German society can give you added credibility in the job search, as well as greatly enhancing your stay in the country.

Unemployment

Like much of the rest of Europe, Germany continues to struggle with a traditionally high rate of unemployment. In March 2003, it reached 11.3 per cent – its highest rate for five years. This figure masks a sharp disparity between the regions of the former Federal Republic and those of the erstwhile German Democratic Republic or (*Deutsche Demokratische Republik/DDR*), now called the *neue Länder*, where the unemployment rate is over double that in the former West Germany. In the old DDR, everyone had the right to a job by constitutional decree, so most of the state-run companies were vastly overstaffed. Unemployment soared in the wake of the closure, reorganisation and privatisation of these former state-owned industries, and the entire population had to be re-educated in free enterprise, market economics and western-style management. Despite the strides made in the east since reunification, there's still a lingering sense of 'foreignness' between the *Ossies* (residents of the former East Germany) and the *Wessies* (those from the former West Germany) which is likely to persist for some time.

In both parts of Germany, massive over-production of qualified people in many occupations adds to unemployment. There simply aren't enough new jobs created each year to absorb the influx of highly-trained, highly-skilled workers into the labour force. Official statistics show that more than half a million foreigners are already in the ranks of the unemployed.

Economy

Germany is one of the world's wealthiest countries, despite currently enduring its worst economic problems for almost half a century, with one of the highest per capita gross domestic products (GDPs) in the EU at $26,600, its place as the second biggest exporter in the world after the US is secure, and its inflation (1.2 per cent in the 12 months to March 2003) invariably among the lowest in the industrialised countries.

Thanks in part to its generous social safety net, along with the distaste of Germany's wealthy classes for conspicuous consumption and their tendency to understatement, widespread extremes of wealth and poverty aren't apparent as in some other European countries. Cynics may claim that it's difficult to become rich in Germany because of the high tax rates, particularly on income from 'speculative' activity and it's true that those who have made fortunes have almost invariably built them up through hard work over the longer term and that becoming a millionaire overnight is rare. This minimises social resentments. There's also somewhat less stigma attached to receiving social benefits here than elsewhere, and the state benefits system provides a decent, if not exactly luxurious, standard of living for those who have fallen on hard times (although more people fall through its safety net than casual observers notice).

The Germans are justifiably proud of their successes in what they refer to as a 'social market economy'. Less *dirigiste* than their French counterparts, German governments have fostered competition in the marketplace and encouraged enterprise among individuals and businesses. However, the government exercises considerable control over business, both by direct regulation and through relatively high taxes on income and capital. Its purpose is to protect economic equilibrium by promoting price stability, high employment, balanced imports and exports, and continuous growth.

A good deal of Germany's success over the last 50 years has been due to the rise of middle-size companies – family-owned and operated industries often started after the war. Many of these companies made excellent use of German engineering skills to produce high quality industrial products known and sold around the world. At the start of the new millennium, however, many of these highly successful companies are facing a crisis of transition, as the founders reach retirement age and must decide whether to keep the business in the family, sell it or merge with larger companies or corporations. Their children often aren't interested in carrying on the family business or face considerable difficulties in changing the company culture and image to reflect their own management ideas.

The reunification of Germany in 1991 carried an enormous price tag, particularly given the government's decision to integrate the two radically different economies as quickly as possible. Much of the infrastructure of the former East Germany had to be rebuilt, with concepts of efficiency and profitability introduced into what for the previous 50 years had been a centrally planned economy. The one-for-one exchange rate agreed for the Ostmark and the Deutschmark meant that the East lost its considerable export markets and competitive edge in eastern Europe, while any incentive to invest in eastern Germany was lost because there was no economic advantage to it. Even the West's greater congeniality came fully into play.

Among the many unpleasant surprises to hit West Germans on reunification was the damage done to the environment in the east. Pollution of the air, water and land was much worse than many had expected, and the cost of the clean-up operation, combined with the creation (almost overnight) of an elaborate benefit structure in the former DDR, have meant that taxes in Germany, on business and personal income as well as capital, are now among the highest in Europe. This further restricts the ability of businesses to create and sustain employment.

This lack of foresight about what reunification would involve financially has left the German government today in a difficult situation. Taxes urgently need to be reduced to encourage economic activity and employment but this cannot be done because the money is needed to pay off the cost of reunification. The only logical escape route is increased borrowing, but Germany cannot do this because of the already excessive levels of public debt – its current borrowings are the highest in the EU in relation to GDP – and the constraints imposed by the euro. The government's commitment to keep public borrowing below 3 per cent of GDP as part of the Euro Stability Pact – something which it ironically insisted upon itself – is exacerbating its problems. It is currently borrowing at a rate of 3.7 per cent, despite strenuous efforts, which are sharply circumscribing its ability to alleviate its unemployment problem. German companies have been forced to put expansion on hold, transfer parts of their operations to cheaper countries, contract out, or in some cases go bust. Nevertheless, inward investment has recently outstripped that into the UK, which was previously by far Europe's most attractive location for foreign business people.

Despite all the gloomy news though, Germany remains the leading exporter in the world besides the US, with over €596 billion in exports annually, more than half of which goes to other EU countries (73 per cent to Europe as a whole), 14 per cent to the US, and some 2.4 per cent to Japan. Rather less than 2 per cent goes to Africa. In 2001, Germany's balance of trade was an incredible €94.2 billion in the black and its balance of payments in credit by €2.3 billion. German products are world renowned for their quality, reliability and state-of-the-art engineering. They rarely compete on price, but provide good value given the standards they exemplify.

Manufacturing and service industries predominate, and Germany is the third-largest producer of motor cars in the world (including Audi, BMW, Ford, Mercedes, Opel, Porsche and Volkswagen). Other major sectors include chemicals, iron and steel, transport equipment, electrical machinery, generators, machine tools, communications equipment, food and beverages. Agriculture, forestry and fishing form a relatively small part of the economy, employing 2.4 per cent of the workforce and contributing just 1.2 per cent of GNP, yet Germany is still almost 90 per cent self-sufficient in food. Service industries, on the other hand, account for over 60 per cent of all jobs.

Industrial Relations

Strikes in Germany are fairly rare, although much more frequent than they used to be. Like many other aspects of society they're strictly controlled by laws and regulations. Civil servants (*Beamte*) aren't permitted to strike at all.

Germany has a number of large, powerful national unions, which negotiate regional contracts with employers' groups representing specific industries. A regional contract is binding on all companies within that industry and region, whether they're part of the employers' group or not, although it has recently been proposed that firms be allowed to negotiate wage rises according to their financial situation.

In the last 50 years, relations between the unions and employers' organisations have tended to be cordial and constructive, both sides willing to compromise in the interest of saving or creating jobs. The more stressful economic situation of recent years is, however, threatening to erode this consensual approach.

All businesses with more than a few employees must establish an elected works council (*Betriebsrat*), made up of worker representatives, who have an advisory role in management affairs. The works council must be consulted on all significant management decisions, including the hiring and firing of key executives, lay-offs and plant closures, and must be regularly informed about the state of a business. Individuals serving on a works council enjoy special privileges and guaranteed job protection under labour law; in larger companies representatives of the works council are guaranteed a certain number of seats on the board of directors. They may work closely with local unions but aren't required to be members themselves. Works council decisions can override even those of regionally organised trade unions under certain circumstances.

Workforce

German employees enjoy high salaries and excellent working conditions thanks to years of negotiation and co-operation between employers and national trade unions. The Germans have taken great pride in their role as leaders of the European economy and champions of industrial productivity and engineering excellence. The title of engineer (*Ingenieur*) carries considerable prestige, and degrees and other qualifications are proudly displayed on business cards and letterheads. Education is highly prized in Germany and many engineers in industry have earned doctorates. (It's common for engineers to become company bosses.) German national apprenticeship and on-the-job training programmes are the envy of the world, and for good reason. German workers are renowned for their high levels of skill and efficiency.

In the 1960s and 1970s, the Federal Republic recruited large numbers of foreign workers, euphemistically called 'guest workers' (*Gastarbeiter*) and mostly from Mediterranean countries, in response to labour shortages. Many guest workers stayed on as long-term residents, so that by the end of 1994 there were over 2 million foreigners employed in western Germany, the largest national groups being (in diminishing order) those from Turkey, the states of the former Yugoslavia, Greece and Italy. The now defunct German Democratic Republic recruited a number of Vietnamese workers, several thousand of whom now live and work in what was formerly East Germany.

Nowadays, from the outside, the German labour market looks completely self-sufficient, with none of the shortages of unskilled labour of the type that made the *Gastarbeiter* necessary, and German companies involved in international markets don't have to look to foreigners for general language skills, as local schools turn out enough individuals fluent in English and other foreign languages.

Work Attitudes

Traditional German companies – particularly small and medium-size enterprises, whose owner-managers comprise a recognised social class, called the *Mittelstand* – often have a strict hierarchical structure with formalised relations between management and workers. Jobs and job titles are often strictly defined by regional industry contracts, with legal distinctions between workers and management. Neither group is keen to take on responsibilities outside their defined duties. Experience, maturity and loyalty are highly valued and the frequent changing of jobs as a way of increasing your salary or promotion prospects is rare. However, this is beginning to change, particularly in high-tech industries and multi-national companies.

It's expensive to hire and fire employees in Germany, and the works council (*Betriebsrat*) often has the right to review candidates and offer suggestions regarding personnel decisions, even where upper management positions are involved. The process of hiring new employees (particularly managers and executives) and making business decisions is slower in Germany than in many other western countries. This is due more to the various levels of review and approval required than to indecision or inherent faults in the system.

Many foreigners, particularly Americans, find that they must adjust to a slower and more deliberate pace of working life in Germany. Snap-decision making is considered suspect, and German managers generally prefer to rely on careful planning and a rational, considered approach to solving problems.

German managers and executives rarely take work home, and they never work at weekends, which are sacrosanct. Many businesses close for two or three weeks during the summer, and employees are generally expected to take the bulk of their annual leave during this period. Many union contracts stipulate the closing dates each year to coincide with the region's school holiday calendar.

Time spent in the office or on the job is generally highly productive, with little or no time wasted on socialising or idle chatter, except during official (and short) break periods. Socialising with colleagues is often done primarily in formal settings such as the annual company outing, holiday gatherings and other events planned and run by the *Betriebsrat* as a part of its official 'social function'.

Working Women

Women in Germany comprise over 40 per cent of the workforce and generally enjoy legal protection from discrimination in the hiring process. However around a third of the female workforce works only part-time, compared with just 3 per cent of men. There are a number of laws designed to protect women (*Frauenarbeitsschutz*) from dangerous jobs, excessive overtime or late-night working hours. Maternity leave is generous and time off for family matters (including caring for sick children) is written into the law as a basic worker's right. This can work against women, as many employers are reluctant to hire women of child-bearing age for jobs involving heavy lifting, etc., which would have to be modified during pregnancy (and the law requires a female employee to notify her employer as soon as she knows she's pregnant). Other employers may fear losing a key supervisor or manager to extended maternity leave at a crucial point in the business cycle.

Women have professional and salary equality with men, although there are still few top-level women managers and executives, and women continue to hold the majority of part-time and lower paid jobs, as in other countries.

On the other hand, women are well represented in the political sphere in Germany and there's an active women's movement. However, there's less apparent interest among women in preparing for management or other non-traditional occupations. Women enter the German university system in roughly equal numbers to men, but far fewer complete the rigorous business and engineering programmes required for managerial and executive level jobs. Women in management fields may have some difficulty establishing credibility with older, more 'traditional' bosses or colleagues.

GERMANY & THE EU

Germany was one of the six founder members of the European Community (now the European Union or EU) in 1957, along with Belgium, France, Italy, Luxembourg and the Netherlands. Since then Austria, Denmark, Finland, Greece, Ireland, Portugal, Spain, Sweden and the United Kingdom have increased the number to 15. The German government has been a driving force behind the extension of EU membership to ten new countries in eastern and southern Europe, including its neighbours the Czech Republic and Poland, who are set to join on 1st May 2004. (The other new members will be Cyprus, Estonia, Hungary, Latvia, Lithuania, Malta, the Slovak Republic, and Slovenia.)

Nationals of EU states have the right to work in Germany or any other member state without a work permit, provided they have a valid passport or national identity card and comply with the member state's laws and regulations on employment. EU nationals are entitled to the same treatment as German citizens in matters of pay, working conditions, access to housing, vocational training, social security and trade union rights, and their families and dependants are entitled to join them and enjoy the same rights.

There are, however, still barriers to full freedom of movement and the right to work within the EU. For example, certain jobs in various member countries require job applicants to have specific skills or vocational qualifications. The EU has developed a general system for the recognition of professional and trade qualifications and guidelines for mutual recognition of qualifications (see below). Nevertheless, there are restrictions on employment in the civil service, where the right to work may be limited in individual cases on grounds of public policy, national security or public health. Differences persist among the various German states regarding the civil service status of some occupations, particularly teachers and health professionals.

QUALIFICATIONS

A remarkable range of job titles is regulated, at least to the extent of requiring a formal qualification. Most qualifications involve a training programme lasting at least two or three years, with or without supervised on-the-job experience or a formal apprenticeship. Germany has a world-renowned apprenticeship system and offers its young people a dizzying array of training programmes when they finish their school careers. The system of job-related qualifications is so pervasive that you may hear Germans making jokes about how even jobs such as toilet attendant or road sweeper require a two-year training programme these days. Qualifications can be very specific, making it difficult to change jobs unless you've taken a supplementary training programme meeting the particular requirements of the new job. Employers are required by law to provide continuing training for employees, and a company's annual educational plan must be approved by the works council.

Germany abides by the EU's general system for recognition of diplomas and qualifications, which means that, if your field of work is regulated in Germany, you must have your home country's qualification formally recognised before you will be allowed to work in that field. This obviously applies to professionals such as doctors, nurses and teachers, but recognised qualifications are required to work in many other areas as well: as an electrician, computer technician or in building trades, for example.

Generally speaking, to have your home country qualifications formally recognised in Germany, you must contact the competent authority (usually a guild, trade association or professional society) for your trade or profession. They will provide you with their requirements, which usually involve the submission of your diploma, certificate or other documentation confirming your training or work experience. You must be able to show that the qualification from your home country is equivalent to the German one, in terms of both duration and subject matter. If there are significant differences in the practice of your profession between the two countries, you may be asked for evidence of mastery of specific areas considered significantly different in your home country. This can take the form of job experience, an aptitude test or additional training. Under German law, the competent authority has four months to respond positively to your application; no response after this period is legally equivalent to a refusal, but you're entitled to know the reasons for any negative decision.

All EU member states issue occupation information sheets containing a common job description with a table of qualifications. These cover a large number of professions and trades and are intended to help someone with the relevant qualifications to look for a job in another EU country. You can obtain a direct comparison between any EU qualification and those recognised in Germany from the *Zentralstelle für Ausländisches Bildungswesen*, Nassestrasse 8, 53113 Bonn, ☎ 0228-5010). In the UK, information can be obtained from the Comparability Co-ordinator, Occupational Standards Branch – OS5, Room E454, The Training Agency,

Moorfoot, Sheffield S1 4PQ. A series of fact sheets called *Citizens First Guides* can be downloaded from the EU website (🖥 http:// citizens.eu.int); these provide detailed information on the European and German procedures for recognition of experience and qualifications.

GOVERNMENT EMPLOYMENT SERVICE

The German Federal Labour Office (Bundesanstalt für Arbeit, also known as the BA or Arbeitsamt) provides a wide range of employment-related services through its 181 offices in Germany. The Arbeitsamt publishes lists of jobs available throughout Germany and abroad, and provides vocational training, assessment and re-integration services for disabled people, and vocational guidance for students and others. It also administers various benefit programmes related to employment, compiles labour statistics and conducts market and labour research. Once you find a job, it's the Arbeitsamt that issues your work permit (if required – see page 77).

The Arbeitsamt provides its services free to both job seekers and employers. If you're already in Germany, you can pick up a copy of their weekly magazine, *Markt und Chance*, at their offices. This publication includes job vacancies and a 'jobs wanted' section, where job seekers can place adverts. You can find similar information on the Arbeitsamt website (🖥 www.arbeitsamt.de). The Arbeitsamt has a special department for foreign applicants seeking work in Germany, called the Zentralstelle für Arbeitsvermittlung (ZAV), which also handles placements for Germans abroad. The main office of the Arbeitsamt is at Regensburger Strasse 104, 90478 Nuremberg, ☎ 0911-1790). The ZAV is located at Villemombler Strasse 76, 53123 Bonn, ☎ 0228-7130, 🖥 www.arbeitsamt.de/ZAV.)

There's also a European Employment Service (EURES) network, members of which include all EU countries plus Norway and Iceland. Member states exchange information regularly on job vacancies, and local EURES offices have access to extensive information on how to apply for a job and living and working conditions in each country. The international department of your home country's employment service can put you in touch with a Euroadviser, who can provide advice on finding work in Germany. Euroadvisers can also arrange to have your personal details forwarded to the Arbeitsamt. The Citizens First website (🖥 http:// citizens.eu.int) contains information about EURES and EURES-related agencies in many European countries.

Given the high level of unemployment in Germany, EURES is rarely the fastest or the most efficient way of finding a job there, especially from abroad. As can be expected, national employment services give priority to their own nationals and jobs don't generally get referred to EURES or other national agencies until after all prospective local candidates have been considered.

RECRUITMENT AGENCIES

Until 1994, the Arbeitsamt (see above) was the only legal recruitment agency in Germany, although many intermediaries posted vacancies in German newspapers as 'employment consultants', mostly for management level jobs. In larger cities today there are branches of many of the major international executive recruitment firms or 'head-hunters' (*Kopfjäger*). Michael Page, Korn/Ferry and Heidrick & Struggles all maintain offices in Germany, although they don't normally accept CVs unless in response to a specific vacancy.

There's a variety of small to medium-size recruitment agencies in the US and UK which specialise in international placements. Agents advertise in daily and weekly newspapers and trade magazines, but don't mention the client's name, not least to prevent applicants from approaching the company directly, therefore depriving the agency of its fat fee!

In a few instances, agencies may advertise directly in international publications to assemble a stable of potential job candidates. International companies may list management positions in Germany with recruitment agencies in the UK, particularly if they're seeking multi-lingual or highly experienced or mobile executives.

Most legitimate recruitment services charge the employer a fee based on the annual salary negotiated for the candidate. Fees can run to as much as 40 or 50 per cent of a year's salary, which the head-hunter may have to refund if employees don't survive the initial probationary period (anywhere from one to six months). **Be extremely wary of recruiters that demand a fee up front from job applicants or expect you to reimburse them for postage, telephone costs or other charges incurred during the course of the job hunt.**

Temporary Agencies

In addition to recruitment agencies for permanent positions, there are temporary private employment agencies in Germany, such as Manpower and Adecco, handling either jobs in specific industries or fields only or general jobs. To be employed by a temporary agency, you must be eligible to work in Germany and have a social security number (see page 287). You must register with most agencies, which entails completing a registration form and providing a CV and references (you can register with any number of agencies). Always ensure you know exactly how much, when and how you will be paid. Deductions for income tax and social security will be made from your gross salary. Because of the long annual holidays in Germany and generous maternity leave, companies often require temporary staff, and a temporary job can frequently be used as a stepping stone to a permanent position. Look in the yellow pages under *Aushilfe, Interim* or *Personalberatung*.

Online Agencies

The rapid development of the Internet has led to a big increase in the number of online recruitment agencies and job search sites. Some sites charge a subscription fee to access their vacancy lists, but many permit job seekers to view and respond to vacancies free of charge. It's also possible to post your CV online (again, usually free), but it's wise to consider the security implications of this move. By posting your home address or phone number in public view, you could be opening yourself up for nuisance phone calls or even worse.

A number of Internet sites that regularly list vacancies in Germany are:

- 💻 www.arbeit-online.de/index.htm;
- 💻 www.stepstone.de;
- 💻 www.jobs.com or http://jobs.de;
- 💻 www.jobnet.de;
- 💻 www.monster.de;
- 💻 www.job-office.com;
- 💻 www.overseasjobs.com.

Note that German sites (those ending .de) usually don't include an English-language version unless a major organisation is involved. However, if your German skills are still rudimentary, you can obtain a rough-and-ready translation using the (free) Babel Fish translator provided by the search engine company Alta Vista. Enter 'http://babelfish.altavista.digital.com' in your browser, then enter the address of the website that you wish to visit in the Babel Fish dialogue box that appears; you will then be presented with an instant translation of the web page in question.

TEMPORARY & CASUAL WORK

Temporary and casual work (*befristete Arbeit*) is usually for a fixed period, ranging from a few days to a few months (or work may be intermittent). Casual workers are often employed on a daily, first-come-first-served basis. Anyone looking for casual unskilled work in Germany must usually compete with newly arrived Turks and eastern Europeans, who are often prepared to work for less money than anyone else. Many employers illegally pay temporary staff in cash without making deductions for social security, insurances and taxes (see **Working Illegally** on page 45), although casual work earnings are subject to the same taxes and other deductions as full-time employment.

Temporary and casual work includes the following:

- Office work – well paid if you're qualified and generally the easiest work to find due to the large number of temporary secretarial and office staff agencies;
- Work in the building trade – this can be found by applying directly at building sites and through industrial recruitment agencies such as Manpower;
- Jobs in shops over Christmas and during sales periods;
- Gardening jobs in private gardens, public parks and garden centres, particularly in spring and summer;
- Peddling ice cream, cold drinks and fast food, e.g. in tourist areas or at trade shows and fairs;
- Work as a security guard (long hours for low pay);
- Nursing and auxiliary nursing in hospitals, clinics and nursing homes (temps are often employed through nursing agencies to replace permanent staff at short notice);
- Newspaper, magazine and leaflet distribution;
- Courier work (own transport required – motorcycle, car or van);
- Driving jobs, including coach and truck drivers, and ferrying cars for manufacturers and car hire companies;
- Miscellaneous jobs such as office cleaners, babysitters and labourers – these can be obtained through a number of agencies specialising in temporary work.

Temporary jobs are also advertised in Arbeitsamt offices (see page 29), on notice boards in expatriate clubs, churches and organisations, and in expatriate newsletters and newspapers. See also **Recruitment Agencies** on page 30, **Seasonal Jobs** on page 33 and **Training & Work Experience** on page 41.

Mini-Jobs

Recent labour law reforms have introduced the concept of the 'mini-job', which is one which is poorly paid, exists in a deregulated sphere largely outside the traditional framework, and is without trade union involvement. It's supposed to be for people in transition or who are waiting to get a 'traditional' job, but some would say that its advent is principally designed to reduce the unemployment numbers to save politicians' blushes. See also page 50.

SEASONAL JOBS

Seasonal jobs are available throughout the year in Germany, the vast majority in the tourist industry. Many seasonal jobs last for the duration of the summer or winter tourist seasons – May to September and December to April respectively – although some are simply casual or temporary jobs for a number of weeks. Some fluency in German is necessary for all but the most menial (and worst paid) jobs. Additional languages can be a big advantage, particularly in the tourist industry, as Germany hosts visitors from around the world.

Seasonal jobs include most trades in hotels and restaurants, couriers and representatives, a variety of jobs in theme parks and holiday camps, sports instructors, service staff in bars and clubs, fruit and grape picking and other agricultural jobs. The main job opportunities are described below.

If you aren't an EU national, you should make sure that you're eligible to work in Germany by checking with the German embassy or consulate in your home country before you start looking for a seasonal job. The Arbeitsamt has been gradually reducing the number of seasonal work permits it issues for foreigners in an attempt to encourage the hiring of Germans and other EU nationals, and non-EU nationals may find it difficult or impossible to secure seasonal work. There are, however, a number of international summer and holiday work programmes that offer work permits and placement assistance, particularly for students (see **Training & Work Experience** on page 41).

Foreign students in Germany can usually obtain a temporary work permit for part-time work during the summer holiday period and between school terms.

Summer Jobs

Grape & Fruit Picking: As in many wine-producing countries, grape-picking is a popular late summer job in Germany, despite being boring, badly paid and hard, physical work. The major vineyards are located on the banks of the Rhine and Moselle rivers, where the harvest usually starts in mid to late September, depending on the climate each year. Other fruit-picking jobs include apples and pears, and are mostly in the south (e.g. Baden-Württemburg and Bavaria). Traditionally, farmers have hired fruit pickers from southern and eastern Europe on a casual, day-labour basis, but in these days of high unemployment the Arbeitsamt is trying to crack down on the use of illegal foreign labour, so in theory at least it ought to be easier to obtain a bona fide fruit-picking job.

Holiday Camps & Theme Parks: For those who like working with children, German holiday camps offer a number of summer job opportunities, ranging from camp counsellors and sports instructors to administrative and catering posts. The school summer holidays aren't as long in Germany as in some other European countries, so the season is correspondingly shorter. There are a number of Internet sites devoted to holiday camps, such as ⌨ www.summercamps.de, which lists job openings for the coming season.

Germany boasts a dozen or so theme parks (*Freizeitpark*) which all rely to a large extent on seasonal staff. The larger parks may also provide on-site accommodation for employees (the cost is deducted from your wages). Positions range from maintenance and catering to performing in the shows and pageants that form part of the entertainment. Check local newspapers from January or February for job advertisements for the coming summer season. April is a popular month for parks to hold auditions for performing roles. Most theme parks have websites containing employment information. The better-known parks are listed below.

- Tripsdrill, 74389 Cleebronn/Tripsdrill (☎ 07135-9999, ⌨ www.tripsdrill.de);
- Phantasialand, Bergeiststr. 31–41, 50321 Brühl b. Köln (☎ 02232-36200, ⌨ www.phantasialand.de);
- Europa Park Rust, Europa-Park-Strasse 2, 77977 Rust/Baden (☎ 07822-770);
- Hansapark, 23730 Siersdorf (☎ 04563-7051, ⌨ www.hansapark.de);
- Movieworld Warner Bros, Warner Allee 1, 46244 Bottrop-Kichhellen (☎ 02045-899899, ⌨ www.movieworld.de).

Winter Jobs

While Germany isn't as well known for ski resorts and winter sports in general as its neighbours France, Switzerland, Austria and Italy, many areas have active winter sports areas. Cross-country skiing (*Langlauf*) is particularly popular in the Black Forest and parts of Bavaria, and there are many small inns and tourist centres catering to winter sports enthusiasts.

One of the best ways to find jobs in ski resorts is via the Internet, where the following sites might prove useful:

- ⌨ www.equity.co.uk;
- ⌨ www.jobs-in-the-alps.com;
- ⌨ www.natives.co.uk;
- ⌨ www.ski-jobs.com;
- ⌨ www.skijobs.net.

VOLUNTARY WORK

Voluntary work provides a means for students and young people to visit Germany for a few weeks or months to learn about the country and its people at first hand. The minimum age limit for volunteers is usually between 16 and 18 and they must usually be under 30, although some organisations have no upper age limit. Qualification requirements vary with the organisation and the nature of the work. Voluntary work is unpaid (of course) and you must usually pay a registration fee plus your transport costs to and from the work site. Although meals and accommodation are normally provided, you may be expected to contribute towards the cost of board and lodging. The usual visa regulations apply to voluntary workers (see **Chapter 3**) and you will be informed when applying whether you need one.

Many of the same organisations that arrange training and work experience programmes, such as CIEE (see **Training & Work Experience** on page 41), also host volunteer programmes for students and young people. For those willing to pay their own way, the Earthwatch Institute (680 Mount Auburn Street or PO Box 9104, Watertown, MA 02471, USA, ☎ 617-926 8200, 🖥 www.earthwatch.org or Earthwatch Europe, 57 Woodstock Road, Oxford OX2 6HJ, UK, ☎ 01865-311600, ✉ info@uk.earthwatch.org) provides a variety of volunteer opportunities, mostly in support of environmental and cultural research projects.

The Belgian-based Association of Voluntary Service Organisations (AVSO, rue Joseph II 174, 1000 Brussels, Belgium, ☎ 02-230 6813), which is an international non-government organisation, maintains a directory of volunteer opportunities throughout the world, and the group Action Without Borders, a non-profit-making organisation aiming to increase political, social and environmental awareness, has a website (🖥 www.idealist.org) providing links to other voluntary work organisations.

There are a number of books providing information about voluntary work, including *Doing Voluntary Work Abroad: A Practical Guide to Opportunities Worldwide* (How To Books) and the *International Directory of Voluntary Work* (Vacation Work), a guide to 400 agencies and sources of information on short to long-term voluntary work world-wide.

JOB HUNTING

There are numerous places to look for jobs in Germany, whether you're already in the country or not. Some of the more effective resources are detailed below. As in any other country, the more job applications you make, the better your chance of finding the right job.

Newspapers & Magazines: Obtain copies of German newspapers, most of which contain job advertisements (*Stellenangebote*), often concentrated in weekend editions. The *Frankfurter Allgemeine Zeitung* (*FAZ*) runs the largest and best-known job advertising section in its Saturday edition, available at international news-stands throughout the world. German business publications and trade journals often have job vacancy notices, particularly for positions requiring special qualifications. International newspapers and magazines that sometimes contain advertising for positions in Germany include the *Financial Times* and the *Wall Street Journal* (for business managers), the *Economist* (economic research and university teaching and administrative positions), the *International Herald Tribune*, and occasionally the London Sunday newspapers.

Recruitment Agencies: Apply to international recruitment agencies acting for multi-national or German companies. These companies recruit primarily executives and key personnel, and many have offices world-wide. British and American-based companies often use recruitment agents in the UK to locate managers. Applying to so-called blind ads (i.e. those with only a brief, general job description and no indication of the employer's identity) can lead to valuable contacts with freelance recruiters. **Be careful if you want to avoid having your employer find out that you're looking elsewhere.**

Employment Offices: The Arbeitsamt (see page 29) publishes a weekly list of job opportunities, which is available at any Arbeitsamt office in Germany and also on its website (🖥 www.arbeitsamt.de). If you're an EU national, you can also check with your home country's EURES network office (see page 29).

Current Employer: One frequently overlooked source is your current employer. This will apply mainly if you work for an international company or at least an organisation with one or more offices in Germany. It's far easier for your current employer to justify the transfer of someone to the German office or factory who's already familiar with the company policies and procedures than for him to hire a foreigner in Germany. This can be a particularly avenue if you require a work permit. Make sure that your personnel department knows of your interest in working in Germany, particularly if you already speak and read the language. Mention your interest to any German contacts you have within your own company, who may be willing to mention your name to fill a local vacancy that you would otherwise never hear about.

Internet: Most of the above sources for job hunting can be accessed to some degree via the Internet. German newspapers, in particular, are nearly all available online, with search facilities that enable you to quickly identify vacancies in specific occupational and geographic areas. Several large recruitment agencies are also online (see page 30). There are even websites devoted exclusively to job hunting, such as 🖥 http://jobs.de and www.monster.de, where you can post your CV free of charge and search the available listings.

Many executive recruitment agencies list their website addresses in their advertisements and it's worth checking these sites regularly for new postings that may never make it into print. If there's a particular company that interests you, particularly in the information technology field, don't forget to check their website for job listings by location. Many companies are now using their websites to advertise vacancies, therefore saving themselves advertising and recruitment fees, and several multi-national companies now claim to do most of their hiring via their own websites.

Unsolicited Job Applications: Apply to American, British and other multi-national companies with offices or subsidiaries in Germany. If you're writing to German businesses in English, don't forget to mention your level of German fluency; otherwise, it's likely to be assumed that you don't speak or understand the language at all.

Making unsolicited job applications to targeted companies is naturally a hit-and-miss affair. It can, however, sometimes work to your advantage when, for example, your application arrives just as a position comes available. Make sure, however, to specify the kind of job that you're interested in and qualified for. There's nothing so annoying to personnel departments as a letter claiming that the applicant will 'consider any job' and offering no hint of the skills or experience that may be of use to the company concerned. If you're writing to a manufacturer, for example, be sure to indicate whether you're interested in working in their factory or are looking for office work as a clerk or manager.

CURRICULUM VITAE

The basic job-hunting package consists of a curriculum vitae or resume (*Lebenslauf*) plus a covering letter explaining your interest in the job or company and stating where you saw the advertisement (if you're replying to one) and highlighting any particularly relevant skills or experiences you have to offer.

Whether you use a German curriclum vitae (CV) and covering letter depends on your fluency in the language and the type of job you're applying for. It's generally acceptable to use an English CV when applying to multi-national companies, particularly if English is the company's *lingua franca* or the job advertisement appears in English or mentions the need for excellent English-language skills. You will need a German CV and covering letter for applications to smaller companies, for jobs involving public contact and in much of the *Mittelstand*.

A German CV contains much the same information as a standard CV, but is in a slightly different format to that of a British or American CV, see below:

- You should include detailed personal information, including your date of birth and age, nationality, marital status, number of children and military obligation status (for men).

- Attach a good-quality photograph. Failure to include a photo may be taken by more traditional employers as an attempt to hide something – such as your real age or the fact that you have a bone through your nose. A photograph taken in an automatic photo booth is generally considered inadequate and may eliminate you from the running faster than no photo at all. Instead, you should go to a good portrait photographer, who can produce a professional-looking picture.

- Your educational background section should include training courses completed, including employer-sponsored programmes, although you should limit these to training courses relevant to the job you're seeking. Copies of certificates of completion for each programme (including university diplomas) are often included in the full application package (*Bewerbung*), but Americans should resist the temptation to include grade transcripts. This information is considered personal and inappropriate, particularly if you didn't complete a certificate or degree.

- Your work experience should be listed in chronological order (i.e. earliest first) rather than starting with the most recent. Each job should be listed with your exact job title and dates of employment. Only the briefest description of job responsibilities should be given or none at all if the duties are immediately apparent from the job title. The American style of 'marketing oneself' by listing personal achievements or quantifying cost savings you've implemented may be seen as bragging, particularly in the more traditional family-owned companies.

- Many German job candidates submit copies of their termination review or last annual job appraisal but, due to the many legal restrictions on employee evaluations in Germany, these are generally given little weight by prospective employers.

- It's important to state your earliest available start date (which could be included in your covering letter). German job contracts often specify quite long notice periods for quitting a job, from a minimum of a month to three months for management-level employees. Your ability to start a new job on the date the employer needs the job filled can therefore give you a significant advantage over other candidates. On the other hand, saying you're immediately available can be taken as an indication that you're currently unemployed, although this isn't necessarily regarded as a negative point, particularly by larger employers.

You should of course take care to ensure that any information in your covering letter is consistent with your CV and may wish to enclose your application in a binder, which will normally be returned to you even if you're unsuccessful – in fact as an indication that you've been unsuccessful. (Even if you decide to use a standard British CV or American resume, don't be surprised to receive your application back in the post.) If you've applied through a head-hunter or other employment agency, you may receive a letter asking for permission to keep a copy of your application package on file for reference. This is obviously a good sign, indicating that the agency believes that they may be able to match you with a future job vacancy.

Interview

For all but the most menial or short-term jobs, most employers will insist on interviewing short-listed candidates in person and on site. This is where foreign job candidates may be at a serious disadvantage, irrespective of their background, education or fluency in German or other languages, as employers are expected to reimburse all travel costs to their interviewees. For local candidates, this involves either a per kilometre allowance for motoring expenses or a round-trip train ticket, possibly with a single night's hotel bill and a meal or two. Few, if any, employers are willing to consider flying a job candidate in from London, New York or Sydney for a first-round interview for any but the most rarefied management positions.

If you're serious about job hunting in Germany, you may wish to consider making yourself available for interview at your own expense, perhaps as part of a holiday. Mention this in your covering letter, even if your plans are vague ('I'll be in Frankfurt in the near future...' or 'As I am planning to spend my summer holidays in Germany this year, I will be available to meet with you between . . .'). This tactic, while admittedly expensive, demonstrates your level of interest in the job and in making an international relocation. Assuming you're well qualified for the job in question, you may be able to overcome an employer's unwillingness to consider a foreign candidate simply by being available for a meeting. However, if you go down this route, you should ask your prospective employer what support he would be prepared to give you for your move and resettlement, should you get the job (see **Travel & Relocation Expenses** on page 54).

SALARY

It can be difficult to determine the level of salary you should receive in Germany, as salaries aren't quoted in job advertisements and are kept strictly confidential. However, Germans are among the best paid workers in

Europe, receiving both a 13th month, year-end 'bonus' and a holiday bonus (generally an additional half month's salary or more) during the summer (see **Salary & Bonuses** on page 51). If you're quoted an annual salary, you should therefore divide it by 13.5 (not 12) to determine what your monthly pay will be. On the other hand, the cost of living is also high in Germany, as are taxes and the various social insurances deducted from pay packets (see **Cost Of Living** on page 328, **Social Security** on page 287 and **Income Tax** on page 317).

Usually only starting salaries are negotiable and it's up to you to ensure that you receive the level of salary and benefits commensurate with your qualifications and experience. Minimum salaries exist in many industries for factory or entry-level workers and the industry agreement for the region may cover extras that must be paid for certain experience or qualifications, unsociable hours, overtime, weekend work or home work, and dangerous or unpleasant working conditions. You don't need to be a union member to be subject to the local industry agreement, and pay rises may be governed by the relevant industry agreement, so make sure your starting salary is appropriate for your age and experience. If you have friends or acquaintances living in Germany or who have lived there, ask them what an average or good salary is for your trade or profession.

For many employees, particularly executives and senior managers, their remuneration is much more than what their monthly pay is. Some companies provide benefits such as a company car, interest-free home or other loans, and membership of local clubs or sporting organisations. These benefits are usually taxable, however, and you should take this into account when calculating your take-home pay or comparing job offers.

An overview of salary levels is provided by the current digest (*Datenreport 2002*) of the Federal Office for Statistics (Statistisches Bundesamt), although the figures quoted should be taken as a guide only. Manufacturing workers in western Germany earned an average of €2,409 per month in 2000, while their white-collar colleagues received €3,506, excluding bonuses and overtime (90 per cent of male white-collar workers earned between €3,340 and €4,400; 80 per cent of women between €2,138 and €2,778, although generally for lower level jobs). Comparable workers in the east earned some 73 per cent of western pay levels. The complete digest is available from the Bundeszentrale für Politische Bildung Informations- und Broschürenstelle, z. Hd. Herrn Schwarz, Berliner Freiheit 7, 53111 Bonn (☎ 01888-5150, 🖥 www. bpb.de); the publication reference number is 1376.

SELF-EMPLOYMENT

If you want to work as a self-employed person (*Selbstständiger*) in a profession or start a freelance business in Germany, you must meet certain legal requirements and register with the appropriate organisation, which is usually a trade or craft guild (*Handwerkskammer*). Of course, you must have the appropriate qualification, recognised by the proper authority in Germany, to legally establish yourself as self-employed (see **Qualifications** on page 27). However, those with a record of practical experience, supported by some kind of certificate, in another country are able to set up in self-employment in certain fields, e.g. crafts, retailing (from a shop or mobile unit), catering and hotel-keeping, food and drink production, insurance broking, transport services, wholesale and hairdressing.

Britons should contact the Certificate of Experience Unit of the Department of Trade and Industry, European Policy Directorate, Bay 211/212, Kingsgate House, 66–74 Victoria Street, London SW1E 6SW (☎ 020-7215 4648) to check whether they're eligible for a certificate.

In the building trades, Germany is cracking down on what it sees as abuses by 'cheap' foreign labourers taking jobs away from Germans under the guise of being sub-contracted on major projects. The law requires self-employed construction workers to hold a qualification at least equivalent to that of a German master craftsman (*Meister*) and to have a contract for a specifically defined segment of the building project – down to defining exactly which wall or room the contractor has been commissioned to construct. **Many people who have been lured by the prospect of high wages for short-term construction jobs in Germany have encountered hostility on the job, and there has been an increase in 'accidents' (sometimes fatal) on building sites hiring foreign workers.**

TRAINING & WORK EXPERIENCE

A number of organisations (listed below) run trainee and work exchange programmes for students and recent graduates. For most programmes you must be under 30. Some programmes arrange job placements, while others offer work permits for up to 18 months for applicants who find their own placement and otherwise qualify for the programme.

- Technical and commercial students wishing to gain experience by working in Germany during their holidays can apply to the International Association for the Exchange of Students for Technical Experience (IAESTE) in over 60 countries. Applicants must possess a working knowledge of German and be enrolled at an educational institution as a full-time student of engineering, science, agriculture, architecture or a related field of study, or be undergraduates in their penultimate year of study and aged between 19 and 30. In the UK, applicants should apply to IAESTE UK, c/o Education Section, British Council, 10 Spring Gardens, London SW1A 2BN, ☎ 020-7389 4114, 🖥 www.iaeste.org).

- The Association for International Practical Training (AIPT) also provides a career development programme for university graduates and a student exchange programme for US nationals. Both programmes require applicants to find their own internships or job placements and provide them with work permits for up to 18 months. For further information contact the Association for International Practical Training, 10400 Little Patuxent Parkway, Suite 250, Columbia, MD 21044-3519, USA, ☎ 410-997 2200, 💻 www.aipt.org).

- For students and those within a term of graduation, the Council on International Educational Exchange (CIEE) provides short-term work permits and job search support for over 30 countries, including Germany. CIEE programmes also include study and volunteer programmes. Contact the CIEE (633 Third Avenue, 20th Floor, New York, NY 10017-6706, USA, 💻 www.ciee.org) for information.

- AIESEC is a student-run, non-profit organisation that provides paid internships in business and technical fields in over 87 countries and territories, including Germany. You can contact the AIESEC chapter at your university for details of qualifications and application procedures. In the UK, contact AIESEC UK, 29–31 Cowper Street, 2nd Floor, London, EC2A 4AT, UK, ☎ 020-7549 1800, 💻 www.aiesec.co.uk); the website contains detailed contact information for individual countries.

- For those with an interest in politics, the Bundestag provides an internship programme, which combines work and study in Berlin. Students and teachers interested in exchange opportunities should contact the Deutscher Akademischer Austauschdienst (DAAD) for information about its various programmes. Its website is 💻 www.daad.de and the address of the UK service is 34 Belgrave Square, London SW1X 8QB.

- *Transitions Abroad* magazine, aimed at Americans, is a good source of information about a wide range of educational and exchange programmes. Its website (💻 www.transitions abroad.com) contains country-by-country listings of programmes for study, work, internships, volunteering, language study and other fields, all in searchable form.

- The European Union and EURES have a number of programmes for young people interested in training and work experience outside their home country. Contact your country's national employment services agency or the national trade association for the industry in which you wish to train, who may be able to put you in contact with a suitable German employer. Information on EURES is available on 💻 http://europa.eu.int (see also page 29).

AU PAIRS

People between the ages of 17 and 30 are eligible to work as au pairs for a German family. Technically speaking, this isn't a job at all but a 'cultural exchange experience' for both the au pair and the family involved. The au pair system in Germany is strictly regulated and generally conforms to the terms of the European Council decree on au pairs, although Germany has never officially ratified this decree.

In Germany, as in most of Europe, an au pair is a live-in part-time child minder who may also be expected to perform light housekeeping duties, in exchange for which he or she receives room and board and pocket money. The great majority of au pairs in Germany, as is the case elsewhere, are young women, but male au pairs are generally accepted, particularly in families with young boys. (On the whole, the Germans are rather less anxious about men working in positions such as this than the Americans or British.)

Au pairs must be allowed adequate free time to attend language classes and cultural events and to pursue other activities and interests. The official brochure on au pair work from the Arbeitsamt stresses that an au pair should be considered more of a family member than an employee. There are many cases of successful placements where families maintain contact with their former au pairs for many years afterwards. Unfortunately, there are also regular horror stories of au pairs burdened with long hours of strenuous work, driven to distraction by spoiled, unruly children, or even preyed upon by unscrupulous family members.

While it's possible (if you're an EU national) to arrange for an au pair position directly with a family, it's usually better to use a reliable agency. **Prospective au pairs from outside the EU must be placed by an agency licensed by the local office of the Arbeitsamt.** This ensures that the proper immigration documents have been obtained and that the terms of the contract are in accordance with the applicable laws. Au pairs are generally contracted to work for 10 to 12 months. It also provides you with someone to turn to should problems arise during your stay. Most agencies provide au pairs with a list of other au pairs living in the area, and they may even arrange small social gatherings or excursions to encourage interaction.

You can contact an au pair agency in your home country to assist you with a placement or contact a German agency directly (e.g. by phone, fax or e-mail). Many au pair agencies can be contacted via their websites, although you should check carefully that they're bona fide agencies. Check for affiliation with both the German Arbeitsamt and one or more of the various international au pair associations that monitor practices.

Agencies will ask you to complete an application form. This will request considerable background information about you – hobbies, interests, training, experience of living and working with young children, education, etc. – in order to match you with a suitable host family. You will be required to provide references (sometimes in German) and evidence of good health. Most au pair agencies expect you to have some knowledge of German, even if it's basic. Applicants from outside the EU (except those from the US, Norway and Iceland) must apply for a visa at a German embassy or a consulate in their home country (see page 72). You should allow at least two months for processing and must have the visa **before** you arrive in Germany.

When an agency has matched you with a family, you should receive a written 'invitation' which serves both as an introduction to your host family and as a form of contract for the au pair position. You will be expected to spend up to five hours a day (on average of 30 hours a week) tending the children and performing light household chores. Typical duties include dressing and bathing children, taking them to school and picking them up, preparing light meals or snacks for them, and playing with them or supervising their play. Light housekeeping chores may include cleaning up after yourself and the children, helping with laundry or ironing, and running errands for the family as required. You shouldn't be expected to undertake heavy house cleaning, redecoration of the home or other caretaker-type duties, but you're free to help if you wish. In fact, your stay is likely to be much more enjoyable if you pitch in with family chores and activities.

The host family must provide you with health and accident insurance during your stay, as well as room and board. They must also give you pocket money (*Taschengeld*), currently a minimum of €205 a month, which isn't considered a salary but an 'allowance'. In addition, you're entitled to have your own room in the family home, at least one full day free each week and adequate free time to take language classes, pursue cultural and other activities, and to attend religious services if applicable. You're also entitled to four weeks' holiday during a 12-month contract (somewhat less for a shorter term). This is free time for you to return to your home country or to travel independently of your host family.

Working as an au pair can be a wonderful opportunity to meet people and experience real German family life, or it can be a nightmare, depending on the individuals involved. If serious problems arise between you and your host family, you should contact the agency that placed you. They will attempt to work out any misunderstandings and, if necessary, find you an alternative family. They will also find another au pair to take your place if the arrangement needs to be cut short for any reason. You should never remain with a family if you're unhappy at the way you're treated. Most agencies, however, will hesitate to intervene during the first few weeks that you're in Germany, on the assumption that in the early days of your contract a certain amount of homesickness or culture shock is natural for a young person living away from home for the first time.

There are many au pair agencies in Germany through which you can find an au pair position, including the following:

- Agentur Grenz, Friedrich-Weich Strasse 20, 76189 Karlsruhe, ☎ 721-986 36 82, ✉ vgrenz@t-online.de);
- MAX AuPair International, Rehhagenhof 42, 33619 Bielefeld, ☎ 521-16 00 50, ✉ maxaupair@aol.com).

Websites of interest to those considering an au pair position in Germany include:

- 💻 http://au-pairs.de;
- 💻 www.uapa.com (Universal Au Pair Association);
- 💻 www.iapa.org (International Au Pair Association).

WORKING ILLEGALLY

Working illegally isn't nearly as easy or as lucrative an option in Germany as it is in some other European countries and is more dangerous than in most. Germans tend to be law-abiding people, who are knowledgeable about regulations that apply to the workforce. Industrial workers are also well aware of the threat of cheap foreign labour in a country with a high standard of living. Foreign labourers on building sites have been subjected to harassment and sometimes unexplained 'accidents' resulting in a few fatalities, even when operating within the law. Young women eager for high-paying employment in Germany have been tempted by organised criminal bands promising jobs, only to find themselves part of prostitution or white slavery rings. Until some years ago, even the holding of a second job was considered a form of working in the black economy (*Schwartzarbeit*) and was officially illegal.

Unscrupulous employers use illegal labour in order to pay low wages and avoid mandatory social insurances, particularly for foreigners who are unable to obtain residence visas. Foreigners caught working illegally are subject to deportation and fines. The employer can also be fined and may be required to reimburse the state for any costs incurred in deporting illegal employees. Even if you aren't caught, if you work illegally, you have no entitlement to social security benefits, such as health care, unemployment pay or pension contributions. Without the proper paperwork, you will be unable to open a bank account, seek medical treatment or rent an apartment.

LANGUAGE

Although English is Germany's second language and is taught in state schools from an early age, so that a considerable number of Germans have a reasonable knowledge of English and many job advertisements require good English skills, if you're remotely serious about finding a job in Germany, you must speak German at a basic conversational level at the very least. Outside the major cities and tourist areas, it may be difficult to find information or help unless you speak German, particularly in the eastern states.

German belongs to the Indo-European language group and is the mother tongue of over 100 million people world-wide. The standard form of German, grammatically 'pure' and free of accent, is referred to as High German (*Hochdeutsch*), and is generally considered to be that spoken in the northern part of Germany. It's also the language spoken between Germans from different regions, many of whom have strong accents or dialects. There are several regional accents or dialects, including *Bayerisch* (spoken in Bavaria), *Hessich* (Hessen, Frankfurt), *Schwäbisch* (in the south-west of Germany, roughly around the Black Forest region) and *Sächsisch* (parts of Saxony), and there are distinctive accents in Berlin and Cologne. These can be difficult to understand at first if you've learned *Hochdeutsch* at school. There are also what amount to minor languages, e.g. that of the *Sorb* community in eastern Germany, and *Plattdeutsch* and *Frisian* in northern Germany.

The good news is that Germans are generally fairly easy-going about their language. If your pronunciation is less than perfect or you use the wrong gender (there are three!) or ending for a noun (there can be eight!), it's very unlikely that you will be corrected – at least not in public. Germans recognise that their language can be difficult for foreigners to learn, due to the sheer volume of rules governing everything from word building to irregular verbs. An attempt was made in the mid-1990s to simplify and modernise some spellings – for example, eliminating the *scharfe S* (ß) character. Unfortunately, these changes are being introduced over a period of years, rather than being imposed instantly, and you can expect to see both old and new forms in current use for many years to come, particularly with the number of older Germans who reject such changes as a 'dumbing down' of the language. In fact, the new spelling has been described as madness and has created chaos.

The German language has adopted many English words and terms, particularly from business, computer technology and marketing jargon; for example, 'manager', 'marketing', 'computer', 'online' and many other familiar English words are in common use, both in conversation and in print. Unlike the French, the Germans aren't paranoid about protecting the purity of their language from insidious foreign (i.e. Anglo-Saxon) influences. For information about learning German, see **Language Schools** on page 190.

2.

EMPLOYMENT CONDITIONS

Employment conditions in Germany are governed by German labour law (*Arbeitsgesetze*), collective agreements (*Tarifverträge*), and the terms of an employee's employment contract (*Arbeitsvertrag* – see below). Foreigners are employed under the same conditions as German citizens, although different rules apply to different categories of employee, e.g. directors, managers and shop-floor workers. In general, part-time employees receive the same rights and benefits as full-time employees on a pro rata basis.

German employees enjoy excellent employment conditions and social security benefits, and extensive rights under labour laws, collective agreements and local custom. Labour laws (and there are many) detail the minimum conditions of employment, including working hours, overtime payments, holidays, trial and notice periods, dismissal conditions, health and safety regulations, and trade union rights. Collective agreements are negotiated between unions and employers' associations in many industries, and apply to all workers and employers in the industry, irrespective of whether they're union members. Agreements specify minimum wage levels for each position in the main employment categories for the industry, as well as controlling the permissible working hours and often even holiday periods.

As in many other European countries, all business establishments with more than a handful of workers must have a workers' council (*Betriebsrat*) – see **Unions & Workers' Councils** on page 60.

An employer's general rules and regulations (*Arbeitsbedingungen*) regarding working conditions and benefits applicable to all employees, unless stated otherwise in your employment contract, are usually contained in a booklet provided to employees.

When negotiating your conditions of employment for a job in Germany, the checklists at the end of this chapter will prove useful.

Mini-Jobs

The severity of the unemployment situation combined with the high costs and responsibilities falling on employers when hiring people has prompted the Government recently to introduce significant labour market reforms, which essentially create a subsidiary realm of work where different rules apply: the 'mini-job'. These offer no protection against dismissal, no permanent contract and no union involvement, and are poorly paid – around 20 per cent less than the standard for the industry concerned – but are considered to be 'better than no job at all'. Surprisingly, Germany's powerful unions have accepted the concept.

Employees who earn up to €400 per month don't have to pay any income tax or social security contributions and their employers pay a flat rate of 25 per cent to cover the latter. Those earning between €400 and €800 pay lower tax and social security than those with 'proper' jobs.

EMPLOYMENT CONTRACTS

Under German law, a contract exists as soon as you undertake a job for which you expect to be paid, although employees nearly always have a written employment contract (*Arbeitsvertrag*) to document the existence of a formal work relationship (*Arbeitsverhältnis*). This relationship is regulated by various labour laws (*Arbeitsgesetze*), which contain specific requirements for virtually every aspect of employment.

Employment contracts usually contain a paragraph stating the date from which they take effect and to whom they apply.

The standard employment contract is usually referred to as an 'unlimited' contract (*unbefristete Vertrag*), meaning that it's for an indefinite period. It usually includes a probationary period of one to six months, depending on the job or industry, before the contract becomes legal and binding on both parties.

A 'limited' employment contract (*befristete Vertrag*) is a contract for a fixed term, usually 6 to 18 months. Normally the job ends on the expiration date, which must be stated in the contract, but under certain conditions the working relationship may be extended to up to two years. If an employee continues to work after the end of a limited contract, he automatically falls under the rules for an unlimited contract and is considered a permanent employee of the company, whether or not a written contract exists. Limited contracts are normally used only in cases where a company needs a temporary substitute, e.g. when a key employee is on maternity leave, or to complete a project without taking on additional long-term workers. The laws controlling limited contracts are strict and somewhat complicated.

All employment contracts are subject to German labour law and references may be made to other regulations such as collective agreements. Anything in contracts contrary to statutory provisions and unfavourable to an employee may be challenged in a labour court (*Arbeitsgericht*), but in principle you're allowed to strike an agreement with your employer that waives some or all of your rights under the law or the collective agreement.

As with all contracts, you should know exactly what an employment contract contains before signing it. If your German isn't fluent, you should obtain an English translation or at least have it translated verbally so that you don't receive any nasty surprises later.

SALARY & BENEFITS

Your salary (*Lohn/Gehalt*) is stated in your employment contract, and details of salary reviews, planned increases and cost of living rises may also be included. Salaries in job contracts are normally stated in gross terms (*Brutto*), i.e. before all deductions and withholdings for benefits, taxes and social security. Salaries are generally paid monthly, although they may be quoted in contracts on an hourly, monthly or annual basis, depending on the type of job you're being offered. If a bonus is paid, such as a 13th month's salary or the so-called 'holiday bonus' in the summer, this is stated in your employment contract. If you're quoted an annual salary in your contract, you should divide this by either 13, 13.5 or 14 as appropriate to arrive at your monthly gross pay (see below).

General points, such as the payment of your salary into a bank or post office account and the date of such payments, are usually included in general employment conditions. You will receive a pay 'slip' (usually an A4 document) that itemises your salary, bonuses and any premiums or special rates, and shows tax and other deductions (both your share and your employer's).

Salaries in Germany are generally reviewed once a year, in around November/December, with pay rises taking effect from 1st January of the following year. Annual increases are determined to a large extent by the regional or industry collective agreements that apply to your German employer. Small 'merit' increases above the general negotiated pay rise may be granted to individual employees, but the total amounts available for such increases are subject to close scrutiny by workers' councils.

13th Month's Salary & Bonuses

Most employers in Germany pay their employees' annual salary in 13 (or sometimes 14) instalments and not 12. If your employment contract mentions a 'holiday' bonus, this usually means that a '13th month' is paid – half in the summer (usually July) and half at the year end. In some managerial positions, a full month's salary is paid both in July and at the end of the year, either in December or early in January, amounting to 14 months' salary. In either case, the annual salary quoted in your contract is the total you will receive in a year. Divide this by either 13 or 14 to determine what your 'regular' monthly salary will be. In your first and last year of employment, your 13th month salary or holiday bonus is paid pro rata if you don't work a full calendar year.

Some employers operate an additional annual voluntary bonus (*Gratifikation*) scheme, based on an employee's individual performance or the employer's profits. If you're employed on a contract basis for a fixed period, you may also be paid an end-of-contract bonus depending on the terms of your contract.

Expenses

Expenses (*Spesen*) paid by an employer are usually listed in your employment conditions. These may include travel costs from your home to your place of work, usually consisting of a second class rail season ticket or the equivalent cost, paid monthly with your salary. Companies without an employee restaurant or canteen may pay a lunch allowance or provide luncheon vouchers. Expenses paid for travel on company business or for training and education may be detailed in your employment conditions or listed in a separate document.

WORKING HOURS & OVERTIME

Working hours (*Arbeitsstunden*) in Germany vary according to your employer, your position, the industry in which you're employed and the regional or industry collective agreement. The average is around 37 hours per week, with some industries formally on 35-hour or even four-day working weeks in order to try to preserve as many jobs as possible.

In some industries, particularly in manufacturing or factories, work may start as early as 7 or 7.30am with quitting time at 3.30 or 4pm, depending on the length of the official lunch break. Most business premises are open from around 6.30 or 7am until 6 or 7pm. Companies with a 35 or 37-hour working week may close completely on Friday afternoons.

Coffee or tea breaks (*Pausezeit*) are strictly scheduled in Germany, where the right to break time (like everything else, it seems) is enshrined in both the law and most union contracts. Breaks usually last 15 or 20 minutes and are strictly monitored. Lunch breaks may be only 30 minutes, although 45 minutes to an hour for lunch is usual in most offices. Eating at your desk is generally frowned upon unless you have urgent work to complete. And don't forget to wish your co-workers '*Mahlzeit*' as they leave for their lunch break. (The word literally means 'mealtime' and it can be debated whether it's a wish that they have a pleasant lunch or just confirmation that you've noted the time they started their lunch break!)

If you work more than the standard number of hours in a week, you must usually be paid overtime at a premium of at least 25 per cent (i.e. 125 per cent of your regular hourly rate). The overtime premium often depends on the time of day when the overtime is worked, with overtime after 9 or 10pm subject to higher premiums than overtime worked during 'regular' working hours. Work on Saturdays, Sundays or public holidays is usually paid at premium rates, from 150 per cent ('time and a half') up to 200 per cent ('double time') for Sunday work. Employers can offer time off to compensate for weekend or holiday work and this must be at the appropriate premium rate (e.g. double time off for a Sunday worked, time and a half for a Saturday).

Salaried employees, particularly executives and managers, aren't generally paid overtime, although this depends on their employment contracts and their legal classification within the company. Salaried employees may receive compensating time off, particularly for holidays or weekend days, if their presence was required outside their normal work schedule for some reason.

It may come as a nasty surprise to some foreigners to discover that many German employers (including some large companies) require all employees to clock in and out of work. If you're caught fiddling the clock, you're liable for instant dismissal (subject, of course, to the approval of the *Betriebsrat*).

Flexi-Time

Many German companies operate flexi-time (*Gleitzeit*) working hours. A flexi-time system requires all employees to be present between certain hours, known as the block time (*Blockzeit*), for example, from 8.30 to 11.30am and from 1.30 to 4pm. Block time can start as early as 7.30 or 8am, which isn't early by German standards. Employees may make up their required working hours by starting earlier than the required block time, reducing their lunch break or working later. Smaller companies may allow employees to work as late as they wish, provided they don't exceed the maximum permitted daily working hours. Because flexi-time rules are often quite complicated, they may be contained in a separate set of regulations.

TRAVEL & RELOCATION EXPENSES

Travel and relocation expenses in Germany depend on your agreement with your employer and are usually included in your employment contract or conditions. If you're hired from outside Germany, your air ticket and other travel costs are often booked and paid for by your employer or his representative. You can usually also claim any incidental travel costs, e.g. for transport to and from airports. If you travel by car to Germany, you can usually claim a mileage rate (actually a kilometre rate) or the cost of an equivalent flight.

An employer may pay a fixed relocation allowance based on your salary, position and size of your family, or he may pay the total cost of removal. Most German employers pay your relocation costs up to a specified amount, although you may be required to sign a contract which stipulates that if you resign before a certain period elapses (e.g. five years), you must repay a percentage of your removal costs, depending on your length of service. An allowance should be sufficient to move the contents of an average house (castles aren't usually catered for) and you must normally pay any excess costs yourself. If you don't want to ship your furniture to Germany or have only a few belongings to ship, it may be possible to purchase furniture locally up to the limit of your allowance. For international relocations, it's common to receive an extra month's salary to cover incidentals, such as electrical equipment you must replace. Check with your employer. When the company is liable for the total cost, you may be asked to obtain two or three removal estimates.

Generally you're required to organise and pay for the removal in advance. Your employer usually reimburses the equivalent amount in euros after you've paid the bill, although it may be possible to get him to pay the bill directly or make a cash advance. If you change jobs within Germany, your new employer may pay your relocation expenses when it's necessary for you to move house. Don't forget to ask, as they may not offer to pay (it may depend on how desperate they are to employ you).

INSURANCE & PENSIONS

Social Security

All German employees, foreign employees working for German companies and the self-employed must enrol in the German social security (*Sozialversicherung*) system. Social security includes disability, health, long-term care and unemployment benefits, work accident insurance and pensions. Contributions are usually calculated as a percentage of your gross income and are deducted at source by your employer. The cost of social security contributions is split 50-50 between you and your employer. Social security contributions are high (to cover the comprehensive and generous benefits available) and can easily total 40 per cent or more of gross pay, i.e. your share will be around 20 per cent. For details see **Social Security** on page 287.

Health Insurance

Health insurance is mandatory for all workers in Germany and is considered part of the social security system. Employees can choose from a number of state-run health insurance providers for cover for themselves and their families. Above certain salary levels, employees may choose to have private health insurance, although this must be purchased and paid for through your employer, as if it were part of the state plan. For further information see page 295.

Unemployment Insurance

Unemployment insurance is compulsory for all employees of German companies and is covered by social security contributions. For details see **Unemployment Insurance** on page 290.

Salary Insurance

Salary insurance for sickness and accidents is included under social security, usually as part of your health or work accident cover. For information see **Health Insurance** on page 289 and **Work Accident Insurance** on page 292.

Company Pension Fund

Due to the comprehensive German state retirement plan, private or company pensions haven't been considered necessary and many companies don't offer a private pension scheme. This is starting to change, particularly as the state has been forced to scale back the generosity of its benefits. If you're working for a large international company, you may have the option to continue participation in the company pension plan while you're working in Germany. For further information about private pension plans in Germany (usually through banks or life insurance companies), see **Supplementary Pensions** on page 296.

HOLIDAYS & LEAVE

Annual Holidays

Your annual holiday entitlement (*Urlaubsanspruch*) depends on your employer, and the regional collective agreement (*tarifliche Vereinbarung*) under which he operates. Under German labour law, all employees working a five-day week must receive a minimum holiday allowance of 20 working days (i.e. four weeks) per year. In fact, in most industries, 25 days (or five weeks) is standard. Part-time employees receive a pro rata holiday allowance based on their normal working week. For example, if you normally work three days a week, your annual holiday allowance will be 15 days (five weeks at three days a week). Employers cannot count official German public holidays (see below) as annual holiday.

Some collective agreements provide for longer annual holidays or grant extra days to employees based on their age or long service. In some industries, the collective agreement may call for a summer shut-down, when all employees are required to take the same two or three weeks' holiday while a factory or business is closed. An individual employer may also declare a holiday shut-down, but this must be announced in advance and be approved by the workers' council. Many businesses close between Christmas and New Year, again requiring employees to use part of their holiday allowance.

Be sure to ask about the process for requesting your desired holiday dates in advance, particularly if the bulk of your holiday time is already committed to business closure periods. There's usually a formal process for submitting holiday requests, often surprisingly early in the year. Senior employees are given priority over more junior workers under contract rules or other regulations, but only if they make their preferences known according to the rules. Employees with children usually have priority on taking holidays during local school breaks, and married people are often allowed to schedule their holidays at the same times as those of their spouse, whether they work for the same company or not.

Under German law, new employees are entitled to take holiday time only after six months' work, and most employers won't permit you to take any holiday until you've at least completed your probationary period (anything from one to six months). Before starting a new job, check that your new employer will approve any planned holidays, particularly if they fall within your probationary period.

Public Holidays

Public holidays (*Feiertage*) vary from state to state (*Land*) and sometimes from community to community within a given *Land*, depending on whether the predominant local religion is Catholic or Protestant. The following days are public holidays in all German states (the nine days prefixed by an asterisk are compulsory but Christmas Eve and New Year's Eve are normally also observed) or certain states as noted:

Date	Holiday
1st January	*New Year's Day (*Neujahr*)
6th January	Epiphany (*Heilige Drei Könige*) – only in Baden-Württemberg, Bavaria and Saxony-Anhalt
March or April	*Good Friday (*Karfreitag*) & *Easter Monday (*Ostermontag*)
1st May	*May Day or Labour Day (*Tag der Arbeit*)
May or June	*Ascension Day (*Himmelfahrt*)
	*Pentecost or Whitsun (*Pfingsten/Pfingstmontag*)
	Corpus Christi (*Fronleichnam*) – only in Baden-Württemberg, Bavaria, Hessen, North Rhine-Westphalia, Rhineland-Palatinate and Saarland
3rd October	*Day of German Unity (*Tag der Deutschen Einheit*)

31st October	Reformation Day (*Reformationstag*) – Protestant areas only
1st November	All Saints Day (*Allerheiligen*) – Catholic areas only
24th December	Christmas Eve (*Heilige Abend*)
25th December	*Christmas Day (*Weihnacht*)
26th December	*Boxing Day
31st December	New Year's Eve (*Sylvester*)

In predominantly Catholic areas, there may be semi-official holidays for Mardi Gras (*Karneval*) in February, such as *Weiberfastnacht* in Cologne and Düsseldorf, *Fasching* in Bavaria and Baden-Württemberg, or *Rosenmontag* in Bonn, Cologne and Düsseldorf. Baden-Württemburg and Bavaria are well known as the states with the most public holidays each year, usually 12 or 13.

If a public holiday falls on a weekend, there's no substitute weekday holiday. If a holiday falls on a Tuesday or a Thursday, many workers (particularly civil servants) are also allowed to take the preceding Monday or following Friday off. Many German companies close during Christmas and New Year, e.g. from midday on 24th December until 2nd January, all employees being required to take part of their annual holiday allowance on the days that aren't public holidays.

Sick Leave

Employees are entitled to six weeks' paid sick leave, although the period is generally unlimited provided your doctor gives you a sick note (*Krankmeldung*) stating that you're unable to work. To those from countries with less liberal workplace cultures, it may initially appear that their German colleagues are taking advantage of a generous system, although they would be wise to keep such views to themselves; they will soon discover that coming to work with a cold can make them unpopular – the German attitude is 'keep your germs to yourself'.

Compassionate & Special Leave

Most German companies provide additional days off for moving house, your own and a family marriage, birth of a child, death of a family member or close relative, and other compassionate reasons. Grounds for compassionate leave (*Sonderurlaub*) are usually defined in collective agreements.

Pregnancy & Confinement

Under German law, mothers and mothers-to-be are entitled to a wide range of physical and financial protection in the workplace. This responsibility is taken very seriously and there's even a separate law, called the Mother Protection Law (*Mutterschutzgesetz*, abbreviated as *MuSchG*), which spells out the details.

A woman must notify her employer as soon as she's sure that she's pregnant by submitting a notification form from her doctor to the personnel or human resources department. This notification activates the provisions of the Mother Protection Law, which include not only her right to time off when the baby is born, but also restrictions on the type of work she may do during her pregnancy, protection from being fired, additional rest periods and other benefits guaranteed by the law. Maternity protection is the same for all women, irrespective of their length of employment or marital status.

Pregnant employees may not work in jobs requiring them to bend or stretch, or to lift or carry heavy loads. Neither are they allowed to work at night, on Sundays or holidays, or in any job that exposes them to chemical solvents or any other increased risk of illness or accident. They must be permitted adequate time off to attend doctors' appointments and for tests related to the pregnancy. After the start of the fifth month, pregnant employees cannot be required to stand for long periods.

Maternity leave normally starts six weeks before the projected birth date and continues for eight weeks after a baby is born, although this can be extended on doctor's orders. This is regarded as normal sick leave, during which the employee receives her regular salary, although part or all of it may actually be paid by her health insurance provider.

While pregnant or on maternity leave, an employee cannot be fired for any reason, provided the employer has been properly informed of the pregnancy. In fact, it's almost impossible for a pregnant woman to quit her job during her pregnancy, even if she wants to!

Either parent has the right to (unpaid) child-rearing leave (*Erziehungsurlaub*) of up to two years any time before a child reaches his or her third birthday. During this leave you're eligible for child-rearing benefit (*Erziehungsgeld*). Its calculation is quite complicated and the amount generally reduces after the first six months depending on household income. The standard amount is €307 per month (per child), provided your family income doesn't exceed certain limits and you're the only adult at home with the child(ren). During child-rearing leave, you continue to earn credit in the state pension plan as if you were working. Provided you comply with the notification procedures and don't extend your leave beyond the permitted period, your employer must allow you to return to the same job at the same or a higher salary, taking into account general increases in wages and the cost of living. The agency which officially gives advice on *Erziehungsgeld* varies from state to state; for example, in Baden-Württemberg it's the state credit bank, in Berlin the youth welfare office, in Bremen the social services office, and in three other states the war pensions office (!).

EDUCATION & TRAINING

Employee training is taken seriously in Germany, whether it's conducted in your own office or in some exotic location. Training may include management seminars, special technical courses, language lessons or any other form of continuing education. If you need to learn or improve your language proficiency in order to perform your job, the cost of language study may be paid by your employer.

Most employers in Germany are required by law to allocate a set proportion of their gross payroll for employee education and training, and must develop a formal training plan covering all employees within their facility. The works council (*Betriebsrat*) must review and approve the training plan and ensure that the amounts spent are appropriately distributed to benefit workers at all levels in the company. There's usually a significant portion of the training budget available to members of the works council to attend courses covering labour law, management, finance and other areas related to their responsibilities.

It's in your own interest to investigate courses of study, seminars and lectures that you feel will be of benefit to you and your employer. Most employers give reasonable consideration to a request to attend a course during working hours, provided you don't make it a full-time occupation. If you decide to pursue a formal degree or certification programme requiring several months or years to complete, your employer may agree to pay for the programme (including books, examinations and other costs), but only if you sign an agreement to reimburse him should you leave the company within a certain number of years (generally no more than three to five) after you complete the course. If you leave one German company for another, it's likely that your new employer will reimburse you for any fees you've had to repay in this manner, assuming that your new employer will benefit from your training.

UNIONS & WORKERS' COUNCILS

Trade unions in Germany are highly organised and play an important role in the 'social market economy'. By far the largest and most powerful union organisation is the Deutsche Gewerkschaftsbund (DGB), which is an umbrella group for the eight individual industry trade unions that operate throughout Germany. The DGB unions represent all workers in specific industries, irrespective of their job titles or professions, with around 8.6 million members in total. For example, the well-known and powerful IG (Industriegewerkschaft) Metall negotiates for all workers in the metalworking and information technology industries, including factory workers, janitorial crews, office workers and management, whether or not they're members of the union.

Normally, unions negotiate directly with the industry employer organisations and agreements are concluded which establish terms and working conditions for an entire industry, rather than individual companies or categories of employee.

In addition to the DGB unions, there's a managerial employees' union (Deutsche Angestellten-Gewerkschaft/DAG), with some 500,000 members. There's also a union for German civil servants, the Deutsche Beamtenbund (DBB), which is the main employee organisation for civil servants, with over a million members.

Under German law, unions are allowed to organise on company premises but 'closed shops' are banned. Civil servants (i.e. government employees) aren't permitted to strike in Germany, although they may be members of unions. Most private employees have the right to strike, but due to the system of strict co-operation between workers' councils and management, strikes are rare and usually of short duration (an hour or so – just long enough to hold a march and get everyone back to work). Employees in the private sector (including management employees) cannot be dismissed for striking, although, as usual in Germany, there are rules and regulations governing exactly how and when strikes must be announced and carried out.

Workers' Councils

All businesses with more than five employees must have a workers' council (*Betriebsrat*). The delegates to this council or committee are elected from among the employees and serve as an advisory board to management, with many of their duties and responsibilities spelled out in German labour law. The workers' council must have regular access to all important financial information and be kept informed of a company's major operating and marketing strategies. It must be consulted before any significant decisions are made that affect the workforce, including redundancies, relocation, or changes in working conditions or schedules.

The workers' council is consulted on the need for overtime or reduced hours and many day-to-day administrative matters, including the hiring and firing of employees, including executive managers. The council can even authorise an employer to impose conditions on the workforce that are contrary to labour law or the local collective agreement, if they feel this is necessary to protect the jobs or rights of the employees they represent. The workers' council also handles individual grievances and brings issues affecting the workforce to management's attention.

In large companies with multiple locations, there's usually a workers' council in each location, and there may also be an all-company workers' council, whose representatives are guaranteed a certain number of seats on the company's board of directors (headquarters staff must also have their workers' council).

Delegates to the council at all levels enjoy special protection from dismissal. They're allowed to use work time for council business, attend meetings and take training classes relating to their position. The industry-wide unions work closely with workers' councils and with management, often providing training programmes and general legal advice on key issues.

OTHER TERMS

Probationary & Notice Periods

For most jobs there's a probationary period (*Probezeit*), ranging from one to six months, depending on the type of work, your position and the employer. The duration of the probationary period is limited by law, according to the pay level and legal classification of the employee, and normally isn't renewable or extendable. Normally, the probationary period is stated as part of the employment contract or collective agreement. During the probationary period, either party may terminate the employment contract without notice or financial penalty, unless otherwise stated in the employment contract.

If the employee works even for a few hours or days after the end of the official probationary period, he's deemed to have been hired permanently, irrespective of whether an employment contract exists.

Your notice period depends on your employer, profession and length of service, and is usually stated in your employment contract and general employment conditions. If it isn't stated, the legal notice period applies (both to the employee and the employer). The legal notice period varies from one month (which must end on either the 15th or the last day of a calendar month) to seven months, for employees with over 20 years' service.

It isn't unusual for managers or executives to have contracts requiring them to work to the end of the calendar quarter (i.e. March 30th, June 30th, September 30th or December 31st) following the three months' notice period. This means that, if you submit your notice on 3rd April, for example, you may be expected to work until the end of September. The notice period may rise to six months or even a year after a few years in the job, which, if applicable, will be noted in your employment contract.

It's possible to waive part or all of the notice period if both sides agree, although this normally requires that the departing employee give up his/her right to a redundancy payment, which can amount to several months' salary and is usually at least partly tax-free. If an employer goes bankrupt and cannot pay you, you can terminate your employment without notice. Other valid reasons for not giving notice are assault or abuse of you or a colleague by your employer or other gross violations of the terms of your employment contract.

Part-Time Job Restrictions

Restrictions on part-time employment (*Nebenarbeit*) are usually detailed in your employment conditions. Most German companies don't allow full-time employees to work part-time (i.e. moonlight) for another employer, particularly one in the same line of business. You may, however, be permitted to take a part-time teaching job or similar part-time employment (or you can write a book!).

Changing Jobs & Confidentiality

Companies in a high-tech or highly confidential business may have restrictions on employees moving to a competitor in Germany or within Europe. You should be aware of these restrictions, as they're enforceable under German law, although it's a complex subject and disputes must often be resolved by a court of law. German laws regarding industrial secrets and general employer confidentiality are strict but, like most German labour laws, include considerable protection for the employee. If you breach this confidentiality, you will be dismissed and may be unable to find further employment in Germany.

Acceptance Of Gifts

Employees are normally forbidden to accept gifts (*Geschenkannahme*) of more than a certain value from customers or suppliers. Many suppliers give bottles of wine or small gifts at Christmas that don't breach this rule.

Retirement

Your employment conditions may be valid only until the official German retirement age (*Ruhestand*), usually 65 – depending on your date of birth and sometimes your profession (see page 294). If you wish to continue working after you've reached retirement age, you may be required to negotiate a new employment contract.

Dismissal

The rules governing dismissal and redundancy (severance) pay are complicated and generally depend on an employee's length of service, the reason for the dismissal (e.g. whether misconduct or redundancy) and whether the employee has a protected status, such as that enjoyed by works council (*Betriebsrat*) members, who can only be dismissed for 'serious misconduct'.

After your probationary period, you can be dismissed only for a valid (and stated) reason, and the proposed dismissal must be reviewed and approved by the workers' council before notice is given. The works council can oppose the dismissal of an employee, if they feel that the grounds are unfair or lacking in substance. In the event of an 'economic' lay-off involving a number of employees, an employer is obliged to submit a written plan to the works council, detailing the reasons for the action, the method for selecting the employees to be made redundant and the redundancy package being offered. The council then has to be given time to review the plan and all the supporting documentation, comment and offer suggestions or alternatives for minimising the number of redundancies.

Irrespective of the reason for the dismissal, a strict procedure must be followed. This involves the formal notification of the employee (or each employee in the case of mass redundancies) by letter to his or her home address. The letter must include the official reason for the termination, make reference to any previous disciplinary actions or warnings (if applicable), and indicate the effective employment termination date in accordance with the legal or contractual notice terms. Normally it's expected that the employee will work up to his date of termination, even though that date may be three months or more away. If an employee is being fired for a serious offence (e.g. stealing from the company or assault on a co-worker), he may be barred from returning to work; however, the employer must usually still pay the employee's salary for the full term of the notice period.

A dismissed employee is entitled to accrued holiday pay and a redundancy payment, which is determined according to his normal pay rate, years of service, family situation and any extenuating or unusual circumstances. There's no legally prescribed minimum, but each region and industry has guidelines for what's 'fair' under various circumstances, usually calculated as a number of months' salary. A minimal redundancy can be paid if an employee is dismissed for serious misconduct, but most labour courts will insist on at least a minimum termination payment no matter how serious the reason for dismissal.

If any of the procedural details of the dismissal have been overlooked or poorly carried out (particularly involving the notice period), the employee can go to a labour law court (*Arbeitsgericht*) and demand to be reinstated in his old job (at which point, the employer starts the dismissal process over again, being particularly careful not to miss any of the details this time). A labour law judge can also require an employer to increase the redundancy payment to comply with local standards or to compensate for other injustices committed during the dismissal process.

CHECKLISTS

When negotiating your terms of employment for a job in Germany, the following checklists will prove useful. The points listed under **General Positions** (below) apply to most jobs, while those listed under **Executive Positions** (see page 68) usually apply to executive and managerial appointments only.

General Positions

Salary

- Is the total salary (including expenses) paid in euros or will it be paid in another country (in a different currency) with expenses for living in Germany?
- Is the total adequate, taking into account the high cost of living in Germany? Is the salary index-linked?
- When and how often is the salary reviewed?
- Does the salary include a 13th month's salary and annual or end-of-contract bonuses?
- Is overtime paid or time off given in lieu of extra hours worked?

Relocation Expenses

- Are removal expenses or a relocation allowance paid?
- Does the allowance include travelling expenses for all family members?
- Is there a limit and is it adequate?

- Are you required to repay relocation expenses (or a percentage) if you resign before a certain period has elapsed?
- Are you required to pay for your relocation in advance? This can run into many thousands of euros for normal house contents.
- If your employer fires you before a certain period has elapsed, under what conditions will your repatriation expenses be paid or reimbursed?
- If employment is for a limited period, will your relocation costs be paid by the employer when you leave Germany?
- If you aren't shipping household goods and furniture to Germany, is there an allowance for buying furnishings locally?
- Do relocation expenses include the legal and estate agent's fees incurred when moving home?
- Does the employer use the services of a relocation consultant?

Accommodation

- Will the employer pay for a hotel (or pay a lodging allowance) until you find permanent accommodation?
- Is subsidised or free (temporary or permanent) accommodation provided? If so, is it furnished or unfurnished?
- Must you pay for utilities, such as electricity, gas and water?
- If accommodation isn't provided by the employer, is assistance provided to find accommodation? What does it consist of?
- What will accommodation cost?
- Are your expenses paid while looking for accommodation?

Working Hours

- What are the weekly working hours?
- Does the employer operate a flexi-time system? If so, what are the fixed working hours? How early must you start? Can you carry forward extra hours worked and take time off at a later date or carry forward a deficit and make it up later?
- Are you required to clock in and out of work?

Holidays & Leave

- What is the annual leave entitlement? Does it increase with age?
- What are the paid public holidays? Is Monday or Friday a free day when a public holiday falls on a Tuesday or Thursday respectively?
- Is free air travel to your home country or elsewhere provided for you and your family and, if so, how often?

Insurance

- Is extra insurance cover provided besides obligatory insurance?
- Is free life insurance provided?
- Is health insurance provided for you and your family? What does it include?
- For how long will your salary be paid if you're ill or have an accident?

Company Pension

- What percentage of your salary must you pay?
- Are you able to pay a lump sum into the pension fund in order to receive a full or higher pension?
- Is the pension transportable to another employer or to another location with the same employer?

Employer

- What are the employer's prospects?
- Is his profitability and growth rate favourable?
- Does he have a good reputation as an employer?
- Does he have a high staff turnover? If so, why?

Other Terms

- Are free or subsidised German-language lessons provided for you and your spouse?

- Is a travelling allowance paid from your German residence to your place of work?

- Is free or subsidised parking provided at your place of work?

- Is a free or subsidised company restaurant provided? If not, is a lunch allowance paid? Some German companies provide excellent staff restaurants, which save you both money and time.

- Will the employer provide or pay for any professional training or education required, if necessary abroad? Will he pay for part or the total cost of non-essential education, e.g. a computer or language course?

- Are free work clothes or overalls provided? Does the employer pay for the cleaning of work clothes (including office clothes)?

- Does the employer provide any fringe benefits, such as subsidised in-house banking services, low interest loans, inexpensive petrol, employees' shop or product discounts, sports and social facilities, and subsidised tickets, e.g. for local theatres or sports events?

- Do you have a written list of your job responsibilities?

- Have your employment conditions been confirmed in writing?

- If a dispute arises over your salary or working conditions, under the law of which country will your employment contract be interpreted?

Executive Positions

- Is private schooling for your children paid for or subsidised? Will the employer pay for a boarding school in Germany or abroad?

- Is the salary index-linked or protected against devaluation and cost of living increases? This is particularly important if you're paid in a foreign currency that fluctuates wildly or could be devalued against the euro. Are you paid an allowance for working in Germany?

- Is there a non-contributory pension fund besides the compulsory German scheme? Is it transferable and, if so, what are the conditions?

- Are the costs incurred by a move to Germany reimbursed? For example, the cost of selling your home, employing an agent to let it for you or storing household effects.

- Will the employer pay for domestic help or make a contribution towards the cost of a servant or cook?

- Is a car provided? With a chauffeur?

- Are you entitled to any miscellaneous benefits such as membership of a club or free credit cards?

- Is there an entertainment allowance?

- Is there a clothing allowance? For example, if you arrive in Germany in the winter from the tropics, you will probably need to buy winter clothes.

- Is compensation paid if you're made redundant or fired? Redundancy payments are compulsory for all employees in Germany (subject to length of service), but executives often receive a generous 'golden handshake' if they're made redundant, e.g. after a take-over.

3.

<u>Permits & Visas</u>

If you plan to live or work in Germany and, in some cases, even if you're only visiting, you may require a visa and/or a work permit. To remain in Germany for longer than three months, you require a residence permit, irrespective of your country of origin or the purpose of your stay.

VISAS

The requirement to obtain a visa before entering Germany changes periodically according to the German Foreign Office's assessment of the risk of illegal immigration (according to the outbreak of wars, civil unrest, economic collapse and other global disruptions). It's a very rough rule of thumb that the poorer the country the higher the probability that a visa will be needed for even a short visit, although in most cases visas are required only for stays of more than three months. The regulations outlined below were current in early 2003.

- EU nationals plus those of Iceland, Norway and Liechtenstein (together forming the EEA) don't require a visa to visit Germany for any purpose. After three months in the country, however, they must obtain a residence permit (see page 73).

- Nationals of the former Soviet Union and most African and Asian countries require a visa to enter Germany for any purpose.

- Nationals of American Samoa, Andorra, Argentina, Australia, Bermuda, Bolivia, Brazil, Brunei, Canada, Chile, Christmas Island, Cocos Islands, Cook Islands, Costa Rica, Croatia, Cyprus, the Czech Republic, Ecuador, El Salvador, Estonia, Guam, Guatemala, Honduras, Hungary, Hong Kong (HK-SAR only), Israel, Japan, Korea (Republic of), Latvia, Lithuania, Macoa (RAE only), Malaysia, Malta, Mexico, Monaco, Nicaragua, Nive, New Caledonia, New Zealand, Norfolk Island, Panama, Paraguay, Poland, San Marino, Singapore, the Slovak Republic, Slovenia, Switzerland, USA, Uruguay, Vatican City, Venezuela and the US Virgin Islands don't require a visa for stays of up to three months, provided they don't intend to do any paid or self-employed work. They may not enter Germany as a tourist and change their status to that of an employee, student or resident, but must return to their country of residence and apply for a visa.

Holders of diplomatic passports from certain countries may be exempt from visa requirements.

Visa application forms and full details can be downloaded from German Embassy websites (e.g. 🖳 www.german-embassy.org.uk in the UK). Visas may be valid for a single entry only or for multiple entries within a limited period. A visa is stamped in your passport, which must be valid for at least four months at the time of entry into Germany.

Transit Visas

Those changing planes in Germany require a transit visa if they're nationals of the following countries: Afghanistan, Angola, Bangladesh, Ethiopia, Eritrea, Gambia, Ghana, India, Iraq, Iran, Jordan, Democratic Rep. of Congo, Lebanon, Nigeria, Pakistan, Somalia, Sri Lanka, Sudan, Syria, and Turkey.
Exceptions are:

* those that have 'leave to remain in the UK for an indefinite period' or a 'certificate of entitlement to the right of abode in the UK';
* citizens of India, Eritrea and Turkey if they have a valid visa or residence permit for any EEA country or Canada, Switzerland or the US;
* Iranian diplomatic passport holders.

Au Pairs

EEA and US nationals don't require visas. Others are required to apply for a visa at the German embassy or a consulate in their home country. You should allow at least two months for the application to be processed and be aware that you must obtain the visa before you can enter Germany to take up a position. For further information about au pairs, see page 43.

RESIDENCE PERMITS

Subject to visa requirements (see above), foreigners are permitted to stay in Germany for up to three months without a residence permit (*Aufenthaltserlaubnis*). After this time, all foreigners, must have a residence permit.

No one has an automatic right to a residence permit in Germany. There are no clear legal guidelines, and the issue of permits is largely at the discretion of the local issuing office. If you have a criminal record or a serious contagious disease or have previously violated German law, you're likely to be denied a permit.

Nationals of the EEA, Australia, Canada, Israel, Japan, New Zealand, Switzerland and the US can apply for a permit during their first three months in Germany – if you know from the outset that your stay in Germany will be longer than three months, it's wise to start the process immediately after your arrival – or can apply in advance at a German consulate in their home country if this is likely to be more convenient or if you require a work permit (see page 77). All other nationals must apply in their country of domicile for a residence permit, which cannot be sent to them in Germany.

When applying in Germany, you must first register your residence (see page 85) and obtain the necessary application forms for a residence permit from the local residents' registration office (Einwohnermeldeamt). If there are no problems, the official at the registration office will give you a confirmation form (*Anmeldebestätigung*) as proof of your registration. Once you've completed the required forms, you must compile the necessary supporting documentation, which includes some or all of the following:

- Three passport photographs;

- A valid passport;

- Proof of health insurance;

- Proof that you have a place to live (e.g. a signed statement from your landlord);

- Proof of means of support (usually a letter from your employer). If you're married to a German citizen this isn't usually necessary.

- A 'Certificate of Health for Residence Permit' (*Gesundheitszeugnis für Aufenthaltserlaubnis*), which can be obtained from any registered German doctor or local health office (Gesundheitsamt) and costs between around €100 and €150 from a doctor or around half as much from a health office. In some states, blood must be tested for HIV.

- A 'Certificate of Good Conduct', which can be obtained from your home country's embassy or consulate in Germany.

Exact requirements depend on the state (*Land*) and your marital status. For example, the last two items aren't required everywhere – your local *Ausländeramt* will tell you what you need. Being married to a German citizen makes the process simpler and also means that you're exempt from paying a fee, which is normally €40.

You must then take your completed application forms and documents to your local foreigners' office (Ausländeramt). It's sometimes possible to hand everything in at the Einwohnermeldeamt, but this will involve giving up your passport for up to a month. Check the business hours of the Ausländeramt – most are closed in the afternoons and many are open for just a few days a week. There's usually a long queue and you should plan to arrive at least an hour before closing time. In larger towns and cities, there's usually a queue ticket system in the waiting room, such as you might find at a supermarket delicatessen. If you aren't sure or don't understand the instructions posted in German, ask the receptionist.

If you're an EEA national, your application should be processed quite speedily; in large cities there's usually a dedicated counter or service centre for EEA nationals.

Eventually your turn will arrive and you will be called for an interview, which usually takes around ten minutes, provided everything is in order. (First the official will go through a checklist to confirm that you have brought all the necessary documents; if anything is missing, you will be given a sheet indicating what you need and be sent away!) Assuming your paperwork is in order, he will want to speak to you about your job and planned stay.

Obviously the preferred language is German, but if you have problems with this many officials will probably be able to speak enough English to manage the interview. Even so, if you don't know any German at all, you may want to arrange for someone to come with you to translate. However, the officials aren't particularly concerned with how well you can speak the language, but whether you have a place to live and a job that will adequately support you and your dependants. If you can demonstrate to them that you will be a responsible, law-abiding, tax-paying resident, you will normally be granted a permit.

At the end of this process, and having paid your fee, you will receive a residence permit for a period of between six months and five years – the duration depending largely on your country of origin. For example, EEA nationals are entitled to a five-year residence permit immediately, although you must specifically apply for one and you must have either a job in Germany or evidence of means of support (including proof of health insurance) in order to qualify. Non-EEA nationals are normally issued with a one-year permit.

After five years, EEA citizens are entitled to an open-ended residence permit. Non-EEA nationals can apply for one after five years, unless they have a German spouse, in which case the period is three years. To obtain an open-ended permit, you're required to be able to speak at least basic German as well as have proof of employment or means of support.

Your residence permit must be attached to a current passport in order to be valid. This means that, if your passport expires while you're in Germany, you must go through the process of applying for a residence permit again once you receive a new passport. Therefore, if your passport is due to expire in the near future, it may pay you to renew it in advance to avoid the hassle (and expense) of having to apply for a new residence permit.

Your children must also have residence permits, which are entered individually in their passports, and they must attend the interview with you to be registered. If you have a baby during your stay in Germany, you should obtain a passport for the baby from your consulate before going to the Ausländeramt. Babies must also be registered with the Einwohnermeldeamt, but this is usually done by the hospital where the baby is delivered. You should check with the hospital for the documentation required to register a baby (see also **Registration** on page 278).

Residence permits can be renewed at the Ausländermeldeamt, but you should apply well before your permit expires. Provided they still meet the necessary criteria for residence, EEA citizens receive an open-ended permit once their original five-year permit has expired; non-EEA nationals must renew their permits every year for five years, after which they also receive an open-ended permit. There's a renewal fee of €20.

Students

In order to remain in Germany for longer than three months, all foreign students, including those from EU countries, must have a residence permit. The procedure is the same as for other EU nationals, with registration at the residents' registration office (Einwohnermeldeamt) followed by a visit to the office for foreigner registration (Ausländermeldeamt). The documentation required for students is, however, different and includes:

- two passport photographs;
- a valid identification card or passport;
- proof of health insurance;
- a rental contract;
- proof of adequate financial resources – the minimum amount required varies depending on the area and is around €700 per month;
- a certificate of study (*Studienbescheinigung*) or notice of admission (*Zulassungsbescheid*).

The requirement regarding proof of financial resources is strict. It isn't sufficient to say that you plan to work, even if you've already obtained a work permit. One possibility is to obtain a formal statement of liability from a third party who will assume responsibility for your living expenses, accompanied by evidence that they have sufficient financial resources. Alternatively, you can open a bank account with the required sum for one year deposited in advance.

Foreign students who are EU nationals or come from Honduras, Iceland, Liechtenstein, Monaco, Norway, San Marino, Switzerland or the US can wait until after their arrival in Germany before starting the visa application process. It's best to start it immediately upon arrival, however, as the procedure can take from eight to ten weeks. Other nationals must begin the application process at a German consulate or embassy in their home country and obtain a visa before arriving in Germany. Note that once in Germany, it isn't possible to change a tourist visa to a student visa.

WORK PERMITS

Citizens of EU member countries don't require permits to work in other EU states. Non-EU nationals (including those from the US and Canada), however, must obtain a work permit (*Arbeitserlaubnis*) before they're permitted to start work. There are stiff fines for employers who hire people without work permits, so most will demand that you have one before starting work. In order to obtain a work permit, you must first obtain a residence permit (see above), although this is no guarantee that you will immediately receive a work permit. The application procedure for non-EU nationals is as follows:

- After your residence permit (see above) has been issued, you must take this to the local employment office (Arbeitsamt) and apply for a temporary (three-month) work permit. This can take eight weeks to obtain, so you may apply for both residence and work permits before arriving in Germany.

- If your residence permit is for less than a year, you must return to the Ausländeramt with your temporary work permit to apply for a one-year residence permit.

- Finally, you take the one-year residence permit to the Arbeitsamt and receive a one-year work permit (the system was designed by and for civil servants).

German law prohibits employers from hiring non-EU nationals unless they're unable to find a German or EU national who's qualified and available to fill a position. When a non-EU national applies for a work permit, he therefore requires documentation to support his application. As the work permit is contingent on your having found employment, you require evidence from a prospective employer that he wishes (and is permitted) to hire you. This is typically a copy of an employment contract (*Arbeitsvertrag*), but it can be a letter or written statement offering you a job. You must also provide a detailed description of the job from your employer with a statement explaining why you, a non-EU national, are uniquely qualified for the position. You may also be asked to provide copies of your educational, professional and trade qualifications. Americans are usually able to receive their work permits without much red tape, once employment has been found.

In all cases, work permits are linked to a particular employer and, if you change jobs, you need a new work permit. It's also necessary to renew a work permit before it expires.

If you're a non-EU national married to a German citizen, the procedure is simplified and it isn't necessary to find a job before applying. Your initial work permit will apply to any job, including self-employment, although restrictions apply to the setting-up of certain businesses (e.g. restaurants and other catering establishments), for which you may need a licence. Also, no time limit applies to your permit provided your residence permit remains valid. Processing is also much quicker and simpler, and a permit is usually issued on the day you apply. In addition to your passport and residence permit, you need your marriage certificate and your spouse's passport, but your spouse doesn't need to accompany you (although you may wish to have him or her along for linguistic or moral support).

Self-employment for non-EU nationals is generally restricted, although freelance journalists, writers, artists, tutors and sales representatives are sometimes excepted. Moving to Germany and opening a shop or restaurant, for example, is prohibited. This also applies to non-EU spouses of German nationals – usually for the first three years of residence. Any limitations will be stated on your residence permit, and the official issuing the permit will tell you exactly what's permitted and what isn't. Restrictions are lifted when an open-ended residence permit is issued (see **Residence Permits** above).

If you anticipate being self-employed, you must apply for a trade licence (*Gewerbeschein*) at the local Trade Supervision Office (Gewerbeaufsichtsamt), although some occupations (e.g. artist, journalist, academic and doctor) are exempt from this requirement.

Spouses of non-EU employees who are on assignment in Germany aren't automatically entitled to a work permit. This can lead to frustration, particularly if the accompanying spouse is a professional in his own right, and needs to be considered carefully before a couple moves to Germany. The good news is that there are some exceptions to this general rule. For example, companies that transfer employees abroad may offer assistance in finding employment within their operation for a spouse. A spouse may also be able to demonstrate to an employer that she has unique qualifications to fill a position that cannot be performed by a German or EU national. Non-professional spouses have a number of options for obtaining employment in Germany. For example, in most cities there's a demand for native speakers who can teach English and for British or American citizens there's the possibility of finding employment at a US or British military installation.

It's wise for non-EU nationals to secure employment before arriving in Germany; otherwise, given the high level of unemployment and restrictions on the employment of non-EU nationals, you may end up being forced to return home after three months.

Students

In general, foreign students must be authorised by the Arbeitsamt to work in Germany. Generally they aren't permitted to work during terms (semesters) but may work without a permit during term breaks. Exceptions may be made if there's a close connection between a student's studies and a desired job, in which case a student may work during terms without a permit. This is typically a job on the university campus or one organised by the university. If a student wishes to work before commencing or after completing his studies in Germany, he must obtain a work permit. Otherwise, holding a wage-earning job while a student is illegal and can be grounds for expulsion from the country, even if you have time remaining after completing your studies. If you want to work, you must find a job and apply for a work permit at the Arbeitsamt (see **Work Permits** on page 77).

There are, however, special programmes that allow for the reciprocal exchange of students seeking short-term, paid employment in Germany. The biggest and best known of these programmes is administered by the Council on International Educational Exchange (🖳 www.ciee.org). You must apply and receive your work permit before leaving your home country. There's a fixed fee and opportunities exist for three or, in some cases, six months' employment.

If, at the conclusion of your studies, you have an offer of a permanent job, bear in mind that you aren't permitted to remain in Germany with a student visa. The official policy is that you must return to your homeland before you can apply for a residence visa and work permit. However, if your future employer wants you to start work quickly, it may be possible to expedite the process while you remain in Germany by hiring a lawyer to make a petition on your behalf.

4.

ARRIVAL

On arrival in Germany, your first task will be to negotiate immigration and customs. Fortunately this presents few problems for most people, particularly citizens of a country that's a member of the European Union (EU) or the EEA (see page 72). However, non-EU nationals coming to Germany for any purpose other than as visitors usually require a visa (see page 72). Germany is a signatory to the Schengen agreement (named after a Luxembourg village on the Moselle River where the agreement was signed), which came into effect on 1st January 1995 and introduced an open-border policy between member countries. Other Schengen members are Austria, Belgium, France, Greece, Iceland, Italy, Luxembourg, the Netherlands, Portugal, Spain and Sweden. Under the agreement, immigration checks and passport controls take place when you first arrive in a member country, after which you can travel freely between member countries.

If you're travelling to Germany by road from a non-Schengen country, you should bear in mind that not all border posts are open 24-hours a day, therefore if you plan to enter the country via a minor border post you should check the opening times in advance. In addition to information about immigration and customs, this chapter also contains a list of tasks that must be completed before (or soon after) your arrival, and includes suggestions for finding local help and information. **Note that you should carry an identity card, passport or residence permit with you when in Germany.**

IMMIGRATION

When you arrive in Germany from another EU country, there are usually no immigration checks or passport controls such as those you will encounter when you arrive from outside the EU. If you're a non-EU national and arrive in Germany by air or sea from outside the EU, you must go through immigration for non-EU citizens. In many cases, however, the official will usually do little more than look at your passport to see that you vaguely resemble the photograph. However, at major border posts they may feed your details into a computer to check whether you're wanted for a crime in Germany. Residence and work permits are handled by the local authorities at your final destination, rather than on entry to the country.

CUSTOMS

The Single European Act, which came into effect on 1st January 1993, created a single trading market and changed the rules regarding customs (*Zoll*) for EU nationals. The shipment of personal (household) effects to Germany from another EU country is no longer subject to customs formalities, although it might be useful to have an inventory of the items you're bringing with you.

Visitors

Visitors' belongings aren't subject to duty or Valued Added Tax (VAT) when they're visiting Germany for up to 90 days. This applies to the import of private cars, camping vehicles (including trailers or caravans), motorcycles, aircraft, boats and personal effects. Goods may be imported without formality provided their nature and quantity doesn't imply any commercial aim. All means of transport and personal effects imported duty-free mustn't be sold or given away in Germany and must be exported before the expiry of the 90-day period.

If you cross into Germany by road you may drive through the border without stopping. However, any goods (and pets) that you're carrying must fall within the exempted categories and mustn't be the subject of any prohibition or restriction. Customs officials can stop anyone for a spot check, e.g. to search for drugs or illegal immigrants.

Non-EU Residents

If you're a non-EU resident planning to take up permanent or temporary residence in Germany, you're permitted to import your furniture and personal effects free of duty. These include vehicles, mobile homes, pleasure boats and aircraft. However, to qualify for duty-free import, articles must have been owned and used for at least six months. VAT must be paid on all items owned for less than six months that weren't purchased within the EU, and if goods were purchased VAT-paid within the EU, a receipt must be produced.

To import personal effects as a non-EU national, you must contact the local customs office (*Zollamt*) in the area where you will be resident and provide documentation showing that:

- you've given up your residence outside Germany, i.e. documents showing the termination of your lease or employment, the sale of your home or a statement from your employer stating that you've been transferred to Germany;

- you're establishing residence in Germany, i.e. a lease agreement, a statement from your German employer or your registration receipt (*Anmeldung*) from the local authorities in the area where you will be living;

- you've been living outside Germany for at least 12 consecutive months prior to your entry. This may be waived if there are unusual circumstances, such as when you're transferred abroad and back to Germany by the same employer.

To import a vehicle into Germany duty-free, you must have owned it (had it registered in your name) for at least six months prior to its importation. You may be required to have a vehicle inspected to check that it meets German standards and that local VAT was paid at the time of purchase (if you're coming from another EU country). For more information see page 223.

All items should be imported within one year of the date of your change of residence, either in one or a number of consignments. If there's a specific reason why you cannot bring in all your goods within your first year, you can apply for an exception. In this case your remaining goods must be imported as soon as possible after the problem causing the delay has been resolved, and in any case no later than three years after your actual move.

If you use a removal company (see page 112) to transport your belongings to Germany, they will usually provide all the necessary forms and take care of the paperwork. On the arrival of your shipment, the removal company will ask you to send them copies of the clearance documents (see above) so that they can attend to the formalities with the local customs office before delivering your goods. Always keep a copy of all forms and communications with customs officials, both with officials in Germany and in your previous or permanent country of residence. You should have an official record of the export of valuables (e.g. jewellery, gem stones, original works of art or antiques) from any country, in case you wish to (re-)import them later.

Germany has no currency restrictions, but may require your bank to report on large transfers of funds into or out of the country. There are detailed and strict regulations regarding the importation of guns, rifles or ammunition into the country, and certain kinds of pets and plants require prior approval and health certificates. You're permitted to bring in personal medication, but to avoid problems it's advisable to have a doctor's prescription (if applicable). Prescription medications (including some vitamins and herbal preparations) cannot be sent by post to a personal address in Germany. If you need prescription items that aren't available in Germany, you should arrange for them to be sent to a local pharmacy (*Apotheke*), where they can then be dispenses to you.

Information regarding German customs regulations is available from customs offices. If you enquire at your local German consulate abroad, they can give you the address and telephone number of the appropriate office to contact. However, German embassies and consulates cannot offer authoritative information on customs practices and should refer you to the German customs service. For details of embassies and consulates in Germany see **Appendix A**.

RESIDENCE PERMIT

All foreigners residing in Germany for longer than 90 days must obtain a residence permit (*Aufenthaltserlaubnis*) from the local 'Foreigners Office' (*Ausländeramt*). EU nationals who visit Germany with the intention of finding employment (or starting a business) have three months in which to find a job and apply for a residence permit. Once employment has been found, an application must be made for a residence permit. If you don't have a regular income or adequate financial resources, your application will be refused. Failure to apply for a residence permit before three months have expired is an offence and may result in a fine or theoretically even expulsion from Germany. For further information, see **Residence Permits** on page 73.

COUNCIL REGISTRATION

Everyone in Germany, including German citizens, must register with their local council and there are fines for those who fail to comply with the rules. Citizens of EU member countries and Iceland, Liechtenstein, Norway, Switzerland and the US are allowed to begin the registration process immediately after arrival, while others must begin by visiting a German embassy or consulate in their home country or their country of residence before their arrival in Germany.

Within a week of taking up residence in a private dwelling in Germany (including accommodation with friends), or within two months of taking up residence continuously in the same hotel, you must register with the local authorities. The initial registration (*Anmeldung*) entails reporting your address to the local residents' registration office (*Einwohnermeldeamt*). Hotels usually provide a registration service for long-term guests, whereby you may not be required to attend the registration office in person. Otherwise, look in the phone book under *Stadtverwaltung* to find out in which of the local council's offices the registration office is located. (The *Stadverwaltung* shouldn't be confused with the *Rathaus* – both of which are often translated as 'town hall'; the latter is usually an imposing edifice and has a representative function, whereas the former is a local administration centre, often functional in appearance and not necessarily near the *Rathaus*.)

There are set times in the week for registering, usually before midday, and you should phone to check or look on the notice detailing '*Sprechstunden*', which is usually located in the main entrance area of the *Stadtverwaltung*. On arrival take a number slip from the inevitable machine and wait until your number is called.

When dealing with officials, remember that they embody the state rather than just work for it, as is the case in the UK or US. In the former DDR, some officials will have being performing the same function since before the fall of Communism. Insulting officials (*Beamtenbeleidigung*) is a specific crime in German law and punishment can be severe.

If you move to a different state within Germany, you must de-register before you leave, although when you register in some states, the town where you were previously registered will be notified. De-registration is also required when you leave the country. Fortunately this process is straightforward and the forms can be returned by post.

Church Tax

One item on the registration form to pay careful attention to is the question asking you to state your religion. **If you list a Christian religion or Judaism, you will automatically be registered to pay church tax.** This is calculated as 8 or 9 per cent (depending on the *Land*) of your income tax (*Einkommensteuer*). No one cares whether you actually practise the religion or attend services, so if you wish to avoid this tax, you must answer the question with the word *'keine'* (none) – no justification for your answer is required. Muslims, Hindus, Sikhs and members of other religions can, at present, register their beliefs without being taxed.

If, due to ignorance of the tax implications, you previously indicated a (taxable) faith, your decision can be rescinded, but not without some effort and inconvenience on your part – and, of course, there's a fee. Some states require you to obtain a note from your church saying that they agree with you leaving the church. The church in question is likely to charge a fee for this, as they of course are 'sacrificing' their church tax. This note must be taken to the local *Amtsgericht*, the official office dealing with public legal affairs, who will change your registered religious status and also collect a fee of around €30. Check the procedure where you live before doing anything, however, as obtaining a note from a church may be unnecessary.

Income Tax Certificate

When you register as a resident, you should ask for an income tax certificate (*Lohnsteuerkarte*), even if you haven't started work. This will be required for your income tax calculations. When registering your tax class (*Steuerklasse*), you must show evidence of your marital, family and employment status. The tax certificate must be given to your employer when you start work and will be returned to you at the end of the year with a summary of your annual income; it must be included when you file your income tax return (*Einkommensteuererklärung*). Provided you haven't moved to another district during the year, a new *Lohnsteuerkarte* will be posted to you the following January. For more information, see page 86.

EMBASSY REGISTRATION

Nationals of some countries are required to register with their local embassy or consulate as soon as possible after arrival in Germany. Registration isn't usually mandatory for most though, even if most embassies like to keep a record of their country's nationals resident in Germany. Embassies and consulates (see **Appendix A**) are usually an excellent source of information and if you have a problem with German bureaucracy they can be contacted for help and advice.

FINDING HELP

One of the main difficulties facing new arrivals in Germany is how and where to obtain help with day-to-day problems. For example, finding a home, schooling, insurance and so on. This book was written in response to this need. However, in addition to the comprehensive information provided herein, you will also require detailed local information. How successful you are in finding help depends on your employer, the town or area where you live (Frankfurt's residents are better served than, for example, Baden-Baden's), your nationality and language proficiency.

As you'd expect there's a wealth of general local information available in German, although it isn't usually designed for foreigners and their particular needs, but little in English and other foreign languages. You may find that your friends and colleagues can help, as they're often able to proffer advice based on their own experiences and mistakes. But be careful: though they mean well, you're likely to receive as much false and conflicting information as accurate (not always wrong, but possibly invalid for your particular area or situation).

Your local council is usually an excellent source of reliable information, but you must speak German to benefit from it. Similarly public libraries often have lots of free Government publications (in German) about many different subjects, usually located near the entrance. Some companies may have a department or staff whose job is to help new arrivals settle in, or they may contract this task out to a relocation company. Unfortunately many employers in Germany seem totally unaware of (or uninterested in) the problems and difficulties faced by their foreign employees.

If you're female and American, a good source of information and help are the American Women's Clubs (AWC) located in Berlin, Cologne, Dusseldorf, Hamburg and the Taunus region around Frankfurt. AWC clubs provide comprehensive information in English about both local matters and topics of more general interest, and many provide data sheets, booklets and orientation programmes for newcomers to the area. Membership in the organisations is sometimes limited to Americans or those with active links to the US, e.g. through study, work or a spouse who works for a US company or the US government, but most publications and orientation programmes are available to others for a small fee. AWC clubs are part of the Federation of American Women's Clubs Overseas (FAWCO), which can be contacted through their website (💻 www.fawco.org).

In addition to the above, there are many social clubs and other organisations for foreigners in Germany, whose members can help you find your way around. They may be difficult to locate, as small clubs run by volunteers often operate out of the president's house, and they rarely bother to advertise or take out a phone listing. If you ask around among your neighbours or colleagues, it's possible to find various Anglo-German 'friendship' clubs or English-speaking organisations. Many embassies and consulates (see **Appendix A**) provide information, particularly regarding clubs for their nationals, and many businesses (particularly large multinational companies) produce booklets and leaflets containing useful information about clubs or activities in the area. Bookshops may have some interesting publications about the local region and tourist and information offices are also good sources. Finally, don't forget to check the Internet, where expatriate groups as well as local newspapers, government offices, clubs and organisations ever more frequently have their own websites.

CHECKLISTS

Before Arrival

The following checklist contains a summary of the tasks that should (if possible) be completed before your arrival in Germany:

- Obtain a visa, if necessary, for you and all your family members (see **Chapter 3**). Obviously this *must* be done *before* your arrival in Germany.

- If possible, visit Germany prior to your move to compare communities and schools, and arrange for schooling for your children (see **Chapter 9**).

- Find temporary or permanent accommodation (see **Chapter 5**) and buy a car (see page 229) if you will need one. If you purchase a car in Germany, you must register it and arrange insurance (see **Chapter 11**).

- Arrange the shipment of your personal effects (see page 112) to Germany.

- Arrange health insurance (see page 289) for yourself and your family. This is essential if you aren't already covered by a private insurance policy and won't be covered automatically through your employer.

- Obtain an international driving licence, if necessary.

- Open a bank account in Germany (see page 310) and transfer funds (see page 312) – you can open an account with some German banks from abroad or even via the Internet. It's best to obtain some euros before your arrival, which will save you having to change money immediately on arrival.

- Collect and update your personal records, including medical, dental, schools, insurance (e.g. car insurance), professional and employment (including job and bank references).

- Obtain an international credit or charge card (see page 314), which will prove invaluable during your first few months in Germany.

Don't forget to bring all your family's official documents, including birth certificates, driving licences, marriage certificate, divorce papers or death certificate (if a widow or widower), educational diplomas and professional certificates, employment references, school records and student ID cards, medical and dental records, bank account and credit card details, insurance policies and receipts for any valuables.

You will also need the documents necessary to obtain a residence or work permit plus certified copies, official translations and numerous passport-size photographs (students should take at least a dozen).

After Arrival

The following checklist contains a summary of tasks to be completed after arrival in Germany (if not done before arrival):

- On arrival at a German airport, port or land border, have your visa cancelled and passport stamped, as applicable.

- If you don't own a car, you may wish to hire one (see page 232) for a week or two until you buy one (see page 229). **Note that it's difficult to get around in rural areas without a car.**

- In the few days after your arrival complete the following (if not done before arrival):

  – Register with your local council within one week of arrival (see page 85).

  – Register with your local embassy or consulate (see page 87).

  – Open a post office or bank account (see pages 132 and 310) and give the details to your employer.

  – Arrange schooling for your children (see **Chapter 9**).

  – Arrange whatever insurance is necessary (see **Chapter 13**).

5.

ACCOMMODATION

Finding reasonably priced accommodation can be particularly difficult in Germany due to an enduring housing shortage. Government programmes intended to remedy the situation resulted in a building boom during the 1990's, when in 1993 alone, a total of 455,503 new housing units were completed – an all-time record for the country. But due to the various incentives available, most were in the west rather than in the former East Germany, where in some areas even now the need is still obvious, even if nothing like as acute as before. Many developers took advantage of state aid to build luxury accommodation with rents to match, so that the government still finds it necessary to provide housing subsidies for many citizens. Although housing is generally no longer as difficult to find as it once was, you must be able to pay the frequently high rents and deposits charged.

Home ownership is far less common in Germany – around 37.5 per cent – than in most of the rest of Europe. Over 60 per cent of the population rent their homes with the figure being as high as 90 per cent in Berlin. The law provides tenants with considerable protection. This means landlords are often particular when choosing new ones and most would prefer to leave an apartment vacant rather than rent it to someone who might cause problems or skip town owing several months' rent. Expect to pay around a quarter to a third of your net income for housing in most areas of Germany.

TEMPORARY ACCOMMODATION

On arrival in Germany, you may find it necessary to stay in temporary accommodation for a few weeks or months, perhaps while waiting for your furniture to arrive or for a property to become vacant. Some employers provide rooms, self-contained apartments or holiday houses (*Ferienwohnungen*) for transferred employees and their families as part of their moving and relocation costs, but usually only for a limited period.

Many hotels and bed-and-breakfast establishments cater for long-term guests and offer reduced weekly or monthly rates. Service apartments or apartment hotels are available in most large cities, comprising fully self-contained furnished apartments with their own bathrooms and kitchens, which are cheaper than a hotel and more convenient for families. In more rural areas, particularly in the south of Germany, you can often rent self-catering holiday accommodation by the week or month, although this can be prohibitively expensive or impossible to arrange at short notice during the main summer holiday season.

RELOCATION CONSULTANTS

If you're fortunate enough to have your move to Germany paid for by your employer, he may arrange for a relocation consultant to handle the details.

Relocation consultants generally work directly with large corporate clients who move their employees around on a regular basis, and must make transition periods as smooth and short as possible. Fees can run into thousands of euros per day. If you have special needs or requirements and enough money to pay for their services, you may wish to consider engaging a relocation consultant on your own behalf – although you shouldn't be surprised to find that many of the larger agencies work exclusively with corporations. Most companies that make frequent use of relocation consultants contract for a set package of services for transferred employees.

The main service provided by relocation consultants is finding accommodation (for rent or purchase), arranging viewing and assisting with the negotiations, particularly if you aren't fluent in German. Other services include handling the details of your move; arranging for temporary housing; advising on local schools, health, transport and recreational facilities; and assisting you with various regulations, including immigration requirements. Some consultants offer or can refer you to seminars on living and working in Germany, multicultural living and even language training. If you're interested in finding this kind of help for your relocation, it pays to contact local expatriate clubs. Members can recommend agencies or individuals, very often club members, who offer relocation services and know the area well. In other cases, local expatriate groups host 'Welcome to Germany' programmes for newcomers. These may include presentations by local relocation consultants, removals companies and other professional services.

GERMAN HOMES

Most Germans live in various forms of multi-family housing – apartments, duplex, triplex and semi-detached properties – particularly if they live in or near a major city. Detached, single-family houses (*Einfamiliehäuser*) are normally available only in more rural areas, although housing estates are beginning to spring up on the edges of cities and towns. Most of the available housing is relatively new, having been built since 1950. If you find a property described as *Altbau*, it may mean that it dates back to before 1914, as there was little building done in Germany between the two wars. Genuine *Altbau* homes or buildings generally command a high price, whether for sale or rent, despite their age and (sometimes) lack of modern conveniences, due largely to the romantic attachment to the older styles. Timber and mortar buildings (*Fachwerk*) are particularly popular and can command top prices, even when in poor condition. The term *Altbau* may also simply refer to an existing house or building, as opposed to a new one.

Regulated building standards and the German liking for modern conveniences ensures that new buildings (*Neubau*) are solidly built. In fact, nearly all building in Germany nowadays is in stone or reinforced concrete and wooden or wood-frame buildings are rare. All modern homes have central heating, usually oil or gas. Air conditioning is rarely provided, nor is it often required, given Germany's moderate summer climate. Germans take great pride in their homes and spend considerable effort keeping them and their gardens attractive and tidy.

When it comes to housing in Germany, size really does matter! The price of a home, whether to buy or to rent, is determined by the floor space, measured in square metres (*Quadratmeter*, abbreviated as *qm* or *m²*). Furthermore, as with many things in Germany, there's a strictly regulated method – stipulated by the Deutsche Institut für Normung (German Standards Institute) – for determining the official size of an apartment or house. The following areas are included in the calculation of habitable living space:

- Living rooms and bedrooms;
- Kitchen, bathroom and toilet;
- Entrance halls, hallways and cloakrooms;
- Closets and stairways inside the dwelling;
- Enclosed porch or balcony areas that can be heated for winter use.

The following areas **aren't** included in the calculation of habitable living space:

- Closets or storage areas outside the main living area, for example, those in a cellar or garage;
- Lofts;
- Utility closets or machine rooms, i.e. boilers and water heaters;
- Any floor space where the ceiling height is less than one metre.

The following areas are calculated at 50 per cent of actual floor space:

- Any floor space where the ceiling height is greater than one metre but less than two metres;
- Balconies, porches, roof gardens and uncovered decks or terraces;
- Enclosed porch or balcony areas that cannot be adequately heated during winter.

When comparing the prices of the properties you're considering, it's important to bear in mind the above. For example, a 60m² apartment may effectively have a total of only 55m² of indoor living space, because there's a 10m^2 balcony, while a rooftop unit (*Dachwohnung*) with the same official size of 60m^2 could yield only 45 or 50m^2 of usable living area if it has a massive roof garden.

Of course, the number of rooms is also important in determining whether a given house or apartment fits your needs. Any advertisement or information sheet will include not only the size of a property, but also the number of rooms. Counting rooms is, oddly enough, not subject to DIN standards, but certain conventions do apply. The room count includes only the bedrooms, living room and dining room. A half-room indicates that there's a dining area off the main living room that isn't separated by a door which can be closed (doors are very important in German homes). Kitchens and bathrooms or toilets aren't included in the room count. Thus, an apartment advertised as 3.5 rooms most probably consists of two bedrooms with a living room and dining area. A four-room dwelling usually has three bedrooms plus a living room, but could also comprise two bedrooms, a separate dining room and a living room. Separate dining rooms are quite rare in new properties, but of course there's no reason why you cannot 'convert' a spare bedroom into a dining room once you move in. Bathrooms, showers and toilets are usually listed separately in advertisements.

Households in Germany had an average of 73 square metres at their disposal in the West and 63 square metres in the East in 2,000. This gives you a rough guide to the amount of space you may reasonably expect for yourself and your family. Student apartments can be much smaller than this. In university towns such as Freiburg or Leipzig, you can sometimes find 'apartments' with just 12m^2 of living space, although even this doesn't guarantee a low rent. Generally, a 70 to 80m^2 property is considered the normal size for a small family, a couple or a well-off single person. Larger apartments, particularly those over 100m^2, are considered rather up-market dwellings, if not actually 'luxury'. Larger properties are generally harder to find, become available less often, and are more likely to be listed with estate agents than smaller, more standard-sized properties.

The one big shock for many newcomers to Germany is that you aren't just expected to supply your own light fittings, but must literally provide kitchen furnishings from cupboards right down to the kitchen sink. If you view an apartment or house before the previous tenants have vacated it, you may have the chance to offer to buy the fittings from them – if you like what you see and the outgoing tenants agree to leave them in place. If you don't purchase the kitchen beforehand, however, chances are it will be gone when you move in. The advantage of this arrangement is that you don't have to limit your house-hunting to apartments with dishwashers or a certain kind of cooker, if that's what you want. However, when you first arrive in Germany you must allow extra in your budget to cover the cost of fitting out a kitchen. Sometimes landlords will provide a kitchen and charge you a separate rental for this over and above the normal rent. Otherwise you must provide your own kitchen cupboards and appliances.

Kitchen fittings in Germany come in standard-sized units, so mixing and matching appliances with cupboards isn't difficult. For those tiny student apartments, there are even compact, all-in-one units consisting of a sink, a small refrigerator and a cooker in a single, stainless-steel box. The Germans like modern conveniences and sturdy, well-engineered products, and you will have no problem finding state-of-the-art appliances when shopping for new ones. Ceramic hobs are popular, as are ovens equipped to handle a variety of cooking methods: forced hot air, baking, grilling and microwave, all at the flip of a switch or sometimes programmable in sequence. Most Germans still prefer rather small refrigerators – generally the type that fit under kitchen worktops – but larger upright fridge-freezer combinations are becoming more popular and it's even possible to find full-sized, American-style fridge-freezers in appliance shops, complete with water and ice dispensers in the door. While these may be tempting (particularly to Americans), you should ensure that you can fit such a large item into your kitchen along with all the other appliances, worktops and cupboards you may want. Connecting the water supply may involve running pipes along the walls in full view unless you can place your refrigerator next to the sink – and those automatic ice-makers and self defrosting features may run up your electricity bill more than you realise.

As you may imagine, there's an active market in used kitchen fittings. Most furniture stores and do-it-yourself shops sell new cupboards and appliances, and can usually arrange for installation if you don't feel up to the task. Keep an eye out for store specials – often a display unit will be sold as a set for an attractive price, particularly when new models are introduced. Bear in mind that most shops must order a kitchen, unless you're buying a display model or other special unit, with delivery taking at least 8 to 12 weeks. For safety reasons (and by law) you must have the plumbing and electrical connections for a cooker done by a qualified tradesman. If you hire someone to install your kitchen or have the store where you purchased it do the installation, they will usually organise a plumber and electrician for you. Some independent kitchen installers are certified in all the necessary trades and can handle the entire job.

ESTATE AGENTS

The quickest and easiest way to find a property, whether to rent or buy, is to contact an estate agent (*Immobilienmakler, Wohnungsmakler* or, more often, just *Makler*). However, you should be aware that this approach will cost you dearly. If you rent an apartment or house through an agent, you must pay the finder's fee (*Provision*), which generally runs to two to three months' rent plus VAT at 16 per cent. Therefore, if you find an apartment for €500 a month through an agent, you must come up with an absolute minimum of €1,000 plus VAT of another €160, making a total of €1.160. This is before you pay the first month's rent or the rental deposit! The agent involved in the purchase of a home may charge you anywhere from 2 to 7 per cent of the purchase price (plus VAT). On average, an agent's fee for a purchase is around 3 per cent, so on a purchase price of €300,000 you should reckon on paying around €9,000 as a fee plus €49,440 as tax.

What the agent does to earn this hefty fee can vary considerably, depending on the region and agency. Perhaps surprisingly, the profession itself isn't stringently regulated in Germany. Basically anyone can set themselves up as an agent once they've taken a three-day training course (mostly dealing with settling their own business registration and taxes) and paid the local licensing fee. They don't need to have any other legal, financial or specialist training. What's more, the bill for their services is legally binding and enforceable as long as they've provided either a referral (*Nachweis*) to the property you ultimately rent or buy, or some form of mediation (*Vermittlung*) in the transaction.

In some cases, the agent may do nothing more than provide a list of properties meeting your requirements, along with (possibly) the name and phone number of the current tenant, so that you can arrange a viewing of the property yourself. Others will set up a viewing appointment for you, but may not actually be present when you view a property. Most reputable agents, particularly those used to dealing with foreigners, will handle all aspects of a transaction, including scheduling visits, accompanying you to properties and assisting in negotiations with the landlord or vendor. Officially, the agent is a mediator between the parties and isn't a representative of one side or the other. His ultimate fee, however, is determined by the selling price or monthly rental, so he obviously wants to get the highest price or rent possible.

It's quite possible to find your own accommodation in Germany without incurring an agent's fee, but it takes time and organisation. Many Germans spend weeks, months or even years conducting their own house-hunting searches, whether they're in the market to rent or buy a property. An agent can help you make the most efficient use of a short house-hunting trip and may even help you avoid spending time in temporary accommodation on your arrival. If your German language skills aren't adequate, there are agents who speak English and other languages who can assist with translating and explaining lease or purchase terminology. If your employer is paying your relocation costs, the agent's fees (for a rental property at least) will usually be covered without question, particularly if your employer is keen to have you settle in and start work quickly. This is certainly cheaper than having you and your family stay in temporary housing or a hotel for several months!

To find a reputable agent, the best approach is to ask around. Your employer and co-workers will be able to advise you on those they've used and can recommend or which you should avoid! Most banks have a property (*Immobilien*) department handling both rental and purchase properties. Doing business with a bank's estate agent can be an advantage in that the bank has an interest in protecting its reputation by exercising control over its property agents. When dealing with a bank's property department, you may be given the hard sell to arrange financing or insurance through the bank, but this can work in your favour if you let it be known that you also require banking services.

You can contact as many agents as you wish, but be careful to keep track of which one referred you to which property. If a second agent shows you a listing sheet for a property that you've already seen, you must notify the second agent of the duplication in writing and return any listing sheets or other information you received about the property. If you don't, you may find yourself liable for two agents' fees when you show up to close the deal, although this is more likely when you're buying than renting.

RENTED ACCOMMODATION

Renting is common in Germany, where some 60 per cent of the population rent rather than own their homes. One reason is that the investment potential isn't huge for owner-occupied housing and most Germans don't consider owning their own home to be an investment, but rather a form of insurance for retirement. Most tax benefits go to property owners who let to others. Tenants have considerable security of tenure in Germany and rental costs and practices are strictly controlled by law.

Most rental properties in Germany are let unfurnished. Furnished properties (*möbeliert*, abbreviated as *möbl.* in adverts) are difficult to find, other than for short-term lets or small properties, such as student housing. Unfurnished properties consist of floors, ceilings, windows, doors and walls, and not much more. The bathroom and toilet will have permanently installed fixtures – sinks, baths and toilets – but beyond that you're on your own. Expect to provide your own lighting fixtures, curtain rods and even kitchen fittings, unless you can do a deal with the previous tenants to buy theirs.

Finding A Rental Property

All German local newspapers contain rental advertisements, usually concentrated towards the end of the week in Thursday, Friday and Saturday editions. Advertisements may be placed by property owners seeking to let properties or by vacating tenants looking for someone to take over their lease before the notice period expires (see **Contract Termination** on page 102).

Look out for a notice headed 'Nachmieter gesucht' in the case of the latter. If you don't want to pay a hefty Makler's fee (see **Estate Agents** above), avoid responding to advertisements placed by letting agencies. It's also fairly common in Germany for apartment seekers to place their own advertisements in local papers, hoping to attract the offer of a reasonable apartment before an owner or vacating tenant places his own advertisement This isn't as desperate a ploy as you may think. A 'for rent' advert can easily attract 50 to 100 phone calls in the day or two after it appears, particularly in areas where housing is in short supply. Therefore landlords usually check the advertisements of would-be tenants before subjecting themselves to this kind of onslaught. Placing an advertisement to find a property to rent may be worth trying if you have particular requirements – such as a large apartment (over 100m²), one that accepts large pets, or when you require a ground floor (Erdgeschoss) apartment or wish to be near a particular school or other facility.

German landlords appreciate stability, so if you place an advertisement yourself it may be worthwhile mentioning if you're a professional being transferred by a large company or in some other 'prestige' occupation (professors, doctors, lawyers, etc. are particularly prized). Be sure to ask around among your co-workers, friends and acquaintances, as personal referrals are among the more common ways of finding a place to rent. Many businesses maintain a bulletin board (schwarzes Brett) for the use of employees, which is usually a good way of finding rentals as well as furnishings (or kitchens) for sale. If your German is up to it, you can also find housing listed on the Internet on sites such as 🖥 www.immowelt.de. You should also check the classified sections of local newspapers on the Internet. Some abbreviations used in rental advertisements are shown below:

Abbreviation	Full Term	Meaning
EBK	Einbauküchen	Built-in kitchen
Nfl.	Nutzfläche	Usable space
Stpl.	Stellplatz	Parking space
TG	Tiefgarage	Underground garage
Wfl.	Wohnfläche	Living space
Zi	Zimmer	Rooms
KM or WM	Kaltmiete or Warmmiete	Indicates whether the rent includes heating costs or not
2MMK	2 Monate Miet Kaution	2 months' rent required as a security deposit

Rental Costs

Rental costs vary considerably across the whole of Germany, but are generally related to the size of a property, measured in square metres (m²), rather than the number of rooms or bedrooms. Liveable floor space is calculated in the same way for rental and purchased properties (see page 94). Your local council office (*Stadtverwaltung*) or some estate agents may be able to tell you the typical rent per square metre for a particular town or district (known as the *Mietspiegel*). Some towns even impose upper limits on rental charges, although enforcement may be lax. Statistically the average rent without including heating costs in 2000 was €410 in the west while in the east it remained much less at €320, but unfortunately the amount you must pay in the kind of cities which act as a magnet to people will be far more. In places like Dusseldorf or Munich, per metre base rents are from around €6 to over €9.30 per m² – meaning that the monthly base rent on a 'standard' 80m² apartment can range from €480 to some €750 or more, depending on its precise location, classification and condition. Various websites provide more detailed information on this topic (See **Appendix C**). Germans generally prefer not to commute, so rents are higher in city centres and areas with good public transport.

Rents are normally quoted 'cold' (*kalt* or *Kaltmiete*), which means basic rent for the roof and four walls you will be calling 'home'. Communal charges (*Nebenkosten* – see page 107) are added to the base rent each month for such things as heating (if the rent is quoted as *warm* or *Warmmiete* it means that heating costs are included in the base rent), water, taxes, rubbish disposal and other utilities, and maintenance costs for the building and grounds. A monthly allocation for communal charges will be estimated when you first move in, based on how many people will be living in the property and your estimated use of common resources based on the usage of previous tenants. A single person living alone can probably negotiate slightly lower communal charges if they're at work most days and keep heated rooms closed when they aren't in use.

At the end of each year, (generally January or February of the following year), your actual use of heat, water and other utilities is calculated and you're apportioned your share of the common costs (cleaning and maintenance of common areas, etc.). You receive an itemised bill for the year, with your total monthly payments offset against your share (of the common costs). If there's a shortfall you must pay the difference and if you've overpaid you will receive a cheque or a bank credit. Communal charges (see page 107) for the following year are based on your previous year's consumption plus any anticipated increase in prices.

Besides the *Makler*'s fee of two to three months' base rent (if you happen to use one), you will be expected to pay a security and cleaning deposit

(*Kaution*), which is usually equal to two or three months' base rent. You must place the deposit in a special passbook bank account in your name and give the passbook to your landlord for safe keeping during the term of your lease. It's sometimes possible to negotiate the payment of the security deposit in two or three instalments at the beginning of your lease.

Rental Contract

A rental contract (*Mietvertrag*) is usually a standard document in Germany and can be rather lengthy. Most rental contracts run to seven or more pages of fine print, spelling out the terms and conditions of the rental agreement. Like many contracts in Germany, housing rental contracts are often open ended, although some landlords like to specify a minimum term of a year, particularly for a new tenant. You should read the lease carefully before signing it, and if you have doubts or questions about any of the terms, have them translated or explained to you. Many standard lease forms include marginal signals (exclamation points or asterisks) to flag paragraphs and provisions considered particularly important or most likely to cause problems (for the landlord, that is). Even a lease with a defined lease term (e.g. one year) will automatically be renewed unless you follow the prescribed notice procedure (*Kündigung*).

Notice deadlines (*Kündigungsfrist*) for terminating a lease are strictly enforced. Formerly the same notice periods and conditions that applied to you, also applied to your landlord if he wanted to terminate the lease for any reason, but recently the law has been changed to the advantage of the tenant. Three months' notice is the minimum for terminating a lease, but now it has also become the maximum period of notice which the tenant needs to give in the case of a contract which is not time limited. However, the longer you live in a property, the longer the notice period. It's usually three months initially, after five years it becomes six months, and after eight years it extends to nine months. Despite this enhanced protection ensure you scrutinise the contract termination requirements before signing. (See **Contract Termination** below for details and exceptions.)

The lease will first of all identify the specific property that you're renting. This includes not only the address and number or location of the property, but also lists the official size of the property (in square metres) and what rooms or other facilities or privileges are included in the rent. You should ensure that any garage space or parking place you were counting on is listed, as well as cellar storage, balconies, garden space, and the right to access laundry or drying rooms in a building. If your landlord is providing a built-in kitchen this must also be listed. The lease will include or refer to a list of keys that you're given for a property and its common areas (see **Security & Keys** on page 114).

The lease must list base rent, the monthly allocation for the communal charges (see page 107) and any other things, such as a parking space or garage, to arrive at your total monthly payment (*Gesamtmiete*). You will be given a detailed listing of the items that are included in the communal charges, such as a caretaker (*Hausmeister* or *Hausdienst*), grounds and building maintenance, lift, hallway lighting and maintenance of a building's TV aerials. Future rent increases should be noted in the lease, particularly if you're renting a new property, or (at the very least) the method used to calculate and notify you of future increases.

Most landlords will expect you to pay your rent by automatic bank transfer or standing order (*Lastschrifteneinzugsverfahren*) and this is usually stipulated in the lease agreement, along with the day of the month on which rent is due and the penalty for late payment. **Make sure that your wages are paid into your account in time to cover your rent payment, as fines for late payment are steep and it can take a long time to recover in the eyes of a landlord once he starts suspecting you may be a liability.** If you have a pet or intend getting one, you must ensure that permission is written into the lease. While it generally isn't too difficult to find landlords sympathetic to pet ownership, most standard leases require specific permission (and occasionally a small additional deposit) in order to keep pets legally.

In general, tenants are expected to maintain everything inside their own home, which means that it's up to you to deal with plumbers, carpenters or electricians should anything go wrong in your apartment. Normally you're free to decorate your home as you wish, e.g. paint the walls, hang wallpaper, put up shelves or hang pictures. However, when you move out you must return it to the same condition as it was when you moved in. Some contracts also specify that the tenant must replace the carpeting, repaint walls and complete other renovations at specific intervals during the lease term, e.g. each five years or so. If you move out before major renovations are due, you may still be liable for a pro rata share of the estimated cost, which will be withheld from your deposit unless you make other arrangements. These terms must all be detailed in the rental contract.

Some landlords require evidence that you have adequate insurance to cover *them* in the event of damage to the property or liability for damage to adjoining properties. These policies cover personal effects (*Hausratsversicherung*) and personal liability (*Haftversicherung*) and are widely available from around €130 to €200 per year. Sometimes policies include legal cover, which can come in useful for matters other than housing.

Contract Termination

Most forms of contract in Germany are assumed to be automatically renewable almost indefinitely, which makes it all the more important for you to be aware of how to terminate your lease or any other contract. In Germany you must give a minimum of three months' notice in writing of your intention to terminate a lease. Notice periods, however, normally increase, according to how long the contract has been running (see page 101). But of course there are some transgressions of the contract terms that permit immediate termination of the lease, such as failure of the tenant to pay the rent or the landlord allowing the property to fall into a dangerous condition, but in order to invoke these rights you must follow the correct procedure. If you find yourself in this situation, it's usually best to consult a lawyer. See also **Household Insurance** on page 297.

If you need or want to terminate your rental contract before your official notice period has expired, you have the option of finding someone to take over your lease. Normally, this means you must advertise for a replacement tenant and arrange to show them around at your own expense. If you can find a new tenant who's willing to take over and start paying rent before your notice period expires, then you're off the hook for the last few rent payments – provided your landlord agrees to rent to the person you've found. You can also authorise your landlord to start showing the apartment, in the hope that he will find someone who wants to rent it. Make sure that you let your landlord know if you want to sell your kitchen or other appliances (such as a washing machine) when your move. If you're obliged to terminate your contract because your employer has transferred you elsewhere at short notice, you can (and should) expect help from him in terminating the lease or finding a suitable tenant.

When you move out of an apartment, you're expected to restore it to the same condition it was in when you moved in. This means that you're supposed to not only clean it thoroughly, but also to do any necessary repairs or renovation (*Schönheitsreparaturen*). This includes repairing any wear and tear to the property, stripping off any wallpaper you've put up, patching any holes you've put in ceilings or walls, repainting the walls (usually white or off-white) and generally preparing the apartment for the next tenant. If you've lived in the same apartment for some time, you may also be expected to pay for (or towards) the periodic replacement of wall-to-wall carpeting or other up-grading of the premises as detailed in your lease. This work must be completed before the end of your notice period, so practically speaking you must schedule your move for a week or two before your lease ends. All this needs to overlap rental contracts, plus the cost of signing a new lease while moving and renovating the old apartment – it explains why Germans don't move house very often!

If you move out without completing the renovation work, your landlord will arrange to have it done and bill you. In practice, this generally results in you not getting your deposit back. If the landlord keeps part or all of your deposit, you're entitled to receive an itemised bill for all work done and you can request copies of the invoices paid by your landlord to verify his expenditure. If you haven't been living in a property very long or you have recently made renovations of your own, you may want to do a deal with your landlord regarding how much of your deposit he will keep in exchange for taking care of the renovations. In some cases, you may even be able to persuade the landlord to buy your kitchen so that he can charge a higher rent to the next tenant.

BUYING PROPERTY

Buying a house or apartment in Germany is considered a 'major life decision' and it's something a newcomer should consider very carefully before doing. If you're staying only for a short term, say less than three to five years, then you're probably better off renting. Due to the chronic shortage of housing, the German government has tended to offer financial incentives to builders rather than to home-buyers. You may find that home ownership in Germany carries few of the tax benefits that you're used to in your home country, e.g. the interest paid on a mortgage or other property-backed loan isn't tax deductible unless you're letting the property. Homeowners are allowed a tax credit during the first eight years of buying a home, but even this is limited depending on your family income and the type of property purchased.

There's one other important factor to consider regarding a property purchase in Germany. Buying rather than renting doesn't free you from most of the communal aspects of life in Germany. If you buy your own apartment, you must still deal with the building maintenance company and the onsite caretaker and are still subject to the house rules (*Hausordnung*) – see page 113. In addition to your mortgage or other financing payments, you must still pay the various communal charges – for example, heating, hot water, building maintenance and the caretaker's salary. Even some single-family (detached) houses are part of a neighbourhood-wide builder's community, and while you may not share a wall with your neighbour, you will still have a surprising number of common fees to pay at the end of the year. If you buy an apartment, it's highly likely that some or most of your neighbours will be renting theirs. The house rules (see page 113) apply to everyone living in a building and some home-buyers are unpleasantly surprised to find that they cannot keep pets or must put up a certain type or colour of curtains, even in their own homes!

Due to the mix of tenants and owners in buildings, house hunting can be difficult. You may well find a property you want to buy, but if the owner is letting it to long-term tenants, it could be as much as a year after buying the apartment before you can actually move in, due to the rules and regulations regarding notice periods. Of course, you'd be receiving the rent from the tenants during this period, but you'd need to find your own 'temporary' home in the meantime.

Germans don't generally consider buying their own home to be a good investment, but rather a hedge against inflation for their retirement years. Over the long haul, most properties in Germany increase in value, but only at a rate of 2 or 3 per cent a year in real terms (after taking inflation into account), so you shouldn't expect to make a quick profit when buying property there. In fact, any sale of real estate held for less than ten years is considered 'speculative' and may be subject to higher tax rates. Prices for residential property are already among the highest in Europe and the government's efforts to encourage the building of new housing may cause the prices of existing housing to dip for a period of months or even years. If this happens just when you must sell your home, you can end up losing money. Germans move slowly and cautiously when considering whether to buy property and it isn't uncommon for even the most desirable properties to remain on the market for years.

Cost

If you're determined to buy a home in Germany, you will find that the prices are calculated on the same square metre (m²) basis as rental costs. In a few areas, you might be able to find 60 to 90m² dwellings costing much less than the average price prevalent in the state or country as a whole, but there will be reasons for this. They're extremely likely to be in locations which are undesirable for one reason or another – in rural backwaters which have chronic high unemployment and declining urban areas – or have serious problems necessitating major repairs and renovation which would cost the earth to carry out because of the obligation to employ craftsmen. While you can get a new family house for around €190,000 plus the cost of the land, the upper end of the market can easily reach €10,000 per m² or more (i.e. €800,000 for a standard 80m² apartment) in more affluent areas such as Stuttgart or certain Berlin suburbs. Until fairly recently, would-be homeowners were expected to have a down payment of one-third of the price available in cash. Although times have changed, even now you should expect to have a down payment of 15 to 25 per cent of the price before you approach a bank or other lender. If you use a *Makler* to help find you a home, you must add another 3 per cent to the price for his fee (plus VAT) and must be careful not to commit yourself to paying two or more *Makler* fees (see **Estate Agents** on page 96).

German tax legislation has tended to favour builders and the tax advantages of owning a home are usually greater if you buy direct from a builder rather than from a previous owner. Prices, however, tend to be slightly lower for existing housing in order to compensate for this. Property buyers generally look for the same conveniences and amenities in their homes as tenants, e.g. proximity to city centres, public transport and outdoor recreational areas, and prices reflect this. It generally isn't worth buying a run-down property in the hope of fixing it up for resale. Due to the high cost of artisans and the stringent German building regulations, it's unlikely that you will be able to recover your costs on selling unless you plan to do a lot of the work yourself and to keep the property for a long time.

Conveyancing

Conveyancing (or more correctly, conveyance) is the legal term for processing the paperwork involved in buying and selling a property and transferring the deeds of ownership. In Germany, all transactions involving real estate ownership (*Grundbesitz*) must be registered in the official land register (*Grundbuch*) of the local authority (*Gemeinde*) where the property is located. Contracts for the buying and selling of all property recorded in the Grundbuch must be handled by a public notary (*Notar*), who ensures that all applicable laws have been observed and that registrations and taxes are properly paid and recorded. The notary is an agent of the state and acts as a neutral third party, representing neither the buyer nor the seller in the transaction.

The actual sales document for a property is referred to as the notary contract (*Notarvertrag*), which contains all the terms and conditions of the sale agreed by the buyer and seller. It isn't unheard of to have a home purchase fall through when the notary refuses to validate the contract because specific terms of the agreement haven't been settled between the buyer and seller. Some of the specific issues you must decide before your appointment with the notary include:

- the exact selling price of the property;
- the payment schedule;
- who's paying the notary's fee or how it's to be divided;
- the exact date of transfer of the property;
- any payment of rent between the parties, i.e. if the legal transfer date doesn't coincide with the buyer's or seller's moving dates;
- a list of repairs or other work to be completed by the seller prior to the hand-over;
- any special features or conditions of the sale, e.g. if the seller is leaving the kitchen or other appliances or any improvements in place.

At your meeting with the notary (*Notartermin*), you must provide personal identification (usually your passport and residence permit, if you're a foreigner) and confirmation of your financing. Normally there aren't any restrictions or prohibitions on foreigners buying or selling property in Germany, although financing a property purchase is a complicated business (see **Mortgages** on page 316).

With all these documents and confirmations to hand, the notary will draw up the sales contract and ensure that it's registered with the appropriate offices and bureaux of the local government. Notary's fees are strictly regulated by law and you should receive an itemised list of precisely what you're charged. Normally this consists of a fee for the preparation of the contract based on the sales price, plus four or five fixed fees for registering the sale with each of the various government offices and tax authorities. In general, you should plan on the notary's fees being around 1 to 1.5 per cent of the price of a property. There's also a 2 per cent tax on the transfer of property (*Grunderwerbsteuer*) which must be paid to the notary.

COMMUNAL CHARGES

Communal charges (*Nebenkosten*) are the monthly fees you pay for everything other than your four walls, whether you're renting or have bought your own home. For tenants, this is an agreed amount that's paid to the landlord each month with your rent. If you own your own apartment or a home that's part of a managed sub-division or housing estate, you make monthly payments directly to the builder or management company handling the property. Once a year, a formal apportionment of the common costs is made for each property in the building or complex. You will receive a letter informing you of the date and approximate time of the official meter reading to determine your actual usage of communal services (usually water and heating costs). It's important that you're available to let the meter reader in on the appointed date – if you're going to be away or will have difficulty taking time off work you must leave a key with a neighbour or give the caretaker authorisation to enter your home with the meter reader. The official meter reading is usually done by an outside company (the cost is included with the other communal charges for the year), and if they need to make a separate trip to read your meters on another day, you must pay an extra charge.

Other shared costs (i.e. those which cannot be metered or directly measured in some manner) are apportioned to your property according to the size of your living space in relation to the building or complex. For example, the occupants of an 80m² apartment pay 80 per cent of the allocation of someone who occupies a 100m² apartment. If you've been paying too much towards your share of common costs, you will receive a refund and your monthly contribution for the next year may be reduced. On the other hand, if you haven't paid enough over the year you will receive a bill and your monthly communal charges will be increased for the next year. In any event, you will receive a statement of your actual communal charges for the year, along with the calculations used to determine your share of each item.

Heating & Hot Water

In most apartment buildings heat is supplied by a central heating furnace, usually oil or gas, which is the responsibility of the caretaker. Most modern buildings allow for the regulation of heat within each apartment, usually on a room-by-room basis. In buildings with radiators, there should be a thermostat and control on each one. In newly constructed buildings you may find that you've heated floors, where heat is generated by circulating hot water through pipes running beneath the floor. However, even in this case there's usually a means of controlling the heat in each room and it isn't uncommon to find heated floors in some rooms combined with radiators, particularly in bedrooms. Forced hot-air heating is rare in German homes.

By law, heating is switched on the 1st October and off on the 30th April, and between these dates there are strict regulations requiring the building management to maintain minimum temperatures in apartments. If you can control the level of heat, there will be a meter (often several) somewhere in your apartment, which is usually located in a storage closet or some other out-of-the-way spot. In some apartments you may find there's a meter on each radiator. It's advisable to locate the meters before the meter reader is due to call, just in case you've stacked piles of books or other articles directly in front of them.

Due to the sturdiness of German homes, insulation isn't usually a problem, particularly in new buildings. The Germans are a thrifty people and tend to keep their homes relatively cool, 20°C (68°F) is considered 'room temperature' during the day, and is the legal standard for living areas between 8am and 10pm. Bedrooms are often kept much cooler and any unused or rarely used rooms are generally closed off and are only minimally heated during the winter. Many Germans believe it's unhealthy to sleep in an over-heated bedroom and they may actually turn the heat to the minimum setting on the radiator and keep bedroom doors closed for much of the time. However, if you do this you must take care, as your lease holds you responsible for maintaining an adequate temperature in your home to insure that no damage occurs. If there's a very cold snap while you're away on holiday, you could be liable for burst pipes – not only for the damage to your own apartment but also for any damage caused to neighbouring apartments.

If you have a shared hot water tank, it may have a separate meter, although it isn't uncommon to find that hot water costs are apportioned in relation to your overall water usage. In newer buildings there are sometimes individual hot water tanks in each apartment, in which case you pay directly for the heating of your water through your electricity bills. In older houses and apartments you may find a small water heating unit for each tap where hot water is needed, e.g. one for each sink and a larger hot-water heater for the bath, which you may have to remember to 'fire up' before use. With this arrangement, you will need to buy a special hot-water heater for your kitchen sink if there isn't one installed when you move in. Kitchen water heaters often have a setting to rapidly heat a small amount of water to boiling point, which can be handy for making a quick pot of tea or filter coffee, instant soups or other convenience foods.

It may come as a surprise to some foreigners that household appliances in Germany, such as washing machines and dishwashers, are connected only to the cold water outlet. Hot water from the water heater is intended primarily for kitchen use and for bathing or showering. Appliances that require hot water have a built-in water heater and heat up just the right amount of water for a single cycle. Obviously this means that British and American washing machines and dishwashers aren't suitable for use in Germany. You will also find that German appliances which use hot water have a much longer cycle time. Even the most expensive dishwashers and washing machines require nearly an hour to complete a full cycle, due to the need to heat the water.

Building Maintenance

In German, the word *Haus* generally refers to the building in which a number of residences (such as apartments) are located, whereas *Wohnung* is used for individual homes or apartments. The residences themselves may be owner-occupied or let, but the builder or a property maintenance company retains the responsibility for the upkeep of the building itself, i.e. the common areas and grounds. Most large buildings have a caretaker (*Hausmeister* or *Hausdienst*), who's either resident or lives in a building nearby, e.g. if there are multiple buildings under the same property maintenance company. The caretaker is the on-site representative of a property maintenance company and usually functions as a handyman and general odd job person for building repairs and maintenance. He is paid a nominal salary and given free or subsidised accommodation owned by the property maintenance company or builder. The job of caretaker is similar to that of a building supervisor ('the super') in the US or a caretaker in other countries, but with one very important difference; a caretaker isn't there to do repairs in individual apartments, which is the responsibility of tenants or owners. If your toilet leaks, you must call a plumber yourself, although your caretaker may be able to recommend someone.

The job of the caretaker is to tend to the grounds and arrange or perform the necessary cleaning and maintenance of hallways and other common areas, and shared heating equipment (furnace, oil tanks) or other shared utilities such as water heaters or lifts. If your heating breaks down or you notice a problem in one of the common areas such as a crack in the wall or a broken entry door, you should contact the caretaker. The cost of the caretaker (mainly his salary and the supplies he uses) is listed in the annual reckoning of the communal charges (see page 107) and apportioned according to the size of your apartment. At Christmas, it's traditional in some buildings to offer a small gift or tip to the caretaker, particularly if you've had direct contact with him during the year for any reason.

If you live in a multi-floor building, your lease or house rules (see page 113) may make you responsible for regular cleaning of the common areas on your floor. Generally this means that once a week the landing area and sometimes the steps up to the next floor must be washed or vacuum cleaned. Some contracts also require tenants to clean hallway windows on a regular basis. This duty is the shared responsibility of all residents on the floor, so if there are, for example, two other apartments sharing your floor, you should expect to do cleaning duty every three weeks or so. How formally this duty is assigned and what happens when one or more apartments on the floor is vacant varies considerably. In small buildings without their own caretaker, residents may be responsible for their own garden maintenance and snow removal in winter. Your lease or house rules (see page 113) will indicate whether this is the case.

In some areas of Germany, particularly in the south (Baden-Württemburg, for example), you may be subject to a maintenance ritual known as *Kehrwoche*. In addition to being required to keep your own floor's hallway clean, you will be assigned a week when you have responsibility for cleaning **all** common areas in the building, in rotation with your neighbours. Usually a complete schedule of *Kehrwoche* assignments and responsibilities is posted in the main entrance of the building. *Kehrwoche* is considered a part of the house rules and failure to do your assigned share (or even failure to meet local standards of housekeeping when you do!) may result in a formal reprimand, with or without an accompanying fine. Even if you aren't officially reprimanded by the building management, you will draw considerable disapproval from your neighbours if you don't fulfil your share of the communal cleaning chores and complete them to everyone's satisfaction on the designated days. You're usually required to clean the hallway windows, wash or vacuum the entrance floors, and possibly clean the cellar floors in laundry or drying rooms. For some reason, cleaning and polishing the entry door to a building is a very important part of the *Kehrwoche* routine in many buildings.

Germans generally keep their homes immaculately clean and have very particular ideas about the appropriate 'tools' for cleaning tasks. Washing the windows in the hallway with a spray bottle and paper towels doesn't always meet with local approval. The Germans prefer to use soapy water and a squeegee (one of those rubber blades that scrapes the water off). Sponge mops are often considered inferior tools for washing floors by proper German housewives (*Hausfrauen*), who prefer to use cloth rags. The good news is that if you don't want to be bothered with *Kehrwoche* chores, you can hire a cleaning lady to do them for you, or if you already have your apartment cleaned periodically, ask your cleaning lady to add this to her routine for a small extra fee. In a small building, you may receive an enthusiastic reception from busy neighbours if you suggest sharing the cost of a regular cleaning person to relieve everyone in the building of these chores, which, in the hands of a professional, should take no more than an hour or two each week. Bear in mind that house rules (see page 113) sometimes require *Kehrwoche* chores to be completed over the weekend or by a certain day of the week.

GARAGES & PARKING SPACE

Public transport in most cities and towns in Germany is frequent and convenient. As a result, it's possible to live and work in many areas without owning a car. If you own a car, you will probably have to rent a garage or parking space for it, as on-street parking is difficult to find in most residential areas. Most modern apartment blocks have parking spaces or garage space available for an added monthly fee. You may have the option of buying or renting a garage or parking space in the building itself or within its grounds, and this may belong to someone other than the owner of the apartment. If you're lucky enough to find an apartment with a garage or parking space, the cost of it will be itemised separately on the lease or purchase documents.

The cost of a parking space varies depending on the size, the type of parking (covered garage, open-air parking space, assigned parking or not), location and other factors, such as the security system, e.g. automatic door opener or card key versus an open car park. Generally, you should be able to find adequate parking for around €70 a month. If there are no available parking facilities in or around your building, you may be able to rent a parking space in a nearby covered car park, garage or even in a nearby apartment building. Parking spaces are advertised for rent in local newspapers, but frequently you can find notices for parking or garage space posted in building lobbies or apartment windows.

MOVING HOUSE

Once you've found a home in Germany, it usually takes only a few weeks to have your belongings shipped from within continental Europe. From anywhere else it varies considerably, e.g. four weeks from the east coast of America, six weeks from the west coast of America and the Far East, and around eight weeks or longer from Australasia. Customs clearance is no longer necessary when shipping your household effects from one EU country to another. **However, when shipping your effects from a non-EU country to Germany, you should enquire about customs formalities in advance, otherwise you can encounter numerous problems and delays, and may be charged duty or even fined.** Removal companies usually take care of the administration and ensure that the right documents are provided and correctly completed.

For international removals, you should use a company that's a member of the International Federation of Furniture Removers/FIDI (🖳 www.fidi.org) or the Overseas Moving Network International/OMNI (🖳 www.omnimoving.com), with experience in Germany. Members of FIDI and OMNI usually subscribe to an advance payment scheme providing a guarantee. If a member company fails to fulfil its commitments to a customer, the removal is completed at the agreed cost by another company or your money is refunded. Some removal companies have subsidiaries or affiliates in Germany, which may be more convenient if you encounter problems or must make an insurance claim. Obtain at least three written quotations before choosing a company, and, if you're moving from overseas, give careful thought to how you plan on shipping your belongings. Most employer-sponsored overseas moves allow for a limited air freight shipment of around 250kg (550lbs) or so, which should arrive at your new home within a week or two. **Be careful to include the items that you will need most until the rest of your belongings arrive by sea freight.**

It's sensible to fully insure your belongings during removal with a well-established insurance company. Insurance premiums are usually 1 to 2 per cent of the declared value of your goods, depending on the type of cover chosen, and most insurance policies cover for 'all-risks' on a replacement value basis. Some insurance companies require separate 'riders' for valuable artwork or jewellery, and most insurers won't cover fragile or breakable items unless they've been packed by the removal company. You should make a complete list of all the items you're shipping and insuring, along with the price you paid for each item, purchase dates and the replacement values. This may be required for the insurance company to issue the cover, and will be needed in the event that you need to file a claim. The same list may be required by the removal company to clear your goods through German customs if you're coming from outside the EU.

If you plan to transport your belongings to Germany yourself, check the customs requirements of all the countries you must pass through. Unless your move is simple, it isn't advisable to try to do it yourself. It's no fun heaving beds and wardrobes up stairs and trying to squeeze cupboards or sofas down narrow corridors. German removal companies have an array of specialised equipment designed to hoist large pieces of furniture into rooftop apartments or transport boxes on a sort of conveyor belt through a convenient window or balcony doors.

Bear in mind that moving house rarely goes smoothly and it's a chaotic and stressful time for all involved. You're entitled to a day off from work to move house under German law and you should plan on taking it, if only to enjoy a moment of peace and quiet once the removal van has left!

HOUSE RULES

All apartment blocks have house rules (*Hausordnung*), some of which may be set by your local council and are enforceable by law (particularly those regarding noise and siesta periods). You should receive a copy on moving into your apartment or when you sign your rental or sales contract. They apply to everyone living in a building, whether a tenant or owner, so it pays to check the rules before making an offer on an apartment that you're interested in buying. If you don't understand them, you should have them translated. Some of the more common house rules include:

- A noise curfew between 10pm and 6am.

- A midday siesta during the day, e.g. from noon to 2pm, during which you mustn't make any loud noise, play music or sing, or (most of all) drill the walls or use any sort of power tools. This is to allow young children or pensioners an undisturbed afternoon nap.

- No bathing or showering between 10pm and 6am. Sometimes there's even a restriction on flushing the toilet during these hours, lest you disturb your neighbours' slumber.

- No loud noise on Sundays and public holidays. In some areas (mostly the south), hanging out washing to dry or mowing the lawn is also expressly forbidden on Sundays, even in detached houses. In some areas, hanging laundry to dry on balconies is prohibited if it can be seen from the street.

- Restrictions regarding where children may play or ride their bicycles.

- Restrictions on the storage of bicycles, carts, children's toys or other personal objects in hallways, ground floor entrances or on balconies.

- Proper use of the laundry or drying room facilities, including cleaning after use.

- Residents' responsibilities for cleaning the common areas (*Kehrwoche*), gardening, snow removal or other maintenance chores.

- The requirement that the front door to the building be closed and locked between 8pm and 6 or 7am. Usually the occupants of the ground floor apartments are responsible for locking the front door at the appropriate hour in the evening.

- Rubbish must be properly separated and prepared for collection according to the town's regulations, with 'recyclables' separated into a number of categories (see **Rubbish Disposal** on page 121).

Your neighbours will be familiar with the house rules and be only too happy to point out any transgressions. If you have problems regarding the communal areas, you should contact the caretaker for clarification.

INVENTORY

One of the most important tasks on moving into a new home is to complete an inventory (*Mängelliste*) and condition report. This includes the state of fixtures and fittings, the cleanliness and condition of the decoration, and anything missing or in need of repair. The form should be provided by your landlord (or by the builder if you're buying or renting a new property), and any problems must be listed on this form, which you sign and return by the deadline stated. If the problems or damages noted aren't repaired within a reasonable period of time, you may be entitled to a reduction of your rent for the period they're left unresolved. If you're buying a home, the inventory list should be used to document any unfinished work or repairs that the seller has agreed to remedy. If possible, this list, along with the deadlines for completing the work, should be submitted prior to your meeting with the notary, so that it can be officially registered with the contract and sale.

If you're renting, a property should be spotless when you move in, as this is what your landlord will expect when you move out. Any damages that aren't noted on the inventory list when you move in will be charged to you when you move out, so you should check a property thoroughly and return the list promptly to your landlord. Most landlords in Germany are honest and won't try to cheat you. Nevertheless, it's better to be safe than sorry.

SECURITY & KEYS

An important part of your apartment lease is the listing of keys you've been given. Make sure you actually receive all the keys that you're entitled to. **If you lose any keys to your home, you will be held liable for having the** barrels of the locks changed, and if you lose a key to a common area you will probably be expected to pay for your neighbours' new keys as well! The key to your front door may also open the main entrance to the building or there may be a separate key. If you have a common laundry room where residents are expected to install their washing machines, there may even be a special key to the electrical socket so that you won't be tempted to run your wash on your neighbour's power! Germans are very security conscious. The most important keys will probably be of a special high security type that you won't be able to have duplicated at the local hardware store. Some keys are quite elaborate, making use of small rollers or ball-bearings as part of the mechanism. Other high security keys use three separate machined surfaces to trigger the lock. Main entrance doors are often constructed so that locks cannot be 'jimmied' or by-passed without significant damage to the lock or the door itself. **Obviously, you should be careful not to lock yourself out of your house!** You may need to carry your house key with you at any time you leave your apartment, as entry doors are often set to lock automatically on closure.

You may also notice that in Germany, door locks work only with keys, from both sides of the door. There's no handy little handle or knob to turn from the inside. Thus, to lock your front door at night, you must have your key handy. Many people are tempted to leave a key in the lock at all times so that if there's a fire or another emergency they can quickly unlock the door and get out. If you do this, however, you should be aware that the lock won't operate from one side of the door when there's a key in the other side. In fact, if someone tries to insert a key in the other side of the lock, both keys and the lock are likely to jam, and you will have to call a locksmith to drill out and replace the lock (a €30 to €70 operation at least!).

ELECTRICITY

Energy is a hot topic throughout German government and society, particularly as it's associated with a number of sensitive environmental concerns. Germany is one of the world's biggest consumers of energy, and not surprisingly, Germans pay some of the highest electricity rates in Europe. The electricity companies were privatised in early 1998 and, in theory at least, you're now able to purchase power from any supplier you choose. In practice, what has developed is a network of electricity brokers, who purchase power from the large generating companies and sell it to individual consumers under a variety of tariffs and plans. Within two years of privatisation there were over 900 different electricity companies, mostly brokers, established in Germany. To find a list of local electricity suppliers, look in the yellow pages under *Elektrizitätsgesellschaften* or *Energie-versorgung* (energy supply).

Electricity in Germany is generated using a variety of fuels, primarily lignite, hard coal and enriched uranium. Each one of these presents its own problems in terms of environmental and economic concerns for government and society. The heavy use of lignite for generating electricity was a major source of pollution in the former East Germany, while hard coal produced from German mines is expensive and uneconomical for privatised power companies. Although nuclear power stations supply around 31 per cent of Germany's electricity, the government is publicly committed to closing all nuclear plants, while at the same time encouraging energy conservation, private sector development of alternative and renewable energy resources, and the reduction of air and water pollution levels. Despite privatisation, it seems likely that electricity prices in Germany will continue to remain fairly high in comparison with other European countries.

Power Supply

The electricity supply in Germany is delivered to homes at 220 to 250 volts with a frequency of 50 hertz (cycles). If you're coming from a country that operates on the same voltage, most of your appliances will require only a change of plug or cord to accommodate the German-style socket. Televisions and video recorders are the most notable exceptions, but this relates to the transmission systems in use rather than the power supply (see **Chapter 8**). North American or other 110V appliances aren't usable in Germany unless they can be switched or converted to the higher voltage. Depending on the country you've come from, you may need new plugs or a lot of adapters. Electrical plugs (*Stecker*) have two round pins, usually with two earth (or ground) contacts on the side if an appliance requires an earth. Most electrical sockets (*Steckdosen*) are recessed into the wall (particularly in modern buildings) and have two small earth contacts.

German plugs aren't fitted with fuses. Instead, the circuit for your home will be protected with either a fuse box or a circuit breaker panel. In modern buildings, you're likely to find a circuit breaker panel containing several switches, usually labelled to indicate the circuits or apparatus they control. When there's a short circuit or the system has been overloaded, the breaker is tripped and the power supply is cut. To reset the circuit breaker, you must flip the switch to the 'off' position (when the circuit 'blows' the switch moves only to the half-way position) and then back to the 'on' position to restore power. **Before reconnecting the power, switch off any high-wattage appliances such as a washing machine or dishwasher.** If the power goes out while you're on the computer, it's advisable to switch off both the computer and the monitor before reconnecting the power. Make sure you know where the breaker box is located and keep a torch handy so that you can find it in the dark. In most apartments, the circuit breaker panel is located in the entrance hall to an apartment or in the main hallway connecting the rooms.

When you move into a new home, there will probably be no lighting fixtures, although you may find wires hanging from the ceiling or walls. These wires are colour-coded and must be joined to the same coloured wires in the lamp or fixture you attach to them. Inexpensive lighting fixtures are available in home furnishing, hardware and DIY stores, and the staff will explain how to connect them if necessary. Always ensure that the electricity supply is switched off at the mains when installing lighting and other electrical fixtures, and if you have any doubts about your abilities employ a qualified electrician. As a further safeguard, many hardware stores sell inexpensive small screwdrivers with a lamp in the handle, which glows if the screwdriver touches a live wire.

Converters & Transformers

Electrical equipment rated at 110 volts AC (e.g. from the US) requires a transformer to operate on a 240v system. Small, hand-held appliances, such as hairdryers or curling irons may operate satisfactorily on small travel converters, but for long-term use it's advisable to buy a power transformer. Some electrical appliances (electric razors, hair dryers) are fitted with a 110/240 volt switch. **Check for the switch, which may be inside the casing, and make sure that it's switched to 240 volts** *before* **connecting it to the power supply.** Transformers are available from most electrical retailers and used ones can often be purchased from Americans returning home. Total the wattage of the devices you plan to connect to a transformer and make sure that its power rating **exceeds** this sum by a comfortable margin. Transformers may generate considerable heat when they're connected to the mains, even if the electrical appliances themselves aren't running or switched on. Make sure that you either disconnect the transformer when it isn't required or install it where the heat generated won't be a problem.

An additional problem with some electrical equipment is the frequency rating, which in some countries, e.g. the US, is designed to run at 60 Hertz (Hz) and not at Germany's 50Hz. Electrical equipment without a motor is generally unaffected by the drop in frequency to 50Hz (except TVs – see **Chapter 8**). Equipment with a motor may run satisfactorily, although with a 20 per cent drop in speed; however, electric clocks, record players and some tape recorders are unusable in Germany if they aren't designed for 50Hz operation. To find out whether a piece of equipment will work, look at the label on the back. If it says 50/60Hz, it should be OK. If it says 60Hz you may try it anyway, but first ensure that the voltage is correct as outlined above. Bear in mind that the transformers and motors of electrical devices designed to run at 60Hz will run hotter at 50Hz, so ensure that equipment has sufficient space around it for cooling.

Computers often have a voltage switch, either on the back panel or on the power supply inside the main unit. If your computer doesn't have a switch and is designed to run on 110 volts, the chances are it can be operated successfully using an appropriate transformer. Most other computer equipment can also be run on a transformer, but you should be particularly careful if you have a laser printer. It may be necessary to provide a separate transformer for this to handle its high power requirements. It's also wise to use a power surge protector (preferably one made for electronic equipment) when connecting your computer to the transformer. If you're bringing a portable laptop computer with you, check the charger unit to see whether it will accept a 240volt/50Hz power supply. Many laptop chargers are made to operate on both systems, with just a change of cable or an adapter plug.

In most cases it's simpler to buy new appliances in Germany and sell them when you leave if you cannot take them with you. German appliances are generally of excellent quality, although they may seem a bit expensive, particularly in comparison with their American or British equivalents. You may also find that it isn't possible to fit American-size appliances into German kitchens or laundry rooms. There is, however, an active market in used household appliances and the recognised German brands retain their value well over time. Contact local expatriate clubs and employer organisations, which often hold sales or post advertisements from members selling used appliances.

Tariffs & Bills

Before privatisation, you only had to go down to your local council offices (*Stadtverwaltung*) to sign up for your electrical (and most other) utilities. A monthly or quarterly rate is estimated based on your family size and the size of the property that you're occupying, and you're asked to transfer this amount each month or quarter via your bank to the local electricity utility. At the end of the year there's an official meter reading and you settle with the utility company, who then set a new monthly or quarterly rate for the coming year based on your actual usage. However, following the privatisation of the electricity market, local utility companies are constantly changing their rates and procedures to compete with rivals.

Electricity rates in Germany are among the highest in Europe. Usage, of course, also varies considerably, depending on the types of appliances you use, your personal habits and preferences, and the local customs of the region where you live. But broadly the average annual household consumption for a family of four would be around 4,000kwh compared with 1,500kwh for a single person household. It's no wonder that most large household appliances are rated for power consumption (displayed prominently in store displays and advertisements) and most Germans pay close attention to these when buying new appliances. Most local utilities offer discount tariffs late at night (*Nachttarif*) and you will find that many appliances are equipped with timers or start delay systems so that thrifty Germans can take full advantage of discount power rates at 2 or 3am.

Since May 1998, consumers in Germany have been free to choose their supplier and hundreds of electricity brokers (*Strombrokers*) have responded enthusiastically by offering an array of special rates. Some market themselves as purveyors of 'green' power generated primarily by wind or solar energy. The net effect of so much competition has been to force down prices, or at least those displayed in advertising. The differences in individual pricing structures, however, make direct comparison between brokers' rates and traditional utility company tariffs tricky. There are other factors to take into consideration besides the price per unit at various times of the day, namely the minimum length of the contract you're obliged to sign up for and the notice period you're obliged to give. A useful website is ⌨ www.strom tarif.de, where you can enter your estimated annual electricity usage, in order to bring up a list of the best offers currently available.

For a normal consumption household (that uses around 1,500kwh per year) in March 2003 the best deal was around €270 per year with a 24-month contract and a three-month notice period. A standard 12-month contract with a one-month notice period cost around €280. The most expensive tariff was almost €400. For a household using twice as much energy the lowest tariff was around €500 with a three-month contract and a two-month notice period. The most expensive tariff for this type of consumption was close to €700. The most expensive tariffs usually apply to companies where the energy is produced in environmentally friendly ways.

Note that some companies supply only within a certain areas (e.g. western or eastern Germany).

Sometimes the kwh rate depends on using a minimum amount each month or quarter and some brokers reduce the kwh rate if you agree to a higher monthly fixed fee. These plans may work out as being more economical for heavy electricity users, but it's difficult to evaluate competing claims if you don't know your own usage. Brokers rarely offer night tariff (*Nachttarif*) rates and may require you to report your own meter readings at regular intervals (with penalties for late reporting). German consumer magazines and other publications publish frequent comparisons of companies offering the lowest rates, but for current best buys check the Internet (⌨ www.stromtarif.de).

Naturally, just because a company offers you a lower kwh rate, it doesn't necessarily mean that your electricity bills will reduce if you switch to them. You should evaluate the entire cost of the contract against your own usage.

When you're ready to look for a better deal, take into account the monthly base payment, as well as any minimum usage and the availability or lack of it of night rates and other discount periods. Given differences in housing, appliances and living styles, your monthly usage of electricity may be very different in Germany from what you experienced back home.

Under the circumstances, with prices and the market changing rapidly, you may want to simply sign up with the local utility to begin with. Changing your electricity company later consists only of the paperwork and there should be no need to turn off the power, change your meter or make any physical changes in order to switch suppliers, although you must arrange a meter reading at the changeover date. When you're ready to make use of a private power broker, bear in mind the following when evaluating offers:

- Don't sign a contract committing you to any power company for more than a one-year period, if you want to be able to switch again if prices drop or other circumstances change.

- The notice period (*Kündigungsfrist*) for cancelling a contract or changing suppliers should ideally be no longer than four weeks.

- Ensure that there are no conditions attached to the cancellation of your contract, such as a penalty payment or the need to produce a copy of a signed competitor's contract before you can cancel.

- Make sure that you read and understand all the small print regarding matters such as minimum consumption and your obligations to confirm or report meter readings.

GAS

Gas isn't widely available in homes in Germany, although local utility companies are starting to promote its use as a clean fuel for heating. Special offers are available from gas companies (usually part of a town or regional utility) for homeowners or builders who wish to install gas central heating in new properties or when making extensive renovations to older buildings. If you want to cook by gas, you may be able to find a house that has it, although this will be difficult. In remote areas, homes may have a bottled gas cooker or heater. Most apartment buildings are designed to accommodate only electrical appliances in kitchens and it generally isn't possible to change over to gas in a single apartment within a building.

Mains gas is supplied by local companies; to find a list look in the yellow pages under *Gasversorgung*.

WATER

Water costs are included in the communal charges (see page 107) for all apartments and most houses in Germany. Costs are based on your actual usage and there may be multiple meters, particularly if laundry or other washing facilities are located in a common cellar area. Water in Germany is generally hard, which means that you must have plenty of decalcification liquid on hand to keep your kettle, iron and other equipment and utensils clean. There are a number of filter systems available that can improve the quality of small quantities of water used in cooking and reduce or eliminate the calcium (*Kalk*) build-up on heating elements and in pots and pans. These normally require you to pour water through a filter into a pitcher or other storage container (such as Brita water filters) before using it. Other systems have a small filter fitted to a kitchen tap, which then filters water as you fill your kettle or pan. Filters for both systems are available in supermarkets and other shops, and generally need to be replaced every month or two. It also pays to use special products now and then to clean and decalcify dishwashers and washing machines. Alternatively you can use special detergents for everyday use that include decalcifying agents.

Dishwashers have their own built-in water softener, which requires the regular addition of dishwasher salt to clean and regenerate the softening filters. Rinsing liquid is also essential for dishwashers if you hope to avoid streaky mineral stains on your glasses and crockery. Tap and shower fixtures must be decalcified regularly. Distilled water or water melted from the frost build up in your refrigerator or freezer, should be used in some electric steam irons, although you should check the manufacturer's instructions. Some brands of steam irons are made to be used with unfiltered tap water, and these have a decalcification system of their own which should be periodically cleaned or cleared. It's also possible to install elaborate household decalcification equipment, although systems are generally expensive and aren't practical for installing in rented premises.

RUBBISH DISPOSAL

The Germans have been sorting their rubbish for years and recycling is a way of life. Most cities and towns require the sorting of household rubbish into several categories, including paper, cardboard, glass, plastic and metal (at a minimum). Many towns also collect organic waste (*Biomüll*) separately for composting. You should check with your local *Stadverwaltung* for the exact requirements for each category and how 'recyclables' should be prepared for pick-up, as this can vary from town to town. For example, some councils require that white paper be separated from coloured paper, while others insist only that brown cardboard be kept separate from paper. A few smaller councils require only that recyclable material be separated into 'round' (bottles, cans, jars, etc.) and 'flat' (paper, cardboard, plastic, etc.).

The collection of rubbish and recyclables is usually 'metered' for billing to building owners or maintenance companies, with the cost distributed to building occupants as part of their communal charges (see page 107). Most towns provide each building with standard-size coloured bins for each type of rubbish and recyclable waste. Often bins have a bar-coded label which indicates the 'owner' of the bin, whether the homeowner or the management company of the apartment block. Each time a bin is emptied the bar code is 'swiped' and the owner is charged for the pickup according to the size of the container. A large container costs more to empty each time, so many building owners try to make do with the smallest possible bins, even if they fill up long before the next collection day! **Leaving rubbish in plastic sacks alongside official rubbish bins is a violation of house rules (if not local laws) and you can be fined if you're identified as the culprit.**

Glass deposit bottles are standard throughout Germany for most juices and fizzy drinks, including beer (wine bottles are the main exception). The price of these drinks includes a deposit (*Pfand*) to ensure the return of the bottle and the plastic crate (if you buy in bulk). When you return the empty bottles and cases to the store where you made your purchase (with the receipt), you're refunded the deposit in cash. Other glass bottles (including wine bottles) should be disposed of in the appropriate glass recycling bin. Glass bottles and jars must often be separated by colour (clear, brown, green). Many towns provide bottle banks in car parks or other facilities if you find that your building bins fill up too quickly (which is often the case).

German shops are required by law to take back packaging materials, e.g. boxes, plastic, styrofoam, etc., for each product they sell. Many supermarkets or other large stores provide a bin in the parking lot or near the main entrance to collect this material. If you have furniture or large appliances delivered to your home, the delivery service must take the packaging material away for you. In fact, if you have your household goods moved by a professional mover, they must offer either to take the packing boxes away with them after they've unpacked your belongings, or to pick up the empty boxes once you've unpacked them yourself. On the other hand, empty packing boxes (particularly heavy duty ones used for international moves) can be sold for a couple of euros each to people who are moving or need storage boxes.

Dead batteries can be returned to stores, where they're collected for proper disposal (there's usually a box located near the checkout). Stores are required to provide this facility if they sell batteries or battery-powered devices, and batteries mustn't be put in with regular household rubbish for collection.

Large objects, such as unwanted household furniture, broken appliances or building debris, may be collected once or twice a year during a special pick-up, announced in advance by your local council offices (*Stadtverwaltung*). In many areas, the evening before the pick-up you will see hordes of casual strollers sizing up the items their neighbours have put out for disposal. By the time the trucks show up the next morning, many of the still-serviceable articles will have vanished as if by magic, leaving only the real rubbish to be picked up and carted off by the council. This form of 'direct' recycling is technically illegal, but is tolerated by most local governments and residents. You can usually schedule a special collection of large items (for a fee) by calling your council offices. In some communities this is the only way of disposing of large or bulky items, so you may want to arrange a special pick-up with one or more neighbours in order to share the cost. For the disposal of hazardous items (paint, paint thinner, cleaning solvents, motor oil and etc.), you should take them to the local recycling and disposal centre – a sort of specialised dump. Recycling information published by your local council offices will include the location of the nearest recycling centre, its hours of business and detailed information regarding disposal requirements.

6.

POSTAL SERVICES

There's at least one post office (*Postamt*) in every German city or town, a total of some 13,000, although they're disappearing fast in small villages. As in many other countries, privatisation in Germany has put an end to the traditional image of the post office as the carrier of post, controller of telephones and repository of small savings accounts. The German post office (Deutsche Post AG) no longer runs the phones or operates a bank and it's now responsible solely for delivering post. When the post office was privatised, certain operations were sold off to separate companies and its banking and telephone operations became the Deutsche Postbank AG and the Deutsche Telekom AG respectively. However, it's still possible to open a savings or cheque account at a post office, deposit or withdraw cash, pay bills and perform a number of other banking transactions. Many post offices still have one or more telephone booths, although as they're no longer operated by the same company, and there's a surcharge for using them. The privatised postal service is trying to introduce the concept of customer care to its employees, although the process is far from complete. While many postal employees are courteous and helpful, some (known affectionately as 'stamp dragons') are notably less so!

Deutsche Post has an extremely useful and informative website (🖥 www.deutschepost.de), of which there is now also an English version. It also publishes a number of free publications describing its products and services, the most comprehensive of which is entitled *Serviceinformationen*, available free from post offices.

BUSINESS HOURS

It's difficult to generalise about post office business hours, although they usually open from around 8 or 8.30am until 6pm on weekdays and until noon on Saturdays. Generally, the larger the city, the longer the main post office (*Hauptpostamt*) will remain open. Main post offices are usually located next to main railway stations (*Hauptbahnhof*) and are often open for a limited period on Sundays. Smaller post offices may close for lunch, which is usually between 1 and 2.30pm. Post offices that are part of shops – a relatively new innovation – may open earlier or be open later than regular post offices, depending on the business hours of the stores in which they're located.

Post office opening hours are given at the entrance to each building. However, should you need to establish the opening hours or locate the whereabouts of any particular post office in the country you can obtain the information by phoning ☎ 01802-3333 between 7am and 8pm on weekdays and from 8am to 2pm on Saturdays. The call costs €0.06 from an ordinary fixed line, irrespective of duration or where you're calling from in Germany.

You can also use the search option (*Filialsuche*) on the Online Services page of the Deutsche Post website (⌨ www.deutschepost.de).

LETTER POST

Now that it has lost its responsibility for telecommunications and banking, Deutsche Post concentrates almost entirely on delivering post and remains one of Europe's best postal services. Ordinary letters posted at larger post offices before 9am are usually delivered the next business day anywhere in Germany. Delivery times to other countries are more difficult to estimate as a result of varying service standards in the country of destination, but average 2.2 days for Belgium and the Netherlands, 2.3 days for the UK and 4.3 days for Italy – which says a lot more about Italy's postal service than Germany's! Deutsche Post is also innovative: for example, if you need to get hold of stamps in a hurry, you can visit the Stampit online franking facility, which will enable you to print out postage vouchers on your own PC (⌨ www.deutschepost.de and follow the link on the home page).

Post boxes are yellow with a black stylised post-horn symbol and are usually mounted on building walls. Collections from boxes outside main post offices are usually made every hour or two, while in residential neighbourhoods they may be emptied only once a day (the days and times of collections are displayed on the front of boxes). A sticker on a post box in the form of a large red dot indicates that it will be emptied later than others in the area.

Postal rates for letters are based on a combination of size, weight, quantity (e.g. bulk deliveries), type of delivery, and even the content and purpose. A complete list of rates would be encyclopaedic and beyond the scope of this book, but the most common categories are listed below:

- **Postcard (*Postkarte*)** – A standard postcard must be between 90 and 125mm wide and 140 and 235mm long, and may weigh between 150 and 500g. They cost €0.45 to send within Europe and €1 to the rest of the world and are sent by airmail.

- **Standard Letter (*Standardbrief*)** – A 'standard letter' can be between 90 and 125mm wide and between 140 and 235mm long. It may be no more than 5mm thick and weigh a maximum of 20g. Postage is €0.55 to Europe, €1.50 to the rest of the world by surface mail and €1.50 also by airmail. American readers should note that the standard US 'business size' envelope is 9.5 inches long. This translates to 241 mm or 6mm too long for this category of post. It's therefore advisable to use standard German envelopes.

- **Compact Letter (*Kompaktbrief*)** – This is the next-smaller size, between 70 and 125mm wide and 100 and 235mm in length. The maximum thickness is 10mm and the maximum weight 50g. It costs €1 within Europe and €2 to the rest of the world.

- **Large Letter (*Grossbrief*)** –This is an intermediate size and applies within Germany only. *Grossbriefe* may be between 70 and 250mm wide and between 100 and 353mm long, not more than 20mm thick with a maximum weight of 500g. The postage is €1.44.

- **Maximum Letter (Maxibrief)** – This is the largest size sent to inland destinations. The length can be from 100mm to 353mm, the breadth from 70mm to 250mm, the thickness not more than 50mm, and the weight up to one kilo. It costs €2.20.

- **Maximum Letter International (*Maxibrief International*)** – It can vary between a length of 140mm, breadth of 90mm and a weight of 50g, to a maximum of 600mm on each side and a weight of 2 kilos. Costs vary with weight, destination and the manner of shipment and range from €1.60 to Europe and €36 by air worldwide.

A special category is the *Plusbrief*, an envelope with pre-printed postage. It's available only at post offices and comes in packages of from 3 to 100 envelopes costing between €5.50 to €60.50. The former are stamped to the value of €0.44 and the latter €0.55.

General Information

Note the following when posting letters in Germany:

- If you send a letter with insufficient postage it will be delivered. However, the addressee will be charged a penalty in addition to the postage due. Should the addressee refuse to pay the postage and penalty, you will receive the letter back and be required to pay the penalty and postage due (with no option to refuse).

- Certain materials addressed to blind recipients – Braille texts, audio tapes and similar materials weighing up to 7kg, can be sent free. Special rules apply – enquire at a post office for details.

- There's one postal delivery per day in most of Germany, from Mondays to Saturdays, usually in the morning.

- It's possible to send letters and parcels by express post. Express letters (*Express Briefe*) cost from €7.50 to €10.50 depending on the weight (the maximum is 2kg). Express packages (*Express Pakete*) can weigh up to

20kg and cost an additional €12 on top of the normal tariff. This is given in the parcel post section below. Both letters and packages are normally delivered the next day, unless it's a Sunday or a public holiday. An extra fee of €31 (plus VAT) will ensure delivery on a Sunday or public holiday, otherwise post will arrive on the next working day.

- Postage for express post sent abroad is determined by weight (up to 20kg) and delivery zone. Zone 1 includes EU countries, zone 2 the rest of Europe plus the US, Canada, and Mexico, and zone 3 the rest of the world. Costs run from €38.35 for shipments of up to 200g for a zone 1 country to €437.15 for a 20kg shipment to a country in zone 3.

- Most post offices sell a variety of envelopes in various sizes, including 'bubble-pack' envelopes for sending fragile, but relatively flat items.

- Aerogrammes are available from stationery shops and cost €1 for world-wide delivery. They must not include enclosures of any kind.

- The correct format for addressing envelopes is as follows:

> Herrn Hans Handel
> Goethestr. 12
> D-65193 Wiesbaden
> Germany

Note that the street number goes after the street and there's a blank line between the street and the line containing the post code (*Postleitzahl*) and city. The post code goes before the name of the city. You may occasionally see envelopes with the *Postleitzahl* and city on the second line and the street address in the third. This is an old format and its use is discouraged due to the increasing mechanisation of post processing.

Mechanisation has given rise to a new requirement for the placement of addresses on envelopes: they must begin (not end) no more than 14cm (around 5.5 inches) from the *right* edge of the envelope. This has the effect of moving the address block considerably further to the right than is customary in many countries. Although senders of individual letters can safely disregard this rule, generators of mass postings must be aware of it. The 'bible' for formats and rules such as this is the booklet, *Gut in Form; ganz automatisch*, available free from post offices.

- A list of *Postleitzahlen* (postcodes) is available for inspection at any post office or on the Internet on the Deutsche Post website (💻 www. deutschepost.de).

- There are various kinds of registered (*per Einschreibung*) letter. A letter which is recorded only by the postman (*Einwurfeinschreiben*) costs €1.66 plus postage. if you want a letter signed for by the recipient (*Über-*

gabeeinschreiben), who may not be the addressee, the cost is €2.05 plus postage. For greater security, materials sent as *Übergabeeinschreiben* may also be denominated *eigenhändig* for an additional €1.80. This ensures that delivery is to the addressee or his legal representative only, who must sign for the item. Finally, a return receipt (*Rückschein*), which costs an additional €1.80, must be signed by the recipient and is returned to the sender.

● There are many categories of insurance for various kinds of post. Ask for details at a post office.

● Stamps can be purchased at any post office or from stamp machines located outside post offices. **Note that when buying stamps from a machine, you receive your 'change' in stamps!**

● Stamp collectors can order a variety of subscriptions and special issues via the extensive philately section on the 💻 www.deutschepost.de website, as well as sign up for a free E-newsletter which will keep them abreast of the latest developments.

● Finally, check all your post carefully and don't throw anything away unless you're certain it's junk post, e.g. advertising circulars and free newspapers. What may initially look like junk post may, in fact, be something official and important. Also check for post in between your junk post.

PARCEL POST

The most convenient way to send parcels in Germany is with the standard boxes available in the *Packset*, an assortment of pre-cut and pre-folded boxes available from post offices. The designations, sizes and prices are as follows:

Size (*Grösse*)	Cost (€)
XS (22.5 x 14.5 x 3.5cm)	1.50
S (25 x 17.5 x 10cm)	1.70
M (35 x 25 x 12cm)	1.90
L (40 x 25 x 15cm)	2.20
XL (50 x 30 x 20cm)	2.50
F (bottle size – 37.5 x 13 x 13cm)	2.30

Of course, you can send objects of all shapes and sizes in other boxes, but the Packset boxes, which include address labels and (all but the XS size) sealing tape, are by far the easiest to use. The Deutsche Post permits the sending of alcoholic beverages – a fact that explains the popularity of the 'Size F' box!

The variety of parcel-post categories and rates is even greater than that for letter post. Generally speaking, postage to domestic addresses on parcels weighing from 5kg to 20kg costs between €6.70 and €13. To the most expensive zone abroad it ranges from €35 to €80. In Germany packages normally arrive next day.

POST COLLECTION

If the postman calls with post requiring a signature, payment of import duty, VAT or excess postage when you aren't at home, he will leave a notification form showing the address (not always the nearest post office) where you can pick up the item. Pay particular attention to the entry on the card that begins *'heute jedoch nicht vor...'* followed by a time. You cannot retrieve the post before the time on the day (*heute* = today) you receive the notice. There is, of course, a practical reason for this: the postman won't have completed his route and left the item at the pick-up point until then.

You can receive *poste restante* (*Postlagernd*) post at most post offices. It's held for 14 days, and you may authorise others in writing to collect it for you. Post intended for such delivery should be addressed as follows:

> [Your Name]
> Postlagernd
> [Postcode] [City]
> Germany

Ensure that the address includes the correct *Postleitzahl* for the post office where you want the post to be delivered, from where post can be collected from the *Postlagernde Sendungen* counter. Try to ensure that your correspondents use the German term *Postlagernd* rather than the French *poste restante*, as the French term, while well-known internationally, isn't generally used in Germany.

You can obtain a post office box (*Postfach*) at your local post office for a one-off registration fee of €10. There are no further charges. Post office box addresses should be in the following format:

> [Your Name]
> Postfach [box number]
> [Postcode] [City]
> Germany

Pay particular attention to the *Postleitzahl* of your box, as it's usually different from that of the post office in which the box is physically located! The box number should be written with the digits grouped in twos, e.g. Postfach 23 45 67.

CHANGE OF ADDRESS

If you're moving house, ask your local post office for a 'forwarding form (*Nachsendeantrag*). Ordinary post is forwarded within Germany free of charge, although you must file a request no later than five days before you want the forwarding of post to begin. For holidays and other temporary absences, it's often more practical to ask the post office to simply hold your post until your return. The form to use to request this is a *Lagerungsauftrag*.

POSTCHEQUE ACCOUNT

Although the post office sold its banking operations when it was privatised, the banking company, Deutsche Postbank AG, still transacts most of its business at post offices and has branches at every post office in Germany (a total of 13,000), and a further 7,600 cash machines (ATMs) throughout the country.

Services available from the Postbank include the following:

- Bill-paying, either in person, by post, or electronically (see below), cash deposits and withdrawals;
- Postbank card free with account;
- Free pre-printed forms (*Zahlungsverkehrsvordrucke*), the ones used for money transfers;
- Postage-paid envelopes for the sending of *Zahlungsverkehrsvordrucke* or other transactions;
- Postbank Mastercard or Postbank Visa card – €20 per year. (Currently under 28's with an ordinary account qualify for a Visa card at a special rate of €5);
- Deposit insurance;
- Savings account.

Electronic Banking

Manual transactions are well on the way to becoming obsolete, and extensive investment by the Postbank in 'electronic banking' (the words are almost always written in English) has made it possible for you to do almost everything that can be done at a post office from home via a computer and the Internet (except withdraw cash). Both of the major home-banking software packages, *Microsoft Money* and Intuit Corporation's *Quicken* include banking modules that feature bill-paying, account reconciliation, the creation of standing orders (*Daueraufträge*) and other common banking transactions. One big advantage of these applications is that they post account information directly from the Postbank to your computerised chequebook.

However the option which most people use and one that doesn't require a software package is *Online-Banking* through the Postbank's own website (🖳 www.postbank.de). This allows you to carry out most transactions by simply 'pointing and clicking'. One advantage of the online service is that foreign currency transactions are considerably cheaper. All you need is an Internet browser. Currently the Postbank has 1.6 million online customers.

Signatures are clearly impossible with online banking, but electronic payments are nonetheless quite safe. The Postbank issues you with a PIN (personal identification number), which you must use to access your account, even if you wish only to check the balance. Actual transactions require additional transaction numbers (TANs), which are computer-generated in sheets of 100 and also inserted in special envelopes by machine. Each TAN is valid for a single transaction and an attempt to re-use one generates an error message from the Postbank's computer. The absence of a human element in this process increases the level of security, but leads to the inevitable result that if you lose your PIN or TANs, no Postbank employee can help you. You will simply have to reapply for new ones, a process that can suspend electronic access to your account for up to ten days.

For further information about banking, see **Chapter 14**.

PAYING BILLS

A red-and-white pre-printed form is usually included with all bills you receive by post in Germany. With this form you can pay the bill, either in cash or as a direct debit from your own account, at any post office or through any bank. There's no charge for the transaction provided you have an account with the Postbank or the bank where you're making the payment. Therefore, in order to pay bills at a post office without paying a fee you must have a postal savings account (*Postgirokonto* or *Postsparkonto*). Most *Zahlungsverkehrsvordrucke* are partially completed with the payee's name, account number (*Kontonummer*), branch code (*Bankleitzahl*) and the amount owing printed on them. You usually need only enter your own account number and *Bankleitzahl*. Make sure that you sign the form, however, or payment will be rejected.

If there's no *Zahlungsverkehrsvordruck* enclosed with a bill, you may have to use your own, which the Postbank provides free of charge. These are pre-printed with your name, account number, and the name and branch code of the Postbank branch that maintains your account. You must enter the payee's name and bank data, the amount and your signature. The payee's bank data (*Bankverbindung*) is shown at the bottom of the payee's letter or statement in the following format:

> **Dresdner Bank Stuttgart, BLZ 600 800 00, Ktonr. 987 654 321**

BLZ is the abbreviation for *Bankleitzahl* (branch code) while *Ktonr.* is the abbreviation for *Kontonummer* (account number). If more than one bank is listed, you may make the payment to any of them. It isn't strictly necessary to enter the name of the payee's bank on the form, but if you omit it you must be absolutely certain you've entered the branch code correctly.

If the creditor hasn't sent you a *Zahlungsverkehrsvordruck* and you have none left, you can obtain a blank one from a post office, although in this case you must complete everything yourself.

When writing figures in Germany (or anywhere in continental Europe), you should cross the down stroke of the number 7 in order to avoid confusion with the number 1, which is often written with a leading upstroke and resembles a seven to many non-Europeans. Germans (and other Europeans) write the date with the day first followed by the month and year, not as Americans do with the month first. For example, 1.7.01 is 1st July 2001 and not January 7th 2001. The conventional US form 1/7/01, with the month first and slashes between the digits, is unknown and must **never** be used.

MISCELLANEOUS SERVICES

Some services available at German post offices seem (at least by UK and US standards) somewhat unconventional, and include the following:

● Toy collectors (and indulgent parents) can find an interesting and large selection of model trucks, buses, railway engines and historical postal vehicles for sale at larger post offices. These can also be ordered by post from Deutsche Post AG, Collection, Postfach 201208, 60642 Frankfurt, over the telephone on ☎ 0180-3246 042, or on the philately section of the 🖳 www.deutschepost.de website.

● A new 'gift service' venture between Deutsche Post and a number of German mail-order companies allows customers to order gifts ranging from flowers to books and CDs to wine, spirits and chocolates.

Catalogues, entitled *Geschenkservice*, are updated every few months and available at any post office.

- A number of lottery tickets can be purchased at post offices, where you can by a ticket for a single draw or an annual subscription.
- Post offices are also ticket agencies, where you can buy tickets for concerts, the circus, exhibitions and other major events.
- Useful computer software programs connected with office tasks are available here too.

7.

TELEPHONE

Until a little over six years ago the German telephone network, operated by Deutsche Telekom (DT), was a state-run monopoly, and prices were among the highest in Western Europe, although the service itself had a good reputation for service and reliability. In late 1996, in accordance with new EU legislation, the German government began to privatise Telekom and offered 500 million shares (representing around 26 per cent of the company) to the German public. Despite the reputation of Germans as cautious investors, the privatisation proved wildly successful and provided DT with much needed capital to update and widen its range of services and prepare for competition, which was introduced to the German telecommunications market in 1998. Although over 95 per cent of fixed lines are still owned by and connected to Deutsche Telekom, many people now use alternative long-distance carriers.

While DT investors have seen their shares take a roller-coaster ride after initially doubling in price since privatisation (although DT are now once more in profit), the outcome for telephone users has been rather more clear-cut. Overall, prices have fallen, although the downside is that there are now so many companies competing for business (particularly in the long-distance and international markets) that keeping track of who offers the best deal has become a challenge.

See also **Emergency & Useful Numbers** on page 150.

INSTALLATION & REGISTRATION

The easiest way to get a standard telephone line installed in your home is to visit a DT office and complete an application form. The fee for installing a line in a property is €51.57. If a phone line is already installed and you're able to take it over, the cost is €25.78. In this case your wait for a connection is typically just a day or two rather than the couple of weeks for a new line. For the same price you can have either an analogue or digital (ISDN) socket.

Leasing or buying a telephone from DT costs from €6 to €16 per month (over a three year period) or you can simply purchase one from any retailer. You will find basic phones for as little as €20, although it's important to check that they conform to European specifications: a phone should have a 'CE' and/or a 'BZT' registration number, usually found on a sticker on its base. If you ignore this rule, a DT technician may appear one day and disconnect your 'illegal' phone and Telekom may refuse to continue providing a service to repeat offenders. However, almost any phone you purchase in Germany will be approved by DT.

For ordinary analogue phones, it's the usual practice for DT to install only a TEA (European Phone Standard) connector and to leave it to the customer to decide what equipment to connect to it. However, Germans are rapidly switching to ISDN lines and the digital phone network is already extensive in Germany. DT markets a number of ISDN packages, but the standard one comprises three phone numbers and two lines, which costs €23.16 per month compared with €13.72 per month for a standard analogue line. An ISDN line allows subscribers to use two different services simultaneously, e.g. phone and fax or Internet. It also provides the fastest means of accessing the Internet. The calls themselves are slightly cheaper than with an analogue line.

In some recently developed urban areas, such as parts of Hamburg, there are alternative providers of local phone services.

Cancelling Your Phone Service: To discontinue your phone service with DT, you must cancel the contract in writing and pay the final bill when it arrives. DT is infamous for pursuing ex-customers to the ends of the world to extract outstanding payments!

USING THE TELEPHONE

Using the telephone in Germany is much the same as in any other country, with a few German eccentricities thrown in for good measure. When dialling a number within your own exchange area, dial the number only. When dialling anywhere else the area code must be dialled before the subscriber's number. Some advertisements and company letterheads have spaces between each few digits, while others prefer to separate the area code (*Vorwahl*) from the rest of the number with a dash or full stop or put it in brackets. In this book, dashes are used to separate the code and spaces are inserted every three or four digits.

Answering The Phone

Germans generally answer the phone by stating their last names, so don't expect a cheery 'good morning' at the other end when you ring somebody. When making a call, Germans identify themselves first, before asking for the person they're calling, so if you don't want to be thought pushy or rude, it's best to do likewise. Similarly, it may be considered impolite to ring a private home between 1 and 3pm (lunchtime) or after 9pm.

Nuisance Calls

Nuisance calls are no more frequent in Germany than elsewhere, but they do happen. **The best advice is to hang up as soon as you realise the nature of the call; most telephone pests soon lose interest if they fail to get a response. If the calls continue, you could blow a loud whistle down the line the next time they call.** If nuisance calls get out of hand, you can ask Telekom to use their call tracing service (called *Fangschaltung*), for which there's a fee. **You should also report the problem to the police.**

If you want to 'screen' calls before you pick up the receiver, a caller ID service is included in the basic T-net 100 tariff monthly rental fee of €17. You obviously need a telephone model capable of physically displaying the caller's number, or an ID box which records this in its memory, so that you have a permanent record of who has been phoning you. With the latter you can also associate numbers with names, so that the name of a caller appears on the display rather than just his number. The service doesn't apply to international calls, however, so calls originating from outside Germany are displayed as 'Number not recognised' (*Nummer unbekannt*). Caller ID boxes are available for around €30 upwards from electronics stores such as Conrad (⌨ www.conrad.de) or from specialist phone shops.

Answering Machines

Answering machines cost from around €40, while the most expensive models cost around double this and have a range of special features, including automatic dial-back, call forwarding, remote playback of messages (only accessible by special code), and recording the date and time of incoming calls. If you feel uncomfortable speaking German you can record a message in English or get someone else to record a German message for you. Alternatively, electronics, music and computer stores sell a variety of approved, pre-recorded cassette tapes or CDs for around €10. **Be wary of programming your telephone answering machine with what you would term a joke, which may not amuse Germans!**

Useful Phrases

Listed below are some useful everyday phrases when using the phone:

English	German
I'd like to speak to ___ .	*Ich möchte mit ___ sprechen.*
Could you connect me with ___ ?	*Könnten Sie mich mit ___ verbinden?*
___ is not in.	*___ ist nicht hier/im Hause.*
I will try again later.	*Ich versuche es später noch einmal.*
I would like to leave a message for ___ .	*Ich möchte ___ eine Nachricht hinterlassen.*
You've reached the wrong number.	*Sie sind falsch verbunden.*
Could you ask ___ to call me back?	*Könnten Sie ___ bitten zurückzurufen?*

Recorded Messages

Listed below are some of the most common recorded messages that you're likely to hear:

German	English
Kein Anschluss unter dieser Nummer.	This number is unavailable.
Dieser Anschluss ist vorübergehend nicht erreichbar.	This number is temporarily unobtainable.
Diese Rufnummer hat sich geändert.	This number has been changed.
Bitte, erfragen Sie die neue Nummer bei der Auskunft.	Please ask Directory Enquiries for the new number.
Der Platz ist besetzt; bitte, warten Sie.	The extension is busy; please hold.

LONG-DISTANCE CARRIERS

Since 1998, telephone customers have been offered a wide choice of long-distance services by specialist companies. This competition among carriers has resulted in the lowest phone costs in German history, but as less profitable companies cease trading or go bankrupt prices are likely to rise again. To access a long-distance carrier other than DT, you must dial a five-digit prefix before dialling the area code and phone number. Many carriers don't require you to register before using them. This is known as a 'call-by-call' service (the English term is used in German); others require a minimum monthly fee and some require you to enter into an exclusive contract. The same variety of rules applies to billing practices, some companies billing independently and others (including most call-by-call providers) adding their charges to your regular DT phone bill.

In March 2003, the cheapest national weekday peak time calls within Germany were via Junior Telecom (access number 0190051) and cost €0.022 per minute. However, for the weekday slot from 9pm to midnight their competitors Callax (access number 01077) charged just €0.017 per minute for national calls. The table below indicates typical rates charged for calls to selected overseas destinations in March 2003.

Country	Provider	Access Number	Price Per Minute (€)
Australia	Maestro Telecom	01015	0.025
Canada	Maestro Telecom	01015	0.02
UK/US	SurpriseTel.	0190047	0.029

In order to compare the prices and packages currently offered by each company (which change frequently), go to the excellent website 🖳 www. teletarif.de, which covers all possible permutations.

You can buy a 'call router' that selects the cheapest service provider for a given call, whether domestic or international. Some call routers are updated weekly by data transmission, although this is an optional service that costs extra. For those who must make regular long-distance or international calls and companies who rely on the phone for their business, these devices can be **very** cost effective.

DEUTSCHE TELEKOM CHARGES

Domestic local call charges are based on units (*Einheiten*) which have a fixed price but are allocated a duration in seconds, depending on the distance and time of a call. The first unit is charged when the party answers the phone and further units accrue at regular intervals. This can work out as expensive for long calls but cheap for short calls, because the minimum charge is the same in all cases. National and international calls are charged by the minute. The charging system has mutated in recent years, with Deutsche Telekom currently (March 2003) having a surprisingly complicated variety of tariff periods, which vary according to whether you are making a local ("City") or national ("Deutschland") call.

Local or "City" Rates

The cost is €0.06 per unit or part of a unit, and a city call is defined as one you can make without using an area code. VAT is included in this charge. A unit is equal to the following periods of time:

- **Daytime Standard (Or Peak) Rate** – Mondays to Fridays from 9am to 6pm. Calls made during this period are over two and a half times more expensive than the cheapest rate. Each unit lasts 90 seconds.
- **Leisure Time Rate** – Weekdays between 8 and 9am and between 6 and 9pm. Each unit lasts 150 seconds.
- **Evening Rate** – From 9pm to 8am plus all day on Saturdays, Sundays and national holidays. This is the cheapest rate. Each unit lasts 240 seconds.

National Rates

National (*Deutschland*) rates are charged per minute or part of a minute for calls outside the local area. The rates (including VAT) are as follows:

- **Daytime Rate** – 7am to 6pm weekdays. Calls made in this slot cost almost four times the cheapest rate. One minute costs €0.122.

- **Leisure Time Rate** – 6pm to 9pm. This is almost twice as expensive as the cheapest rate. One minute costs €0.061.

- **Evening Rate** – 9pm to 7am. This is the standard evening rate and reasonably cheap, making this is a popular time for phoning overseas while the significant reduction in local rates also explains why the whole of Germany floods the Internet at precisely 9pm. One minute costs €0.031.

- **Weekend/Public Holiday Rate** – The 9pm to 7am rate is the same as the standard evening rate. However, the period 7am to 9pm is charged at the leisure time rate which is over one third more (one minute costs €0.046).

Other Calls

There are also many special rates for mobile phones, varied international rates, and rates that remain constant at all times, e.g. ship-to-shore. Public telephones charges are by the minute: €0.10 per unit for local and €0.20 per unit for national calls. Calls abroad cost from €0.60 to €2,60 a minute from boxes marked "Ausland".

BILLS

Your telephone bill (*Rechnung*) is issued monthly, whether by Telekom or another provider. It shows the charges for the previous month, based on units, although for an additional fee you can request an itemised phone bill showing all calls made (although this must be explicitly requested due to Germany's privacy laws). A standard phone bill includes the following information (listed in alphabetical order):

German	English
Andere Dienstleistungen	Additional services provided by Telekom
Anschlüsse an . . .	Services to . . . (i.e. other providers' services)
bei Rückfragen Telefon	Telephone number to contact in case of billing discrepancies
Cityverbindungen	Local calls
Deutschlandsverbindungen	National calls not included above under local calls

Inlandsauskunft, Auslandsauskunft	Calls made to information services
Kundennummer	Customer reference number
Mobilfunknetz	Connections made to mobile phone services
Monatliche Beträge	Monthly basic fee, including any rental equipment
Rechnungsbetrag	Total amount due, including 16 per cent value added tax
Rechnungsdatum	Date of billing
Rechnungsnummer	Billing number
Regionalverbindungen	Regional calls
Rufnummer	Customer's telephone number
Weltverbindungen	International calls

Your telephone bill must be paid within 14 days of the posting date. If you're late and receive a reminder by post, there's a penalty of €1. Don't wait too long at this point, as disconnection is just around the corner if you fail to pay promptly after the second reminder. If you're disconnected, there's a fee to be reconnected and your telephone number is likely to change because your previous one may have been given to another customer! If you accrue too many of these extra charges, you may also have to pay an advance (refundable) deposit equal to the amount of your last three telephone bills before your service will be continued. It's no wonder Telekom customers are slightly paranoid about paying their bills on time! Prepayment can be made prior to a holiday or other absence by simply completing a form at a post office and paying the estimated amount for the period in question. Any difference is adjusted the following month.

The most popular way to pay phone bills is by automatic bank payment or direct debit (called a *Dauerauftrag* when done on a permanent basis).You receive the bill for information purposes and the amount due is automatically debited from your bank (Giro) account. You can also pay your phone bill at a post office or bank, but this requires paying in cash and waiting in a queue.

PUBLIC TELEPHONES

Public phone boxes in Germany used to be easy to spot by their bright yellow colour, but only a few of these now remain. New style booths are a pinky lavender hue, and nothing like as common as they used to be. Finding a public phone in Germany can sometimes be a challenge, although they are usually located at post offices, in hotel foyers, hospitals, restaurants, pedestrianised areas of cities, outside the gates of military bases, at *Autobahn* service areas, airports, railway and bus stations, and near sports stadiums.

A sign on the booth indicates whether it can be used for international calls (*Ausland*) or domestic calls only (*Inland*). As elsewhere in Europe, most public phones in Germany no longer accept cash, but require phone cards (*Telefonkarte*). These are available in denominations of €5 and €10 at Telekom offices, post offices and some newspaper kiosks. Units are recorded on the card and subtracted automatically after each call. There are now also far more phone booths in which you can use an international credit card (Kreditkarte), particularly at airports, railway stations and hotels – a full 15,000 say DT.

There are still a few payphones around that accept coins, mainly at airports and railway stations. Some phones are equipped with an illuminated counter indicating the credit remaining and when *Bitte Zahlen* flashes it's time to insert more money. Some phone booths are equipped to receive calls, indicated by the sign of a bell, which are useful when you run out of money and can ask someone to ring you back. As mentioned previously, local calls cost €0.10 a minute, Germany-wide ones €0.20 a minute and calls abroad from €0.60 to € 2.60 a minute.

You can also make calls from phones that are located in post offices. You must register at the counter, make your call from the assigned booth and then return to the counter to pay. If you're making an international call, go to the counter marked *Auslandgespräche*. **Note, however, that you must pay a hefty cash deposit for an international call – even as much as €50 if you're phoning the US.** Germany's phone system is fully automated, therefore operator-assisted calls aren't possible from phone booths, including those at post offices.

TELEPHONE DIRECTORIES

Deutsche Telekom issues a handy free annual book of German and foreign area codes, entitled *Vorwahlverzeichnis, Inland, Ausland* (AVON). AVON is simple to use, provided you know the German spellings of the countries you wish to call, such as 'Kanada' and 'Ungarn' (Canada and Hungary). All Telekom subscribers are entitled to a free copy of AVON, along with their local telephone directory and yellow pages, although they aren't delivered to your door. You must collect copies from your local post office – subscribers receive a postcard explaining the procedure each year. Some post offices accept old directories for recycling, while others expect you to recycle last year's books yourself.

When you receive new local directories you should read the introductions carefully, where information explaining how to use the phone system is provided in seven languages, including English. If you must look up numbers in directories other than your local directory, you can do this at a post office, although the quality of directories varies as some selfish customers simply tear out the pages they want.

Directory Enquiries

The phone number for domestic directory enquiries is ☎ 11833 and for international enquiries it's ☎ 11834. If you need an English language version of national enquiries you must dial ☎ 11837. These services are now free. As an alternative, you may wish to obtain a nation-wide telephone directory on CD-ROM. When Telekom issued its first CD-ROM directory the cost was exorbitant. However, other companies then produced much cheaper versions and Telekom sued them for copyright infringement. Unfortunately for them the courts decided that no organisation had the right to 'own' phone numbers. Nowadays DT's own CD costs just €7.95 and of course there's a web version at 🖥 www. teleauskunft.de which is free.

The yellow pages are called *Gelbe Seiten*, an exact translation of the English title, and while accessible in printed form, going to the website at 🖥 www. gelbeseiten.de is likely to be a better option as some three thousand entries are altered on it every single day.

MOBILE PHONES & PAGERS

Before buying or using a mobile phone, you should be aware that health fears have been raised in some countries over the effects of the electromagnetic fields generated by them. On the other hand, a mobile phone could save your life in an emergency. One other advantage of a mobile compared with a fixed-line phone is that 'installation' is almost immediate. Usually you can use a mobile phone within a few hours of signing a contract and the longest you're likely to have to wait is until the next day.

Mobile phones are called 'handys' in Germany and prices range from around €200 to around €400 without a contract; if you take out a contract, the phone itself is usually 'free'. Needless to say, this apparent benevolence carries a sting in the tail. In the small print of the contract there's a clause committing you to a minimum period with a specific mobile phone service provider. This will be at least one year and possibly three, which allows the retailer to recoup the cost of the phone and (he hopes) make a sizeable profit. A typical mobile phone contract requires you to make a payment of at least €15 a month, even if you don't use your phone at all. Added to this are charges for each call you make, although some 'free' calls may be included in the monthly rental.

You can buy mobile phones from retail outlets, specialist dealers, and department and chain stores. Retailers have arrangements with service providers or networks to sell airtime contracts along with phones, so you shouldn't rely on getting good or impartial advice from retail staff, some of whom know little or nothing about phones and networks. Ask friends and colleagues for their recommendations and shop around, comparing not only phone prices but also the features and additional services on offer (see below). Above all, compare the monthly fees and the charges for calls at different times. Retailers advertise in magazines and newspapers, where a wide range of special offers are promoted.

There's also an active market in secondhand mobile phones. Good places to look are in the shoppers' newspapers that are published once or twice a week, such as *SperrMüll* (🖳 www.Sperrmuell.de) and *das Inserat* (🖳 www. das-inserat.de). The German version of the E-bay website is as popular as its American and British counterparts and offers the opportunity to buy almost anything including mobile phones within a context with which many readers will already be familiar.

Before buying a mobile phone, compare battery life, memory number capacity, weight, size and features. The latter may include alphanumeric store, automatic call-back, unanswered call store, call timer, minute minder, lock facility, call barring, mailbox, messaging services, Internet web-surfing, email and the personal handy phone system (PHS), which operates as a cordless phone in the home (using your home fixed-line number) and a mobile phone elsewhere.

There are three main mobile phone systems in Germany. These are C-Net, which is generally used only in cars due to the size and weight of the equipment; the GSM-900 coded D-Net, which is used mostly for cell phones; and the GSM-1800 coded E-Net, which is for the exclusive use of cell phones. The C-Net has countrywide cover, even in the most remote areas and within the border areas of neighbouring countries. The D-Net has some 'black spots' where communication isn't possible, the exact location of which depend on the company providing the service. If you live outside a major city you must ensure that a company's cover includes the area(s) where you live and do business. The two main D-Net networks are D1 (operated by Deutsche Telekom) and D2 (run by Mannesmann). In eastern Germany, the D1 Net is said to have better cover, whereas in western Germany both are about equal. The E-Net operates mainly in the larger urban centres.

A distinct advantage of the D and E-Nets is that they conform to the GSM digital standard used by most systems internationally (the exceptions being Japan and most of the US). This means that people moving to

Germany from another European country, Africa, Australia or most of Asia can use their existing GSM phone and must purchase only a new coding card. Coding cards can be bought with pre-paid credits, which can be 'topped up' once the existing credit is used, or paid via a monthly bill as with a fixed-line phone service.

Some companies offer a service called E-Plus (one of the E-Net services), where you can decide in advance how much time you plan to spend on your mobile phone each month and sign up for a service providing 20, 60 or 120 minutes per month. The drawback is that these minutes are valid only within Germany and if you don't use all the time you have contracted for in a particular month you must still pay for them. Note also, that any additional minutes you use will cost you extra.

All mobile phone companies will continue to bill you, even if you move from Germany while your mobile contract is active. They will pursue you until the money is paid and are quite prepared to engage debt collectors in other countries if necessary. Most mobile phone companies don't include a cancellation clause in their contracts, therefore, as many foreigners have discovered, customers are stuck with the monthly payments for the full term of their contract. Short-term mobile phone rentals aren't common, but are possible for visiting business people with generous expense accounts (suffice to say, they aren't cheap).

Security

The theft of mobile phones is a huge problem, with stolen mobile phones usually reprogrammed (cloned) to make free calls overseas. You will be held responsible for the cost of any calls that thieves make between the time of a theft and you reporting it to your phone company. Mobile phones should never be left in cars. It's advisable to insure a phone for its real value, because if a rented phone is stolen you will be billed for its replacement cost – not what you paid for it. All phones are provided with a unique serial number, which allows their use to be blocked if they're stolen, and digital phones can also be programmed to stop users making certain calls, e.g. international calls. New, clone-proof mobile phones are now being slowly introduced.

One positive spin-off from the mobile phone explosion is that they have created a new breed of 'cellular Samaritans' who use their mobiles to report emergencies, accidents, crimes, traffic jams and other problems.

Pagers

Pager services for private customers have died a death in Germany in the last few years due to the advent of sms-capable mobile phones, and the main

company still active in this area is concentrating on the business market .
Already the pager is gathering the aura of a collectible electronic oddity.

INTERNET

The Internet is very popular in Germany, confirmed by the number of
advertisements on TV and in print that include email and website addresses.
Internet Service Providers proliferate and the variety of factors involved in
finding the best deal for you, and the permutations of these possible, is
much wider than in the UK. Deutsche Telekom's Internet service, T-Online
(🖳 www.t-online.de), is currently the most widely used, and of its variety of
tariffs, the most basic one, *T-Online eco surfen*, costs €0.0159 per minute
around the clock and has a monthly fee of €3.95.

Both CompuServe and AOL provide services in Germany and both have
large numbers of customers. To sign up, contact ☎ 01805-704070 for
CompuServe (🖳 www.compuserve.de) or ☎ 01805-313164 for AOL
(🖳 www. aol.de). Chances are you will receive free promotional CDs from
both of these ISPs in your post from time to time anyway, and you will
certainly find them on the free CD-ROMs provided with most computer
magazines. Hundreds of smaller ISPs advertise in local newspapers,
magazines and on billboards, and you will also be bombarded with
advertisements on TV and radio. Prices and services vary and you should
be wary of signing up with an 'unknown' new service, as many fail in their
first few months leaving users high and dry.

The cheapest offers in May 2003 for someone wanting to surf for around
an hour a day at peaktime (9am to 6pm), were between €15 and €17 per
month, with companies such as: T-online (✉ kundenservice@t-online.de
🖳 www.t-online.de); Freenet.De (✉ service@freenet.de 🖳 www.freenet.de);
Net.Art (✉ info@net.art.de 🖳 net.art.de; Compuserve Pro (✉ kunden
betreuung@compuserve.de 🖳 www.compuserve.de) and Arcor Spar (✉
info@ arcor.net 🖳 www.arcor.de).

You can also sign up with one of the free, web-based, email services, such
as Yahoo Mail (🖳 www.yahoo.com) or Hotmail (🖳 www.hotmail.com). One
advantage of these services is that you can access your email from any
computer with web access, e.g. at a library or a cybercafe. **However, post
sent to and from such services isn't necessarily secure.**

Modems

Any modems can be used on the German network, although if purchased
overseas you must watch out for the 16kHz timer signal which Telekom
sends to allow you to keep track of phone bills. German modems have

built-in filters for this, but if your modem doesn't you can lose your connection every 90 seconds or so! However, if you don't want the signal you can ask Telekom to switch it off or you can buy special filters from companies such as Teleadapt (🖳 www.teledapt.com) and Blackbox (🖳 www. blackbox.com).

EMERGENCY & USEFUL NUMBERS

There are two nation-wide emergency numbers in Germany. The number for the police is 110, while for the fire and ambulance services it's 112. In some remote areas there are local numbers for ambulance services, although the fire department (on 112) will gladly put you through. You should be able to call either of these numbers free of charge from any public phone, including card phones, although with some very old payphones you may need to insert coins first, which will be returned after the call. In many phone booths you will find a special emergency services connector in a separate case near the phone, which is activated simply by pulling a lever. Pulling it to the green side automatically connects you to the police, the red side to the fire department – needless to say, misuse of this facility is punishable by a heavy fine.

Some other useful numbers to keep by your phone are listed below – those prefixed with an asterisk (*) are free calls:

Number	Service
*011500	Pharmacists (recorded information service)
*011500	Doctors On Call (recorded information service)
*011500	Veterinarian (recorded information service)
01169	ADAC (German motoring club) traffic report
069-252500	Weisser Ring (child abuse hotline)
0611 581242	Ozone levels
01191	Speaking clock

TELEGRAMS, TELEX & FAX

Telegrams can be sent by phone, fax or online at 🖳 www.post.de and delivery is the next working day. You have the choice of a plain cover or, for a small supplement, a festive version suitable for birthday greetings and so forth. Costs are high, starting at €14.83 for a short message of up to ten words to a recipient within Germany. There's also an extra fee of €10.23 for delivery on Sundays or public holidays. To send an inland telegram by phone call ☎ 01805-121210 (€0.12 for each 60 seconds or part thereof) between 7am and 10pm weekdays and 7am and 11pm on Sundays and holidays. The corresponding number for international telegrams is ☎ 0800-330 1133 which is free. Inland telegrams can also be forwarded by fax on 🖳 01805-121211 while for international telegrams connect to 🖳 0800-330 1134. The latter is a freephone number.

Fax is widely used in Germany. There are no special rules for fax machines connected to your normal phone line, but you're required to register your machine if it's connected to a dedicated phone line. The registration process involves simply faxing a printed form to Telekom. Any fax machine using the G3 standard is adequate, but it must have either a CE or the older style FTZ registration number to be legal. If you're bringing your own fax machine to Germany there's no guarantee that it will work.

You can send faxes from post offices where fax machines may be located in the lobby (for which you will need a credit card) or behind the counter, when you must pay in cash. You will also find public (credit-card operated) fax machines in busy places such as airports, railway stations and *Autobahn* restaurants.

Telex is the largest dedicated text message network in the world, with over two million subscribers world-wide in over 200 countries. There are public telex bureaux at city telegraph offices and main post offices, and most hotels with a business clientele also offer telex facilities.

8.

TELEVISION & RADIO

Television (TV) and radio services in Germany are operated by both public and private broadcasting companies. The two public 'national' TV channels, ARD and ZDF, are run by a network of *Länder*-based broadcasters and funded by advertising and TV and radio licence fees, which are collected and distributed by an agency of the federal government. The regional authorities also produce and broadcast programmes targeted at their local audience using the so-called 'Third Channel' of public TV, one for each of the 11 regions that make up the network. Since the 1980s, when broadcasting regulations were relaxed across Europe, many private broadcasters have set up shop in Germany, as a result of which there's as wide a choice of TV programmes as you will find anywhere in Europe.

There was a time, way back, when a good deal of German TV consisted of recycled American series, inter-mixed with locally-produced game or talk shows and political coverage. However, the public broadcasters were among the first to comply with European regulations requiring that at least 51 per cent of programming be European in origin, so now there's an ever increasing amount of programming produced in Germany – everything from soap operas to drama series. One long-standing favourite throughout Europe has been Derrick, a German detective series (usually referred to as a *Krimi*), which ended production only when the star of the series announced his retirement from the acting profession. Derrick has achieved a kind of TV immortality, however, and can still be seen, dubbed into the local language or subtitled, throughout the continent. The game shows, ever popular here, can be quite useful viewing for those learning the language, as many are based on word play or other language skills. The Germans also produce a wide range of talk shows, some of which are indistinguishable from their American counterparts, often right down to the sets used (but with different guests!).

German audiences are keen on news programmes and documentaries, particularly 'investigative reporting' or consumer-oriented *exposés* of overpriced tourist packages, shoddy builders and crooked estate agents. Late night programming is often on the exotic (and erotic) side, with some documentary format shows dedicated to exploring sexual themes. At weekends, don't be surprised to find soft porn films broadcast in the wee small hours – usually starting around midnight, although these are often poorly made or dubbed.

Television Standards

The standard for TV reception in Germany isn't the same as in many other countries. Germany, together with much of the rest of continental Europe and Australia and New Zealand, uses a standard called PAL B/G. This differs from the PAL-I standard used in the UK, the SECAM-L standard used in France, the North American NSTC standard and the SECAM D/K used in Eastern Europe and many African countries. This means that anyone coming from the UK, France or the US will find their old TV of little use unless it's multi-standard or equipped with a satellite receiver. Some TVs can be converted to PAL B/G, but in most cases it isn't worth the expense.

The new European standard, PALplus, which includes a digital 16:9 (wide-screen) image and surround-sound transmission, is gradually replacing the older standards, so purchasing a PALplus set could be a worthwhile investment for anyone planning to remain in Europe. You should look for a model offering features such as teletext and a tele-synchronising clock – and particularly dual channel tone (not the same as stereo) – which will enable you to take advantage of the growing number of programmes transmitted in the original language as well as German. **The German mains supply is 220–240 volts at 50 hertz (cycles), giving an additional problem for those wishing to use equipment manufactured for the US market, which operates at 110 volts, 60 hertz (see page 116).**

German video recorders are capable of playing back all PAL cassettes and some are equipped with an NTSC or SECAM playback capability. Many German TVs are capable of reproducing direct NTSC and SECAM video signals from NTSC or SECAM recorders. Older TVs, however, will only show such recordings in black and white (use the 'video out' and 'sound out' plugs on the recorder and the European SCART plug on the TV). If you want to import a video recorder made for the US market, check that it doesn't synchronise on the AC frequency, as the German mains frequency is 20 per cent slower than that used in the US. British video recorders can also be used to play cassettes on German TVs provided you use the direct video/sound connection. American, French or British recorders cannot be used to record German TV off air, although British VCRs can be used to record from a TV's video output.

For those planning to travel outside Europe after their stay in Germany, a multi-standard set-up is the best buy. Companies such as Bang & Olufsen and Loewe offer multi-standard compatibility across their entire range, while most other companies offer particular (generally more expensive) models only.

Television Licence

It's mandatory for all radio and TV owners in Germany to pay a licence fee (currently €193.80 a year) to the Gebühreneinzugszentrale (GEZ) or Central Office for Licensing Fees for Radio and Television. The licence fee goes toward maintaining the broadcast services of the ARD, ZDF and the regional (Länder) third channels. Registration forms (Anmeldung) are available from banks and post offices, and you can even register and change (but NOT cancel) your TV licence over the Internet (🖥 www.gez.de). The GEZ prefers bills to be paid by standing order from a bank account (quarterly, bi-annually or annually, as you wish). TV and radio registration are done together, as the TV licence fee also covers radios in your household, including your car radio (see also **Radio Licence** on page 165).

A separate licence isn't usually required for additional TVs, provided they're located in a room used by yourself, your spouse or your children who are under 18. If any other adult household member (including any of your children who are over 18) has a TV in their room, i.e. not in the main family room, they're expected to register it in their own name and pay a separate licence fee. There's a separate form to use for reporting changes (*Änderungen*), such as buying a second TV for your holiday home or the children's bedroom. **On leaving the country (or if you decide to live a radio and TV-free life), don't forget to file the licence cancellation form (*Abmeldung*) to stop your standing order to the GEZ.**

Registration should be made within a week or two of installing a TV. The registration form asks you for the month and year you first bought or installed your TV or radio and if there's any cause for doubt you may be asked to prove this date, either by producing a receipt for your TV or radio or verification of when you arrived in Germany. **You will be fined if you have a TV or radio without a licence when an inspector calls.** If your TV is used only for video playback or as a computer monitor, no fee is payable, but you must be able to show that it's incapable of receiving any signals from broadcast, cable or satellite channels.

Television Channels

In most cities and many rural areas, the majority of buildings are wired for cable TV (see below), which enables households to receive over 30 TV stations and at least as many radio stations. Without cable or satellite TV, you will normally be able to receive only the three public broadcasters (ARD, ZDF and the local regional channel). plus perhaps the third channel of a nearby region. Most private broadcasters are available only by cable or satellite. The network of local broadcasters making up the ARD, ZDF and the third channel stations (NDR, WDR, HR, SR, BR, etc.) are responsible for producing and relaying programmes throughout Germany. If you're in an area that receives more than one regional station, don't be surprised to find that both (or all three) regional channels are showing the same programmes at the same time. It's one way they combine their resources and make maximum use of shared production facilities. Public stations are permitted to show commercials only during scheduled breaks between programmes and at certain hours during the day.

Private broadcasters in Germany come in all shapes and sizes. There are channels dedicated to children's programmes (such as Ki.ka), to music (Viva Plus), shopping (Home Shopping Europe), news (N-TV), as well as the more general stations such as Pro7, RTL, Sonnenklar TV, Vox and many similar counterparts. To receive private commercial stations, you need either a satellite dish or cable. Private stations are financed by advertising revenue and the limitations on the frequency and duration of advertising are much less restrictive than those of public broadcasters. Commercial breaks can extend to 10 or even 15 minutes. Until quite recently, the private commercial stations in Germany relied heavily on recycled American series, and you can still find Columbo and Kojak in infinite re-runs. Nearly all imported shows are dubbed into German. A single actor is used to provide the German voice for each foreign star whose career is therefore intimately linked with that of his or her voice-over alter ego. The studios take great care in matching the voice quality of the original actor, so don't be surprised to hear radio spots that sound as though they're Telly Savalas or Peter Falk speaking German!

The German public is also fond of classic British comedy. Not only will you find frequent re-runs of Monty Python and Fawlty Towers, but they even have the decency (or good sense) to run subtitles rather than try to dub them. You will find quite a number of English-language channels on both cable and satellite, but only American Forces Network (AFN TV), on air. Even this is available only in areas where US military installations are present, and you will need an NTSC standard TV or VCR to receive it. With a standard cable or satellite set-up, you can usually receive CNN International, NBC Giga (which rebroadcasts selected English-language US programmes – usually documentaries and talk shows, combined with German language programmes), SkyNews, MTV and BBC World. If you have access to digital TV, you can receive EuroNews with an English-language soundtrack.

Programme Guides

There's a bewildering choice of TV guides in Germany, some of which are published weekly and some fortnightly. They come out early, so once you're a day or two into the current issue it's often too late to buy it, and all you will find on the shelves will be the next week or fortnight's issues. Some magazines include satellite and cable programmes, whilst others include radio programmes. Certain publications concentrate on films while others are dedicated solely to series, soaps or police series. The best idea is to try a few different magazines to see which you prefer, starting with oldies such as *HörZu* or the quite intelligent *TV Today*.

A new radio and TV listing magazine is launched at regular intervals while others fold, therefore just as you find one you like it could disappear from sight. There's no need to go specifically to a newsagent's for programme guides as most supermarkets stock a wide selection. There are even a number of Internet sites where you can design your own programme guides according to your tastes and the cable or satellite programmes you can receive. One particularly comprehensive website is 🖳 www.eurotv.com, which has the added advantage of being in English, although it carries programme listings for nearly all European countries. Nearly every TV station in Germany (and elsewhere) has a website these days, and some German websites even offer some programme information in English.

Cable Television

Cable television is widely available in most of Germany, though not nearly as popular as its satellite equivalent, and is still dominated by Deutsche Telekom in one way or another. In theory, you can request a cable connection to anywhere in Germany, but the cost in a remote rural area will be very expensive if cable TV isn't already installed locally – in any case it will cost far more than satellite TV (see below). In most urban areas, apartment buildings are equipped with a communal aerial that can also be connected to cable TV. To have the cable connected is as easy as informing the building superintendent that you want it. In some apartment blocks, the entire building is wired for cable and all you need to do is connect your TV to the cable outlet. The cost of the connection is either billed to you as part of your monthly service charges (*Nebenkosten*) or directly by Deutsche Telekom. Cable fees range from around €13 to €15 per month, depending on the options you choose. You can save a substantial sum by paying the charges annually or every six months in advance, rather than quarterly or monthly.

Cable TV comprises a selection of some 30 channels from German and international state or private broadcasters. The exact selection varies depending on the region, and now and then Deutsche Telekom makes changes to the offerings, depending on local needs and tastes. The most popular German and international stations, such as ARD, ZDF, RTL, MTV, VIVA, Eurosport, CNN International and NBC Giga, are usually available, and the remainder are selected according to local interest. In border areas, you're likely to find public TV channels from neighbouring countries, as well as Arte (formerly a French-German co-operative channel, but now becoming a truly pan-European enterprise) and channels appealing to local ethnic groups.

There are some scrambled stations on cable (e.g. Premiere which shows top new films) that require a special decoder. An additional monthly fee is payable for this service (occasionally on a pay-per-view basis) directly to the pay-TV company. Details about how to subscribe to pay TV channels are available on TV (adverts) or from TV stores.

Satellite Television

Although many people complain endlessly about the poor quality of TV in their home countries, some find they cannot live without it when they're abroad. Fortunately, the advent of satellite TV in the last few decades means that most people can enjoy TV programmes in English and a variety of other languages almost anywhere in the world. There are a number of satellites positioned over Europe carrying many hundreds of stations broadcasting in a variety of languages. A large proportion of the satellite channels serving Germany are unencrypted, which means you need only a standard satellite receiver to pick them up anywhere in Europe.

Although it wasn't the first in Europe (which was Eutelsat), the European satellite revolution really took off with the launch of the Astra 1A satellite in 1988 (operated by the Luxembourg-based *Société Européenne des Satellites* or SES), positioned 36,000km (22,300mi) above the earth. TV addicts are offered a huge choice of English and foreign-language stations, which can be received throughout Germany with an 85cm dish (a larger dish may be required for some areas for digital satellite reception). Since 1988, a number of additional Astra satellites have been launched, greatly increasing the number of available channels to hundreds. For more information contact their information hotline (☎ 0180-511 0000). A bonus is the availability of radio via satellite, including the major BBC stations (see **Satellite Radio** on page 165).

Among the many English-language stations available on Astra are Sky One, Movimax, Sky Premier, Sky Cinema, Film Four, Sky News, Sky Sports (three channels), UK Gold, Channel 5, Granada Plus, TNT, Eurosport, CNN, CNBC Europe, UK Style, UK Horizons, The Disney Channel and the Discovery Channel. Other stations broadcast in Dutch, German, Japanese, Swedish, Arabic, Spanish, Polish, Portuguese, Catalan, Italian and various Indian languages. The signal from many stations is scrambled (the decoder is usually built into the receiver) and viewers must pay a monthly subscription fee to receive programmes. You can buy pirate decoders for some channels.

Sky Television

You must buy a receiver with a Videocrypt decoder and pay a monthly subscription to receive Sky stations except Sky News (which isn't scrambled). Various packages are available costing from £12.50 to over £38 a month, with Sky Sports 1 plus Sky Premier and Sky MovieMax coming to

£35. A wide variety of permutations can be selected. To receive scrambled channels such as MovieMax and Sky Sports, you need an address in the UK. Subscribers are sent a coded 'smart' card (similar to a credit card), which must be inserted in the decoder to activate it (cards are periodically updated to thwart counterfeiters). Sky won't send smart cards to overseas viewers as they have the copyright to show films only in the UK and Ireland (overseas residents need to obtain a card through a friend or relative in the UK). However, a number of satellite companies in Germany (some of which advertise in the expatriate press) can provide genuine Sky cards.

Sky Digital Television

Digital TV was launched on 1st October 1998 by BSkyB (now Sky) in the UK. The benefits include a superior picture, better (CD) quality sound, wide-screen cinema format and access to many more stations. To watch digital TV you require a Digibox and a dish. In addition to the usual analogue channels (see above), digital TV offers BBC 1, BBC 2 and Channel 4 (but not ITV or ITV2), plus many digital channels (a total of 200 with up to 500 possible later).

German Digital Television

Digital satellite TV was launched in 1998 in Germany by DF1. The following year DF merged with Premiere, a pay-TV broadcaster, to form Premiere World, which is still by far the biggest player among the digital satellite providers. To watch digital TV you need a digital decoder, called a d-box, which you can either buy for around €100 plus or rent from your provider for around €7 a month in addition to your subscription. Premiere's current best offer is one year of Premiere Start along with a d-box for €99. You will also need a satellite dish, although it isn't always necessary to get a special one for digital reception. Premiere World offers a wide range of programme packages besides the one mentioned, which feature specialised (mostly German language) channels. Most of the foreign-language channels are available unencrypted in Germany and are part of the basic monthly package which includes all the regular unencrypted German TV channels. Customers must usually sign up for a 12-month subscription and it's recommended that you have a phone line available if you want to use interactive services. **As with any contract in Germany, you should pay careful attention to the cancellation notice period, which is usually three months.**

Eutelsat

Eutelsat was the first company to introduce satellite TV in Europe (in 1983) and it now runs a growing fleet of communications satellites carrying TV stations to some 100 million homes. Until 1995, they broadcast primarily advertising-based, clear-access cable channels. However, following the launch in March 1995 of their Hot Bird 1 satellite, Eutelsat set out to become a major competitor to Astra, although its channels are mostly non-English language. The English-language stations on Eutelsat include Eurosport, BBC Prime, BBC World and NBC Europe. Other stations broadcast in Arabic, French, German, Hungarian, Italian, Polish, Portuguese, Spanish, Turkish, Rumanian, Russian, Serbo-Croat, Slovak, Czech, Swedish, Flemish, Greek, Kurdish and Macedonian.

BBC Worldwide Television

The BBC's commercial subsidiary, BBC Worldwide Television, broadcasts two 24-hour channels: BBC Prime (general entertainment) and BBC World (24-hour news and information). BBC World is free-to-air and is transmitted via the Eutelsat Hot Bird satellite, while BBC Prime is encrypted and transmitted via Eutelsat Hotbird 5. BBC Prime requires a Viaccess compatible decoder. Smartcards are available directly from the BBC. The annual subscription costs £75 plus a one-off payment of £12 for the card and the inevitable VAT at 17.5 per cent. There are currently plans afoot to make BBC Prime available in Germany via digital cable.

For more information and a programming guide contact BBC Worldwide Television, Woodlands, 80 Wood Lane, London W12 0TT, UK (☎ 020-8433 2000). A programme guide is also available on the Internet (🖥 www.bbc. co.uk/schedules) and both BBC World and BBC Prime have their own websites (🖥 www.bbcworld.com and 🖥 www.bbcprime.com). When accessing them, you must enter the name of the country (e.g. Germany), so that schedules appear in local time.

Equipment

A satellite receiver should have a built-in Videocrypt decoder (and others such as Eurocrypt, Syster or SECAM if required) and be capable of receiving satellite stereo radio. A basic Astra system costs from around €200, not including installation. Shop around as prices vary considerably. With a 1.2 or 1.5 metre motorised dish, you can receive hundreds of stations in a multitude of languages from around the world. If you wish to receive satellite TV on two or more TVs, you can buy a satellite system with two or more receptors. To receive stations from two or more satellites simultaneously, you need a motorised dish or a dish with a double feed antenna (dual LNBs). There are many satellite sales and installation companies in Germany, some of which advertise in the expatriate press. Shop around and compare prices. Alternatively, you can import your own satellite dish and receiver and install it yourself. Before buying a system, ensure that it will be able to receive programmes from all existing and planned satellites.

Location

To receive programmes from any satellite, there must be no obstacles between the satellite and your dish, i.e. no trees, buildings or mountains must obstruct the signal, so check before renting an apartment or buying a home. In Germany, the Astra satellites are located at around 12° east of south at an elevation of 35° (depending on location, e.g. in Hamburg the elevation is lower than in Munich and the direction also varies). If you're in doubt, ask at your local TV shop, where they will be able to advise you on the local requirements. Before buying or erecting a dish, check your lease or house rules regarding whether you need permission from your landlord or if there are restrictions on the size or visibility of a satellite dish. You can now buy flat dishes in a variety of colours and patterns which blend into the background and are virtually invisible, and may meet the requirements in buildings that don't want dishes sprouting from every balcony.

Satellite Programme Guides

Many satellite stations provide teletext information and most broadcast in stereo. Satellite programme listings are provided in a number of British publications with names such as *What Satellite*, and *Satellite TV* (probably the best), which are available on subscription. A number of satellite TV programme schedules can also be displayed via German TV teletext. The annual *World Radio and TV Handbook* (Billboard) contains over 600 pages of information and the frequencies of all radio and TV stations world-wide. See also **Programme Guides** below.

Videos & DVDs

Videos are readily available to rent or buy in Germany. To rent a video, you generally must join a rental club and pay an annual fee, after which you can rent videos for prices ranging from €1 (for an old 'classic') up to €12 per night for the latest Hollywood blockbuster. The only drawback for someone still learning German may be that videos on offer very naturally have German soundtracks (apart from rock music performances!). Almost every shop or petrol station sells videos these days for prices ranging from €10 to €25 or more, but (as with rentals) it can be difficult or impossible to find videos in English. Check with local expatriate clubs for English-language videos available for sale or swap. You can buy English-language videos over the Internet and through mail-order book and video catalogues.

DVD players and films have become very popular in Germany. While they're still more expensive than videos, they often have added features such as extra scenes, multiple language soundtracks and subtitling. Be particularly careful, however, to buy DVDs for the correct 'zone', as films intended for an American audience (zone 1) won't play back in a European (zone 2) DVD player unless it has been modified, and zone 1 versions often don't contain the alternate soundtracks and subtitling. There are multi-zone DVD players available, and it's also possible to modify many single-zone players to handle multiple-zone DVDs.

RADIO

The good news for radio enthusiasts is that radios have the same standards the world over, meaning there are generally few problems with equipment compatibility. The only significant difficulties are likely to be experienced by Americans, who may find that their VHF radios with digital tuning don't work properly in Europe. The reason for this is that the American broadcasting standard calls for a broader tuning bandwidth than in Europe (9 kHz in Europe, 10 kHz in the US). Many modern radios can be switched from 10 to 9 kHz bandwidth, but not all.

FM (VHF) stereo stations flourish in Germany, to the extent that it's currently almost impossible to obtain a broadcasting licence due to the lack of available frequencies. Medium-wave (MW or AM) and long-wave (LW) bands are also in wide use throughout Europe. A short-wave (SW) radio is useful for receiving international stations such as the BBC World Service, Voice of America, Radio Canada and Radio Sweden. The BBC World Service and Voice of America are also available via cable and satellite radio (see below). Portable digital radio receivers are now widely available and provide good reception, particularly on short wave, and expensive 'professional' receivers are capable of receiving stations from almost anywhere. If you're interested in receiving radio stations from further afield, obtain a copy of the *World Radio TV Handbook* (Billboard).

German Radio

There's a wide choice of German radio stations, both public and private, although most are regionally orientated. All musical tastes are covered, from classical to youth and all-oldies stations. If you're located near a US or British military base, you will be able to pick up English-language stations, e.g. in the Lüneburg-Osnabrück area there's the British Forces Broadcasting

Service (BFBS) of the Rhine Army broadcasting in English, while those living in central and southern Germany can receive AFN Radio catering to the American forces in Europe. The latter is a popular source for country-and-western music among German listeners, as well as homesick Americans. There's also Deutsche Welle, the equivalent of BBC World Service, broadcasting on short-wave and satellite in German and English (as well as in many other languages) across the globe.

BBC & Other Foreign Stations

The BBC World Service is simultaneously broadcast on short wave, medium wave, long wave and FM frequencies, and you should be able to receive a good signal on one of them. The signal strength often varies depending on where you live in Germany, the time of day and year, the power and positioning of your receiver, and atmospheric conditions. The FM signal, which is re-broadcast by local stations mainly in eastern Germany, tends to be the best, and a list of the latter with their own frequencies is on the BBC website (🖥 www.bbc.co.uk/ worldservice) Short wave frequencies are also listed and come into use at different times of the day, but 12095, 9410 and 6195 Khz are usually worth trying. The medium wave frequency, 648 Khz, is only worth bothering about in north-west Germany roughly north of Bonn and west of Osnabrück. Reception is very variable. The long wave frequency, 198 Khz, boasts BBC Radio 4 during the day and the World Service between 1 and 5.30am and again this can get quite 'crackly'. The BBC World Service plus BBC Radio 1, 2, 3, 4 and 5 are also available on the Astra (Sky) and Eutelsat Hot Bird 6 satellites. For a free BBC World Service programme guide and frequency information leaflet write to BBC World Service (BBC Worldwide, PO Box 76, Bush House, Strand, London WC2B 4PH, UK. ☎ 020-7240 3456). The BBC also publish a monthly magazine, *BBC On Air*, containing comprehensive programme listings for BBC World Service radio, BBC Prime TV and BBC World TV. It's available on subscription from the BBC (On Air Magazine, Dept Sub, Room 310NW, Bush House, Strand, London WC2B 4PH, UK, ☎ 020-7240 4899, ✉ on.air.magazine@bbc.co.uk) and from some newsagents in Germany. You can also buy it over the Internet on the BBC website or simply download an order form so as to conveniently fax back your details. Of course self-evidently today all schedules for Germany are also available on the World Service website 🖥 www.bbc worldservice.com. You key in the city or region in which you're located for real precision about what you can receive.

Many other foreign stations also publish programme listings and frequency charts for expatriates desperate for news from home including Radio Australia, Radio Canada, Denmark Radio, Radio Nederland, Radio Sweden International and the Voice of America. Don't forget to check for similar websites, where you can often download and hear broadcast material as well as check schedules.

Satellite Radio

If you have satellite TV you can also receive many radio stations via your satellite link. For example, BBC Radio 1, 2, 3, 4 and 5, BBC World Service, Sky Radio, Virgin 1215, NPR (National Public Radio from the US) and many non-English language stations are broadcast via the Astra satellites. Satellite radio stations are listed in British satellite TV magazines such as What Satellite and Satellite TV Europe and schedules can also be found on the Internet. If you're interested in receiving radio stations from further afield you should obtain a copy of the *World Radio TV Handbook* (Billboard). Both digital and regular TV satellite services offer a range of radio stations, often from around the world.

Cable Radio

If your apartment is wired for cable TV (see page 158), it will also be wired for cable radio, providing reception of more than 30 stereo stations. Many cable networks provide the BBC World Service, BBC Foreign Language Service, and Voice of America, in addition to a wide selection of FM stereo stations based in Germany and Austria. All you must do is connect your radio or hi-fi tuner aerial to a special wall socket (cables are available from TV stores).

Radio Licence

A radio licence costing €63.84 a year (€5.32 a month) is required by all owners of radios. Registration is done with the same form (*Anmeldung*) as for TV licence registration (see page 155), although if you pay for a TV licence there's no additional fee for a radio licence for your household. TV and radio registration can be done at the same time. The radio licence fee is payable monthly, quarterly or annually by bank standing order. The licence fee covers any number of radios used in your home by members of your immediate household (which means spouse and children under 18). It also covers the radio in your car, although if you have a company car or use your personal car for business, the rules get a bit more complicated (basically, you're likely to have to pay extra). If any other adult member of your household (including your children who are over 18) has a radio in his room, he should register it and pay an additional licence fee in his own name. **Failure to register can result in a fine.**

9.

EDUCATION

Germany was one of the first countries to introduce compulsory schooling but has no national education system, as education is a responsibility of the individual states (*Länder*). Consequently, there are as many school systems as there are states, all with differing structures and methodologies. This has led to some apparently bizarre conflicts, most prominent of which was Bavaria's refusal to recognise the grammar school diplomas of some other states, because their examinations were less demanding than its own. The introduction of a unified school system for the whole of Germany has been a perennial topic of discussion among the chattering classes but up to now little has come of it.

Until recently, Germany has been proud of its educational standards, but the 2002 OECD Program for International Student Assessment (PISA) study of the achievements of 15-year-olds in 32 mainly industrialised countries sent a tidal shock-wave across the country when German children came 21st in reading, 20th in maths and 20th in science. The different German states were assessed in a separate league table, at the top of which was Bavaria. But even Bavaria only managed to reach a mid-table position in international comparisons. The PISA also showed that German pupils were less positive in their attitudes about their school experience than their counterparts elsewhere. These results have led to collective soul-searching among federal and state authorities and have given fresh impetus to proposals to change many long-standing educational traditions.

Education is compulsory in Germany for at least nine years (ten in some states), children beginning full-time education at between five-and-a-half and six-and-a-half, depending on the time of year they were born. Education in German state schools is free, from primary school through to – and including – university. Free education is also provided for the children of foreign residents in Germany, although non-resident, non-EU students require a student visa (see page 72). Unlike some other Europeans, Germans have always viewed their education as almost entirely egalitarian. There are special schools for those with mental and physical disabilities, but every attempt to create special schools for exceptionally intelligent or gifted children has been met with fierce opposition, both from the general public and politicians. However, although there are no close equivalents of France's élite Grandes Ecoles and Britain's prestigious universities, there are nonetheless good universities, which are recognised as such, and universities which have a relatively poor reputation – and the differences between them can be considerable.

Critics of the German education system complain that, unlike British and US schools, which emphasise developing the whole person, the German system is solely focused on career and academic achievement. Most German schools offer little in the way of extra-curricular activities, leaving sports clubs, musical activities and certain arts to other organisations. Inter-school sporting competitions are rare, although there may be the occasional track-and-field contest.

The teaching style is generally more formal than in many countries, including the UK and the US, with pupils in eastern Germany in particular still required to stand by their desks when a teacher enters, and little contact between pupils and teachers outside classrooms. In some city schools, discipline has become a problem in recent years, owing partly to tensions arising from the high proportion of children from ethnic minorities, who constitute 50 per cent or more of the school rolls in some districts of large cities.

On the plus side, academic standards are generally high (notwithstanding the PISA results), with well-qualified teachers and commendable results – over 90 per cent of all pupils achieve a school-leaving certificate and around 25 per cent the general university entrance qualification. German schools have also been quick to embrace the potential of new technology and the Internet, most of the country's schools having ISDN connections.

The German school system may be more disciplined and less flexible than that of many other countries, but each child, whatever his level of natural ability, is given the opportunity to study for a trade, diploma or degree.

Nevertheless, the education system highly competitive and selective and separates the brighter students from the less academically gifted at an early age – often as young as ten. Formal tests are conducted each year from primary school upwards, and the results carry considerable weight in determining the type of education (and hence the likely future career) a child can expect. A strong emphasis is placed on training, and few school-leavers go directly into a job without training. It's normal practice for those leaving school at 16 to attend a technical college or train as an apprentice, and everyone up to the age of 18 must attend some form of educational institution (full or part-time). In today's highly competitive labour market, both parents and students are acutely aware that qualifications and training are of paramount importance in obtaining a good (or any) job, although these don't have to be academically orientated. A graduate of a *Fachhochschule*, where studies have a strongly technical bent, is more likely to get a job than a university graduate.

Generally, the younger your child is when he enters the German school system, the easier he will cope. Conversely, the older he is, the more problems he will have adjusting, particularly as the school curriculum is more demanding at a higher level. Teenagers often have considerable problems learning German and adjusting to German school life, particularly children from America or the UK who haven't already learnt a second language. In some schools, foreign children who cannot understand the language may be neglected and just expected to get on with it. In your early days in Germany it's important to check exactly what your children are doing at school and whether they're making progress (not just with the language, but also with their lessons).

As a parent, you should be prepared to support your children through this difficult period. If you aren't fluent in German, you will already be aware how frustrating it is being unable to express yourself adequately, which can easily lead to feelings of inferiority or inadequacy in children as well as adults. It's also important you to ensure that your children maintain their English or other native language, as it can easily be neglected (studies show that the children of English residents in non English-speaking countries are losing their ability to read and write English).

For many children, the experience of living in a foreign country is a stimulating change and a challenge they relish, and it provides invaluable cultural and educational experiences. Your child will become a 'world' citizen, less likely to be prejudiced against foreigners and foreign ideas. This is particularly true if he attends an international school with pupils from many different countries (many state schools, particularly in the larger cities, also have pupils from a number of countries and backgrounds). Before making major decisions about your child's education, it's important to consider his ability, character and individual requirements.

Further information about German schools, both state and private, can be obtained from German embassies and consulates abroad, and from foreign embassies, educational organisations and government departments in Germany. Local school information can be obtained from the Stadverwaltung (the municipal administration centre), or the education office (Amt für Schule or Behörde für Schule, Jugend und Berufsbildung), which is usually located at the Stadverwaltung but may be in a separate building. The Behörde für Schule, Jugend und Berufsbildung in Hamburg (Postfach 76 10 48, D-22060, Freie und Hansestadt Hamburg) provides an English-language leaflet explaining the different kinds of school and outlining the counselling services which can help parents decide a child's future education.

STATE OR PRIVATE SCHOOL?

State education is generally perceived to be of a higher standard than private education, parents usually sending their children to a private school for religious or philosophical reasons, to get them off their hands if they're 'difficult', or if specific help is needed that's unavailable in a state school. If you're able to choose between state and private education, the following checklist will help you decide:

- How long are you planning to stay in Germany? If you're uncertain, it's probably best to assume a long stay. Due to language and other integration problems, enrolling a child in a German state school is recommended only for a minimum of a year, particularly for teenage children who aren't fluent in German (see **Language** below).

- Bear in mind that the area where you choose to live will affect your choice of school(s). For example, it's usually necessary to send your child to a state school near your home; if you choose a private day school, you must take into account the distance from your home to the school.

- Do you know where you're going when you leave Germany? This may be an important consideration regarding your child's language of tuition and system of education in Germany. How old is your child and what age will he be when you plan to leave Germany? What long-term plans do you have for his education, and in which country?

- What educational level is your child at now and how will he fit into a private school or the German state school system? The younger he is, the easier it will be to place him in a suitable school.

- How does your child view the thought of studying in German? What language is best from a long-term point of view? Is schooling available in Germany in his mother tongue?

- Will your child require your help with his studies and, more importantly, will you be able to help him, particularly with his German?

- Is special or extra tutoring available in German or other subjects, if necessary?

- What are the school hours? What are the school holiday periods? Many state schools in Germany have compulsory Saturday morning classes. How will the school holidays and hours affect your family's work and leisure activities?

- Is religion (or the lack of it) an important aspect in your choice of school? Most German state schools have compulsory religious education; most international schools, in contrast, don't.

- Do you want your child to go to a single-sex or co-educational school? Nearly all German state schools are co-educational.

- Should you send your child to a boarding school? If so, in which country?

- What are the secondary and further education prospects in Germany or another country? Are German examinations or the examinations set by prospective German schools recognised in your home country or the country where you plan to live after leaving Germany? If applicable, check that the German *Abitur* examination is recognised as a university entrance qualification in your home country.

● Does a prospective school have a good academic record? Most schools provide exam pass rate statistics.

● How large are the classes? What is the pupil-teacher ratio?

Obtain the opinions and advice of others who have been faced with the same questions and problems as yourself, and collect as much information from as many different sources as possible before making a decision. Speak to teachers and the parents of children attending the schools on your shortlist. Finally, most parents find it pays to discuss the alternatives with their children before making a decision. See also **Choosing A Private School** on page 181.

Language

There are many considerations to take into account when choosing an appropriate school in Germany, not least the language of study. The only schools in Germany using English as the teaching language are a few foreign and international private schools. For most children, however, studying in German isn't such a handicap as it may at first appear, particularly for those aged below ten. Many young children adapt quickly and some may become quite fluent within six months (if only it were so easy for adults!). However, all children don't adapt equally well to a change of language and culture, particularly children aged over ten (at around ten years of age children begin to learn languages more slowly), many of whom encounter great difficulties during their first year.

It should be borne in mind that the German state school system generally makes little or no concession to non-German speakers, e.g. by providing intensive German lessons. This can make the first few months quite an ordeal for non-German-speaking children. In areas with a large foreign population, schools may offer special classes for those requiring additional German language lessons, but this is far from the rule. It may be worthwhile inquiring about the availability of extra German classes before deciding where to live. Note that while attending special language classes, children may fall behind in other subjects.

Once your child has acquired a sufficient knowledge of spoken and written German, he's integrated into a regular class in the local school. Foreign children are tested (like German children) and put into a class suited to their level of German, even if this means being taught with younger children or slow learners. However, a child of six or seven must be permitted to enter the first year of primary school (*Grundschule*), even if he speaks no German.

If your local state school doesn't provide extra German classes – and outside large cities this is very likely to be the case – your only choice will be to pay for private lessons or send your child to another (possibly private) school, where extra tuition is available. Some parents send a child to an English-speaking school for a year, followed by a state school. Other parents find it's easier to throw their children in at the deep end than to introduce them gradually. It all depends on the character, ability and wishes of the child.

Whatever you decide, it will help if your child has some intensive German lessons before arriving in Germany (see **Language Schools** on page 190). It may be possible to organise an educational or cultural exchange with a German school or family before coming to live in Germany, which is a considerable help in integrating a child into the German language and culture.

STATE SCHOOLS

Each state (*Land*) develops its own education programme, determines its own educational objectives and sets its own standards. The education ministers of German states meet periodically to debate current issues and establish minimum standards, although all attempts to institute a unified state education system have been vigorously opposed.

The German state education system has traditionally been very highly regarded, and is for the most part well organised and adequately funded (not that teachers would ever agree!), although the PISA results (see above) must call into question its efficiency.

Attending a state school helps children to integrate into the local community and learn the language. Pupils usually go to local nursery (*Kindergarten*) and primary schools, but attending secondary school often entails travelling long distances. One of the consequences of the depopulation of rural areas in the last few decades has been the closure of many schools.

Co-education (mixed classes of girls and boys) is normal in German state schools and is even required by law in some states. There are very few all-male or all-female schools, and most of these are private schools operated by the Catholic church.

A general criticism of German state schools often made by foreigners is the lack of extra-curricular activities such as sport, music, drama, and arts and crafts. State schools have few if any sports clubs or teams and, if your child wants to do team sports, he must join a local club. This means that parents must ferry children back and forth for games and social events (Americans will be used to this!). A list of organised activities for children and young people can usually be found at the town hall, and the local church may organise some activities.

Children at German schools are regularly tested in a range of subjects and each year receive two reports (one at the end of each term). Performance levels are traditionally indicated by a grade from 1 to 6, as follows:

Grade	Assessment	Meaning
1	*Sehr gut*	Very good
2	*Gut*	Good
3	*Befriedigend/zufriedenstellend*	Reasonable/satisfactory
4	*Ausreichend*	Sufficient
5	*Mangelhaft*	Deficient/unsatisfactory
6	*Ungenügend*	Poor/insufficient

Having made the decision to send your child to a state school, you should stick to it for at least a year to give it a fair trial. It will take a child at least this long to begin to adapt to a new language, the change of environment and the different curriculum.

Enrolment

Enrolling your child in a German school is usually straightforward. In fact, provided you're officially registered as German residents (see page 85), your local school will write to you some time before the start of the school year inviting you to register your child for classes (this applies if you move to Germany from abroad or within Germany). You will be told of any medical certificates that you must provide and any provisions you must buy (see page 177), and you're then required to visit the school during normal office hours to complete the necessary forms. Even if you've decided to send your child to another (e.g. private) school, you must notify your local state school and tell them what alternative arrangements you have made.

School Hours

Most state schools operate only in the morning and early afternoon from Mondays to Saturdays. Saturday may be a normal school day, reserved for extra-curricular activities or a completely free day, depending on the school district. There's never school on Sundays. The standard school day is from 8am until 1pm, with a maximum of half an hour's variation either side of these times. The original rationale for this arrangement was that the afternoon and early evening would be devoted to a demanding homework regime, although, as the social climate has become more relaxed, children increasingly tend to look upon this as 'free time' for sport and leisure. This, of course, places additional demands on parents, who must be available to provide lunch for their offspring and supervise them during the afternoons.

Some schools, however, have classes on several afternoons (e.g. until 3.30 or 4pm on three or four days). There are around 1,600 such schools, where midday meals are provided. 'All-day' schools were introduced by the Communist authorities in Saxony Anhalt, where there are almost 50. The number of all-day schools in other states varies; Lower Saxony has none, for example. Partly as a consequence of the PISA results (see page 168), there are plans to greatly increase the number of all-day schools.

The situation is made even more difficult for parents by the fact that school hours can vary from day to day. In most schools, children don't go to school in the early morning if they have no classes scheduled – and if their last class finishes before the end of the school day, they're free to go home. Similarly, if a teacher is off sick and the school cannot arrange a replacement (an increasingly common occurrence), children may be sent home without warning. Parents with two or more children face even greater difficulties, as each child may have quite a different school schedule. If both parents work, one must be home by around 2pm or some other form of supervision for children during the afternoons must be arranged.

Holidays

Summer holidays, which normally last six weeks, are scheduled with a few weeks' difference between states. Each year a schedule for the whole of Germany is issued, which changes from year to year. In general, the northern states start their summer holidays in mid-June and the southern states as late as the end of July. (Before the introduction of this system, almost all Germans tried to have their holidays at the same time, causing monumental traffic jams on motorways and congestion on public transport.) It's still commonplace for Germans to go on holiday the day after the school holidays commence and return the day before school starts again.

In addition to the summer holidays, there are the following school holidays:

- Two weeks in autumn, which used to be termed 'harvest holidays' and were originally intended to give children in rural areas time off school to help their parents with the farm work;
- Two to three weeks' at Christmas;

- Rose Monday (the day before Shrove Tuesday, which itself is the day before Ash Wednesday or the beginning of Lent) and Hag Thursday (the Thursday of the week preceding Rose Monday). In regions where *Fasching* (Carnival) plays a major role, holidays can extend from Hag Thursday to Rose Monday or even Ash Wednesday.

- A one-week break at Easter, which usually starts on the Monday before Easter and ends the Tuesday after;

- 10 to 14 days' holiday around Pentecost (in May or June).

There are additional short holidays of two to four days that vary from state to state. Schools are also closed on church, state and national holidays that don't fall within a holiday period (see **Public Holidays** on page 57).

Some states allow you to withdraw your children from school for special reasons and/or to observe religious holidays that aren't provided for by the state. All absences from school (including those due to illness) must be justified in writing. It's wise to co-ordinate any planned absences with the teacher in charge of your child's class so that he doesn't miss any special activities or annual tests. **Removing your child from school for a period of more than a day or two without prior agreement with school officials can lead to a substantial fine, and, for persistent offenders, imprisonment for parents and the placement of a child in foster care!**

Summer camps, so much a feature of a child's upbringing in North America, aren't part of the state educational system in Germany. There are, however, some summer camps organised by Boy and Girl Scout organisations, certain church groups and political parties.

Health & Accidents

As a rule, there's no school nurse in German state schools and health problems are generally referred to a family doctor (see page 272) or the hospital nearest to a school. Vaccination programmes exist in each state, but only a few are mandatory. Some states have a school doctor, who makes regular examinations and provides vaccinations at a school, while others leave health care to the discretion of parents. As dental care is covered by German health insurance, it's left to parents to decide whether to send children to the bi-annual dental checks held at schools. All school health programmes are free of charge (which may be why so few are mandatory).

Schools are insured for accidents that occur on their premises during school hours and on the way to and from school, provided children take the shortest route between their home and school, and don't interrupt the journey for any non-school-related reason. Other accidents should be covered by a family's health insurance, which is mandatory for all wage and salary earning employees and some self-employed people (see **Health Insurance** on page 289).

Provisions

The items required to start school in Germany vary from state to state, although all pupils require the following:

- School bag (a rucksack is most commonly used);
- Pencil case, pencils, coloured pencils or crayons and a fountain pen (most German schools and teachers are opposed to the use of ballpoint pens during primary education and some schools insist on the use of fountain pens throughout a child's education);
- An assortment of lined writing pads or notebooks, graph paper for mathematics and plain (unlined) paper for drawing;
- Gym shoes (plimsolls), a T-shirt and a towel for sports and exercise periods. Some states also require a jogging suit. A sports bag is also required if the above doesn't fit into the normal school bag.

There are mandatory school books for all ages, which are provided free by schools in some states, while in others parents must pay for them. In some cases books are provided free of charge only if a child's parents earn less than a certain amount. If you have several children, it's therefore advisable to tell them to look after their books, so that they can be used by their younger siblings (the required book for a particular level seldom changes). Parents must also be prepared to pay for the cost of materials for cookery and handicraft lessons.

There may be a need for a sleeping bag or similar for the annual school excursion, which may be a day trip to a nearby site or a few days of camping or staying at youth hostels (billed to the parents, of course). The excursions tend to get longer the older the children get, and a week's holiday in Majorca just before graduating from secondary school isn't uncommon.

School uniforms are extremely unusual, although students usually devise their own 'uniform' and in some areas the theft (e.g. by 'mugging') of designer clothes by gangs is widespread and has resulted in children being told to dress down and not wear expensive clothes to school.

Parents are required to provide their children with food for mid-morning breaks, although snacks may be available from vendors who visit schools during breaks or from local shops. School cafeterias are rare, as most children are home by lunch-time. Some schools offer a 'milk-for-breakfast' programme, through which parents can arrange for their children to be given warm milk or a chocolate drink during break periods.

Nursery School

Attendance at nursery school (*Kindergarten*, meaning literally 'children's garden') is voluntary in Germany and parents are required to pay a fee. While there are sufficient nursery school places available in the eastern states, in some western areas there aren't nearly enough to meet demand. Indeed, some parents go to the lengths of enrolling their children at birth to ensure a place. Nursery school generally lasts from two to three hours in the morning, unless there are special requirements – for example, both parents are working – in which case children can be taken care of for eight to nine hours. Naturally, the fee for this is correspondingly higher.

In some towns there are *Kinderkrippen* (a kind of crèche) for children under three, providing the same service.

Children normally attend nursery school five days a week (Mondays to Fridays), although some nursery schools are also equipped to look after the children of shift and weekend workers. Nursery school is generally a good way to integrate your pre-school children into German life. However, in many nursery schools all children from the ages of three to six play together, with no attempt to segregate them into groups or activities. This means that children must be prepared to face a degree of rough-and-tumble; as one expatriate parent in Germany commented: "Kindergarten is wonderful for the children – they really learn how to defend themselves!"

Primary School

Children start primary school (*Grundschule*) between the ages of five-and-a-half and six-and-a-half depending on the month they were born. In some states they can start at five. A child may be held back one school year due to health or other considerations (such as lack of maturity).

The first day of primary school is considered a very important event in a child's life in Germany and a degree of ceremony accompanies it, including pictures by professional photographers. It's customary to provide children starting school with a bag of sweets (*Schultüte*) resembling a colourful dunce's hat upside-down with an inscription such as 'my first day at school' (in German). These bags can be purchased at stationery shops and supermarkets in a variety of colours and sizes, but are sold empty and must be filled with treats purchased separately.

The total number of weekly lessons at primary school varies from 20 to 30 depending on the class (i.e. the age of the child). The main subjects are reading, writing and arithmetic. In addition, children receive a basic introduction to other subjects they will be studying at secondary school, including history (*Geschichte*), geography (*Erdkunde*), social studies (*Sozialkunde*), biology (*Biologie*), physics (*Physik*), chemistry (*Chemie*), music

(*Musik*), art (*Kunsterziehung*) and sport (*Sport*). Religious education classes (*Religionslehre*) are mandatory almost everywhere with the exception of some former eastern states, where they've been substituted by a non-religious equivalent called 'ethics'.

There's a strong Catholic tradition in southern Bavaria and, if your child attends a state school in this region (except in Munich, which is more cosmopolitan), you will probably have to accept this as part and parcel of his education. Despite a recent ruling by Germany's supreme court, which ruled that crucifixes on the walls of classrooms infringe on religious freedom and should be removed, there's hardly a classroom in the area without one.

Primary school normally lasts for four years (six in Berlin and Brandenburg). After this, in most states, parents receive a recommendation from the child's teachers concerning the type of school most appropriate for his continuing education. This is based on the teachers' assessment of the child's performance, abilities and interests, and teachers can veto the admittance of a child to a grammar or intermediate school if, in their view, he hasn't achieved the necessary standard. In some states, failing to pass a year (grade) precludes a child from attending grammar school, and failing the same year twice or any grade three times means that a child is automatically enrolled in a special school for slow learners.

Secondary School

After primary education, children normally go to one of three types of school: a *Hauptschule*, a *Realschule* or a *Gymnasium*. In Bavaria, however, *Grundschulen* and *Hauptschulen* are amalgamated into *Volksschulen*. In some states, there are *Gesamtschulen*. The different types of secondary school are described below.

Hauptschule: This type of school is designed for those who are less academically gifted, who are expected to enter a manual trade on leaving school. The main subjects studied are German, arithmetic, history, work studies (*Arbeitslehre*) and crafts. In some states, the *Hauptschule* curriculum also includes a foreign language (English, French or Russian). The total number of weekly lessons is between 30 and 33.

After five or six years, a *Hauptschule* graduate generally enters an apprenticeship (*Lehre*) in a manual trade, although those with very good grades may apply for an apprenticeship in a commercial or medical profession. Once a *Hauptschule* student has achieved his school certificate (*Hauptschulabschluss*), he can go on to study part-time for vocational qualifications at a *Berufschule*.

Realschule: This is designed for those who will be entering an apprenticeship in a commercial trade or medical profession such as nursing.

Here the emphasis is more on mathematics and language skills than on crafts. In most states, at least two foreign languages (usually English and French) are taught, with the total number of weekly lessons between 30 and 34. *Realschulen* include specialised schools such as trade schools (*Handelsschule*). The school-leaving certificate is called the *Mittlere Reife* and is awarded after a final examination.

Gymnasium: Equivalent to a British grammar school, this is the type of school for students with the most academic promise and is designed to prepare them for university or a 'high-end' apprenticeship. This is the most demanding type of schooling, with lots of homework and pressure to perform and between 32 and 40 hours of lessons per week.

Classes at a *Gymnasium* consist of a group of mandatory subjects, including English, French, German, mathematics, chemistry, physics, history, religion/ethics, and a group of optional subjects (electives), such as advanced chemistry, advanced physics, advanced mathematics, Greek and Latin. The optional subjects selected depend on the career intentions of the student (a classical language for example may be compulsory for those hoping to pursue a career in medicine).

Gymnasium concludes with the *Abitur* examination, which includes four subjects. Upon passing the *Abitur*, a student is awarded the *Zeugnis der allgemeinen Hochschulreife*, which entitles him to study the subject of his choice at a university or equivalent institution (provided a place is available).

Because German university education is free, there's a tendency to filter out all but the best in the *Gymnasium*, and it's possible that after one or two years your child's teachers may recommend that he transfers to a *Hauptschule* or *Realschule*. It may be wise to accept this suggestion, because in Germany it's much better to have a lower level graduation than no graduation at all. In most states, failing two years at any point in your school career automatically sets you back to a lower level education and in all states a child is allowed just two attempts to pass the final examination.

The *Abitur* is generally reckoned to be more demanding than UK A levels but is less demanding than the French *baccalauréat*. It's widely (but not universally) recognised as an entrance qualification to universities worldwide, although a student may need to prove his capabilities in the teaching language (e.g. English for the UK or US, French for France).

Gesamtschule: These are found in some parts of Germany (particularly the east) and are equivalent to a comprehensive school in the UK, where education for children of all abilities is carried out under one roof, with some common classes.

The traditional three-track system (*Hauptschule, Realschule, Gymnasium*) still applies, leading to three levels of graduation, although there's more opportunity for a late-developing child to move to a higher level of schooling within a *Gesamtschule*.

PRIVATE SCHOOLS

There are various alternatives to the state school system in Germany, although most aren't strictly private and some claiming to be so are in reality dependent upon government funding and may operate under the same rules as state schools. Many 'private' schools are located in Bavaria and North Rhine-Westphalia, where, from time to time, a debate breaks out about reducing government funding to such schools. The largest network of private schools in Germany is the *Walldorfschule*, which are 'alternative' schools based on the philosophy of Rudolf Steiner, known as anthroposophy. Similar in many respects to Montessori schools, which generally extend from kindergarten through to the early years of secondary education, Walldorf schools emphasise the importance of developing creativity in a child and the curriculum places considerable emphasis on the arts. Walldorf schools have spread across the world since the first was founded in Stuttgart in 1919, but they're most heavily concentrated in Germany (although Steiner was Austrian), where there are around 160.

Religious schools can also be found throughout Germany, although most depend on state funding for their survival. They operate to a large extent like German state schools, although with a greater emphasis on religious and moral instruction. Catholic schools constitute the largest group in this category, although the Lutheran Church has a nation-wide network, and there are Jewish and Moslem schools. Religious schools are heavily oversubscribed, as they're perceived as being more effective than normal state or other private schools. There's no need for a family to be practising members of a particular faith for their children to attend a religious school, but the children must show due respect for its beliefs and traditions and will, of course, be required to abide by its customs (e.g. concerning diet or dress).

There are currently only around 12 boarding schools in Germany.

Choosing A Private School

The following checklist is designed to help you choose an appropriate private school:

- Does the school have a good reputation? When was it established?
- Does the school have a sound academic record? For example, what percentage of pupils receive good examination passes and go on to university?
- How large are the classes and what's the student-teacher ratio? Does the class size tally with the number of desks in the classrooms? What are the classrooms like? For example, their size, space, cleanliness, lighting and

furnishings – including computer equipment. Are there signs of creative teaching, e.g. wall charts, maps, posters and students' work on display?

- What are the qualification requirements for teachers and what nationality are they? Ask for a list of the teaching staff and their qualifications.

- What is the teacher turnover? A high turnover is generally a negative sign and suggests underpaid teachers and/or poor working conditions.

- What extras (e.g. art supplies, sports equipment, outings, clothing, health insurance, textbooks and stationery) must you pay for? Different schools have different policies.

- Which countries do most students come from?

- Is there religious education and, if so, in what faith?

- What language is used? Are special classes offered to students who need tutoring in German?

- What languages does the school teach as required or optional subjects?

- What is the student turnover?

- What are the school terms and holiday periods? These won't necessarily coincide with those of state schools.

- What are the school hours? Ask to see a pupil timetable to check the ratio of academic to non-academic subjects. Check the number of free study periods and whether they're supervised.

- What are the withdrawal conditions? A term's notice is usual.

- What does the curriculum include? What examinations are set?

- What sports instruction and facilities are provided and where?

- What are the facilities for art and science subjects, e.g. arts and crafts, music, computer studies, science, hobbies, drama, cookery and photography? Ask to see the classrooms, facilities, equipment and some students' projects.

- What sort of outings and holiday celebrations does the school organise?

- What medical facilities does the school provide, e.g. infirmary, resident doctor or nurse? Is medical and accident insurance included in the fees?

- How is discipline handled?

- What reports are provided for parents and how often?

A limited number of pupils can attend Department of Defense Educational Activity (DODEA) schools (called – for reasons known only to the DODEA

– K-12 schools), run by the US Department of Defense, which are located on American military bases throughout Germany. Normally these schools are for the children of US (and some other NATO) military personnel and other government workers. All others must apply for permission and relatively few are approved (the admission criteria are – intentionally? – nebulous). Fees at K-12 schools are high, but they provide extensive sports facilities and instruction (basketball, American football, wrestling, track and field, and sometimes hockey and baseball) for both boys and girls. The comprehensive DODEA website (💻 www.odedodea.edu) has sections of interest to parents and potential pupils (and to those seeking teaching positions), and is frequently updated with news.

Other private school options include international schools in Germany (see below), private day schools in neighbouring countries, e.g. France or Switzerland, and boarding schools abroad.

Before making a final choice, it's important to visit the schools on your shortlist during term time and talk to teachers and students (and, if possible, former students and their parents). Try to find answers to the above questions in person and don't simply rely on a school's prospectus to provide the information. If you aren't happy with the answers, look elsewhere.

Having made your choice, keep a check on your child's progress and listen to his comments and complaints. Compare notes with other parents. If something doesn't seem right, try to establish whether the complaint is well-founded or not, and, if it is, take appropriate action to have the problem resolved. Don't forget that you (or your employer) are paying a lot of money for tuition.

Make applications to private schools as far in advance as possible. You're usually requested to send previous school reports (or transcripts), exam results and records.

Before enrolling your child in a private school, make sure you understand the withdrawal conditions in the school contract!

International Schools

Germany's 27 international schools can be found in cities or regions with a high concentration of diplomats or multinational firms. Most use English as their main teaching language and are based on the American educational system. Schools range from kindergarten level to American high school diploma or International Baccalaureate. Tuition fees are generally around €9,000 or €10,000 per year, with other fees such as transport, registration and extra-curricular activities adding a further €2,500 or so. Among the most popular international schools are:

- Bonn International School (Martin-Luther-King Strasse 14, 53175 Bonn, ☎ 0228-308540);

- Frankfurt International School (An der Waldlust 15, D-61440 Oberursel, ☎ 06171-2020, ▭ www.fis.edu), which has a second campus in nearby Wiesbaden (see below). The brochure claims an average class size of 20 students.

- International School Berlin/Potsdam (Lentzeallee 12/14, D-14195 Berlin, ✉ info@private-kant-schule.de, ▭ www.berlin-international-school.de). This school has become very popular due to the relocation of the German government from Bonn to Berlin. Foreign embassies having moved their staff to Berlin accordingly, many pupils are from the families of diplomats.

- International School of Stuttgart (Sigmaringer Str. 257, D-70597 Stuttgart, ☎ 0711-7696 000). Many of the parents of pupils enrolled at this school work at the Daimler Benz and IBM plants. The school boasts relatively new buildings, opened in 1998.

- International School Wiesbaden (Rudolf-Dietz-Str. 14, D-65207 Wiesbaden, ☎ 06127-99400).

Enquire at your country's embassy or consulate about international schools near where you will be living and about costs.

APPRENTICESHIPS

The vast majority of German school-leavers go into an apprenticeship (*Lehre*) rather than straight into a job. There are around 375 state-recognised occupations in Germany, ranging from publisher to ladies' tailor, carpenter to dental surgery assistant and photographer to car mechanic. All require a two to four-year apprenticeship, the exact length of which depends on the demands of the job. Participants who have passed the *Abitur* examination (see page 180) may have their apprenticeship shortened by six months or even a year if they perform exceptionally well.

An apprentice receives a low salary, which is increased annually. Roughly half the working week is spent on the job and the other half at a vocational school (*Berufsschule*), where the apprentice learns the theoretical and practical skills officially required for his occupation (although not necessarily used in the workplace!). The syllabus is set out in detailed national training regulations for each occupation drawn up by the relevant federal ministries in consultation with employers' organisations, business associations and trade unions with the aim of ensuring a uniform qualification for the practitioners of each occupation in Germany.

An apprenticeship concludes with an examination marked by a board of examiners comprising employer and employee representatives and vocational school teachers. Successful candidates are awarded a certificate of fellowship (*Gesellenbrief*) in manual trades, a business assistant's certificate (*Kaufmans Gehilfen Prüfung*) in commercial occupations, or a medical assistant's diploma (*Abschlussprüfung zur Arzthelfer/Apothekergehilfe*) in the case of medical assistants and chemists' assistants.

In recent years, there has been a marked shortage of available apprenticeship positions, which in certain cases has reached the point where a young man or woman wanting to be, say, a carpenter in Bremen might only be able to find a place as a men's hairdresser in Dresden. This shortage of apprenticeship positions has led to a kind of 'inflation' among educational qualifications, whereby only those with the highest grades and best qualifications are considered for even relatively lowly positions. Many banks, for example, are nowadays only taking on trainee cashiers with a top-level technical school qualification, or even an *Abitur*.

Cross-training programmes (*Umschulung*) are offered by the German labour office (*Arbeitsamt*) for people trained in occupations which are gradually becoming obsolete, to enable them to move to another field offering better prospects.

Master Programmes

After working for three years as a qualified tradesman (*Geselle*), you can attend classes to become a master tradesman (*Meister*). There are two types of *Meister* programme, one designed for someone wishing to run his own skilled trade business and the other for someone wanting to manage a company's apprentice programme. In most trades it's mandatory to have a *Meister* or engineer managing the business and an 'industry master' (*Industriemeister*) in charge of apprentices. There's no master tradesman qualification in medical or commercial professions. For the latter a special licence (*Lehrberechtigung*) is required to train apprentices. Any doctor, dentist or chemist is authorised to train assistants. For those wishing to attend these classes full-time but who lack the funds, there's a Federal Tuition Assistance Programme from BAFöG (see **Student Loans** on page 189).

Further Education

For those who have successfully completed an apprenticeship and want to obtain a higher level qualification in their chosen field, there's the *Fachabitur*, which enables a student to attend a polytechnic (see below). A *Fachabitur* can be obtained by attending a vocational school, either full or part-time. There are specialised schools for many fields of the medical professions; these are often private, meaning that students must pay for their board and tuition. For information on loans that may be available, see **Student Loans** on page 189.

HIGHER EDUCATION

Germany has over 220 higher education institutions, including state universities (traditional and technological), private universities and colleges of education, as well as a large number of specialised establishments, such as colleges of theology, colleges of art, polytechnics and colleges of public administration (the latter admitting only graduates). Anyone who passes the *Abitur* (see page 180) is guaranteed entry to one of these institutions, which are attended by some 30 per cent of secondary students (around 1.8 million).

The duration of higher education courses depends largely on students themselves. The period prescribed is usually four to six years, but most students take longer over their courses, which are completed at an average age of almost 28 in comparison with 25.5 in the US and 22.8 in the UK.

State Universities

German state universities include Augsburg, Bayreuth, Berlin, Bielefeld, Bonn, Bremen, Cologne, Dortmund, Dresden, Dusseldorf, Erlangen, Essen, Frankfurt, Frankfurt-an-der-Oder, Göttingen, Hamburg, Hanover, Heidelberg, Kaiserslautern, Karlsruhe, Leipzig, Mainz, Mannheim, Marburg, Munich, Münster, Osnabrück, Passau, Potsdam, Rostock, Saarbrücken, Stuttgart, Tübingen, Ulm, Weimar and Würzburg. Germany's oldest higher education institutions are the universities of Heidelberg (founded in 1386), Leipzig (1409) and Rostock (1419).

German educational policy has been to open up higher education to as wide a spectrum of the population as possible and since 1960 over 20 new universities have been built to further this aim. In the last few years the total number of students has fallen slightly, but many universities suffer overcrowding, with lecture halls packed to the rafters and many courses heavily over-subscribed. The situation hasn't been helped by the budgetary cuts which many universities have been forced to make. Nevertheless, in international comparisons German universities still score well in terms of results.

Only students with the highest *Abitur* grades may choose the university they wish to attend; all others are allocated places by the Central Office for the Allocation of Study Places (Zentralstelle für die Vergabe von Studienplätzen/ZVS) in Dortmund. The allocation depends on two factors: your *Abitur* grades and the length of time you spend waiting for a place. The *Abitur* is graded from 1 to 6, where 1 is the highest and 6 is a fail; the better your grades, the better the university you will be sent to. However, many fields of study have access restrictions. For example, if you wish to study medicine, you must usually have at least a grade of 1.5. If your grade is too low for direct admission, you can sometimes still obtain access to a university education by learning a related profession first. For example, doing a three-year apprenticeship as a medical technical assistant greatly improves your chances of getting into medical school if you have low *Abitur* grades. If you fail to gain admission at your first attempt, you can improve your chances by reapplying a term or a year or two later; presumably, the fact that you're prepared to wait for admission means that you're unusually keen to obtain a place – and the longer you wait the more likely you are to be accepted.

If you wish to study at a German university but have non-German educational qualifications, your prospects will depend largely on whether your qualifications were awarded inside or outside Europe. All European qualifications (including British A levels and the International Baccalaureate) are recognised as equivalent to the *Abitur* for the purposes of university admission. Non-European qualifications, however, including those from the US and Canada, require additional certification for recognition. Each state's ministry of education has a different policy for evaluating such qualifications, with costs likely to include an administration fee plus the cost of official translation of school reports and other documents and the qualifications themselves. Without a BA, BBA or equivalent, an American will usually have difficulty obtaining a place at a German university. Foreign students number around 165,000 or just over 9 per cent of the intake to higher education establishments, over a third of whom obtained their university entrance qualification in Germany (so-called resident foreign students).

This is a good time to apply to a German university, because the government, anxious that the country will suffer academic isolation, is keen to attract more foreign students, and a knowledge of German is no longer required. Many courses leading to internationally recognised bachelors and masters degrees are now available in English. Even for foreign students, tuition is free, and graduates are encouraged to remain in Germany to help bridge the country's skills gap.

Private Universities

Germany also has a number of private universities, which fall into three categories.

- **Private universities** are similar to state universities but usually affiliated to a religious organisation and focusing on subjects such as theology. You must pay the tuition costs yourself.

- **Elite, industry-sponsored institutions** are designed to train the second-level management of large corporations. Gaining access to these is even more difficult than to state universities but, once you're in, a glittering career in senior management is all but guaranteed.

- **International universities**, mostly of US origin, include the well-known Schiller International University in Heidelberg (Bergstrasse 106, 69121 Heidelberg, ☎ 06221-45810, 🖳 www.siu.heidelberg.de). International universities mostly offer US-style diplomas, which aren't automatically recognised in Germany or the rest of the EU, and are designed largely to allow American students a period abroad. Tuition fees are high.

Polytechnics

Polytechnics (*Fachhochschulen*) were originally intended to improve the skills of blue-collar workers but are now fully-fledged university-level institutions. However, one tradition remains, which is that only technical subjects are taught there. Many firms and institutions (e.g. Deutsche Telekom) run their own polytechnics to train their engineers. Some states insist that the diploma contains the letters *FH* to show that it was obtained at a *Fachhochschule*.

Some graduates from traditional universities refer rather disparagingly to polytechnic graduates as 'narrow gauge scholars'. However, an *FH* designation often isn't a disadvantage for a graduate, but quite the opposite. Many employers seek those with *FH* degrees because of the practical skills and experience they have, and such individuals are more likely to find employment shortly before or after graduation than those from regular universities.

Accommodation

After gaining a university place, your next challenge will be to find a place to live. Although university and polytechnic courses are free, accommodation can be expensive and difficult to find. Many universities have halls of residence (*Studentenwohnheim*), but few have anywhere near enough places to meet demand and getting a room is almost equivalent to winning the national lottery! (Not many years ago, one university had to give homeless students 'containers' originally designed for earthquake victims.) If the cost of accommodation is likely to be a problem for you, as it is for many German students, you should apply for a place at a university in a smaller town rather than a large city, as rents are usually lower.

Degrees

There are essentially three types of degree: an MA, which is a purely academic qualification, usually in an arts subject; a *Diplom*, which is similar but in a science subject; and a *Staatsexamen*, which is taken by future teachers and tests their knowledge of the relevant school curriculum. Teacher-trainees must also take a second (*zweites*) *Staatsexamen* after practical experience in the field. After six terms (semesters), you take an intermediate exam (*Zwischenprüfung*), which is often regarded as the equivalent of a British BA degree, although it confers no qualification.

The highest qualification is a doctorate, which is highly prized – almost all Germans who have achieved a doctorate wish to be addressed as '*Herr/Frau Doktor*'. Those with doctorates from other EU countries have the right to use the title also, but those with an American Ph.D can call themselves 'Doctor' in Germany only if their qualification has been recognised by a state's Ministry of Education. The procedure for this can be more or less complicated, depending on the state. In some states (Berlin, for example) it's as simple as sending a copy of your diploma to the registrar's office, while in others you may feel as if you're doing your thesis all over again (and you must have documents translated by officially-recognised translators at considerable cost).

State Subsidies

Most German students were given grants until the early 1980s, when funds were first limited to those who couldn't afford to study, then geared to the level of their financial needs, and finally converted into a loan which must be repaid (after finding your first job). The situation which applies today is some way from the original intention, which was to allow anyone capable of studying at a university the opportunity to do so. Student subsidies are administered by the Bundesausbildungsförderungsgesetz (BAFöG), which roughly translates as Federal Promotion of Education Act but is also the name for the assistance it provides as well as for the authority that dispenses it. The Act stipulates the kind of aid a student is entitled to in order to enable him to study or learn a trade or profession.

To qualify for a subsidy, you must 'earn' less than €377 per month if you live with your parents (or a parent) or €466 per month if you don't. To apply for a subsidy up to this amount, you must provide statements showing not only your own financial means but also the means of anybody who may reasonably be expected to support you. Those under the age of 27 must provide earnings statements from their parents, and a divorced person may even be required to supply an earnings statement for his ex-spouse. If your means are below the qualifying limit, the state pays the balance – 50 per cent in the form of a grant and 50 per cent as an interest-free loan, which you have up to 20 years to repay (up to a maximum total of €10,000; exemptions and reductions also apply to certain categories of student). Applications are processed locally in the town or city where you wish to study and full information is available (in German) on the BAFöG website (💻 www.bafoeg.bmbf.de).

The qualifying limits haven't been increased in line with inflation for well over a decade, which means that anybody trying to survive on a subsidy will barely exist above the poverty line – in some cities (e.g. Munich, Frankfurt and Berlin) the BAFöG subsidy hardly covers the average room rent. Consequently many German students must have at least one part-time job, which is one reason why they take much longer than their European counterparts to complete their studies.

DISTANCE LEARNING

Although magazines in Germany are filled with advertisements for correspondence schools, there's only one German state institution whose certificates are recognised by all European countries. This is the Fernuniversität Hagen (💻 http://fernuni-hagen.de), which is roughly equivalent to the UK's Open University and broadcasts some lectures via the third TV channel (see **Television Channels** on page 156). The Fernuniversität is designed for people who can't afford to take time off work to study, and conditions are a little more relaxed than at normal universities. The disadvantages are that it usually takes longer to earn a diploma than through a 'normal' university and the subjects available are somewhat limited.

Graduates of other distance learning universities, particularly those located overseas, may have more trouble getting their qualifications recognised in Germany. However, because of the many distance-learning programmes throughout the EU, some of the stricter German rules regarding recognition are likely to be relaxed in the future.

LANGUAGE SCHOOLS

If you want to make the most of the German way of life and your time in Germany, it's essential to learn German as soon as possible. For people living in Germany permanently, learning German isn't an option but a necessity. Although it isn't a particularly easy language to learn, even the least linguistically-talented person can acquire a working knowledge of German. All that's required is some hard work, help and perseverance, particularly if you have only English-speaking colleagues and friends. **Your**

business and social enjoyment and success in Germany will be directly related to the degree to which you master German.

Most people can help themselves a great deal through the use of books, tapes, videos and CDs. However, even the latest interactive language-teaching programs cannot (yet) answer your questions or correct your pronunciation. For most people, attending a course (combined with one or more of the other methods listed above) is likely to be the best solution. There's certainly no shortage of possibilities. Teaching German is big business in Germany, with classes offered by language schools (including franchises of big corporations such as Inlingua and Berlitz), German and foreign colleges and universities, private and international schools, foreign and international organisations, local associations and clubs, and private teachers. Tuition ranges from language courses for beginners through specialised business-related or cultural courses to university-level courses leading to recognised diplomas. If you already speak German but need conversational practice, you may prefer to enrol on an art or craft course at the local *Volkshochschule* (see **Evening Classes** on page 350). You can also learn German via a telephone language course, which is particularly practical for busy executives and those who don't live near a language school.

There are language schools (*Sprachschulen*) in all German cities and large towns. Most run various classes, from which you can choose according to your language ability, how many hours you wish to study a week, how much money you have to spend and how quickly you want or need to learn. For those for whom money is no object (hopefully your employer!) there are courses where you study for up to nine hours a day, five days a week at a cost of between €1,500 and €2,000, depending on the school. Note, however, that not everyone benefits from such intensive study and it's generally better to spread your lessons over a longer period.

Language classes generally fall into the following categories:

Category	No. Of Hours Per Week
Extensive	4 – 10
Intensive	15 – 20
Total immersion	20 – 40+

One of the most famous German-language teaching organisations is the Goethe Institut, now Goethe Institut Inter Nationes (Dachauer Strasse 122, 80637 Munich or Postfach 19 04 19, 80604 Munich, ☎ 089-159210, 🖳 www.goethe.de), a government-funded, non-profit making organisation with 141 branches in 76 countries across the world and 17 centres in Germany. The Goethe Institut runs general, specialist and intensive courses. The recommended method (not always possible in practice) is to start with a course in your home country at level one (*Grundstufe 1*), followed by courses at levels 2 and 3 in Germany. Courses cover speech, pronunciation, reading, writing and grammar. All Goethe Institut instructors are university graduates with additional training in teaching German as a foreign language. Many have studied abroad or worked at an overseas branch, and the high quality of the teaching is widely acknowledged. Unfortunately the costs are also high (e.g. a two-week total immersion course costs €1,725). The Goethe Institut publishes a free annual leaflet, *Learn German in Germany*, which contains up-to-date information about the courses available at its centres in Germany, with an overview of course content, dates and prices. The leaflet is available in American-English, British-English, French, German, Greek, Italian, Japanese, Polish, Portuguese, Russian, Spanish and Turkish.

You may prefer to have private lessons, which are a quicker, although generally more expensive, method of learning a language. The main advantage of private lessons is that you learn at your own pace and aren't held back by slow learners or left floundering in the wake of the class genius. You can advertise for a teacher in your local newspapers, on shopping centre/supermarket and university notice boards, and through your or your spouse's employer. Don't forget to ask your friends, neighbours and colleagues if they can recommend a private teacher. Private lessons by the hour cost from around €50 at a school or €20 to €30 with a self-employed tutor.

Another possibility is to find someone who wants to learn (or improve) his English and work out some kind of reciprocal arrangement with them. This can be a very economical way of learning German, although it depends on your having the time (and inclination) to give 'lessons' as well as take them.

UK citizens wishing to visit Germany to study the language and culture might be interested in programmes offered by the Central Bureau for Educational Visits and Exchanges, a division of the British Council. The Central Bureau also organises a range of international education and training exchange programmes, including the English Language Assistants Programme, which enables Modern Language graduates and undergraduates to spend a year working as a language assistant in a foreign school. The Central Bureau publishes a range of guides, including *Home From Home – The Complete Guide to Homestays and Exchanges* and the annual *Working Holidays*. These guides contain practical information on a wide range of opportunities to work and study abroad. For information contact the Education Section of The British Council, 10 Spring Gardens, London, SW1A 2BN, UK (☎ 0131-524 5770, ▭ www.britishcouncil.org).

10.

PUBLIC TRANSPORT

Public transport (*öffentlicher Verkehr* or *öV*) in Germany is efficient, clean, safe, comfortable and comprehensive. Integration between different modes of transport is good, although perhaps not quite up to the standard of Switzerland. The main modes of public transport within Germany are air, train, tram, bus, and underground (subway). There are also river and lake ferries and cable-cars, although these tend to be localised and usually cater more for tourists than residents. Inter-city services are provided largely by air and rail, and inter-city bus services are virtually non-existent, although Germany is served by a network of international bus services provided by companies such as Eurolines.

Urban transport is generally of a high standard, with full integration between transport and ticketing, where one ticket is accepted on all modes of transport within a city or region. Rural transport, by contrast, can be patchy, with infrequent services outside school starting and finishing times. Weekend services, particularly outside tourist areas, can be very limited.

The level of fares within Germany may be considered high by some foreigners, but for others (e.g. Britons) this won't be the case. Rail fares aren't simply based on distances, but may also take into account the quality and speed of trains, which means that money can be saved by choosing slower trains when time isn't of the essence.

In major cities – and to an increasing extent in rural areas also – public transport is organised and paid for by a public transport authority (*Verkehrsverbund*), which contracts services out to different companies and is responsible for integrating fares within the region. In general, fares are zonal, allowing through journeys with changes of mode (bus to tram to underground, for example) with the use of a single ticket.

Newcomers are sometimes confused by the terminology used in Germany for rail systems, which include main-line railways (*Eisenbahn*), trams (*Strassenbahn*), underground (*U-Bahn*) and light rail (*Stadtbahn* or more commonly *S-Bahn*).

TRAINS

The railway (*Eisenbahn*) network in Germany is extensive and has seen huge investment in recent years, high-speed lines being built and others upgraded to cater for high-speed trains. Most main lines are electrified, as are suburban lines around the main conurbations. After unification, the railway systems of East and West Germany were merged to form Deutsche Bahn AG (DB AG). However, following directives from the European Union (EU) that were intended to increase competition, the operating arm of DB AG was split into several companies, the most important of which are DB Reise & Turistik AG (long-distance passenger) and DB Regio AG (local passenger traffic).

Among the major projects in recent years have been the construction of new high-speed lines from Würzburg to Hanover, Mannheim to Stuttgart and Hanover to Berlin, while route sections between Nuremberg-Munich and Stuttgart-Munich have been upgraded.

However, the biggest single investment has been in the direct high-speed line from Frankfurt to Cologne, costing some €5 billion, which opened recently. Trains reach top speeds of 300kph (186mph), and it reduces the time for the 226km (140mi) journey between the two cities by an hour.

The opening of the new line means that Frankfurt airport now has two stations – see page 218). There's full co-ordination between trains and flights, so that passengers holding both rail and air tickets can check in their luggage at certain DB stations for direct loading onto planes in Frankfurt.

Internationally, rail links between Germany and other European countries continue to improve. Probably the most significant is the construction of the new high-speed route between Brussels, Aachen and Cologne, which means that high-speed Thalys trains (owned jointly by France, Germany, Belgium and Holland) can operate at a full 300kph (186mph) on routes between Amsterdam, Brussels, and Frankfurt. In Brussels, there's a direct connection with the Brussels-London Eurostar service, providing high-speed rail connections from Germany to Britain for the first time. Other international links upgraded or being upgraded include Berlin-Prague-Vienna, Berlin-Poznan-Warsaw (with the potential for onward connections to Minsk and Moscow) and Paris-Strasbourg-Karlsruhe.

Investment isn't restricted to high-speed routes. In many conurbations, a new generation of rolling stock for *S-Bahn* and regional trains has been introduced, providing new standards of comfort and security. Several rural lines are benefiting from tilting trains, enabling higher speeds in situations where new infrastructure cannot be justified.

The post-war history of Berlin meant that the railway network serving the city was split between its western and eastern halves. Since reunification, there has been major investment in a new north-south rail link, together with a completely new *Hauptbahnhof*, sited near the historic *Reichstag* in the centre of the city. Additionally, the major interchanges at Berlin Ostbahnhof and Lichtenberg – both in the east of the city – have been completely rebuilt and now offer full facilities, including hotel accommodation at Ostbahnhof. Not to be outshone by the investment in mainline railways in Berlin, the *S-Bahn* network is rapidly being restored to its original extent, with the addition of new lines that have been opened in the east since the war.

Perhaps one of the most innovative local train services in Germany in the last decade has been in the Karlsruhe area, where specially-designed trams operate not only on the streets of the city but also on main DB lines to many surrounding towns and cities, providing a true centre-to-centre service. A few years ago, tramlines were re-introduced in central Heilbronn, allowing trams from Karlsruhe to travel all the way into Heilbronn city centre. The same idea has been used in Saarbrücken, trams running on tramlines in the city centre and on DB tracks outside the city. (A novelty here is that one of the lines crosses the border into France at Sarreguemines.)

In addition to DB, there are a number of private railway companies in Germany, operating branch lines or small self-contained networks. Many are fully or partly-owned by the states and in several recent cases have been successful in obtaining operating contracts for regional passenger services from the *Verkehrsverbünde*, whereby they're now fully integrated into the local transport network. More rail-based competition was expected in Germany as new or foreign companies were given the opportunity to take advantage of the EU open-access policy, but this has come to little so far.

In contrast to some other European countries, first class rail travel is popular in Germany, and not only among expense-account businessmen. One reason is that discount fares also apply to first class tickets and many people consider the extra comfort and space well worth the extra cost.

General information is available on the DB website (🖳 www.bahn.de), which has links to many other information pages, plus timetables.

Types Of Train

Passenger trains are classified according to their speed, the distance they cover, and the type of service they offer, as shown below:

- **ICE (*InterCity Express*)** – Deutsche Bahn's flagship trains travel at up to 280kph (174mph) on selected routes, usually with regular-interval timetables. Seating, entirely of the reclining variety, is arranged in either compartment or open-plan style carriages, with panoramic windows and air conditioning. You can plug a headset into the audio system in your armrest to access six music/ radio channels, while individual video screens and a copy of the *Financial Times Deutschland Kompakt* are available free in first class. In the latest version, the even more plush *ICE 3*, first class passengers can sit in a lounge directly behind the driver with a view right through the cockpit onto the track ahead. The *ICE T* is a tilting train which takes bends at up to 220kps (138mph).

  ICE Sprinter services connect Frankfurt with Berlin, Hanover/Hamburg and Munich every morning, with a journey time of under 3.5 hours. A complimentary snack, soft drinks and daily papers are available to passengers travelling in first class. Hire car bookings with Avis, Eurocar, Hertz and Sixt can be made from these trains an hour before arrival. Your car will be waiting at the station on arrival.

- **IC (InterCity)** – express trains operating on major internal routes at a speed of up to 200kph (124mph), at regular intervals and with first and second class carriages. They usually include a restaurant or bistro car.
- **EC (Euro-City)** – IC trains serving destinations outside Germany;
- **IR (Inter-Regio)** – limited-stop trains connecting regional centres, with a minimum two-hour frequency and an average speed of at least 90kph (56mph); these now only run on the secondary Dresden-Goerlitz-Wroclow route;
- **D (Schnellzug)** – other limited-stop fast trains;
- **SE (StädteExpress)** – limited-stop local trains linking with the main conurbations;
- **RE (RegionalExpress)** – local trains operating a limited-stop service;
- **RB (RegionalBahn)** – local trains stopping at all stations along their route;
- **S-Bahn** (originally **Schnellbahn**) – suburban services inside the *Verkehrsverbünde*.

Each train has a unique number (like the flight number for aircraft) which is prefixed by one of the above abbreviations, so there should be no confusion about the type of train or the fares applicable. Most trains have a sign on each coach giving its destination and route details. *ICE* trains usually have an on-board electronic display with the same information, as well as an information screen in the entrance area to coaches, which can be used to obtain details of connections and other information. When it isn't otherwise in use, the screen shows the train's speed, which can be a plus or a minus depending on your disposition. Restaurant or bistro and trolley facilities are available on *IC*, *ICE* and *EC* trains. *IR* trains also normally have a bistro car, as well as a trolley service. A small number of *RE* and *SE* trains offer a limited refreshment service from a trolley. Double-decker trains, helped by the generous loading gauge in Germany, are becoming increasingly common on *RE* and *SE* services. These trains have been in use much longer in eastern Germany and are often to be found there on rural services.

The 'Metropolitan' train, introduced a few years ago, connects Cologne and Hamburg in around 3.5 hours. This service is operated by an ostensibly independent railway company, Metropolitan Express Train GmbH (☎ 01805-905805, 🖥 www.met.de), which is in fact a business unit of DB AG. The Metropolitan (which has three different 'comfort categories' in first class) runs four times daily in each direction during the week, with one return journey on Saturdays and two on Sundays. The marketing clearly targets business users and fares include a 'business snack', non-alcoholic drinks, newspapers, easy luggage stowage, a 220V electricity socket and a service call button at each seat, not to mention card telephones. There are also a cocktail and espresso bar, and a Europcar car rental terminal. The distance between rows of seats is 100cm (42in). However, a second class category has now been added to what was formerly a first class only service.

Accommodation is divided into four zones, which you choose when booking your ticket and seat:

- **Office Zone** – Clear mobile telephone reception, fax service and business magazines for sale;
- **Silence Zone** – Quiet atmosphere (mobile telephone and computer-free), seats in rows, a choice of radio/music programmes with headphones, and blankets and pillows available;
- **Club Zone** – Individual choice of films (DVD players), clear mobile telephone reception, area for families with children and one coach specially equipped for disabled passengers;
- **Traveller Zone** – The second class area.

Tickets

The rule in Germany is that you buy a ticket before travelling by train. If you don't, you will end up paying a higher fare or even a penalty. Bear in mind that ticket checks are routine, as each train usually has a team of staff rather than a single conductor. Tickets for train travel can be purchased from a variety of sources:

- Travel centres or booking offices at stations;
- Authorised travel agencies (note that you may be charged an additional handling fee by the agency);
- Ticket machines at stations. These are usually 'touch screen' with the full range of tickets available and tickets may be purchased with cash (notes and coins) or by credit card.
- Via the Internet (🖳 www.bahn.de) using credit card payment; tickets can be posted to you, collected at a nominated station, or printed at a machine by entering a personal identification number. You can also print them out on your computer at home if you're a *Bahncard* holder or have a credit card.

Tickets can also be bought on board some long-distance trains, where a surcharge for this service is payable. This varies from €2 to €10. Payment isn't permitted on local trains operated by a *Verkehrsverbund*, and anyone discovered travelling without a ticket is regarded as a fare dodger (*Schwarzfahrer*) and liable to an on-the-spot fine. Fines vary according to the *Verkehrsverbund* but average around €30.

RE, SE and *S-Bahn* trains operating within major conurbations can be used with tickets issued by the *Verkehrsverbund*. Many of these trains offer first class compartments, for which you pay extra.

Fares

DB's new fare structure (introduced in 2003) was intended to be simpler than the old one but not everyone has found this to be the case, and a pocket calculator is still a useful accessory for travellers. A wide range of passenger fares is offered, and there are many discounts, some of which can be utilised simultaneously. (This is usually where that calculator comes in handy.) Prices are based on the speed and comfort offered as well as the distance covered. Premium trains attract premium fares and there's no set per kilometre tariff; the further you travel, the lower the kilometre price. The most common fares, tickets and concessions are summarised below:

- **Standard (Basic) Fares** – These vary with the length of the journey, longer journeys costing less per kilometre, so that the new prices are often cheaper than the old ones. There are no discounts on these fares, except for 'mini groups' (see below). You may either exchange your ticket for another or obtain a full refund if you decide not to travel, as long as you do this before the day of validity. No charge is made.

- **ICE Fares** – These vary with the journey but are generally the most expensive. You travel on DB's state of the art trains and are treated like a VIP.

- **Kostenloser Kindermitnahme** – Children up to 14 can now travel free when accompanied by their parents or grandparents. If they're on their own, they receive a 50 per cent discount. They can receive a further 25 per cent discount if they have a *Bahncard* (see page 203).

- **Mitfahrer-Rabatt** – One person pays the full fare and up to four others travel for half price. The minimum fares before this offer applies are €15 in second class and €22.60 in first class. For groups of six and more the *Gruppe und Spar* tariffs apply (see below). To assist travellers in taking advantage of this offer, DB have instituted a *Mitfahrer-Boerse*. Give DB your travel date and they will find one or more people going to the same place at the same time who can combine with you to take advantage of it. Contact details are sent by e-mail.

- **Plan Und Spar** – These discounted tickets are subject to availability and, although you may cancel, a fee of between €15 and €30 is thereby incurred, depending on how late this is done. Two under-14s count as one adult.

- **Plan Und Spar 10** – You book the ticket the day before you use it and get a 10 per cent reduction. The outward and return legs are booked individually.

- **Plan Und Spar 25** – Book three days before travelling and get a 25 per cent reduction. Valid for return trips.

- **Plan Und Spar 40** – Book seven days in advance and get a 40 per cent reduction. Valid for both legs of the journey but there must be a Saturday in between.

● **Gruppe Und Spar** – Fares apply to six or more people travelling together (two under-14s counting as one adult) and are subject to availability. There are three types of ticket:

- **Gruppe Und Spar 50** – Buy the tickets at any time and get a 50 per cent reduction.

- **Gruppe Und Spar 60** – Buy the tickets seven days in advance and get a 60 per cent reduction.

- **Gruppe Und Spar 70** – Buy tickets 14 days in advance to get a 70 per cent reduction.

● **Schönes-Wochenende-Ticket** – Valid on Saturdays and Sundays from midnight to 3am the following day (27 hours total), e.g. from midnight Friday to 3am on Sunday, for unlimited travel on local trains (*RE*, *RB*, *SE*, *S-Bahn*) in second class. The cost is just €28 for up to five people travelling together, or for parents or grandparents with an unlimited number of their own children or grandchildren up to 14 years of age, which must be one of the best bargains in Germany! If you buy it aboard the train, you must pay 10 per cent extra. (Don't forget that within local transport networks you must buy tickets before boarding.) You can also bring a bike with you on all the trains you catch for an additional one-off payment of €3. The *Schönes-Wochenende-Ticket* is also valid on the *U-Bahns*, trams and buses of many local transport systems.

● **Länder-Ticket** – This is a 'rover' ticket for an entire federal state and costs from €21 to €25. It's valid from Mondays to Fridays on a day of your choice from 9am to 3am the following morning on local trains (*RE*, *RB* and *S-Bahn*) in second class, along with the other forms of transport of many local transport authorities. Up to five people, or parents/grandparents with an unlimited number of their own children or grandchildren up to the age of 14, can use it. The supplement for using *IR* and *D* trains is €13. Conditions vary slightly from state to state.

● **Local Transport System All-Inclusive Tickets** – Usually up to 48 hours' unlimited travel in a particular city and surrounding area, using the entire local transport network. Prices vary but are usually an excellent bargain; they're listed on the Deutsche Bahn website: pick the state and then the local area to view the details.

● **Other Special Tickets** – Rail & Fly tickets are airline tickets that include free or reduced rate travel on German railways. Other tickets offer reduced prices for journeys to specific destinations at specific times, such as the annual carnival in Berlin. They're explained in detail on 💻 www. bahn.de.

Bahncard

This network card, also valid in Austria and Switzerland, gives a 25 per cent discount on all fares, including the Mitfahrer-Rabatt, Kostenloser Kindermitnahme and the Plan Und Spar options (see above). Get your calculator out! *Bahncards* cost €50 second class and €100 first class. When a parent buys one, the other parent and children are entitled to buy their own for €5 each. An additional payment of €15 annually means that *Bahncards* can also be used in 28 more European countries to get an equivalent 25 per cent discount. The standard *Bahncard* will also get you a 25 per cent discount from DB-owned regional bus companies.

Recent additions are the *Bahncard 50*, which entitles you to a 50 per cent reduction on fares and costs €200 for second class and €400 for first class (half price for partners, children and students, senior citizens and the disabled), and the *Bahncard 100*, which allows you (and four of your children under 15) to travel anywhere at any time 'free' (it costs €3,000 for second class and €5,000 for first class!).

Booking

Bookings can be made for all *ICE, IC, EC, IR* and *D* trains, from three months in advance up until a few minutes before departure. The latest *ICE* trains have automatic booking systems allowing seats to be reserved even after a train has left its starting station. Bookings are highly recommended on the inter-city routes, particularly on Fridays and Sundays, when trains can become very crowded, even in first class. In second class you're liable to find yourself surrounded by soldiers either going home for the weekend or returning to barracks at these times (you can tell which by whether they're cheerful or gloomy).

The current booking fee is €2.60. If you want to reserve one of the special seats available for disabled people and their companions contact the Mobilitäts Service Zentrale, whose telephone number is ☎ 01805-512512 (calls cost €0.12 per minute).

Train Accommodation

Accommodation on trains varies with the train type. *ICE* trains have coaches that are mostly 'open', with two or three compartments at the end of each coach. *EC* and *D* trains have carriages with either compartments or open accommodation, whereas those on *IR* trains have mixed seating in compartments and semi-open 'bays'. On *ICE* trains, you can book a particular seat, whereas on other trains you can choose only between a compartment or open carriage, window or corridor seat and (if you want two seats) facing or adjacent seats. In all cases, smoking or non-smoking is an option, although the number of smoking seats on *ICE* trains is relatively low. Note that you cannot choose a forward facing or backward facing seat, as many trains change direction during the course of their journey, although in older *IC* trains, seats in first class 'open' carriages are reversible.

The majority of coaches in *EC* and *IC* trains are air-conditioned, as are all *ICE* trains and the latest generation of *S-Bahn* trains. Virtually all trains, including some *S-Bahn* trains (although not in Berlin) have both first and second class carriages. Many trains have toilets with wheelchair access. *ICE* trains have two toilets per carriage (male and female) in second class.

Sleeping Cars

You can take a sleeping car on many long-distance routes, and services include the following:

- DB AutoZug GmbH operates DB NachtZug, offering the biggest choice of routes within Germany, with 11 standard routes.

- EN (EuroNight) operates trains on international routes such as Berlin-Vienna-Budapest, Hamburg-Vienna, Cologne-Warsaw and Vienna-Ostend.

- CityNightLine (CNL) operates trains to Austria, Holland and Switzerland in purpose-built couchette and sleeping cars, connecting Zurich with Berlin, Dresden, the Ruhr area (in summer also Nordeich-Mole) and Hamburg, Dortmund with Vienna, Amsterdam with Zurich and Munich and (on winter weekends) Garmisch-Partenkirchen.

- Urlaubs Express (UEX) runs seasonal trains to holiday destinations such as Italy.

- Sleeping car and couchette coaches are also attached to normal international *D*-class trains. These trains link many major cities in western and eastern Europe and include through coaches to Rome, Warsaw and Budapest.

Accommodation in sleeping car trains includes the following:

- *Ruhesessel* – a reclining seat, normally in an 'open' coach;
- *Economy Vierer* (economy four) – four berths in one compartment;
- Economy Double or Single;
- Eco Family – two adjacent Economy Double compartments linked;
- Deluxe Double or Single (with shower and WC);
- *Liegewagen* – a couchette, first or second class, the former with four berths and the latter with six berths per compartment.

Fares for these services can be found on 🖥 www.dbnachtzug.de along with other information. In calculating fares, the type of accommodation and the time of year (peak periods are more expensive) are prime factors along with the distance. Breakfast is included in the price.

Car Trains

DB AutoZug GmbH operates a network of car-carrying trains from selected centres within Germany to popular holiday destinations. The timetable differs considerably between summer and winter, the destinations offered in winter being mostly ski and winter holiday resorts. As most operate overnight, the trains consist of couchette and sleeper coaches and double-decker, car-carrying wagons. Daytime travel when it takes place is all in first class.

Prices vary according to the date of the journey (peak holiday seasons are more expensive), the size of the car, the number of passengers travelling together and the type of accommodation (sleeper or couchette). Bookings can be made via the Internet on 🖥 www.dbautozug.de, where you can view all possible permutations and pay by credit card.

Bicycles

Bicycles can normally be taken on local trains (*RE*, *SE*, *S*, *RB*) in luggage and entrance areas, provided space is available, although in some cases their carriage is subject to the rules of the *Verkehrsverbund* concerned, which may differ from Deutsche Bahn standard rules. Long-distance trains are individually designated 'with' or 'without' cycles in all timetables. For those taking a bicycle, booking is recommended at peak holiday times between the beginning of March and the end of November. Reserving a place for your bike is obligatory on some long-distance trains but doesn't cost anything. DB provides advice and assistance on its cyclist's hotline (☎ 01805-151415 – €0.12 per minute). The current charges for cycles are:

- International trains – €10 (but €15 on the night train 242/243 from Berlin to Paris);
- Long-distance trains (*EC*, *IC*, *D* and sleepers) – €8 or with a *Bahncard* €6;
- Local and regional trains (*IR*, *RB*, *RE* and *S-Bahn*) – €3 with some variations according to the *Verkehrsverbund*.

If you don't want the hassle of taking your own bike with you, you can hire one on arrival through DB's new Call-A-Bike service. It's currently available only in Berlin, Munich and Frankfurt, but if successful will be extended. According to DB, 3,700 modern bikes with eight gears are available for hire. When you call the local Call-A-Bike office to register, you will be given a code, which you enter into a gadget attached to a bike to release the lock. Bikes can be found at major road junctions as well as the railway stations in the towns mentioned. When you've finished with your bike, you leave it at the station or any main junction. You lock it and de-register with another telephone call to the Call-A-Bike office. Bikes are thus available 24 hours a day. You're charged according to the exact amount of time you've spent with the bike (at €0.06 per minute) and regular users can pay monthly. A seven-day hire costs €60. *Bahncard* holders receive a 33 per cent discount. More traditional bike hire companies usually operate close to stations, but these aren't connected with DB and rates vary.

Luggage

Accompanied luggage up to 30kg (66lb) is carried without charge. (In fact, it's unusual for the weight to be checked unless an item is extra-large.) Luggage can be sent in advance using the *KurierGepäck* service, for which there's a standard fee of €14.30 per 'normal' item (up to 30kg/66lb in weight and 165cm/65in in length) or €23.50 for 'special' items (cycles, skis, wheelchairs, etc.). Additional items cost €9.20 and €18.40 respectively. The service is available door-to-door, with payment made in advance at a DB ticket office.

Station Facilities

The main station in each town is called the *Hauptbahnhof* (abbreviated to *Hbf*). In the major cities these offer a range of facilities, including a *Reisezentrum*, which is a large combined ticket, enquiry and information office, left luggage lockers, a manned left luggage office, a travel agency (often from the associated DER chain), a currency exchange counter (run by the in-house Deutsche Verkehrs-Bank), usually a post office, plus a variety of book shops, magazine stalls, cafes, bars and restaurants. Another important feature of large stations is the *Markt im Bahnhof* ('market in the station'), where you can buy fresh food and vegetables seven days a week, without concern for Germany's restrictive shop trading hours.

Luggage can be transported on trolleys located at strategic points in stations. You simply insert a 50 cent or €1 coin to free a trolley, which is returned when you replace the trolley at a collection point. Alternatively, you can sometimes hire the services of a porter.

Recently, DB has been putting a lot of effort into improving station waiting areas with the introduction of DB Lounges. These are quiet waiting areas for first class passengers, similar to business class lounges in airports (complete with comfortable seats, drinks, newspapers, magazines, television and a screen displaying train times) with adjacent office areas equipped with desks, telephones and sockets for laptops. Conference rooms for meetings or presentations are also available.

The DB Lounges at Frankfurt, Frankfurt Airport AIRrail and Cologne stations now offer a 'Rail&Mail' service, providing Internet access. Laptops can be hired at the lounges. By the end of 2003 all DB Lounges should be equipped with Rail&Mail' facilities.

DB Lounges can be found at the following main stations: Bremen, Cologne, Frankfurt, Frankfurt AIRrail (airport), Hanover, Leipzig, Mannheim, Nuremberg and Stuttgart. They're open every day from 7am to 9pm. Customers with Metropolitan or Thalys (Comfort 1) tickets can also use the DB Lounge at Cologne, while Lufthansa customers (first class) have access to the lounge in Stuttgart.

Another innovation is the 'ServicePoint/ServiceTeam'. Located in over 90 DB stations, these are places where passengers can send faxes, post letters and arrange courier deliveries, etc.. A DB ServiceTeam is on hand to provide transport and local accommodation information.

Travel Information

Information about train services can be obtained at all stations with a manned ticket office. In an attempt to help passengers orientate themselves at stations, large colour-coded metal figures (*Stahlmenschen*) display different types of information, as follows:

- **Blue** – welcome signs and temporary information;
- **Red** – timetables (sheets showing departures (*Abfahrt*) are yellow, while those showing arrivals (*Ankunft*) are white);

- **Yellow** – station plans showing facilities and city maps;
- **Green** – exhibitions and shows in the city and/or station.

Large electronic displays show train departure and arrival details and platform information. Note, however, that only a limited number of stops for any given route are shown on these. At the entrance to platforms there's a separate display board indicating the next arriving or departing train, again with main (but not all) stopping points. On the platform itself there's usually a *Wagenstandanzeiger*, a diagram showing every carriage in each train stopping at the platform with its number (and destination, if different from the rest of the train), alongside a series of letters from A to E. These letters relate to sections (*Abschnitte*) on the platform surface, so that it's easy to see precisely where your carriage will stop. This is important on long platforms where trains may stop only for a few minutes and you won't have time to rush from one end to the other looking for your carriage. This information also appears in simplified form on the platform display screen.

An increasingly popular way to find train and bus information is via the Internet. DB has an easy-to-use website in German and English (🖳 http://bahn.hafas.de), which provides extensive details of train times and categories of trains. If you don't want the expense of an *ICE*, for example, you can exclude this type of train, or any other, from your timetable search. It's also possible to make bookings and buy tickets online. DB's latest development is 'Surf and Rail' (🖳 www.surfandrail.de), where tickets purchased online can be printed on your own printer. DB's online information isn't restricted to Germany and information about all European railways can be accessed via DB's website, together with a range of bus and other local transport information.

BUSES & TRAMS

Regional Services

Regional bus companies are owned mainly by Deutsche Bahn (DB) and tend to offer inter-urban (although not inter-city) services, as well as services linking major towns to outlying villages. In most cases these operate in conjunction with regional train services and generally the bus terminus is adjacent to the railway station. However, the service is severely limited on some rural routes, with the frequency of services calculated per week rather than per day. Many services cater particularly for schoolchildren, although anyone can use them, and therefore they may operate only from Mondays to Fridays or Saturdays at the start and end of the school day, and not at all during school holidays.

In some towns, local bus services are also provided by a DB subsidiary company. Some can be identified by a variation on the old DB bus livery of strawberry pink and grey, although many companies are now introducing their own styles. You should ask if the service is run by DB or a subsidiary if you have a *Bahncard* (see page 203), as you're entitled to a 25 per cent fare discount on all DB services.

City Services

In all major cities, and in many smaller towns, bus services are provided by a division of the local authority (*Verkehersbetriebe* or *Stadtwerke*). The scale of these operations varies enormously, from the extensive route networks of Berlin, Hamburg and Munich to just two or three routes in small satellite towns. Services are mainly operated with buses, although trams (*Strassenbahn*) are used in the larger cities and trolleybuses in Eberswalde (north-east of Berlin), Esslingen (south of Stuttgart) and Solingen (in the Ruhr). In neighbouring Wuppertal there's the *Schwebebahn*, a suspended monorail operating along the River Wupper, which, despite its novelty, is an integral part of the local transport system.

Many large cities operate tram services, an increasing number being banished underground in city centres. Sometimes, as in Stuttgart, Frankfurt and Cologne, these have developed to become an underground railway (*U-Bahn*) and the stations are distinguished by large signs showing a white 'U' on a blue background. In the Ruhr, high-speed tram lines are also referred to as the *U-Bahn* but confusingly often have the word *Stadtbahn* superimposed on the U. Only Hamburg, Berlin, Munich and Nuremberg have constructed genuine undergrounds from the start, all other cities having upgraded from tramways.

Running alongside the underground network (or superimposed on it) may be the *S-Bahn* (an abbreviation of the original *Schnellbahn*). These often go underground in the city centre and can be distinguished by a sign showing a green circle with a white 'S' in the centre. Most *S-Bahnen* are operated by DB under contract to the *Verkehrsverbund*. Stopping points are normally further apart than on the *U-Bahn* and trains are generally less frequent – every 15 to 20 minutes is typical – with routes extending into the surrounding towns and countryside. Nevertheless, both the *U* and *S-Bahnen* are fully integrated into city transport systems and can be used with normal city transport tickets.

U and *S-Bahn* services are both numbered, in contrast with similar services in other countries, where a line may have a name and/or a colour allocated to it. (In Germany, things are often numbered rather than named.) *U-Bahn* routes, not surprisingly, are numbered with a U prefix, *S-Bahn* lines with an S prefix. Peak hour or less-frequent services on branch lines have a different number, usually an extra digit; for example, the S11 may be a peak hour variation of the S1. At a main station the *S-Bahn* often runs from underground platforms (*Gleis*) separated from the main part of the station and accessible via an escalator or lift.

In the major conurbations transport services are co-ordinated by the regional *Verkehrsverbund*, common fare systems and timetables covering all public transport within the area. The largest example is the Verkehrsverbund Rhein-Ruhr, covering an area of over 5,000km² (1,930mi²) in the industrial Ruhr area, and incorporating more than 800 routes providing services to over 20 major towns and cities in the region. Such services are also co-ordinated with local trains (*S-Bahn*) provided by DB.

Tram and bus services don't generally operate between around 1 and 5am, but most larger cities have an hourly night bus service covering the more popular destinations, often with planned interchanges so that a small number of vehicles gives the maximum cover. A higher fare is usually payable on these routes.

Fares & Tickets

Fare systems vary between cities and regions, but generally operate on a zone basis, where you purchase a single ticket that's valid from the start of the journey to the end, irrespective of the number of changes you make, provided you remain within the designated zone(s). Normally, a central city area will be within one zone and therefore subject to a single fare. Fares for journeys crossing a zone boundary may be more complex, but ticket machines usually show a simplified route map or list of possible destinations to help you select the right ticket.

In most large towns and cities, it's compulsory to buy a ticket from a machine before boarding a vehicle – buying tickets from the driver is the exception, although it's more common on rural routes where traffic doesn't justify the cost of installing a machine at each stop. The rule is: if there's a machine, use it! Because of the differences in systems between cities, it isn't possible to give precise instructions for using machines. For example, in the Rhein-Main area (the area surrounding Frankfurt) you enter a four-digit destination code on a numerical keypad and then press one of around ten buttons for the type of ticket required. Other cities have a simpler, colour-coded route map, where you press a coloured button corresponding to your destination area. In each case the fare is displayed on a screen and you then insert the necessary coins; an increasing number of machines accept banknotes and credit cards. Change is usually given. When change runs out, a sign is displayed, usually in red.

In some cities, such as Munich and Berlin, you may find a ticket machine on board trams (rather more rarely on buses). These function in the same way as machines at stops and, as there are no conductors, you must use them. Having purchased your ticket, it's usually necessary – depending on the city – to validate it (*entwerten*) in a special machine or slot after you've boarded a vehicle. If a ticket has a space on it for a machine stamp (generally marked with an arrow), it probably needs to be validated. If in doubt, ask the driver or another passenger. **If you don't validate your ticket, you're riding illegally and can be fined.** Random inspections by teams of plain-clothes ticket inspectors take place regularly, with a fine of around €30 for offenders, payable on-the-spot (or by bank transfer if you can prove that you have a German bank account).

Children up to the age of six travel free, those aged from 7 to 14 travel at reduced fare (but rarely half) and those 15 and over pay full fare. In many cities *Auszubildende* or *Azubis* (youths aged 15 and over in full-time education or training) are able to purchase season tickets at reduced prices, typically 20 to 25 per cent below the full fare. Many cities allow the transport of bicycles without an extra charge, although this may be restricted to off-peak times and may be at the discretion of the driver if the vehicle is full or otherwise too small (such as a minibus).

Special Tickets

There's usually a wide range of tickets available and it's worth checking which is the best value. For example, if you're commuting regularly, it's worth buying a weekly, monthly or even an annual ticket. Many transport systems grant extra privileges to season ticket holders, such as allowing other family members to accompany them free of charge during the evenings and at weekends. In addition, these tickets aren't usually issued in an individual's name, which allows other family members or friends to borrow them and travel independently. The only drawback is that there's no automatic replacement if a ticket is lost or stolen. You can use these tickets for travel at any time on all modes of transport within the designated zone(s), with the exception of long-distance DB trains.

Other special tickets include 24-hour or day tickets (*Tageskarten*), which are excellent value for a day trip to explore a city. It's worth checking whether a ticket is in fact valid for a day (usually until the last normal bus or tram) or for 24 hours, as the latter can be used on the following day up until the time printed on it. Take care when using these tickets, as in some cities they must be both validated and signed. The machine (or ticket) should tell you; if in doubt, ask. Family tickets (*Familienkarten*) are economical when travelling with your spouse and children.

Some cities offer a cheaper off-peak ticket, but you don't need to worry about the calculation, as the tariff will automatically be calculated by the ticket machine or bus driver according to the time of day. (In some towns, it isn't unusual to see groups of people waiting at a stop for the cheaper tariff to start, pressing the buttons on the ticket machine every few seconds to see whether the cheaper fare applies.) In some cities you can buy a short-distance (*Kurzstrecke*) ticket, usually for journeys of less that 2km. The ticket machine will know whether this is valid for the journey you want to make or will list the destinations served by such a ticket.

If you've invested in a *Bahncard* (see page 203), you may also be entitled to a cheaper fare if your journey within a conurbation involves train travel only (*S-Bahn*, *RE* or *SE* services), although it's usually necessary to check the small print of the tariff regulations or ask station staff.

Finally, you will find that most cities with an *S-Bahn* network also offer first class carriages. If you want to take advantage of the exclusivity (it's rarely any more comfortable than standard class), you must buy a *Zuschlag* ticket from a machine to cover your journey.

Access

Germany is at the forefront of investment in easy-access buses and trams, normally referred to as *Niederflür* (low entrance) vehicles. These originally involved merely a shallow entrance step to the main seating area, but the most recent vehicles have a completely flat floor, with direct access to most seats from the low floor area. Most of the latest vehicles also have a retractable wheelchair ramp, usually at the centre door, and a special wheelchair storage area with clamps. Many drivers lower ramps obligingly at stops, even for (apparently) able-bodied people. Modern buses and trams are usually also air-conditioned.

In general, access to buses and trams can be made through any door. The exceptions are buses on rural routes, where the driver may want to check your ticket or sell you one, and on city buses after 8pm, when you should enter by the front door. When you want to get off, you normally just press the button marked *Haltewünsch* on buses and some trams. A sign, '*Bus hält*' (bus stopping), will be illuminated. On some buses and trams you must push an additional button to open the doors, while on others they open automatically.

It isn't usually necessary to signal the driver to stop if you're at a bus or tram stop, as there are few 'request stops'. Sometimes, however, a driver may not realise that you're intending to board, so it's wise to put an arm out if he doesn't seem to be slowing down.

FERRIES & SHIPS

There's a variety of ferry (*Fährboot*) and shipping services in Germany. Major rivers, such as the Rhine and Main, have a number of cross-river ferries for cars and foot passengers, and some major cities include ferry services in their range of public transport services, which are usually covered by a standard ticket. Examples are the river services in Hamburg and the lake services in Berlin, each of which forms an integral component of the local public transport system. Lake services on the Bodensee are provided by a Deutsche Bahn associate company. The Bodensee Pass gives 50 per cent reductions on transport in this area, including the ferries.

North Sea ferry services operate internationally from Hamburg/ Cuxhaven to Harwich in England (see ⌨ www.dfdsseaways.co.uk for details and timetables) and in the Baltic between eastern Germany and Sweden, Finland, Lithuania and Latvia. There are also good connections from the German mainland to the outlying Friesian islands, usually run in conjunction with trains or express buses.

A variety of shipping companies provide tourist services on Germany's lakes and rivers. Trips range from a few hours to several weeks. The two biggest operators are the Weisse Flotte (White Fleet) in Dresden, specialising in vintage steamboats on the Elbe River, and KD in Dusseldorf, which mainly operates in the Rhine/Main/Mosel regions.

CABLE CARS & FUNICULARS

Cable cars (*Seilbahnen*) and rack railways (*Zahnradbahnen*) can be found in the more mountainous areas of Germany, particularly the northern Alps in Bavaria. Here you will find the famous *Zugspitzbahn*, an electrified rack railway running some 18.6km (12mi) from Garmisch-Partenkirchen and climbing 1,945m (6,381ft) to the top station at 2,650m (8,694ft) above sea level. Funiculars (*Drahtseilbahnen*) are found in several of the hillier towns in Germany and include the *Nerobergbahn* in Wiesbaden, operated by a water-balance system, the two-stage line in Heidelberg and an ancient line in Stuttgart. Stuttgart also has the only rack railway (actually a tramway) to be integrated into a city transport network (at Degerloch on Route 10). In summer, a trailer is attached for the transportation of bicycles. Dresden has a hill-climbing *Schwebebahn* (suspension railway) and a more conventional funicular.

TIMETABLES

Comprehensive timetables are published by the major public transport authorities and cover all services in a region, although they're usually in several volumes. Similarly, DB produces a national timetable known as the *Kursbuch*, in addition to more manageable regional timetables. However, the trend is towards publishing timetable information electronically, such as on the DB website (🖳 www.bahn.de), and most *Verkehrsverbünde* have their own websites. There's a move towards producing a co-ordinated national enquiry system, so that it will soon be possible to obtain 'door-to-door' timetable information between any two towns in Germany (and indeed Europe) from a single Internet enquiry.

DB and the major *Verkehrsverbünde* also publish their timetables on CD-ROM. It's possible to take out a subscription so that the most up-to-date information is always available, and indeed many authorities offer updates by e-mail or by downloading a single file from a website. Most transport authorities and DB have telephone enquiry services, sometimes providing recorded announcements for the most popular routes. DB has a single national enquiry number (☎ 11861). This enquiry service costs on average €0.60 per minute but can be accessed 24 hours a day throughout the year. There is also a freephone number (☎ 0800-1507 090) for spoken timetable information – spoken by a machine, not a person!

TAXIS

Taxis are easy to identify in Germany, where they're painted in a standard cream livery and have an illuminated 'Taxi' sign on the roof. Many are Mercedes or other quality makes. Fares are shown on a meter inside the vehicle and usually consist of a minimum fare plus a variable kilometre or elapsed time rate. Rates for evenings and weekends are usually higher, although there are basic rates between towns that are fixed by the local authorities. Taxis cannot usually be hailed on the street and must be hired from an official taxi stand found at railway stations, airports, bus and tram termini, and other designated areas. Taxis can be summoned to your home by telephone at no extra charge. Several public transport authorities offer the facility of booking a taxi to meet a bus or tram at a nominated stopping point, particularly during the evening or night. This is usually arranged with the driver of the tram or bus. There's usually no extra charge for this service.

AIRLINE SERVICES

Germany is well served by airlines, both domestic and international, and boasts the second-busiest airport in Europe, as well as numerous smaller airports.

Lufthansa

Lufthansa, the national airline, is one of the world's largest passenger and freight carriers. It flies to around 340 cities in some 90 countries and operates over 300 aircraft. Although the company made healthy profits immediately after privatisation in 1997, it's currently losing money – in common with many airlines – but optimistically increasing its operational fleet. To strengthen its international ties, since 1997 Lufthansa has been a leading player in the 'Star Alliance' with other major airlines, including Air Canada, Air New Zealand, British Midland, Singapore Airlines, SAS Scandinavian, Thai, United Airlines and Varig. One of its most successful innovations in recent years has been the 'Miles and More' frequent flyer reward programme, which also recognises air miles flown with other Star Alliance members. (More information is on ⌨ www.miles-and-more.com). There are reputed to be some 3 million participants world-wide.

Flights within Europe offer business and economy classes, while intercontinental flights also include first class. Lufthansa aircraft are equipped throughout with leather seats, which can be widened in business class to give additional room. All flights are non-smoking. Passengers travelling in first or business class can make bookings via the Lufthansa InfoFlyway website (⌨ www.lufthansa.com), which also provides flight information, timetables, news of special offers and other details. Economy seats can be reserved on intercontinental flights (on European flights seats are allocated at check-in). Flights are often fully booked at school holiday periods, which are listed in most diaries and calendars.

In addition to standard check-in facilities, Lufthansa provides a late-night check-in service at main railway stations in Bonn, Dusseldorf, Cologne, Nuremberg and Würzburg for passengers travelling to Frankfurt by train the following morning. Look out for the 'Moonlight Check-in' sign. Similar late night check-in services are also provided at 12 German airports (although flights to Tel Aviv are excluded for security reasons). Since May 2003 passengers can also check in at any time at Cologne central station, handing in their luggage and receiving their boarding cards, in conjunction with the AIRail service to Frankfurt Airport on the new ultra-high speed route. The service also operates in reverse with the customs check at Cologne station. Trains run hourly. Telephone or fax check-in is also possible on international flights from Germany for first and business class passengers calling from anywhere in Europe with only hand baggage by ringing ☎ 0561-993399. At Frankfurt, Munich and Dusseldorf, first and business class passengers (with or without baggage) may check in at drive-in desks located outside the terminal building adjacent to the taxi set-down point. Valet parking and porter service is available here.

Many airports around the world provide dedicated lounges for holders of Lufthansa first, business and status cards (Senator or Frequent Traveller). There are some 55 Lufthansa lounges and at a further 80 airports you can use the executive lounges of its partner airlines. Since March 2003 Lufthansa has been installing broadband cable-less Internet facilities in their lounges.

Lufthansa CityLine

CityLine (formerly DLT) has been a Lufthansa subsidiary since 1993 and serves routes in continental Europe with 80-seat Avro RJ85 and 50-seat Canadair Jets. It transported over 6 million people in 2002. The operation is based at the head office in Cologne and most routes are centred on Cologne/Bonn airport.

Condor

Condor is Lufthansa's holiday airline, most of whose flights are sold as part of a complete holiday package. It's the largest such airline in Germany and provides around 500 weekly flights during the peak season to over 70 international destinations. Its modern fleet consists of Boeing 757, 767, DC10 and Airbus A320 aircraft.

Other Airlines

Germany is served by most major international airlines, several of which co-operate with Lufthansa on joint promotions and marketing (see **Lufthansa** above). Also based in Germany are Deutsche BA, a subsidiary of British Airways, which operates mainly from Berlin Tegel, and a number of large charter holiday airlines.

Airports

The main international airports in Germany include Berlin (Tegel and Schönefeld), Cologne/Bonn, Dusseldorf, Frankfurt (see below), Hamburg and Munich. There are also many smaller airports that provide limited international services, including Dresden, Hanover and Leipzig/Halle, although some cater only for charter rather than scheduled flights. This is not the case with Hahn (served from Stansted in England by Ryanair), which is described rather ingenuously as Frankfurt (Hahn), although in fact it's over 80km (50mi) from Frankfurt. Hahn is set to become Ryanair's second continental hub. (Lufthansa recently took the Irish airline to court over the latter's description of Hahn as Frankfurt/Hahn.)

Long and short-term parking is available at all major airports, including reserved parking for the disabled, and all major airports have wheelchairs and ambulance staff on hand to help disabled travellers, although it's wise to make arrangements in advance. Lufthansa also provides stewardess services for children over five who are travelling alone, for an additional fee.

International airports have shopping centres that are usually open for around 12 hours a day, seven days a week. The table below gives the telephone number for flight information and details of bus or rail services to the city centre from the main airports.

Airport	Telephone Number	Transport To City Centre
Berlin Tegel	0180-500 0186	Express bus X9 or bus109 (20 – 25 minutes)
Cologne-Bonn	02203-400	Shuttle bus 170 (20 minutes)
Dusseldorf	0211-4210	*S-Bahn* S7 (13 minutes)
Frankfurt	069-6900	*S-Bahn* S8 or S9 (12 minutes)
Hamburg	040-50750	Airport Express bus (25 minutes)
Hanover	0511-9770	*S-Bahn* S5 (12 minutes)
Munich	089-97500	*S-Bahn* S1 or S8 (40 minutes)
Stuttgart	0711-9480	*S-Bahn* S2 or S3 (25 minutes)

Frankfurt

Frankfurt International is Germany's most important airport and the second-busiest in Europe (after London Heathrow), handling well over 40 million passengers a year. The airport is huge, although every imaginable service is available. There are two terminals (a third is being discussed), five 'halls' (A–C in Terminal 1, D and E in Terminal 2) and six floors (four in Terminal 1 and two in Terminal 2); finding your way around can be difficult and you may have to walk long distances. Finding unoccupied information desks isn't unusual, and airport staff are often less than helpful. Looking at the airport website (🖳 www.frankfurt-airport.de) is worthwhile, and printing the map of the airport recommended. Most Lufthansa flights use Terminal 1.

The two terminals are linked by the 'Sky Line Shuttle', a driver-less, elevated electric train, which runs every two minutes (also the length of the trip). The shuttle is free, but you cannot take luggage trolleys on it. The Sky Line 'station' in Terminal 1 is situated above the Departure Hall B and in Terminal 2 it's on Level 4. You must take the shuttle to get from Hall C to Hall D.

For passengers requiring overnight accommodation, there's a Sheraton Hotel in the terminal complex and at least 15 other hotels nearby, many directly accessible by courtesy shuttle buses and taxis. There's a hotel information and booking desk in each terminal, but the one in Terminal 1 is open later than that in Terminal 2. Several hotels offer a 'Park & Fly' service, with a room rate combined with short or medium-term secure parking.

Access: The airport is well served by public transport and has good road access.

- **By Train** – There are two railway stations: *Frankfurt Flughafen Regionalbahnhof* and *Frankfurt Flughafen Fernbahnhof*, the latter also called the 'AIRail terminal'. The first is served by local and regional trains and the second by long-distance inter-city trains. The *Regionalbahnhof* is situated directly beneath Terminal 1 (Hall B). Local *S-Bahn* trains operating on the Frankfurt city underground loop leave every 15 minutes, while main line trains to the *Frankfurt Hauptbahnhof* depart at frequent intervals, with an 11-minute journey time. The *Fernbahnhof* is situated almost half a mile from the airport, although with covered pedestrian access from Terminal 1, and is the terminus for the new Frankfurt-Cologne ultra-high-speed rail line, which became fully operational in May 2003. Deutsche Bahn claims that all major cities in Germany – and many abroad – can be reached from here with a maximum of one change of train.

- **By Bus** – There are bus stops at both terminals: opposite Hall C (on Level 0) at Terminal 1 and opposite Hall E at Terminal 2. Buses generally call at both terminals in both directions. They also run to many nearby destinations. Lufthansa operates regular connecting buses to the neighbouring urban centres of Heidelberg, Heilbronn, Kaiserslautern, Mannheim, Saarbrücken and Sinsheim.

- **By Road** – The airport is conveniently situated close to *Autobahn 3* (Cologne-Munich) and *Autobahn 5* (Hanover-Basle), with well-signposted slip roads. However, local access is provided from the parallel but less-congested B43 dual-carriageway, which can be used for the entire journey when travelling to or from Frankfurt city.

  There are multi-storey car parks in both terminals open 24 hours a day. Fees at both terminals are €1 for 30 minutes, €3 for an hour and €21 per day. Facilities are available for the disabled, including designated parking places (currently in the P31 car park close to Terminal 1).

  Taxis are plentiful and can be found on the forecourts of the terminals. Although you sometimes need to queue, you rarely have to wait long. Arriving taxis at Terminal 1 generally drop off at one of the Halls on Level 2 (departures) and depart from Level 1 (arrivals). At Terminal 2, taxis usually stop on the terminal service road on Level 2. The fare from central Frankfurt to the airport is around €20 to €25 and the journey normally takes around 20 minutes.

Departures: Luggage trolleys are plentiful, a situation which has improved considerably in recent years, and some escalators accommodate them, saving constant loading and offloading. Large information boards show where your check-in desk is located. Most Lufthansa check-in desks are in Hall A and other airlines' desks in Hall B, while Hall C (with fewest facilities) tends to be the refuge of small charter and holiday airlines. There's no logical allocation between Halls D and E in Terminal 2, and it isn't always possible to establish which terminal you must go to before travelling to the airport.

After checking in, you will find the gate number for your flight (if known) on your boarding card. Gate numbers consist of a Hall letter (A to E) and a number. It's wise to locate your gate well in advance of the departure time, as it may be a long walk.

Airport authorities state that X-ray machines used for hand baggage at German international airports are safe for film. However, a manual search is normally possible on request and is recommended if you're carrying high-speed film (over 400ASA). Note that film shouldn't be transported in hold baggage, which is subject to more powerful X-ray machines, and computer hard and floppy disks can be damaged by X-rays. You may be asked to switch a computer on, so it's wise to charge it up beforehand.

Arrivals: If you arrive on a flight with a high proportion of transit passengers, the airport staff may decide not to run the luggage carousel. If this is the case, you must go to the 'oversize luggage' (*ISperrgepäck*) claim area and ask whether your luggage is there.

If your luggage doesn't arrive at all or is damaged, go to the 'baggage tracing' kiosk (*Gepäckermittlung*) and report your loss and show your baggage tags. If your luggage is damaged, this is likely to be the only opportunity you will get to report it and claim damages. Generally, lost luggage appears a day or two later and is usually delivered to you directly by the airline; you don't need to return to the airport to collect it.

11.

MOTORING

Germany has one of the highest rates of car ownership in Europe, with 516 cars per 1,000 inhabitants – a level exceeded only by Italy (545) and Luxembourg (582) – and a total of over 40 million registered cars. Not surprisingly, although the country has an excellent road system, which includes some 226,500km (140,312mi) of main roads, it's notorious for its traffic jams (*Staue*), which can be encountered at any time. In addition to the expected congestion during rush hours, the roads are usually clogged on school and public holidays, when millions of Germans take to their cars. Add to this the German propensity for high-speed driving and, irrespective of your level of motoring experience, you're likely to find motoring in Germany a challenging, and at times, nerve-racking experience (unless you're Italian or Portuguese or Spanish . . .).

Germany's motorway (*Autobahn*) network covers 11,500km (7,132mi) and provides direct connections between most German cities. There's no official speed limit on motorways (although there are 'recommended' speed limits), which can be exciting for fast drivers but frightening for drivers who aren't used to traffic moving at such high speed. Cruising speeds in excess of 160kph (100mph) are commonplace and high performance cars can be seen – if you don't blink – zooming by well over 200kph (125mph). Not surprisingly, there are a lot of road accidents in Germany, where around 7,500 people are killed annually and some 500,000 injured. (Germany ranks 'behind' Portugal, Spain, Italy and France in the western European league table of the number of road deaths relative to the distance travelled by motorists but well 'ahead' of the UK, which has around half as many.)

The German authorities are serious about traffic laws and police them assiduously and effectively, using not only patrol cars but also cameras, which are more common than in any other European country. Cameras are stationed at strategic points (such as traffic lights) throughout the country, and photographs show not only your number plate and the date, time and location but also your face! You may not be aware that you've been caught until a traffic ticket arrives in the post a few days later. (The pictures used to be sent to the offender's home along with the ticket, but this practice was dropped when many partners opened the envelopes and saw photos of their spouses with someone of the opposite sex whom they didn't recognise! Now, in order to see the incriminating picture, you must go to a police station.)

Traffic information is readily available from radio and TV announcements and German TV's teletext information service. Recorded traffic information is also provided by the German motoring organisation ADAC (☎ 011-69). Signs on motorways show the local radio frequency on which road and traffic bulletins are broadcast.

In case of an accident or breakdown, emergency telephones are located at 1.5 to 3km (1 to 1.5mi) intervals along motorways. Black directional arrows on white posts on the hard shoulder indicate the direction of the nearest phone box. An operator will answer as soon as you pick up the receiver, so you should be ready to give the number of the motorway, the direction in which you're travelling and the identification number marked on the telephone box.

Vehicle Documents

Under German law, you're required to carry your vehicle registration certificate (*Kraftfahrzeugschein* or *Kfzschein* – see **Registration** on page 225) and driving licence and at all times when driving a vehicle. It's wise to take copies of these documents (in case the car and/or your documents are stolen) and to keep the originals on your person or locked in the glove box. If you're stopped by the police without the required papers, you can be fined. When driving outside Germany, it's wise to have a green card from your insurance company with you (see page 239). It's also prudent to keep a blank accident report form in your car; these can be obtained from your insurance company.

IMPORTING A VEHICLE

If you plan to bring a motor vehicle or motorcycle to Germany, either temporarily or permanently, you should be aware of the latest regulations. All vehicles manufactured outside Germany must meet German specifications (see **General Operating Licence** on page 225) and may therefore need to be modified. The problem of finding parts and service facilities for foreign-made vehicles should also be considered before deciding to import a car rather than buying one in Germany. Add to this the cost of import duty and VAT (see below) and you may think twice (or three times) about bringing a car with you!

You're permitted to drive an imported vehicle with foreign number plates for up to 12 months, provided the vehicle's registration remains valid, but the use of the vehicle is duty and tax-free for six months only. A registration document with a German translation is required.

Duty & VAT

Motor vehicles registered in a non-EU country are normally subject to import duty (*Zoll*) and value added tax (*Einfuhrumsatzsteuer*), either when entering Germany or at a later date. There are two exceptions:

- Under certain circumstances, vehicles imported for private use for a maximum of six months (which doesn't need to be consecutive) in any

12-month period are exempt from taxation. It's strictly forbidden to lend, hire, give or sell a temporarily imported vehicle to a citizen of an EU member country. In this case, VAT must be paid at the time of import and it's refunded by the customs office upon departure.

- If you're moving from a non-EU country and establishing residence, your vehicle may be considered part of your household goods and therefore exempt from taxation provided the following criteria are met:
  - You can prove that you've been resident outside the EU for the last 12 months;
  - You register your residence in Germany (see page 85);
  - The vehicle is for personal use only;
  - The vehicle is immediately registered with the local motor vehicle office (see **Vehicle Registration** below);
  - The vehicle has been in your possession and was registered abroad by you at least six months before your arrival in Germany;
  - The vehicle isn't given away, sold, lent or hired for a year after its importation.

If no duty or tax is payable, a customs exemption certificate (*Unbedenklichkeitsbescheinigung*) is issued. This document is required when registering the vehicle in Germany (see below).

For those who don't qualify for exemption under the above criteria, the following charges are levied, irrespective of the type of vehicle being imported:

- Import duty of 10 per cent, based on the purchase price (see note below), plus freight costs and insurance to the place of destination in Germany;
- Value added tax at 16 per cent, based on the purchase price plus freight costs and import duty.

You're required to present a dealer's invoice as evidence of the purchase price of the vehicle. If, however, customs officials don't consider this a fair and accurate representation of the vehicle's market value, they may calculate their own figure by reference to a dealer's car buying guide (the standard one is the *Schwacke Liste*) or obtain a certified appraisal (*Wertgutachten*). The authorities recommend that private importers without a recent invoice for their vehicle or who ship an uncommon type of car should have their vehicle appraised before declaring its value. If necessary, appraisals can be arranged in Germany with local branches of the Dekra organisation (listed in the telephone book).

Some shipping agencies will complete the clearance and customs formalities on your behalf (for a fee).

Once payment has been made, a customs receipt or clearance certificate (*Zollquittung*) is issued, which is required when registering the vehicle in Germany (see below).

VEHICLE REGISTRATION

You must register your vehicle if one or more of the following apply:

- It was purchased in Germany.
- You've imported it but plan to stay longer than 12 months.
- You've imported it but its foreign registration has expired.

Only residents and resident companies can register a car, either directly or via an authorised representative with power of attorney.

General Operating Licence

Vehicles can usually be registered only if a general operating licence (*Allgemeine Betriebserlaubnis*) for the model has been issued by the Federal Motor Vehicle Authority (Kraftfahrtbundesamt or KBA), which certifies that the model has passed a general inspection, including safety and emissions tests and conforms to German technical, safety and pollution-control standards. The general inspection is usually instigated by the manufacturer or importer when a new model is launched. The KBA issues a specification (*Kraftfahrzeugbrief* or *Kfz-Brief*) for each model, listing its principal technical features, a copy of which is automatically issued to car buyers by the manufacturer or a dealer. If you don't have one, a copy can be obtained from the local motor vehicle licensing office (Kfz-Zulassungsstelle). **You're strongly advised not to make any substantial modifications to a licensed vehicle without obtaining expert advice, or you could invalidate the general operating licence.** If you feel compelled to turn your hatchback into a roadster, you can engage a KBA certified expert (*Kfz-Sachverständiger*) to issue the necessary title after performing a technical inspection, but be warned: such 'private' general vehicle inspections don't come cheap.

Even when an imported model has been granted a general operating licence, modifications are likely to be necessary to meet German safety and environmental standards.

Foreign vehicles (particularly those manufactured in America and Japan, few of which are sold in Germany) imported privately don't usually have the required operating licence. If a licence hasn't been issued, it's your responsibility to supply the necessary technical data. To avoid the time-consuming and expensive procedure of establishing the technical specifications of a car via a general inspection, you should contact the manufacturer of your vehicle before shipping for information about the VIN (vehicle identification number), year of manufacture, vehicle type, and other technical data, including:

- engine capacity;
- power (in horsepower or kilowatts);
- maximum speed;
- emissions data;
- admissible wheel and tyre sizes;
- admissible gross front/rear axle weight.

If the vehicle doesn't have valid number plates, you need to request special red licence plates (*rote Kennzeichen*) from the local motor vehicle licensing office in order to drive it to the inspection station. Note that the date of the vehicle's first registration determines the legal standard that applies, and you must provide this date.

Procedure

To register a vehicle in Germany, you must apply at the local motor vehicle licensing office in the town were you live, with the following documents:

- Proof of identity and residence, e.g. passport and registration card;
- A customs clearance certificate stating payment of, or exemption from, the relevant duty and tax (see **Duty & VAT** on page 393);
- Proof of ownership, e.g. a bill of sale or commercial invoice;
- Proof of liability insurance cover, which takes the form of a copy of your policy (*Versicherungsdoppelkarte*), obtainable from your insurer;
- An export permit (from your previous country of residence) if applicable;
- Vehicle documents, including the specification (*Kfz-Brief*) if one is available; if not, a blank specification form will be issued, which must be completed by a certified expert;
- The technical inspection and emissions test certificates (see below).

Fees: You must pay a fee of between €10 and €45 in cash (the authorities don't accept payment by credit or debit cards), and you will be been given a receipt and your vehicle registration certificate (*Kfz-Schein*) as well as three stickers to be affixed to the number (licence) plates, which must be purchased (you will be told where you can obtain them). They cost between €20 and €30, depending on their size (non-standard plates are available for certain makes of car). The stickers show the validity of the vehicle registration and that the vehicle has passed the technical inspection (on the rear plate) and the emissions test (on the front plate). Nothing should be stuck on your windscreen. Be prepared to attach your plates before driving away!

Number Plates

The first one to three letters of a German number plate indicate the district (*Kreis*) where the vehicle is registered. Large cities generally have a single registration letter (e.g. F for Frankfurt and S for Stuttgart), while smaller districts have two or three letters. Locals can use these letters to determine whether a vehicle is 'foreign' to their region. Number plates must be changed if you move to a new district for longer than three months. Standard plates show the letter 'D' for *Deutschland* and the EU logo, so no country code sticker is required.

SAFETY INSPECTION & EMISSIONS TEST

A regular safety inspection (*Fahrzeughauptuntersuchung*) made by a certified expert is required by law for every vehicle registered in Germany. An inspection must be made when a car reaches three years of age and thereafter at least every two years. The Technischer Überwachungsverein (TÜV) and the private Dekra organisation (💻 www.dekra.de) maintains test centres in most towns and cities (listed in telephone books). (If you have an older vehicle which may be due for some repair, folk wisdom suggests that you should take it to a Dekra centre, as they have a reputation for being slightly more lenient on older cars.) The inspection currently costs €42 and re-inspection after a failure costs €27.10. The car's mechanical condition is checked for compliance with relevant safety standards, which cover brakes, lights, chassis rust, shock absorbers and tyres. The vehicle is also tested for general roadworthiness. You don't need an appointment and can just drive your car to an inspection centre and ask for the inspection to be carried out on the spot.

If your vehicle doesn't pass the inspection, you will be told what repairs or alterations are necessary before it can be re-tested. When your vehicle is approved, a small circular sticker (*TÜVplakette*) is affixed to the rear number plate by the test centre and a certificate issued; these state the expiry date (the number in the inner circle indicates the year when the next inspection is due and that in the outer circle the month). The certificate for cars and motorcycles expires two years after the inspection and it's the responsibility of the owner to renew it. If you're apprehended driving a vehicle with an expired inspection sticker, you can expect to be fined. You will be given a brief period in which to have the car tested; if it isn't tested within this period, you won't be permitted to drive it until it passes the inspection. You must also pay a premium of up to €40 for an overdue inspection. After any major alterations or accident repairs, a vehicle must be checked to determine whether the modifications or repairs influence the handling or operating characteristics, in which case its certificate can be revoked.

An exhaust emissions test (*Abgassonderuntersuchung* or *AU* – unofficially referred to as the *ASU*) is required after the first three years and thereafter every two years for modern petrol and diesel-powered vehicles. Older cars (generally those manufactured before 1980), which weren't designed to meet recent EU norms, must be tested annually. The test costs €36.30, which includes any necessary minor repairs, and is carried out by the same centres as the safety inspection (see above) as well as at authorised garages (displaying an *ASU* or *AU* sign). As with the safety inspection, you don't need to make an appointment and there's a penalty of up to €40 for an overdue test.

Certificates for both the safety inspection and emissions test are required when registering a motor vehicle (imported vehicles usually have both inspections at the same time) and must be carried with the vehicle or driver at all times.

VEHICLE TAX

Vehicles registered in Germany are subject to an annual tax (*Kfz-Steuer*), which is payable soon after registration. An 'application' for the tax is filed automatically with your registration and you will receive a bill (*Kfz-Steuerbescheid*), which should be paid to your local tax office (*Finanzamt*). The amount payable is determined by the size of your vehicle's engine as well as the environmentally friendly (or unfriendly) features it possesses.

Rates are high compared with similar taxes in other countries: the tax for cars is currently between €5.11 and €23.06 for every 100cc or part thereof (in 2004 these figures will rise to €6.75 and €27.35) according to whether they're diesel or petrol-powered and, if the latter, equipped with a catalytic converter (the lowest tax for a diesel car is currently €13.80 per 100cc). If you have a petrol-engine car that meets European Standard 3, the tax will be €6.75 per 100cc in 2004, i.e. a total of €202.50 for a 3,000cc engine. A petrol-driven car with a similar size engine but only meeting Standard 1 would cost you €15.13 per 100cc or a massive €453.90 per year. A different calculation is used for lorries, depending on the size of the loading surface. Motorbike owners pay €1.84 for every 25cc irrespective of engine type.

BUYING A CAR

After you discover what's required to import (see page 223) a vehicle into Germany, you're likely to decide against bringing a car with you, unless you're pathologically attached to your existing car, and will therefore need to hire (see page 232) or buy one in Germany.

New Cars

Germany is the world's third-largest producer of cars in the world and possibly the largest producer of high-quality cars. German-made cars aren't necessarily cheaper to buy in Germany than elsewhere, although prices are generally lower than in the UK.

Haggling over the price of a new car is possible, although significant discounts aren't easy to negotiate; you may have more chance of success by saying that the price is acceptable only if some options are included. Note, however, that you should expect to pay not only the list price but also several fees, including shipping charges, VAT (*Mehrwertsteuer* or *MWSt* – see below) and 'dealer preparation'. Dealer preparation fees cover the cost of the final factory inspection of a car and can run from around €200 to €400. Registration fees (see page 226) and insurance premiums (see page 239) must also be paid before you can put a new vehicle on the road. When you buy a new car, a dealer can assist you with the registration process – all you need to do is provide the necessary documents.

In contrast with most other items sold in Germany, VAT isn't always included in the list price of new cars, so you should make sure you know the total price, including taxes and fees. There are, however, certain circumstances that allow exemption from VAT, e.g. diplomats and military personnel enjoy tax-free status irrespective of how long they remain in Germany. German law also permits non-EU nationals to avoid paying VAT on cars if they leave the country within 12 months of the purchase date (see **Importing A Vehicle** on page 223).

When considering a new car purchase in Germany, it's important to take into account your intended length of stay. If you expect to be in Germany for longer than six months or more, you're likely to be better off purchasing a car with German specifications in local currency. Those in Germany for a short period only and those who expect to qualify for a tax reduction or exemption may wish to consider a purchase scheme such as those offered by the dealerships of the Swedish car companies Saab and Volvo, who offer expatriate, diplomatic and military sales programmes that can save customers who qualify between 10 and 30 per cent of standard pre-tax prices and tax-free purchase programmes for EU nationals planning to leave Germany within the year for a non-EU country, as well as favourable terms for shipping a car. Details are available on the respective websites (💻 www. saab.com and 💻 http://expat.volvocars.com). Among the German manufacturers, Audi and BMW have discounts for diplomats and other visiting short and longer-term residents, while BMW, Mercedes-Benz and Porsche offer a 'tourist delivery programme' for US residents through their dealers in the US. The car is paid for in the States, picked up by the owner in Germany and later dropped off at a handling agent, who ships it to the US for no extra charge.

Used Cars

Buying a used or secondhand car (*Gebrauchtwagen*) in Germany usually offers good value, as vehicle inspection standards are relatively stringent, meaning that cars are generally maintained in good condition. Nevertheless, the precautions necessary when buying a used car are the same as in any country and, whether you're buying privately or from a dealer, you should check:

- that the car has valid safety inspection and emissions test certificates (see page 227) and preferably that it isn't due to be re-tested for a year or more;
- that it hasn't been involved in a major accident and suffered structural damage. You can ask for a written declaration that the vehicle is 'accident-free' (*unfallfrei*).
- that the vehicle identification number on the chassis is the same as the identification number on the vehicle registration certificate (*Kfz-Schein*);
- that the service coupons have been completed and stamped, and that servicing was carried out by an authorised dealer;
- that the price roughly corresponds to the *Schwacke Liste* value or some other reputable guide to used car prices (secondhand car prices are fairly standard throughout Germany, but you may be able to negotiate a better deal in the former eastern bloc states, as their economies are still not as strong as those in the west).
- that import tax and duty have been paid (if applicable);
- whether a written guarantee is provided;

You should obtain a written purchase agreement, even if the vehicle is purchased privately. The agreement should state the odometer (km) reading at the time of sale and confirm that it's accurate.

Notwithstanding the above, you should have the condition of all major systems checked by a car mechanic or someone with a good knowledge of cars. If you don't know someone who can help you check a car before buying it, the German motoring club ADAC (see **Motoring Organisations** on page 261) provides an inspection service (*Standartgebrauchtwagen-untersuchung*) for prospective buyers costing €75 for members and €95 for non-members.

When buying a car from a garage, some protection is afforded if the dealer is a member of the German Motor Trade Association (Deutsche Kraftfahrzeuggewerbe). In addition to the points noted above, members should provide a detailed list of items that are checked before a used car is sold. A reputable garage should also provide a warranty or guarantee, typically three months or 4,000km (2,500mi).

If you purchase a used car through a dealer, they can handle the paperwork and register the car in your name. If you buy privately, you must complete the registration procedure (see page 226).

A type of used car peculiar to the German market is the *Jahreswagen*, which is a vehicle bought at a discount by an employee of a large firm and sold after a year or so (*Jahreswagen* means literally 'year car'), usually at a low price and often in excellent condition. Some dealers operate a *Jahreswagen* service (*Jahreswagenvermittlung*).

SELLING A CAR

The main points to note when selling a car in Germany are the following:

- The number plates stay with the car when you sell it and either you or the new owner must change the registration of the vehicle. If you sell the car to someone you know and trust, it may be easier to let him register as the new owner of the car. However, if you have any doubts at all about the reliability of the buyer, you should cancel the registration before selling a car.

- Inform your insurance company once the registration has been changed. Your insurance for a vehicle is automatically cancelled when your registration is cancelled.

- Insist on payment in cash; this is standard practice in Germany.

- Include in the receipt the price paid, the car's odometer (km) reading and the fact that you're selling the car in its present condition (as seen) without a guarantee (*ohne Garantie*). The new owner may ask for a declaration in writing that the car is accident-free (*unfallfrei*). This refers to major accidents causing structural damage and not slight knocks.

You can advertise a car for sale in local newspapers, on free local notice boards, in major newspapers (the Saturday editions are best) and in many motoring newspapers and magazines. There's a range of publications consisting entirely of lists of used cars (and possibly other items) for sale.

There's also a growing number of Internet-based advertising sites. If you belong to any clubs or organisations that publish a newsletter, they usually have a classified advertising section (even if you aren't a member, many accept advertisements for a small fee). The best place to advertise a car depends on its make and value. Cheap cars are probably best sold in local newspapers, while expensive and collectors' cars are better advertised in the national motoring press. Buyers will usually travel a long way to view a car that appears good value (if nobody phones, you will know why!).

CAR RENTAL

The major international car hire (rental) companies, such as Avis, Budget, Europcar and Hertz, are all represented in most German cities, although Budget goes by the name of Sixt in Germany (it's popular for its competitive rates.) Cars can also be hired from local garages and offices in most towns – look under *Autovermietung* in the yellow pages. Business hours vary with the location of the office, those at airports having the longest opening hours. There are no special number plates for hire cars in Germany, as found in some other countries.

Although far from cheap, car hire is not as expensive as in some other European countries. The daily rate with unlimited mileage for a VW Golf is currently between around €55 and €70. The same car can be hired for a week with unlimited mileage for around €210. Although some car hire companies offer lower daily rates, they charge for each kilometre driven, possibly with the first 100km/62mi 'free', so the value will depend on the distance you intend to cover.

Hire costs not only vary between companies but also depend on where you hire a car. Hiring from an airport is generally more expensive – around 17 per cent of the basic rate – and, if you can get to a city by public transport, you will almost certainly get a better deal. Older cars can be hired from garages at lower rates than those charged by the national companies.

Most car hire companies in Germany require drivers to be aged over 21 and some even have a minimum age of 25. It isn't necessary to hold a German driving licence or even a licence from an EU country, but your home licence must be valid. However, if you're resident in Germany and your home licence (although still valid) is no longer recognised because of the length of your stay, you aren't permitted to use it to hire a car in Germany (see **Driving Licence** on page 234). By law, non-residents are required to possess an International Driving Permit (IDP), although in practice few companies will ask to see it.

It's usually necessary to pay for car hire with a credit card, which is preferable in any case, as it may cover your uninsured excess (deductible) in the event of an accident, in which case you don't need to pay for the (usually exorbitant) collision damage waiver (CDW) option. However, this may apply only to US-issued credit cards and you should check in advance. If you don't have a credit card and the company still allows you to hire from them, you should expect to pay a deposit of at least €150.

German hire cars usually have manual transmission; if you want (or need) an automatic, you must state this when booking and be prepared to pay extra. You must usually pay extra for an additional driver.

Most major companies allow you to collect a car in one city and drop it off in another for no additional fee, although if you want to do this you must ensure it's permitted before you hire. If you plan to travel outside Germany, this must also be allowed and noted in the contract. You will also need to check that the vehicle is properly documented for international travel, even within the EU. Most companies permit travel to other western European countries but not anywhere east of Germany (except Austria).

Vehicles should be equipped with the necessary emergency equipment (i.e. warning triangle and first-aid kit) and you may want to check that you have a parking disk (see **Parking** on page 253). In winter, hire cars are fitted with winter tyres and you can usually request snow chains and ski racks if you're heading for a ski destination. Car phones and baby and child seats are available from many companies for a fee, e.g. €10 per day for a child seat, which is required in Germany (see **Rules Of The Road** on page 245).

Remember to check what type of fuel a vehicle uses and the octane rating. Before venturing onto the road, you should ensure that you know where all the important controls are – they are likely to be different from those in your own car, especially if you're used to driving on the left. (It pays to be able to differentiate between the windscreen wiper control and the indicator switch before you get onto an *Autobahn*.)

You should also check a car thoroughly for any damage, including any marks on the bodywork, and have them noted on the hire contract form.

In addition to standard cars, you can hire a four-wheel drive vehicle, estate car (station wagon), minibus, luxury car or convertible. Vans and pick-ups are also available from major hire companies and some local companies by the hour, half-day or day.

If you want to hire a car but don't want to drive it yourself, the major companies offer various options. Sixt provides a chauffeur service for those who would rather concentrate on business than the road, and they offer a welcome service so that visitors can be picked up in style. Private sightseeing tours are available in a chauffeured car – a pleasant (if expensive) way to take in the city's highlights.

The German websites of the major car hire companies are 🖳 www.avis.de, www.e-sixt.de, www.europcar.de and www.hertz.de.

DRIVING LICENCE

Ensuring that you're licensed to drive in Germany can be either very simple or infuriatingly complicated depending mainly on whether your licence originates from a country inside or outside the EU. Those in the former category should have few problems (see **EU Licences** below). On the other hand, if you're coming to Germany from outside the EU and plan to live there for longer than six months, obtaining a German driving licence (*Führerschein*) may be one of the most frustrating experiences of your stay.

EU Licences

Residents of the EU now enjoy reciprocal recognition of driving licences for an unlimited period and you don't need to obtain a German licence even if you become a permanent resident in Germany. If you wish, you can obtain a German licence from a driving licence office (*Führerscheinstelle*) without needing to take either a written or road test, a privilege known as *Prüfungsfreiheit*, although this will cost a small fee. However, if you have a driving licence of a category other than class B (e.g. allowing you to drive professionally or in an HGV) and want to exercise the same privilege in Germany, you must obtain the appropriate German licence.

Non-EU Licences

If you have a valid non-EU driving licence, you can legally drive in Germany for up to six months. However, you must obtain an official transcription of your foreign driving licence (see **Transcription** below) and carry it with you when driving. Once your initial six months have elapsed, you must have a German licence. Therefore, if you plan to stay for longer than six months, you should start the process of applying for a German licence as soon as possible after your arrival, as it can take some time.

Those with licences issued in the following countries or states (irrespective of their nationality) can obtain a German licence without having to take either a written or road test, a privilege known as *Prüfungsfreiheit*: Andorra, the Channel Islands, Hungary, Iceland, Japan, Liechtenstein, Malta, Monaco, New Caledonia, Norway, French Polynesia, San Marino, Slovenia, South Korea, Switzerland and some states of the US (see below). However, even if you can take advantage of *Prüfungsfreiheit*, you must still obtain an official transcription of your foreign licence, although the procedure is slightly less complicated (see **Transcription** below).

You should beware of obtaining a licence from one of the above countries or states after becoming an official resident in Germany. If you're an official resident of Germany when your foreign licence is first issued, the licence won't be recognised as valid for transcription to a German licence. (This regulation was enacted to stop the flood of Germans going to one of the above countries to avoid the time and expense of obtaining a licence in their home country.) Similarly, if you renew your licence after becoming officially resident in Germany and cannot prove that you had a licence before the renewal, your transfer application will be denied.

Those with licences issued in another country must take a German road and written test (see **Driving Test** on page 237) in order to obtain a German licence.

American Licences: Some American states enjoy *Prüfungsfreiheit* (known to Americans as 'full reciprocity'), while others have partial reciprocity, but the majority (including some of the most populous states) have no reciprocity at all.

The following states currently have full reciprocity: Alabama, Arizona, Arkansas, Colorado, Delaware, Illinois, Kansas, Kentucky, Louisiana, Massachusetts, Michigan, New Mexico, Pennsylvania, South Dakota, Utah, Virginia, Wisconsin and Wyoming, and also the commonwealth of Puerto Rico.

Holders of licences from the following states are exempt from the practical test but must take the written examination: Connecticut, Florida, Idaho, Mississippi, Missouri, Nebraska, North Carolina, Oregon, Tennessee and Washington DC. This list has been growing, so check with a US consulate for the latest situation. The local driving licence office (*Führerscheinstelle*) will inform you of your situation when you apply, but it's wise to get an update from the consulate before you apply, as information on reciprocity agreements can take time to percolate down to local offices.

Transcription

If the country or state where your licence was issued enjoys *Prüfungsfreiheit* (see above), to have your foreign licence transcribed you must take the following documents to the driving licence department (*Führerscheinstelle*) of your local district administration office (*Landratsamt*):

- A valid passport or identity card with a residence permit;
- A passport photograph;
- A translation of your driving licence made by an official translator with approval from the German courts or by a recognised German motoring club;
- The results of an eye test (*Sehtest*) not more than two years old stating that your eyesight is acceptable. You can have the eye test done at most

opticians or optometrists for around €12 and must take your passport with you.

- The original and one copy of your foreign driving licence.

If your foreign licence wasn't issued in a country enjoying *Prüfungsfreiheit*, you must take the following **in addition to** the items listed above:

- A certificate stating that you've participated in a training course on 'first-aid techniques at the scene of an accident'. These courses are offered by many organisations and last for almost a full day. Many centres offer package deals, where for around €30 you receive the first-aid course and, during coffee breaks, can have your eye test performed and passport pictures taken. Don't worry if your German isn't good; it only seems to matter that you sit in the room, bring the dummy back to life when it's your turn and pay your fee in cash. Check in the yellow pages or with any driving school for a list of local course providers. If you want to take the course in English, contact the American Red Cross, which offers courses in conjunction with the US military (e.g. at its bases in Ramstein, Landstuhl and Kaiserslautern/Kleber/Kapaun).
- The name of the driving school through which you plan to take your driving test (only a licensed driving instructor can register you to take the tests).

In a large city, the office is likely to be crowded and you will need to take a number from a dispenser and wait for it to be called. The official will examine your paperwork and tell you if anything isn't in order. If your driving licence has been renewed since you arrived in Germany and the date your licence was first issued isn't printed, you will need proof that your driving history pre-dates your arrival in Germany – either an expired licence or a letter from the licensing authority. If you cannot prove that you've held your existing licence for more than two years, you will be given only a probationary licence. This will greatly increase your insurance premiums, so it's worthwhile obtaining proof of your driving history.

Once the paperwork has been deemed acceptable, there are some additional forms to complete and a fee of €35 be paid. You will be notified when your paperwork has been processed and the licence can be collected or, if required, the driving test taken (see below). This should take six weeks but can take 12 or more – another reason to begin the process as early as possible.

The German licence-issuing authority considers that once you have a German licence, your original licence is no longer valid. Therefore they may ask you for your original licence and, if you have one, your IDP. They may then return your original licence to the issuing authority with a note stating that you now have a driving licence in Germany, or they may just stamp it to indicate that you also have a German licence and return it to you.

Driving Test

If you're required to take a German driving test, you can start studying for the written test and taking whatever driving lessons you require while waiting for the necessary paperwork to be processed. You aren't obliged to attend the classroom sessions that new drivers must attend but, depending on the degree of 'reciprocity' of your licence (see **Non-EU Licences** on page 234), you may have to take the written test as well as the road test, in which case a driving school can order a set of 28 questionnaires in English with all the possible questions for you to study.

The written test consists of 30 questions taken randomly from the possible questions. Most are multiple choice but there are a few 'fill-in-the-blank' questions requiring you to know certain figures. The test is by no means easy, as each time you answer a question incorrectly you lose points, and to pass you may not lose more than eight points in total. The fee for the written test in English is €40, but this will also include a separate test of German driving-related vocabulary. Don't forget to take your passport with you to prove your identity. If you fail the test at your first attempt, the fee for a re-test is much higher!

Only after you pass the written test are you permitted to take the road test. You can register to take both tests on the same day but, if you fail the written test, you aren't permitted to take the road test and your registration fee of around €100 will be forfeited. Once again, remember to take your passport with you for identification. The road test is administered by an examiner from the Technischer Überwachungsverein (TÜV), who sits in the rear right-hand seat and gives instructions. Your driving instructor sits in the front passenger seat, and, if necessary, can translate for you. The test takes place on public roads and lasts from 30 to 45 minutes. After you've finished, the examiner will tell you whether you've passed and, if not, why not.

Once you've passed, you're given a card stamped by the examiner as proof and must return to the *Führerscheinstelle* to obtain your German licence. An instructor or other representative from your driving school may accompany you if you require help. Take your passport to prove your identity and your foreign driving licence. As with a transcription (see above), either you will be given your old licence back with a stamp or it will be taken from you. You must pay a fee of €10 if you want a temporary licence valid immediately; otherwise you must wait around a week for your permanent licence to arrive.

If all this bureaucracy sounds too much for you, Germany has an excellent public transport system (see **Chapter 10**)!

Penalty Points

As in many other countries, if you infringe the rules of the road, you're liable for penalty 'points' on your licence. Once you've amassed a certain number of these, you must attend a course designed to correct your driving habits and, if continue to incur penalties, your licence can be withdrawn. **You should be particularly careful if you're driving with a foreign licence (see Driving Licence on page 234), as penalty points don't apply and you can have your licence withdrawn for even a fairly minor infringement**; there's no option to obtain a local licence and have the penalty points deducted from that, as in France, for example. See also **Drinking & Driving** on page 257.

CAR INSURANCE

Car insurance in Germany is strictly regulated by law and supervised by the state authorities. The following categories of car insurance are available:

- **Third Party** (*Haftpflichtversicherung*) – the most basic insurance, which covers you for the cost of third party damage or injury in accidents for which you're responsible. This cover is compulsory for all motor vehicles.

- **Part Comprehensive** (*Teilkasko*) – known in the UK as third party, fire and theft cover and similar to comprehensive cover in North America. It includes cover against fire, natural hazards (e.g. rocks falling on your car), theft, broken windscreen and damage caused by a collision with animals. You can usually choose to pay an excess (*Selbstbeteiligung*), e.g. the first €200 to €1,000 of a claim, in order to reduce your premium.

- **Fully Comprehensive** (*Vollkasko*) – as in the UK and equivalent to the combination of comprehensive and collision cover in North America. It covers everything included under *Teilkasko* and also damage to your own car for which you're responsible. Again you can pay an excess to lower your premium. Fully comprehensive cover is compulsory when you lease a car or purchase one on credit. Experts recommend this cover for new cars up to three years old, after which you need to consider whether it makes financial sense due to the high premiums.

To ensure that any passengers injured in your car are well provided for, extra passenger insurance (*Insassenversicherung*) is recommended. For a small extra charge this provides higher financial cover for passengers than is provided by third party cover.

Although EU regulations allow you to insure your car with any EU insurer (and therefore possibly save money), a vehicle licensed in Germany must be insured with an insurer 'registered' in Germany.

If you take out third party insurance with a German insurance company and wish to increase your cover to fully comprehensive later, you aren't required to do this through your third party insurance company but may shop around for the best deal.

Motorists insured in any EU country are automatically covered by third party insurance in all EU countries, as well as in the Andorra, Croatia, Cyprus, the Czech Republic, Hungary, Iceland, Liechtenstein, Norway, the Slovak Republic, Slovenia, Switzerland.

Green Card: Under recent EU regulations, possession of a international insurance certificate (commonly referred to as a 'green card', although in many countries it isn't green) is no longer compulsory within the EU. However, it's still wise to obtain one from your insurance company, as it can help prevent problems and delays in the event of an accident in another country, and if you're travelling outside the EU it may be obligatory. In most countries you need only inform your insurance company that you need a green card to prove your cover and they will provide one free of charge (some insurance companies provide them automatically). If you're insured in Britain, however, your insurance company may provide a free green card for a limited period only, e.g. 30 or 90 days. (This is to discourage the British from driving on the continent, where they're a danger to other road users – most of them don't know which side of the road to drive on!)

If you have fully comprehensive insurance, you should obtain a green card, as without one you will be insured only for third party damage. Note also that a green card must be signed to be valid.

Schutzbrief: Even if you're covered by your insurance policy when driving in other EU countries, an additional protection (*Schutzbrief*) can be well worth the extra cost. Costs vary quite widely but, for example, the ADAC *Schutzbrief* costs €33.23 and provides good coverage. The *Schutzbrief* is offered by most insurance companies and motoring clubs. The benefits offered vary between companies, but the most important is the return of your car to Germany after an accident or mechanical fault outside the country rendering it unfit to drive. The policy also provides for the transport of you or your passengers to hospitals in Germany if hospital treatment is necessary. Additional benefits may include breakdown assistance and a hire car while your vehicle is off the road. Check before buying, however, as the price of most new cars includes protection similar to that afforded by a *Schutzbrief* for the first three years.

Premiums & No-Claims Bonus

The cost of car insurance in Germany is high. Basic annual premiums vary with a number of factors – not least the insurance company. (The same car, driver and circumstances can attract quotes which differ by over 30 per cent.) A male driver who has a child at home will pay less (apparently fathers are calmer drivers than childless men), especially if he's a civil servant, but, if he drives a car which thieves have a propensity to steal (e.g. a VW Golf), it will cost him more. Premiums are also higher for cars with expensive replacement parts but lower in areas with a low theft rate. A novice driver will normally pay 25 per cent more than the standard rate, while someone with the best possible record – 18 or 21 years without a claim – will pay just 30 per cent of the standard rate. (You must normally have a year of accident-free before you qualify for the standard rate.) The average standard rate across the 20 most popular new cars for an average driver is currently around €300 for third party insurance, €500 part comprehensive and €650 fully comprehensive. Note that these rates are estimates only and the various discounts that you may be able to take advantage of, depending on your circumstances, can make a huge difference.

When buying car insurance (or any other kind of insurance), it's wise to shop around a number of insurance companies and compare rates and cover. Note that an insurer may offer excellent rates for certain classes of vehicle and/or drivers but may be uncompetitive for others. It's also sensible not to be too strongly influenced by discounts offered for such considerations as off-road parking because, although a company may offer a 10 per cent discount if you keep your car in a garage, another may have a lower rate even without a discount.

If you had a no-claims bonus with a previous insurer, this is usually taken into account by a German insurer, although German insurance companies aren't obliged to do so. However, you must obtain a letter from your previous insurer stating how many years you've driven without making a claim. In Germany, no-claims discounts apply only to third party and fully comprehensive cover. You're placed in a 'no-claims class' (*Schadenfreiheitsklasse* or *SF*) according to your number of years without a claim. For each claim-free year you're automatically moved into a higher SF class, which usually leads to a premium reduction. If you're involved in an accident for which you're deemed wholly or partly at fault, you may lose some or all of your no-claims bonus and can expect your premiums to rise significantly the following year.

High discounts take longer to accrue in Germany than in some other countries, and you may need 21 years claim-free driving to achieve the maximum discount of 65 or 70 per cent (compared with as little as five years in the UK, for example).

German drivers must complete a two-year probationary period after passing their test, and during this period they must pay the highest rates. The rate for third party cover can be as high as 240 per cent of the standard rate. If you're in this category, it pays to shop around, as there are huge differences in premiums between providers.

If you discover that you can obtain better rates in your particular classification from another insurance company, you're permitted to switch, but only at the end of your insurance year. If you're switching third party cover, you must give written notice a month in advance, while terminating part or fully comprehensive cover requires three months' notice. Notice can be sent by fax but a fax should be followed by a registered letter (*Einschreiben*) requiring a signature to indicate receipt by your insurance company. Your new insurance must begin no later than one day after the last day of your old insurance. Be sure to arrange this well in advance of the date you need the policy to commence, in order to allow time for billing and payment processing. Bills are usually sent out 30 days in advance to ensure that payment is received by the due date.

BREAKDOWN INSURANCE

Breakdown insurance (*Pannenservice*) in Germany and other European countries is provided by car insurance companies and German motoring organisations (see page 261), as well as by some car manufacturers. If you are or have been a member of a motoring organisation in another country, check with them before you move whether they have a reciprocal agreement with a German motoring club. If you've purchased a new car in Germany, you may already have breakdown cover, at least during the initial warranty period, which is provided through the manufacturer. Some credit card companies (e.g. American Express and Diners Club) offer this type of insurance for their members. If you have a company car, breakdown cover is usually provided by your employer. Some organisations also provide economical annual motoring policies for those who frequently travel abroad.

ROAD SIGNS

Germany generally adheres to the international road sign system. With a few exceptions, most signs conform to the following shapes and colours:

Design	Meaning
Red triangle	Warning
Red circle	Restriction
Blue circle	Requirement
Square/rectangle	Guidance
Diamond	Priority
Octagon	Stop

German road signs generally use words quite sparingly. Some of those you're most likely to come across are listed below:

German	English
Abblendlicht	Dipped headlights
Abstand halten	Keep your distance
Achtung	Warning
Alle Richtungen	All directions
Anfang	Start, beginning
An geraden Tagen	On even days (see **Parking** on page 253)
An ungeraden Tagen	On odd days (see **Parking** on page 253)
An Sonn und Feiertagen	On Sundays and holidays
Anleiger Frei	Except residents
Anschluss	Junction
Ausfahrt	Exit
Bauarbeiten/Baustelle	Roadworks
Belegt/Besetzt	Full
Durchfahrt verboten	No through traffic
Einbahnstrasse	One-way street
Einfahrt	Entrance
Fahrbahnwechsel	Change lanes
Gefahr/gefährlich	Danger/dangerous
Glatteisgefahr	Risk of ice
Grenze	Border
Grenze Kontrolle	Customs inspection
Haltestelle	Bus/tram stop
Keine Einfahrt	No entry
Landschaftsschutzgebiet	No parking
Licht einschalten	Switch on lights
Lieferverkehr frei	Delivery vehicles only
Links einbiegen	Turn left
Radweg kreuzt	Cycle path crossing

Raststätte	Service area
Rechts einbiegen	Turn right
Rechts fahren	Keep right
Sackgasse	Dead end, cul-de-sac
Seitenstreifen nicht befahrbar	Do not use hard shoulder
Sperrgebiet	Restricted area
Überholen verboten	No passing
Umleitung	Detour
Unfall	Accident
Verengte Fahrbahn	Road narrows
Vorfahrt/Vorrang	Priority (right of way)
Vorfahrt beachten	Give way (yield)
Vorsicht	Be careful
Zentrum	Town centre
Zufahrt frei	Access permitted

SPEED LIMITS

Maximum speed limits are posted on signs with red circular borders, while a blue circular sign with a number within it is a minimum speed limit. The latter most commonly show 60kph (37mph), the minimum speed on motorways. There are also blue square signs, which show recommended maximum speeds that aren't compulsory. Note that speed limits aren't always posted and it's up to motorists to know the prevailing speed limit in the absence of signs.

In cities and towns, the maximum speed limit for all vehicles is 50kph (31mph) unless otherwise posted. Many residential and school areas are designated as '30 Zone', where the maximum speed limit is 30kph (18mph); the 30kph limit remains in effect on all streets within the zone until you pass a 30kph sign with a diagonal line through it, indicating the end of the zone. Even more restrictive are the traffic calming zones found on some residential streets, which are indicated by blue signs showing an adult playing ball with a child in front of a house. Traffic here is limited to walking speed or no faster than 7kph (4mph).

Outside cities and built-up areas, the speed limit for vehicles under 3.5 tonnes without trailers on a normal two-lane road is 100kph (62mph). If a vehicle is being used to tow or is between 3.5 tonnes and 7.5 tonnes, the maximum permissible speed is 80kph (50mph), and above 7.5 tonnes the limit is 60kph (37mph).

Despite their reputation for being unlimited, you will frequently find zones on German motorways where speeds are regulated. Speed limits of between 90 and 120kph (56 to 75mph) are typical on stretches with constant heavy traffic, near urban areas, or with dangerous curves. Construction zones (*Baustelle*), which seem to be everywhere, can have limits as low as 60kph (37mph). There are also sections with night and wet-weather speed restrictions. Trucks and vehicles with trailers are limited to speeds of between 60 and 110kph (37 to 68mph). Generally speaking, trucks and trailers of less than 7.5 tonnes are permitted to go slightly faster than those above this weight. If there are no special exceptions, indicated by a sticker on the back of the vehicle, a truck or car with a trailer weighing less than 7.5 tonnes may travel at up to 80kph (50mph); those above this weight are limited to just 60kph (37mph).

Where there are no signs stating otherwise, drivers are advised (although not compelled) not to exceed 130kph (82mph). The absence of a general motorway speed limit isn't without controversy. The Green Party, with its strong environmental platform, has pushed for a national speed limit as low as 100kph (62mph) and claim that the air pollution created by high speed driving has caused widespread destruction of trees and forests. As a compromise, some limits have been set in heavily forested areas, but a limit remains unlikely. It appears that the government fears the reaction of the millions of citizens who own luxury cars and have a predilection for high-speed driving. No matter how highly petrol is taxed, it doesn't seem to persuade many drivers to slow down.

When fog reduces visibility on any type of road, the maximum speed is reduced to 50kph (31mph).

Speed Traps & Fines

Speed zones are patrolled by various methods. Some small towns use cameras controlled by a measuring system built into the road surface. More common are radar-linked cameras, which are found along various stretches of the motorway system, usually on the busiest sections, and indicated by a large yellow or grey box showing an orange circle and a flash sign. They can take a picture at any time of the day or night showing you and your car, together with a record of your speed, the date, the time and the location. There are various rules about the distances between cameras and the location on the road where the picture is taken and, if you can prove that the camera that took your picture fell outside these guidelines, the evidence will be invalidated (good luck!). As in most of Europe, the use of radar detectors by motorists is illegal.

Police also set mobile speed traps controlled by radar or laser, which have a range of several kilometres, depending on the road. Green and white police cars are typically used for this type of control, and traffic often slows down 'mysteriously' when such a vehicle is in their midst. Harder to spot are the unmarked cars used to set mobile traps in some cities.

Speeding fines range from €10 to €425 depending on the speed at which you were travelling, how far it was above the legal limit and whether you have any previous convictions. If you're stopped directly by the police (as opposed to having your picture taken by a camera), you may be asked to pay a fine of up to €35 on the spot; this applies particularly if you're a foreign visitor. If you don't have the money with you, you may be allowed to pay within a week, but you will probably be required to pay at least a deposit immediately. If you can't pay even this, your vehicle will be impounded (at an additional cost, of course). If you're caught significantly exceeding the speed limit, not only may the fine be the maximum of €425, but you can also lose your driving licence for a period – usually a month.

RULES OF THE ROAD

The following rules apply to driving in Germany generally:

- The Germans drive on the right-hand side of the road; it saves confusion if you do likewise!

- All motorists must carry a red breakdown triangle (*Warndreieck*), which must be stored inside the car within reach of the driver's seat and not in the boot (trunk), which could be damaged and jammed shut in an accident. If you have an accident or breakdown, the triangle must be placed behind the car at the edge of the road, at least 50m (160ft) away on secondary roads, 100m (325ft) on major roads and 200m (650ft) on motorways.

- You must also carry a spare bulb kit (*Ersatzglühbirnen*) and a first-aid kit (*Erstehilfekasten* or *Verbandkasten*). It's wise to buy the latter in Germany, as there are specific requirements for the kit's contents, e.g. they must include impermeable gloves to provide protection from HIV infection. Kits are available from the ADAC (see **Motoring Organisations** on page 261) and petrol stations.

- If you need to wear glasses or contact lenses when motoring, it will be noted on your German driving licence and you must always wear them and carry a spare pair.

- When motoring outside the country in which your car is registered, your vehicle must display either the new EU-style number plates, which incorporate a letter or letters showing the country of registration surrounded by the EU yellow stars, or a separate nationality sticker affixed to the rear. For vehicles registered in Germany the identification letter is D (for *Deutschland*). You can be fined on the spot for not displaying this, although judging by the number of cars which fail to do so, this law is seldom enforced. Cars must show only the correct nationality sticker and not an assortment.

- The wearing of seatbelts is mandatory and includes passengers in rear seats when seat belts are fitted. In the event of an accident, a German insurance company isn't obliged to pay the whole cost of damages when it appears that those injured weren't using their seat belts (benefits may be reduced by up to 50 per cent). The driver and each passenger who isn't wearing a seatbelt can be fined €30 if they're apprehended by the police. Children up to the age of 12 and shorter than 150cm (59in) are permitted to ride in a vehicle only in an approved safety seat that's appropriate for their size. They may not ride in the front seat if they can be accommodated in a back seat. The driver of a vehicle who is carrying children who aren't properly secured can be fined €40.

- All drivers must give way to police cars, ambulances and fire engines in emergencies (with flashing lights and wailing sounds) and trams and buses when they're leaving stops. You may also not pass a school bus when its red lights are flashing.

- On secondary roads without priority signs (a yellow diamond on a white background, used throughout most of continental Europe), you must give way to vehicles coming from your right. **Failure to observe this rule is the cause of many accidents.** The priority to the right rule usually also applies in car parks.

- In a situation where all motorists at a crossroads must give way to the motorist on their right, it isn't necessary for them to wait there forever. The drivers may agree among themselves who has priority, generally on the basis of who has been waiting the longest.

- Vehicles on a roundabout have priority and not those approaching it, who will be faced with a give way sign. Traffic flows anti-clockwise around roundabouts and not clockwise as in Britain and other countries where motorists drive on the left. Roundabouts aren't as popular in Germany as in some other countries, although they have become more common in recent years.

- Driving in bus, taxi or cycle lanes is prohibited unless it's essential to avoid a stationary vehicle or obstruction, and car drivers using these lanes must give priority to authorised users. For obvious reasons, you should stay clear of tramlines and outside the restricted area around them, marked by a white line.

- Dipped (low beam) headlights must be used in tunnels, fog, snowstorms, heavy rain and when visibility is less than 200m (640ft). It's illegal to drive only on side (parking) lights at any time. Front fog or spotlights must be fitted in pairs at a regulation height and should be used only when visibility is less than 50m (160ft). Rear fog lamps are officially permitted on the offside only, to prevent following vehicles mistaking two fog lamps for brake lights. **Although many cars are equipped with two, only the offside lamp should be fitted with a bulb.** A vehicle's hazard warning lights (both indicators simultaneously) may be used to warn other drivers of an obstruction, e.g. an accident or traffic jam.

- Headlight flashing has different meanings in different countries. In Germany, it's likely to mean 'Get out of my $*@!# way!'.

- Within a city or town border you must ensure that your vehicle can be seen when parked at night. This means you will be required to leave your car's side lights on if street lighting is inadequate or doesn't remain on all night – a red-and-white band around the post indicates a street lamp that doesn't stay on all night. (Many cars allow you to turn on your parking lights on one side of the car only, by using your direction indicator.)

- Traffic lights (*Verkehrsampel* or *Ampel*) are usually located on the same side of the road junction as the approaching traffic. They're often mounted above the road as well as to the left and right. The sequence of lights is: red, red and amber (yellow), green, amber, and back to red, as in the UK. Amber means stop at the stop line; you may proceed only if the amber light appears after you've crossed the line or when stopping may cause an accident. Red and amber together mean prepare to go, but you may not actually move off until the green light appears (although most drivers ignore this rule).

  Road junctions often have traffic lights marked with arrows showing the permitted directions of travel. If the lights at a junction show these arrows and you don't see a signal with an arrow for the direction you want to go, travelling in that direction may not be permitted; look for other signs. A full green signal without any arrows generally means you may travel straight ahead or make a right or left turn unless otherwise prohibited by a sign. Always give way to pedestrians and cyclists when turning left or right. There's often a flashing yellow signal with a pedestrian symbol to warn you that pedestrians have priority.

  Sometimes you will see a yellow and green left-pointing arrows (one mounted above the other) or just a green arrow on the far left of a road junction. These signals are used when a left turn can change from permitted (you may make the turn only if there's no other traffic) to protected (you have the right of way). When both green and yellow signals are used, a flashing yellow arrow indicates that a left turn is permitted but not protected and you must therefore proceed with caution. When the green arrow is on, the turn is protected. On its own a green arrow indicates a protected left turn. If the arrow is off, you must obey the signals for straight-through traffic.

Right turns on red aren't generally permitted in Germany. Such a turn is allowed only at junctions with a separate filter light to the right of the red stop light with a green arrow pointing right. If this is illuminated, you're allowed to make a right turn, but only after coming to a complete stop and giving way to other traffic and pedestrians.

Amber flashing lights are usually a warning to proceed with caution, for example, at roadworks and non-functioning traffic lights. They're also used to indicate speed restrictions, particularly on motorways. Many crossroads and road junctions have traffic lights that operate only during peak periods. At night and weekends (in particular) lights may be switched off or the amber light may be set to flash constantly as a general warning to drivers to look out for other road users. When lights aren't functioning, control is provided by the traffic signs mounted to the right of the traffic lights (when lights are functioning, they overrule any other signs). Signs also provide regulation in the rare event of a traffic light malfunction. A flashing amber light will usually be accompanied by a give way or stop sign. There's no flashing red signal in Germany.

Rather confusingly, many locations (usually at railway or tram crossings) have signals consisting of just red and amber lights. If you come upon one of these signals, obey it as you would any other traffic signal. When neither red nor amber is lit, ignore the signal and obey any other signs or signals displayed; in the absence of these, follow the default right-of-way rules

● When two vehicles meet on a narrow mountain road, the ascending vehicle has priority and the other must give way or reverse as necessary. On roads where passing is difficult or isn't permitted, slower traffic is required to pull over when possible to allow faster traffic to pass.

● On-the-spot fines (*Strafgeld*) can be imposed for traffic offences such as minor speeding (see **Speed Traps & Fines** on page 244), not being in possession of your driving licence or vehicle documents (see **Vehicle Documents** on page 223), failing to remove the ignition key when leaving a vehicle unattended, not using dipped headlights at night and parking infringements. The police are permitted to collect on-the-spot fines of up to €35.

● If you're annoyed by someone on the road, you'd be wise not to show it with finger or other hand signals. If it's proven that you showed a fellow driver a particular finger, you can be fined over €1,000. Tapping your forehead or passing your hand in front of your eyes is considered equally injurious and, if you call a police officer or other uniformed traffic official an idiot in German (or any other language that they can understand – Swahili is usually pretty safe), the fine is €1,500. (The German police has an official list of offensive phrases and corresponding fines – presumably derived from long experience of being insulted!)

- Although using your mobile phone when driving is permitted in Germany (though forbidden in neighbouring Austria and Switzerland), if it's proved that you caused an accident while on the phone, your insurance may provide only partial cover and the courts will reduce damages due to drivers who have suffered as a consequence.

- If you witness an accident, you must stop and give assistance.

- Motorists must signal before overtaking and when moving back into an inside lane after overtaking, e.g. on a motorway.

- Take care when crossing railway lines, particularly at crossings with no barriers, which can be very dangerous. Approach a level crossing slowly and STOP at the St. Andrew's Cross (*Andreas Kreuz*) as soon as the barrier or half-barrier starts to fall, or as soon as the red warning lights are illuminated or flashing or the warning bell is ringing, or when a train approaches! Your new Audi or Mercedes may be built like a tank, but it won't look so smart after a collision with a 70-tonne locomotive.

  A heavy vehicle that's slowing traffic is required to stop at the '300 metre' sign before closed level crossings, to allow other vehicles to overtake it.

- Be wary of cyclists and moped riders. It isn't always easy to see them, particularly when they're hidden by the blind spots of a car or are riding at night without lights (illegal, but it happens). When overtaking cyclists or motorbikes, give them a **WIDE** berth. By law there must be at least 150cm (59in) of space to the right of your vehicle when you overtake a cyclist or vehicle. If you knock a rider off his bike, you may have a difficult time convincing the police that it wasn't your fault.

- Drive at no faster than walking speed (*Schritt Tempo*) when passing a stationary tram or bus, particularly a school bus. Where passengers must cross a road to reach a pedestrian path, e.g. from a tram stop in the middle of the road, you must stop and give way to them.

- In a city or town you may not use your horn except when necessary to avoid a collision.

- Vehicles with a gross permitted weight of 7.5 tonnes or more are prohibited from public roads on Sundays and public holidays from midnight until 10pm, i.e. from midnight Saturday until 10pm Sunday evening.

The following regulations apply on German motorways:

- Vehicles with a maximum speed of less than 60kph (37mph) are prohibited from using motorways, as are bicycles, mopeds, and pedestrians.

- Overtaking on the right is prohibited. Slower vehicles must move to the right to allow faster traffic to pass. The left-hand lane is for overtaking only and as soon as you have completed your manoeuvre you must return to the right-hand lane.

- Stopping, parking, U-turns and reversing are prohibited, including hard shoulders and entrance and exit roads.

- In traffic jams, motorists must leave a gap between the left-hand lane and the adjacent lane for emergency vehicles. This is accomplished by traffic in the left-hand lane moving as far to the left as possible and traffic in the adjacent lane moving as far to the right as possible.

- It's illegal to run out of petrol on a motorway (you can be fined for doing so) or use full beam (high beams).

- You must stop for a pedestrian waiting at a crossing if he shows any intention of crossing the road. Pedestrian crossings that aren't at traffic lights are indicated by thick black stripes on the road known as zebra stripes (*Zebrastreifen*). It's prohibited to overtake on or near the zebra stripes or to park your car on them.

For further information on traffic rules and regulations, you can purchase a driver's education manual at a driving school or obtain a copy of the *Strassenverkehrsordnung*, which is distributed by the Federal Transport Ministry and available from book shops. See also **Pedestrian Road Rules** on page 262.

WINTER DRIVING

Most of Germany doesn't experience winter as severely as many of its neighbouring countries. Except in a few high altitude regions such as the Bavarian Alps and the Black Forest, driving conditions aren't usually hazardous for prolonged periods during winter. If you live in a city such as Frankfurt and don't need your car for commuting to work, you can probably make it through the winter without snow tyres (*Winterreifen* or *Schneereifen*), which have metal studs embedded in the rubber. However, most motorists who rely on their cars for regular transport fit snow tyres at the start of the winter. In some rural areas, roads aren't cleared of snow by the authorities, making snow tyres a necessity. Snow tyres may be used on vehicles of up to

3.5 tonnes from 1st November until 31st March; vehicles are restricted to 80kph (50mph). **If you have an accident on snow in a vehicle which isn't fitted with such tyres, you may be considered at fault if the other vehicles involved have snow tyres, irrespective of other circumstances.**

In towns and cities, many roads are salted or gritted during the winter. Due to the risk of corrosion, many motorists change to steel wheels in winter rather than fit snow tyres to their expensive alloy wheels. Shop around for the best buys in winter tyres and steel wheels, as prices vary considerably.

If you're driving in an area where there are signs showing a tyre covered by chains, this means that it's compulsory to fit snow chains (*Schneeketten*) in winter conditions. These signs are generally found only at the highest altitudes, but even if you don't see them it's wise to fit chains in mountainous areas in winter. If you will be driving in such regions, buy good quality snow chains and practise putting them on and removing them before you get stuck in the snow; even getting the container undone can be a trial when you have numb fingers, let alone fitting the chains. Note that vehicles with chains may not exceed 50kph (31mph).

In mountainous areas, the edges of many rural roads may be marked by two-metre high poles. These fulfil an essential function in areas with heavy snowfall, as without them even a light snowfall can obscure the edges of the road.

Skis carried on roof racks should have their curved front ends facing towards the rear of a car.

GERMAN DRIVERS

Ever since Carl Benz invented the first practical motor car in 1885, Germans have been in love with their cars and care for them like a member of the family (often better). Only Americans are more devoted to their cars, and it's said that depriving a German of his car is like amputating one of his limbs. On the other hand, the Germans, being more ecologically-minded than many other Europeans, are prepared to forego their cars for more environmentally-friendly means of transport, when this is practicable. The number of Germans who own bicycles and use them surprises most visitors. And it's a common sight to see them sitting on top of or tied behind their cars for use at a weekend or holiday destination.

Germans take it for granted that anyone driving in Germany will stick to the rules of the road, and the rigorous process of earning a driving licence contributes greatly to the general competence of motorists. Predictability is as important in this sphere as it is in every other in this country. Thus Germans drive precisely, if not always with any particular degree of courtesy or understanding beyond that specifically called for by the rules of the road.

Although Germans are proud of their driving skills, they come only fifth in the current ADAC league table of safe driving countries in the EU, top of the league being the British by a considerable margin. Despite the high speeds permitted on motorways, there are relatively few serious accidents on them. Most serious crashes occur on ordinary roads outside built-up areas, and speeding or impatience are frequently a prime cause. Sixty-four per cent of fatalities take place on such roads annually, although the number of minor traffic incidents is much greater within urban areas. Significantly, recent statistics from the Federal Office of Statistics show that the city-states of Hamburg and Bremen have annual road-death rates of 24 and 35 per million inhabitants respectively, whereas the rate for the almost entirely rural state of Mecklenburg-Vorpommern and similar states is over 200.

Patience isn't common among German drivers and, although sounding your horn is prohibited within city limits (except in an emergency), this regulation is overlooked by many. Aggressive drivers are identifiable by their fondness for tailgating and reminding you with their horn that the light may turn green at any second.

When driving on the motorway, you may feel that you've strayed onto a race track. Even if the traffic in the 'slow' lane is moving at the recommended maximum speed of 130kph (82mph), some drivers will constantly change lanes, often cutting in with no more than a few metres to spare. The one thing that preserves some kind of order in this potential chaos is the German respect for the 'car hierarchy'. In the outside lane, where tailgating is the norm, there's an unwritten code that a VW will yield to an Audi, which will yield to a Mercedes, which will yield to a BMW, while the kings and queens of the highway drive Porsches (German cars don't give way to foreign vehicles, whatever their make!).

MOTORCYCLES

To drive a motorcycles up to 50cc with a maximum speed of 45kph on German roads, you require a class M licence and must be at least 16 years old. Obtaining a licence involves attending a driving school, as you must pass a written rules test and prove to the satisfaction of an examiner that you're capable of riding the vehicle in a practical test. Most driving schools teach motorcycle as well as car driving, although specialist motorcycle driving schools exist. If you already have a class A1, A, or B driving licence, however, you can ride any vehicle in class M without obtaining further permission. Once you're authorised to take your bike on the road, you can obtain a number plate from an insurance company at the same time as paying your road tax and obtaining the mandatory third party insurance. In addition, you must wear a crash helmet at all times when riding.

There are two classes of driving licence for motorcycles over 50cc: A1 and A. To apply for the restricted A1 classification, you must be at least 16 and, if you're under 18, your bike must be capable of a speed no greater than 80kph (50mph). Irrespective of your age, you may not drive a motorcycle with an engine capacity of more than 125cc or an engine power exceeding 11kW.

If you wish to drive a larger motorcycle, you must have a class A licence. If you're aged 18 to 25, obtaining this is a two-stage process: first you must take instruction and pass written and road tests entitling you to ride motorcycles with an engine power not exceeding 25kW and a power-to-weight ratio of not more than 0.16kW/kg for two years after obtaining your licence; after two years' experience without any major accidents, you're permitted to ride any motorcycle. If you're over 25, you needn't undergo the two year 'probationary period' but may ride any bike after undertaking the required practical training and passing the corresponding test.

The registration procedure for a motorcycle is the same as for a car (see page 225). Your motorcycle must also pass a safety inspection and emissions test every two years (see page 227) and you must pay annual vehicle tax (see page 228).

Motorcyclists are required to use dipped (low beam) headlights at all times and must have at least third party insurance.

PARKING

Once you've successfully navigated the roads and reached your destination, you may find yourself with a new challenge: finding somewhere to park. In heavily populated residential areas and business districts, there's usually an acute lack of parking space. In many larger cities, areas are reserved for resident parking (as in other countries) during morning and afternoon rush hours. In order to park in places reserved for residents during these times, you must go to the town hall and prove your residence before you can buy a permit (*Anwohner Parkausweis*). Recent legal challenges to this system led to the courts declaring it illegal. This caused much annoyance, but the authorities simply introduced new regulations which effectively restored the status quo ante.

Parking is prohibited:

- on or within 5m (16ft) of a pedestrian crossing;
- within 10m (32ft) of stop and give way signs and traffic signals, if parking would obstruct other motorists' view of the sign;
- within 5m of a junction;
- within 15m (50ft) of a bus or tram stop;

- within 50m (160ft) of a railway level crossing outside a built-up area or within 5m of a pedestrian crossing in a built-up area;
- on a main road outside built-up areas;
- in front of entrances or exits;
- adjacent to a traffic island or roundabout;
- on railway level crossings (for obvious reasons!), taxi ranks and motorways;
- anywhere there's a 'No Parking' sign (a blue circle with a red border and a single red diagonal line).

Legal street parking is indicated by a blue sign with a white P, although wherever you park there must be at least 3m (10ft) between the middle of the street and your car. This may require that you park partly or completely on the pavement. When this is permitted (for vehicles up to 2.8 tonnes only), it's indicated by a sign with a P showing a car parked on two levels. There must be sufficient room left for pedestrians on the pavement. Parking is normally permitted only in the direction of the traffic. Cars may park on both sides of a one-way street, provided there's room for vehicles to pass between them.

Parking Vouchers, Discs & Meters

If the time permitted for parking on a street or in a car park is limited, parking will be controlled by one of the following methods:

- **Parking Voucher** (*Parkschein*) – When you see the sign *'Nur mit Parkschein'*, you must buy a parking voucher from a nearby machine (*Parkscheinautomat*) before leaving your vehicle. The most modern machines accept debit cards and money cards (see page 314); otherwise, a notice will tell you what coins or notes are accepted. Vouchers must be placed behind your windscreen where they can clearly be seen, and you must return to your car before the expiry time printed on the voucher.
- **Parking Disc** (*Parkscheibe*) – In shopping areas in particular, you will often see a sign requiring the use of a parking disc. These can be obtained free or for a nominal cost from petrol stations, motor accessory shops, news-stands and kiosks, and from the ADAC and other motoring organisations (see page 261). You must turn the dial to indicate the time of your arrival (you may round it up to the next half-hour) and put it behind your windscreen. The time by which you must leave is automatically shown on the disc.

- **Parking Meter** (*Parkuhr*) – These aren't as common as the other two methods and operate in the same way as in other countries. Coins must be put into the meter for the amount of time you wish to park. If a meter is defective, you're permitted to park with a disc. You may remain for the maximum period allowed by the meter.

If you're caught exceeding your allotted time, you will be fined between €5 and €40. It's illegal to return once your time has expired to insert more coins into a meter or to adjust your parking disc, penalties for which are similar to those for over-staying your time.

Car Parks

Blue-and-white parking signs not only indicate street parking, but are also used to give directions to off-street car parks (*Parkplatz*). A covered car park (*Parkhaus*) is designated by a similar sign with an inverted (and flattened) 'V' over the P to indicate a roof. In many larger urban areas there are electronic signs indicating which car parks and garages have spaces available (*frei*) and which are full (*besetzt*). These signs may also show the number of spaces available.

Most covered car parks are completely automated, whereby you pull up at the entry gate and take a time-stamped ticket, upon which the gate rises allowing you to enter. You take your ticket with you when you leave your car and when you're ready to leave you find a payment machine (*Parkenkasseautomat*), which is usually near the pedestrian entrance. Insert the ticket in the direction shown by the arrow and the amount payable is displayed. Once you've inserted your payment, your ticket is validated and returned to you. You then have around 15 minutes in which to return to your car and leave the garage. At the exit gate, you insert your ticket into the machine and the gate will open (you hope). Payment at the exit isn't possible and you will be extremely unpopular with the motorists behind you in the exit queue if you forget to pre-pay!

There are exceptions to this general principle, as some garages still have people who collect payments. Even so, they aren't at the exit gate but rather in a booth at a pedestrian entrance, so you still need to pay them and have your ticket validated before returning to your car.

Remember to check the opening hours if you're planning a late night, as some car parks close at 11pm or midnight and you will have to wait until the next morning to retrieve your car if you fail to return in time!

Using a car park usually costs around €3 or more for an hour (although additional hours are cheaper), particularly in areas where there's little or no on-street parking.

ACCIDENTS

Knowing the correct procedure in case of an accident is very important in Germany, particularly as motorists who see an accident are required by law to stop and render assistance. If you drive by the scene of an accident, fail to stop and are later reported to the police, you can be severely penalised. The basic procedure is as follows:

1. Stop and secure the scene of the accident.
2. Attend to the injured.
3. Call for help.

If you are involved in an accident, stop immediately and pull over to the side of the road if possible. Place your red warning triangle at the edge of the road at least 50m (160ft) behind your car on secondary roads, 100m (325ft) on major roads and 200m (650ft) on motorways. If necessary, e.g. when the road is partly or totally blocked, switch on your car's hazard warning lights and dipped (low beam) headlights and direct traffic around the hazard.

If anyone is injured, call immediately for emergency help. For an ambulance or the police, dial ☎ 110. If someone is trapped, or oil or chemicals have been spilt, dial ☎ 112 for the fire brigade. If someone has been injured more than superficially, the police must be notified. Don't move an injured person unless absolutely necessary, and don't leave him alone except to call for help. Cover him with a blanket or coat to keep him warm.

If there are no injuries and damage to vehicles or property is relatively minor, it isn't essential to summon the police to an accident scene. However, it's usually wise to call them and obtain an official report; even if the other parties involved admit that they were at fault, they could 'forget' what happened when questioned by an insurance company. They may also give you false information. However, don't sign any police statements unless you're certain you understand and agree with every word.

Always use your insurance company form (*Unfallbericht*) to report any accident involving your vehicle. Don't forget to sign it and to obtain a new accident form.

Under no circumstances should you admit guilt, even if you know you did something wrong. Restrict yourself to telling what happened, and let the police and insurance companies decide who was at fault. **If you admit responsibility, either verbally or in writing, it can absolve your insurance company from responsibility from paying a claim under your policy.**

If the other driver has obviously been drinking or appears incapable of driving, call the police immediately!

If either you or the other driver(s) involved decides to call the police, avoid moving any of the vehicles unless they present a hazard. In such a case, try to record the positions of the vehicles before you move them. If there's a camera available take pictures; otherwise make drawings or, if you can find some chalk, mark their positions on the road. The accident form from your insurance company will require drawings of all the vehicles involved, so it's wise to keep a record somewhere other than in your memory.

Check whether there are any witnesses to the accident and try to obtain their names and addresses, making a particular note of those who support your version of events. Note the registration numbers of all vehicles involved and their drivers' names, addresses and insurers. In return you will be expected to give your details to any other drivers involved.

If you damage a parked car or other property, leaving a note with your name and address isn't sufficient. You can wait a reasonable amount of time for the other party to return, but if they don't you must note the registration number and the damage and report it to the nearest police station.

If you're the victim of a hit-and-run accident, you should report it to the local police immediately and, if possible, summon them to the accident scene before moving your car. They will inspect your vehicle and take photographs and paint samples, which will help them to catch the culprit as well as assisting you with your insurance claim.

DRINKING & DRIVING

The laws regarding drinking and driving are taken just as seriously as the beer in Germany. If you want to go out and enjoy a few drinks, it's wise to have someone with you who will remain sober to drive you home or to use public transport. Riding a bicycle isn't an acceptable alternative; if you're caught riding a bike on public roads while over the legal limit for driving, your driving licence can be taken away.

The legal limit in Germany is 0.5mg per 100ml of blood and the penalties for driving while under the influence are severe. Random breath tests can be performed by the police at any time and those found in violation of the law can lose their licence for a first offence and also receive a high fine. If you're stopped for a random check, even without driving erratically, you can be fined €250 and receive penalty points on your driving record (see page 238) if you're over the limit. You can also be banned from driving for a month.

If you have 1.1mg (or more) of alcohol per 100ml of blood, you can lose your licence for three months, in addition to more points and a higher fine. If you're driving erratically or are involved in an accident, the penalties are even higher. **The courts may decide that alcohol was a factor in an accident even when a driver's blood alcohol content was below the legal limit, and anything above 30mg is likely to put you at fault.**

If you have an accident while under the influence of alcohol, it will be expensive. Your insurance company isn't obliged to pay for damage to your car or any other vehicle that you damage. You can also be held personally liable for all medical expenses and property damage resulting from an accident. There will also be a fine, starting at several thousand euros, and if you're unable to pay it you may find yourself facing a jail sentence of up to five years!

Driving under the influence of 'recreational' drugs also isn't taken lightly. If you're apprehended driving with traces of marijuana, hashish or cocaine in your system, your licence will be withdrawn for at least a year. Penalty points will also be allocated to your driving record, fines imposed and you will need to undergo a psychological examination before you receive your licence back.

It goes without saying that it doesn't make any sense to do anything but stay sober in Germany if you want to drive, or have alternative transport if you want to indulge!

CAR CRIME

Car theft is a significant risk in Germany, with well over 100,000 cars stolen annually. In addition, there are hundreds of thousands of incidences of items being stolen from parked cars. Of the stolen cars, some two-thirds are recovered, but usually not before they've been burnt out or badly vandalised. The police recommend that you observe the following rules, irrespective of where you park your car:

- Never leave handbags, cameras, mobile phones, wallets, cash or other items of obvious value visible to those passing by your car.
- Be sure to lock your car when parking in quiet areas, such as back-street car parks or deserted side streets.
- Never leave your car windows or sun-roof open.
- When stopping overnight at a hotel, empty your boot of all luggage and try to park in a brightly lit or secure area.
- If you have an alarm or other security system, get into the habit of turning it on each time you park your car.

FUEL

Unleaded (*Bleifrei*) petrol and diesel (*Diesel*) are available at all garages in Germany. (Leaded has been phased out.) Typical current fuel prices are:

- Diesel – €0.90 per litre;
- Super (*Super Bleifrei*), 95 octane – €1.10 per litre;
- Super Plus (*Super Plus Bleifrei*), 98 octane – €1.15 per litre.

Depending on where you fill up, the price of petrol varies by up to ten cents per litre. As you would expect, petrol stations on motorways are the most expensive. The best places to fill up tend to be petrol stations associated with supermarkets, and, of course, in areas where there's lots of competition.

Although diesel fuel is much cheaper than petrol, vehicle taxes for diesel cars are higher (see page 228).

Petrol stations in Germany are usually self-service; if you find one of the few exceptions, you will pay extra for the pleasure of sitting in your car watching someone else fill the tank and splash petrol on his hands and shoes. Opening hours vary, but they aren't controlled like those of shops. Some are open from 7 or 8am until 10 or 11pm, although many are open 24 hours a day, so when filling late at night you can take the opportunity to buy grocery items. Many petrol stations are more interested in selling you goods (at high mark-ups) than petrol, on which they make the bulk of their profits.

Payment is usually made after petrol has been purchased and to a person rather than a machine. Petrol pumps that accept credit cards are still rarer in Germany than in neighbouring European countries. As long as a petrol station is open, it's usually manned by at least one person. When you've filled your tank, you go to the cashier and tell him the number of your pump. Unless otherwise stated, garages accept payment in cash or by debit card. Most petrol stations accept credit cards, although you shouldn't rely on paying by credit card in rural areas. If a garage is in an area with a high risk of robbery (especially after dark), you may be required to pay in advance; if you pay in cash, no change may be given, as all money is deposited directly into a safe (which the attendant is unable to open) to prevent robberies.

If you're worried about running out of petrol, you're permitted to carry up to five litres with you, but only in an approved petrol can. However, different rules apply in other countries, so check with a German motoring club before taking a can of petrol over the border. **It's illegal to run out of fuel on a motorway, for which you will be fined if caught.**

The main operator of motorway petrol stations is the Tank & Rast company, which has over 700 outlets across the country offering (as the name suggests) fuel and relaxation. A free booklet, which includes a map showing the location of all services, is available at motorway service areas or from Autobahn Tank & Rast GmbH & Co KG, Andreas-Hermes-Str. 7-9, D-53175, Bonn (🖳 www.tank.rast.de – an English-language version is available).

GARAGES & SERVICING

As in most other western countries, car dealers, private garages and petrol stations with workshops all offer servicing and repairs. If you require only a simple oil change, tune-up, new exhaust or tyres or other minor service, there are numerous places you can take your car with little or no advance notice. Pit Stop is one of the most popular chains and has outlets in cities and towns throughout Germany. Don't expect to find a garage open on a Sunday, but otherwise opening hours are usually generous. Many service stations open as early as 7am (or you can drop your car off the evening before) and closing time is usually around 6.30pm, although special arrangements can usually be made. Many garages also open on Saturday mornings.

Prices vary, as does the quality of service, and it will pay to obtain recommendations if it isn't an emergency. Ensure that you obtain an estimate for any work to be done before you approve it, or you may be in for a nasty surprise when the bill is presented. Main dealers are typically the most expensive, but their work is guaranteed, although other reputable garages also offer a guarantee and can be much cheaper. Be wary of using 'back street' garages unless they're highly recommended by someone you can trust, as the money you save may well be exceeded by the amount you need to spend on repairing their work later.

If you need a car while yours is being serviced or repaired, most garages will hire you one for a nominal fee or make arrangements with a local car hire company.

Recent EU regulations forbid dealers to insist that cars they've sold are serviced by them (in order for the warranty to remain valid) and in theory this applies in Germany. In practice, however, the government has vehemently opposed this ruling and it may be slow to be implemented, so you're advised to check with your dealer whether you may have your car serviced elsewhere.

ROAD MAPS

Good road maps are readily available in Germany and reasonably priced. Falk publishes an excellent hard-cover atlas and CD which covers all of Germany and sells for around €25. The most popular street atlases are those published by Shell. The average hard-cover Shell edition sells for around €15, with soft-cover versions available from €7 to €13. The ADAC motoring club (see **Motoring Organisations** below) provides maps at nominal prices for anywhere in Germany and also many other countries.

Street maps and atlases can be purchased at book shops, newsagents and kiosks everywhere, while there are shops specialising in maps in the major cities. Other sources of maps include your telephone book, where you will find local street maps with indexes, and tourist information offices.

MOTORING ORGANISATIONS

There are two main motoring organisations or clubs in Germany – the Allgemeiner Deutscher Automobil Club (ADAC) and the Automobilclub von Deutschland (AvD) – plus a few smaller organisations, such as Auto Club Europa (ACE). The ADAC, which celebrated its 100th anniversary in 2003, is by far the biggest and best known, and provides products and services extending well beyond the usual road and travel necessities. It has a large network of shops selling road maps and motoring accessories, and also maintains driving practice areas for learners and foreigners who need to take practical driving tests. The ADAC also provides translations of foreign licences. Many services aren't, however, included in the basic membership fee, although members are usually entitled to a discount. Basic services offered by ADAC, AvD and the other smaller clubs include:

- emergency roadside assistance;
- lock-out service;
- estimation of repair costs and verification of repairs/servicing and bills;
- travel bureau and ticket office services;
- hotel planning and reservations;
- road maps, tour guides and tourist information;
- advice on buying cars and valuations of used cars;
- car insurance;
- travel insurance.

There are two types of ADAC membership: standard (costing €37.84 per year) and *Plusmitgliedschaft* (€71.07), the latter including its invaluable *Schutzbrief* (see below). If you want other family members to be covered, they need their own membership, although discounts are provided. Basic annual membership of the AvD costs €54. Entitlements vary with the organisation and, if you want anything more than basic emergency breakdown cover, it pays to shop around and compare the benefits offered.

Basic membership of the ADAC covers roadside assistance in Germany up to €154 and towing away without any monetary limit. Its higher category of membership provides you with more extensive cover and assistance outside Germany through reciprocal agreements with other national breakdown services.

Even if you aren't a member, a German motoring organisation will come to your rescue if you call for help via the *Strassenwacht* emergency breakdown service. To summon assistance you go to the nearest emergency phone, indicated by arrows along motorways and other main roads, pick up the receiver and tell the operator you require assistance and which (if any) motoring organisation you belong to. If you're a member, have your card handy and be ready to give your membership number. If there isn't an emergency phone nearby, the number to call is ☎ 222-222 on a mobile for the ADAC. The number to call from a fixed line is ☎ 0180-2222 222. The equivalent for the AvD is ☎ 0800-9909 909.

German motoring organisations offer a comprehensive international travel insurance known as a protection letter (*Schutzbrief*), which covers you against most likely travel problems. The ADAC version costs €33.23. It covers repairs, removal of a damaged vehicle, emergency car-hire, the train fare home, and repatriation by air of the sick and injured. This protection could be indispensable if you do a lot of driving in other European countries. The ADAC provides legal advice regarding accidents and other motoring-related problems, with the initial consultation free to members. You can purchase motoring legal protection (*Rechtschutz*) for around €46 per year, which covers your legal costs in the event of an accident. See also **Car Insurance** on page 238.

The main motoring club head offices are listed below (check your phone book for local branches):

● Allgemeiner Deutscher Automobil Club (ADAC), Am Westpark 8, D-81373 Munich (☎ 089-76760, 💻 www.adac.de);

● Automobilclub von Deutschland (AvD), Lyoner Str. 16, D-60528 Frankfurt (☎ 069-66060, 💻 www.avd.de);

● Auto Club Europa (ACE), Schmidener Str. 227, D-70374 Stuttgart (☎ 0711-53030, 💻 www.ace-online.de).

PEDESTRIAN ROAD RULES

The following rules apply to pedestrians (*Fussgänger*) in Germany:

● You must wait for a green light before crossing the road at a crossing with a pedestrian traffic light, irrespective of whether there's any traffic. You can be fined €5 for failing to do so or for crossing the road dangerously, although it isn't likely.

● Pedestrian crossings that aren't at traffic lights are indicated by thick black stripes on the road known as zebra stripes (*Zebrastreifen*). Although motorists must (and in Germany usually do) stop when you're waiting at a crossing if you show any intention of crossing the road, you should never assume that a car will stop.

If an accident results from your crossing the street without proper regard to traffic controls, you're liable for any resulting damages and, not surprisingly, you can take out special liability insurance (*Haftpflicht*) against this eventuality.

MOTORING ABROAD

If you're travelling across the border into other European countries, you should make yourself aware of the rules and regulations that apply. The following general hints and tips are designed to help you survive a trip across the border:

- Don't forget your car registration and insurance papers, passports, identity cards, visas, children and inoculation certificates for pets. Make sure you have sufficient local currency for petrol, road tolls, border insurance, food, fines, etc.. If you're planning to use Swiss motorways, you must buy a pass costing around €25.

- Check that you have valid insurance. A green card (see page 239) is compulsory for Andorra, Bulgaria, Poland and Rumania and strongly recommended for Greece, Italy, Portugal, Spain and Turkey. A green card is available at no extra cost when you're insured with a German insurance company.

- Holiday or travel insurance (see page 298) and breakdown insurance (see page 241) is recommended when travelling abroad. If you're a member of a German motoring organisation (see page 261) you will usually be covered when travelling elsewhere in Europe through reciprocal agreements with national breakdown services. When motoring in some countries, it's wise to have legal protection insurance.

- Note that the procedure following an accident (see page 256) isn't the same in all European countries, although most western European countries use the standard European accident report form (*Unfallbericht*) provided by German insurance companies. As a general rule, it's wise to call the police for anything other than a minor accident. **In eastern European countries you should always call the police.**

- Check that your car complies with local laws and that you have the necessary equipment, e.g. warning triangles, first-aid kit, fire extinguisher, petrol can (plastic cans are forbidden in some countries) and headlight beam deflectors (for the UK and Ireland). Check the latest regulations with a German motoring organisation.

- Make sure that you have sufficient spares such as bulbs, fan belt, fuses, and clutch and accelerator cables, particularly if you're driving a rare or 'exotic' model (e.g. most American and British cars).

- Seat belts must be worn in all European countries. In Finland, Norway and Sweden, dipped headlights (low beam) must be used at all times.

- In the UK and Ireland traffic drives on the left. Fortunately the majority of British and Irish motorists are quite civilised and most foreigners don't find it a problem (but you must adjust your brain and lights).

- If your car doesn't have an alarm system or immobiliser fitted, use a visible lock, e.g. a for the steering wheel or gear stick. This may not deter a determined thief but will usually discourage a casual joy rider or opportunist. In some countries, thieves will queue up to steal your shiny new BMW, Mercedes or Porsche.

- A good map will come in handy, particularly when you're lost.

- If you're planning a long journey, a mechanical check-up for your car is recommended, particularly if it's some time since its last service.

- The maximum legal blood/alcohol level is lower in some countries than in Germany, and the beer may be stronger. The permitted level usually varies from 0.2 to 1mg of alcohol per 100ml of blood, although in some countries it's zero!

- An international driving permit (IDP) or a translation of your German or foreign driving licence is necessary in some countries (check with a German motoring organisation).

When driving anywhere, **NEVER** assume that you know what another motorist is going to do next. Just because he's indicating left doesn't mean he's actually going to turn left; in some countries he's more likely to be turning right, stopping or about to reverse and in many countries motorists make turns without any indication at all! Don't be misled by any semblance of road discipline and clearly marked lanes. Try to be courteous, if only in self-defence, but don't expect others to reciprocate.

The most dangerous European countries to drive in include Portugal, Spain and Italy, but that doesn't mean you're safe in any other country. Driving in some European cities can be totally chaotic. If in doubt about your ability to cope with the stress or the risks involved, you'd be wiser to fly or take a train and use public transport on arrival.

12.

HEALTH

The German health care system is widely acknowledged as being among the best in the world, although it may not be as good as it once was. It provides near-universal cover and ensures that almost everyone, irrespective of income or social status, has the same access to health care. Statistics underline its excellence. The infant mortality rate in Germany is five deaths in the first year for every 1,000 live births, one of the lowest in the world and down from 34 as recently as 1960. Thirty-seven mothers died in childbirth in total in 1999 in contrast to 1,030 in that same year of 1960. Average life expectancy at birth is now 74.7 for a man and 80.7 for a woman, figures exceeded by very few other nations.

The system is, however, an enormous financial drain on the government and private industry (which foots part of the bill) as well as individuals, and cost-cutting reforms have been constantly mooted – and occasionally implemented – over the last 25 years. One such reform was recently made and more are in the pipeline or being urgently discussed in parliament, as the financial situation makes this unavoidable. (A proposal to levy a fee of €20 for each visit to the doctor, in order to discourage abuse, was deemed too radical by the present Health Minister!)

Such reforms and proposed reforms inevitably meet stiff resistance from a population unaccustomed to paying anything for their health and medical needs other than through their health insurance (see page 289). As in most western countries, a declining birth rate has unbalanced the system so that a decreasing number of workers must pay for the extended life spans of an increasing number of retirees. Employee contributions have now reached 14.5 per cent of gross income, with employers paying the same amount, and further reforms are inevitable. Nevertheless, for the time being at least, Germany has a surplus of hospitals and medical personnel, and waiting lists for treatment are rare.

One area in which Germans are surprisingly less than health-conscious is smoking, with over 28 per cent of the population as a whole and a massive 37 per cent of those aged 17 to 40 regularly inhaling the weed. Non-smoking areas are provided in a only few restaurants, and the practice is still uncommon. For a smoke-free meal out you must head for somewhere expensive or an American fast food franchise such as McDonald's or Burger King. You will notice many people ignoring 'Rauchen Verboten' signs, and polls show that the great majority of Germans are opposed to legislation banning smoking in public places. Nevertheless, such sentiments didn't hinder the recent imposition of ferocious tax rises on cigarettes – partly inspired, it must be said, by the need to replenish health service coffers, although the government is well aware of the need to place far more emphasis on preventative rather than curative medicine.

Paradoxically, despite their general salubrity, most Germans are regularly anxious about their health. They worry about most medical problems known (and many unknown) to modern man and visit the doctor frequently, fully covered by their health insurance. (The average number of visits made in a year by each citizen is around 11.5, and a recent reform proposal to reduce benefits for those who didn't visit their GP more than 12 times in a year met with understandable derision.) An employee need only inform his employer that he has a doctor's appointment to be allowed time off work to attend, although current job market uncertainties are making employees less inclined to take advantage of the system. Employees are generally entitled to unlimited paid sick leave provided their doctor provides them with a sick note (*Krankmeldung*) stating that they're unable to work (see **Sick Leave** on page 58).

Perhaps the biggest health mystery in Germany is a 'disease' unknown to the rest of the world called *Kreislaufstörung*. This roughly translates as 'circulatory disorder' and covers everything from mild headaches and tiredness to heart problems. In some cases it can also mean 'I don't feel like going to work today but don't want to use any of my annual leave'. Since the disease is so vague and all-encompassing, some Germans claim a form of it regularly, and it's often difficult to determine how serious the underlying health problem is – "if any!" the sceptic might add.

EMERGENCIES

In a life-threatening emergency, you should call for an ambulance (dial ☎ 112 from anywhere in Germany), which will take you to the nearest hospital accident and emergency (A&E) department. Germany has a public ambulance service, which is efficient, and you will normally be attended to without delay at A&E. If necessary, ambulance crew will begin treatment en route and, if you're able to, you should give them details of your health insurance (see page 289).

If you need a doctor outside regular surgery hours, you should first try to contact your family doctor (keep the number by your phone). If the surgery is closed, there should be a recorded message telling you how to reach your doctor or a locum or service standing in for the practice. This of course will be in German, so it's wise to ask in advance how a practice handles emergencies. If you don't have a family doctor or yours cannot be reached, there are two possible courses of action:

● Call the 'Emergency Doctors Service' (*Ärztlicher Notdienst* or *Ärztlicher Bereitschaftsdienst*), a free 24-hour public service. The number for your service will be at the front of your yellow pages. The GPs in a district usually take it in turns to act as emergency doctor (*Notarzt*) at night. They will offer advice and, if necessary, visit you or send an ambulance.

- You can go to the A&E department of a nearby hospital, but it's wise to call the Emergency Doctors Service (see above) for advice first.

When visiting a hospital or clinic, take proof of your health insurance, although you're unlikely to be refused treatment if it's urgently required.

If you have an existing medical condition which cannot easily be seen or recognised, e.g. a heart condition, diabetes, a severe allergy (e.g. to penicillin) or epilepsy, or you have a rare blood group, you may wish to join the Medic-Alert scheme. Medic-Alert members wear an internationally recognised identification bracelet or necklace. On the back of this are engraved brief details of your medical condition, your membership number and a 24-hour emergency phone number. When you're unable to speak for yourself, doctors, police or paramedics can obtain vital medical information from anywhere in the world by phoning this number. Medic-Alert is a registered charity. Members pay for the cost of the bracelet/necklace (in the UK £30) and a small annual fee. For more information contact the Medic-Alert Foundation, 1 Bridge Wharf, 156 Caledonian Road, London N1 9UU, UK (☎ 020-7833 3034).

If you have a dental emergency or your pet is in dire need of medical attention, there are emergency numbers in your yellow pages for these services, listed under *Zahnärztlicher Notfall Dienst* (dental emergencies) and *Tierärztlicher Notdienst* (animal emergencies).

ACCIDENTS

If you have an accident resulting in an injury, either to yourself or a third party, inform the following as required:

- A doctor if treatment is necessary;
- The police;
- Your accident insurance company;
- Your employer (if you have an accident at work, report it to your manager or boss as soon as possible).

An accident report form must be completed for all accidents where medical treatment is necessary and which result in a claim on your insurance (e.g. car, health or third party liability). Your health insurance policy will normally pay out for medical treatment only if you remain in Germany, and journeys abroad while undergoing a course of treatment as the result of an accident may require the consent of your insurance company.

HOSPITALS & CLINICS

Hospitals are denoted by the international sign of a white 'H' on a blue background. To find a list of hospitals in your area, look in your phone book under the heading *Krankenhäuser* (the singular is *Krankenhaus*). Hospital care is excellent in Germany, but you may notice a number of differences in admission and other procedures from those you're used to in your home country. Your family doctor will request a bed for you, but your care will be taken over by a doctor at the hospital and you shouldn't expect to see your GP during your hospital stay. Either your medical records will be transferred to the hospital or, if you're undergoing a regular operation, you will be given your records to take with you and hand over during registration.

The kind of room you're allocated depends on whether you're enrolled in the compulsory state insurance plan or have private insurance (see pages 289 and 295). A privately insured person is usually assigned to a single or double room, while those with state insurance will usually share with two or three others. You can request a single room, but you're required to pay the extra cost yourself.

As a consequence of the growing concern over the cost of state organised health care in Germany, patients are expected to pay a small percentage of hospital bills. Patients over 18 must pay a fee of €9 per day for the first 14 days of their stay in any given year (to a maximum of €126), after which there's no further charge. They're also required to pay the first €13 of the cost of travel for necessary medical treatment. People on low incomes are exempt from these charges.

Some insurance companies are also ending the widespread practice of admitting patients the day before surgery, by refusing to pay the bill for the extra night unless it's shown to be necessary. Nevertheless, Germans stay in hospital longer than people in many other countries.

Because German doctors aren't usually inclined to discuss treatment with their patients, it may pay you to read up on your condition and possible treatment alternatives before entering hospital. If you don't speak fluent German and cannot find any useful books in English, you may wish to check the Internet, where there's a wide range of English-language sites, including American Virtual Hospital (⌨ www.vh.org) and UK Patient (⌨ www.patient.co.uk). German doctors will, of course, answer your questions or address any concerns you may have, but you must know what to ask. If language is a problem, you may also wish to take a German-English dictionary with you. Most doctors can speak at least some English, but nurses and other hospital personnel may not, although there will usually be someone around to interpret if there's a major problem.

Germans tend to be less concerned about privacy than most English-speakers. Gowns aren't issued during examinations, and there are usually no curtains surrounding beds. Be sure to bring a night-dress or pyjamas, dressing gown and slippers, and also come prepared with towels and toiletries. Don't, however, bring too many things, as you will have only a small locker in which to store them.

Visiting hours vary with the hospital, the level of care that you require, and whether you're in a private room. In a hospital ward, visiting hours are usually from 2 to 8pm. Small children aren't welcome as visitors. If a child must go into hospital, a parent can usually spend the night. A telephone on which you can make outgoing calls is normally provided next to the bed, but to activate it you must buy a card from a machine in a public area on your floor. This can cost anywhere from €10 to €25 and there's a fee for just turning the phone on, after which charges for calls are deducted from the card. If you have unused time, the card machine will refund your money when you leave.

Meals and meal times in hospitals conform to the usual German practice, breakfast consisting of rolls or bread with jam, meat or cheese. (Expect to be woken up at crack of dawn.) Large hot meals are served at lunch time and supper is a simple meal based on bread or rolls. There's usually a choice of menus and you may also keep your own food and drinks by your bed, although if you're on a special or restricted diet this will determine what and when you're permitted to eat or drink.

DOCTORS

Just as you would be careful when selecting a doctor (*Arzt*) in your home country, the same care should be taken in Germany. There are many excellent German doctors, although not all of them will be right for you. In general, German doctors aren't particularly open to discussion and questions about your treatment, so if this is important it may take some searching before you find someone who meets your needs. There's a chronic surplus of doctors – one for every 280 inhabitants – so finding someone willing to take the trouble to meet your needs shouldn't be impossible.

If possible it's preferable to obtain recommendations from colleagues or friends. If you don't know anyone you can ask, start by checking at your consulate or in guides published by local English-speaking organisations. Doctors are listed by their specialities in the yellow pages under *Ärzte*. Many if not most doctors in Germany have at least a basic level of English, but this is far less the case with nurses and nursing assistants. If this is a significant factor for you, check before making an appointment.

The health care system allows you to visit any doctor you choose, which means you may consult any doctor or specialist who will accept you as a patient. However, it can be difficult to obtain an appointment with certain specialists without a referral from a general practitioner (*Praktischer Arzt*). If you're unhappy with the diagnosis or treatment given by a doctor, you're free to consult another to obtain a second opinion.

Once you've found a doctor you like, it's preferable to visit him regularly in order to establish a relationship with him and for the convenience of having your medical records in one place. Most people have a regular or 'house' doctor (*Hausarzt*).

Doctors' surgeries are usually open during normal office hours, with perhaps one day a week when there's a late afternoon or early evening surgery. City doctors usually have longer surgery hours than those in small towns and villages, where hours may be more sporadic. When you call a doctor's surgery for an appointment, you're usually given an appointment time (*Termin*) or occasionally told to come any time during surgery hours (*Sprechstunden*). The latter operate on a first-come-first-served basis but there's usually no difficulty in obtaining an early appointment.

If you have German health insurance, your insurer will issue you with a plastic ID card, which you must sign and take with you when you visit a doctor. There's a micro-chip in the card, where your medical data are stored and, when you register, the doctor's receptionist will enter these into a computer. If you're enrolled in the statutory health insurance programme, there are currently no charges made to you when you visit a doctor, although a standard charge of €10 per visit will be introduced early in 2004. **Note, however, that some doctors don't accept payment via the state system, so you should check when making an appointment.** Signs outside the surgery will also indicate this; look for '*Kassenarzt*' or '*Alle Kassen*', which will indicate that patients from all the public health insurance providers or *Krankenkassen*, are accepted. Absence of this indicates either that the doctor is a high-flying specialist or that he hasn't been able to obtain the official blessing of the *Krankenkassen* because the maximum number of doctors they will accept in any district has been reached. It doesn't necessarily indicate a higher quality of service.

If you're treated by anyone other than a *Kassenartzt*, you will receive a bill that you must pay yourself, and the state health insurance scheme won't reimburse you. If you have private insurance, you must still pay and then submit the bill to your insurance company for reimbursement.

COMPLEMENTARY TREATMENT

Complementary medicine has a long tradition in Germany, although it certainly isn't accepted as an alternative to regular medical care by any more than a few. Nevertheless, you may find the surgeries of both a doctor and an alternative practitioner (*Heilpraktiker*) in the same building, and it isn't unknown for someone who has first consulted the latter to move on to the former (or vice versa). A small but growing number of GPs offer complementary therapies in addition to conventional medicine. Check in your local yellow pages, where these services are listed under the doctor's name. Doctors (and their specialisms) are also listed on the Internet (🖳 www.netklinik.de/aerzte-liste/index.htm).

The most widely available alternative therapy in Germany is homeopathy, which should come as no surprise given that it was founded by a German doctor, Samuel Hahnemann (1755–1843). Homeopathy operates on the controversial principle that a substance that's toxic in large quantities can act as a remedy in smaller measures – rather like a vaccination. Approval for homeopathic treatment in Germany dates back to a law passed in 1939, allowing a homeopath to practise in conjunction with an authorised medical doctor, provided he has passed a qualifying examination. Obtaining a diploma is still necessary to establish a homeopathic practice in Germany, which is awarded after an examination at the end of a two-year training course.

Standard health insurance – whether state or private – doesn't cover the cost of treatment by a homeopath or other alternative practitioners. If, however, such a practitioner recommends or starts a treatment that's subsequently taken over by a GP, your insurance may cover the cost. (Some *Kassen* are more inclined to do this than others, so it's best to find out before choosing one – see page 289.) If you wish to turn to alternative medicine, there can therefore be a considerable financial advantage in registering with a doctor who offers such therapies, rather than going to an alternative practitioner who isn't medically qualified. Some doctors however, might offer alternative therapies despite limited knowledge of them. If this is important to you, check before making an appointment.

Spas

The spa process is more of a ritual in Germany than in any other country in the world. *Spa* is a German word. Going to 'take the cure' was originally made popular by noble families of central Europe, and the German bourgeoisie of the 19th century were behind the construction of the majority of spa resorts still found in Germany today. They were built around the dozens of mineral springs that had been discovered on German soil, the waters of which were thought to provide cures for arthritis, gout, hypertension and gynaecological problems. Today, there are over 300 health resorts with spas (*Kurort* – meaning literally 'cure place') in Germany, where the word Bad before the name of any town is an indication that it has a 'curative' spa (although 'bad', they're supposed to be good for you!). There are four different types of spa in Germany:

- **Health Resort With A Mineral Spring (*Kurbad*)** – These are springs with at least 1g of dissolved mineral substances per litre of water, where the water coming from the ground is at a natural temperature of at least 20°C (68°F). Various special treatments are offered at these establishments, some of which are also pleasant for bathing.

- **Climatic Health Resorts (*Luftkurort*)** – These are health resorts situated in densely wooded areas that claim to have fresh air free of industrial waste gases. Landscaped trails are provided so that you can concentrate on enjoying the scenery, rather than the challenge of reaching your destination.

- **Seaside Spas** – Sea water, seaweed and mud are used in the therapeutic treatments here. Most of the patients at these resorts are being treated for circulatory problems, heart disease, post-operative weakness and skin diseases.

- **Kneipp Spas (*Kneippkurort*)** – These spas are operated in accordance with a formula developed by Sebastian Kneipp in Bad Wörishofen. The treatment is based on strengthening the body's immune system and encouraging a natural and harmonious 'macrobiotic rhythm'. Cold water is used for stimulation and warm water for relaxation. There are five basic components to the system:
  - Hydrotherapy for exercising the vascular and circulatory systems and for strengthening the immune system;
  - Natural whole foods to ensure regular metabolism;
  - Medicinal herbs to activate self-healing powers;
  - Physical training and physiotherapy to improve cardiac activity and blood circulation;
  - 'Adjustment' therapy to create a balance in life and harmony of the body and spirit.

If you feel that you will benefit from a spa treatment and can convince your GP, he can prescribe a visit for you. At one time, a visit to a spa was a pleasant little holiday at the expense of the *Kasse*, but recent health reforms mean that there must now be a clear and valid medical reason for you to take the cure, or your insurance won't cover the cost. In any event, you will have to pay a contribution.

If you go for the cure, don't expect wild nightlife or a day filled with activities – you're meant to be recuperating and relaxing!

Even if you don't need a spa for medical reasons, it's well worth visiting one for a leisurely break. Many spa resorts have luxurious hotels where you can enjoy a fine meal, stay overnight and stroll around the beautiful grounds. Others have casinos, where you can gamble the night away. Casino and spa combinations are a long tradition in Germany, where resorts such as Bad Homburg, Baden-Baden and Wiesbaden have achieved world-wide fame and popularity (see also **Gambling** on page 344).

MEDICINES & CHEMISTS'

Prescription and most non-prescription medicines are sold by chemists or pharmacies (*Apotheke*), denoted by a sign showing a large red 'A' with a white symbol of a serpent and a dish on the left-hand side. Apart from throat lozenges, vitamin preparations and some therapeutic lotions, most medicines are (by law) available only from an *Apotheke*. This includes homeopathic products and items that you may be used to buying at your local corner shop or supermarket at home, such as aspirin and cold cures. Even if it doesn't require a prescription, you must usually ask for the product you want by name or describe your symptoms, and the chemist (*Apotheker*) will offer a suggestion. This system tends to drive up the prices of even simple things such as aspirin, so it will pay you to bring an ample supply of non-prescription painkillers, cold remedies and other preparations with you to Germany.

Chemists' opening hours correspond more or less with normal shop opening hours (see page 376), although if a number are located in one area they usually take turns in opening during the evening. In smaller towns and villages some chemists' are closed on Wednesday afternoons. Chemists' display a duty roster on their doors or windows and at least one will be available at night for emergencies when others are closed. This information is also published in local newspapers under the heading *Apothekennotdienst*. Another alternative is to check the yellow pages for the number that provides a recorded list of chemists' open outside normal hours (again under *Apothekennotdienst*).

If you're privately insured, you must pay for all medicines and reclaim the cost from your insurer by sending the receipts. Some chemists offer a service whereby they keep your records on file and at appropriate intervals prepare a print-out of your purchases for submission to your insurance company (therefore encouraging you to visit them for all your medicines).

If you're insured under the state scheme, the process is simple. You can take a prescription to any chemist and, provided they have the medicine in stock, they will fill it for you. You must usually show your insurance card at the time of purchase and make a contribution of between €4 and €5 depending largely on the package size. (This contribution is likely to increase in the near future.) Similar charges apply to non-prescription items. Not all medicines are covered by health insurance. If your doctor recommends you to use something that isn't covered by state insurance, you must pay the full price at the time of purchase.

Although you may associate a shop called a *Drogerie* with an America drugstore, this is in fact a shop that sells household goods, baby care items, cosmetics and personal hygiene products, but no medicines. You may be able to find some of these items at your *Apotheke*, but prices are generally higher. For health foods and other 'natural' food products, look for a *Reformhaus*; for perfumes and cosmetics, a *Parfümerie*.

DENTISTS

It's wise to be cautious when choosing a dentist (*Zahnarzt*), as recent reforms in the state health system have greatly reduced the cover and reimbursement for dental procedures. For example, preventative cleaning is no longer covered by state health insurance. Patients are therefore cutting back on treatment and even travelling to other European countries where costs are lower for 'dental work holidays'. This in turn has encouraged some dentists seeking to replace lost business to recommend procedures that may be unnecessary (a common practice in all countries).

Many foreign residents schedule dental visits during their trips home, as they fear being pressured into undergoing unnecessary dental work, despite the fact that most German dentists are excellent (on the basis 'better the devil you know . . .'). In any case, treatment is likely to be cheaper in your home country than in Germany (a check-up costs around €80 and you can pay €4,000 for a set of dentures!). However, if this isn't possible or practicable and you need dental care while in Germany, try to obtain a recommendation from someone you can trust. If it's important to find a dentist who speaks English, check with your country's consulate or local English-speaking organisations to see whether they maintain lists. Dentists are listed in the yellow pages under *Zahnärzte*.

Before committing yourself to expensive treatment, it's wise to obtain a second opinion and in any case to ask for a written estimate of all costs. Note, however, that two dentists rarely agree exactly on what treatment is necessary. It may be possible to negotiate the price with a dentist to some extent, but you shouldn't try too hard.

OPTICIANS

If you just want to have your vision examined or check whether your prescription has changed, you can visit an optician or optometrist (*Optiker*), who are associated with most businesses selling prescription glasses and contact lenses. An optician will usually adjust your glasses free of charge.

Ophthalmologists (medical doctors who specialise in examining and treating diseases of the eye) can also do a vision check but will charge more than an *Optiker*. Ophthalmologists are listed in yellow pages and other directories under *Augenärzte* (singular *Augenarzt*). You don't need a referral from a GP to visit an ophthalmologists and if you have state health insurance the cost will be covered automatically (with private insurance you will be reimbursed after paying the bill).

On the other hand, state heath insurance covers only a small proportion of the cost of frames and lenses, both of which are expensive in Germany. For example, you will probably pay twice as much for glasses in Germany as you would for a comparable pair in the US and even Germans have been known to take their prescriptions with them on holidays to the States. The cost difference for contact lenses isn't as marked. Note, however, that there are several large optical chains in Germany selling glasses at lower prices than small shops. Fielman is probably the best known name, thanks to their widespread advertising, and Apollo is another well-established chain.

CHILDBIRTH

Once pregnancy is confirmed by your gynaecologist, you will be issued with a 'mother's passport' (*Mutterpass*), which is similar in size to a passport and contains all the important details of your pregnancy. It starts with your medical history and, each time you go for a check-up, information such as your blood pressure, weight and ultrasound results is recorded. Your *Mutterpass* must be taken to all pre-natal medical appointments and to the hospital for the birth itself. If you're pregnant, you're advised to carry your *Mutterpass* with you at all times in case an emergency should arise.

In your home country, it may be customary for the obstetrician who provides your pre-natal care also to deliver the baby. However, this isn't the case in Germany, where the discontinuity can be unsettling to some parents. A woman visits her regular gynaecologist (*Frauenarzt*) for pre and post-natal care, but the baby is delivered at a maternity clinic by the medical personnel on duty there. If you're privately insured, however, you can arrange to be cared for throughout the pregnancy and birth by the chief obstetrician of the hospital's delivery team. With private insurance, it's also possible to hire a midwife during a pregnancy, to assist with the birth preparation and accompany you to the hospital.

You must decide where you want to have your baby. Options include regular hospitals with maternity units, special 'birthing centres' and your own home, under the supervision of a midwife. An invaluable magazine entitled *Wo bekomme ich mein Baby?* (Where do I have my baby?) is available from maternity clinics and gynaecologists' offices and provides a list and description of all the options in your area for having a baby, including information about the type of equipment available in the labour and delivery rooms, the anaesthesia and medication offered, childbirth preparation classes and post-natal services, and parking and public transport facilities. It's available only in German, so if you don't understand this and don't have anyone to help you translate, check with your local embassy or consulate to see if they have any information in English. Women's clubs, such as the American Women's Club (🖥 www.fawco.org) may also be able to help.

In addition to published information, most hospitals offer at least one 'open house' evening per month, when expectant mothers and partners can obtain details of the services available and inspect the facilities. After you've chosen the hospital or clinic for a birth, you must register with them.

When preparing your things to take to the hospital, you should include the passports of both parents and your marriage certificate. If the latter is in English, you will need a certified German translation. The hospital will then register the birth, but be sure to ask where it has been registered, as it may be necessary to go there in person to collect the birth certificate (*Geburtsurkunde*).

If you have a baby while resident in Germany, it's essential also to register the child with your consulate or embassy, for which you will require the birth certificate. Check the procedure with them, or a child may later be denied citizenship in your home country. US passport-holders must bring their baby to the US consulate, where the Consul General must see the baby in person. It's wise to make an appointment as soon as the baby is born, as it can be a month or so before you receive an appointment. You must also register a baby with the German authorities at the *Einwohnermeldeamt* and apply for a residence permit on his or her behalf (see **Residence Permits** on page 73).

For a normal delivery, a woman usually spends six days in hospital. Recent changes in state health insurance law have increased the post-natal care to which a mother is entitled. All German health insurance plans now pay for a daily midwife visit for the first 11 days after a birth, plus a further 16 visits until a baby is two months old. Two house calls and two telephone conferences during weaning are also included.

COUNSELLING & SOCIAL SERVICES

Counselling and general welfare assistance is widely available in Germany. In all major metropolitan areas, you can find help for problems such as alcoholism (Alcoholics Anonymous), drug addiction, compulsive gambling, marriage and relationship problems, and eating disorders. There are also special centres for women or children who are suffering abusive family situations.

For a list of qualified professionals, you can check first with your family doctor or, if you have health insurance in Germany, your insurance company. Also check the yellow pages under your local social services department. Key words to look for include *Jugendamt* (department for juvenile programs), *Sozialamt* (department of social services), *Sozialhilfe* (social help) and *Sozialdienst* (social work).

If you need counselling in English, you may be able to obtain advice from your local embassy or consulate or an expatriate club, such as the American Women's Club.

HOME NURSING SERVICES

If you or someone in your family requires care in the home, it's covered by a special home care insurance (*Pflegeversicherung*). You can either have the regular state insurance or buy a separate private policy for additional cover. The premiums for state insurance are deducted from your salary. If you have private insurance, you must negotiate a separate home care policy with your insurer.

Since the introduction of home care insurance in 1995, there has been a rapid growth in the number of private home care agencies (*Pflegedienste*) in Germany. Your insurance company can assist you in choosing one and there are various seals of approval that indicate a high quality agency, such as the *Qualitätsgeprüfter Ambulanter Pflegedienst*. This award indicates that agency personnel are well trained and qualified for demanding care situations and are regularly monitored by external auditors.

The following services are usually provided by a home nursing service:

- **Body Care** – bathing, oral hygiene, hair care, shaving, and help with other bodily hygiene functions;
- **Nutrition** – preparing food so that it can be easily eaten and swallowed, and feeding;
- **Mobility** – getting in and out of bed, getting dressed and undressed, help with standing and walking, stair climbing, accompanying on excursions outside the home;
- **Household Needs** – shopping, cooking, cleaning, dishwashing, changing and washing bed linen.

A basic requirement for the cost of home nursing to be covered by insurance is that the patient requires help for a period of at least six months. The one exception to this rule is when the life expectancy of the patient is less than six months. The level of reimbursement depends on the amount of care required. There are three levels defined by law, and your insurance company will determine which applies according to the evaluations of qualified medical personnel.

SEXUALLY TRANSMITTED DISEASES

As in most countries, AIDS and other sexually transmitted diseases (STDs) are a concern in Germany. It's estimated that since the beginning of the 1980s, over 56,000 people in Germany have been infected with the HIV virus, which can lead to AIDS, and the numbers are growing at a rate of some 2,000 per year. According to the Federal Office for Statistics, some 18,240 people were suffering from AIDS in 1999. The vast majority were men in the former West Germany.

Condoms (*Kondome*) are widely available in a variety of shops and kiosks, and there are dispensing machines in public toilets.

AIDS-related advertising campaigns targeted at the most vulnerable sectors of the population (the young and gay men) are widely shown on TV and in the press. Information about AIDS and organisations in Germany working to combat the disease and assist sufferers and their families is available from a number of organisations in major cities and via the Internet (e.g. ⌨ www.hiv.info.de and ⌨ www.aidsfinder.org).

The number of cases of other STDs has fallen dramatically in the last 25 years: in 1975, there were 77,500 cases of STDs other than HIV/AIDS and in 1999 a mere 3,450.

DEATHS

If a foreign national dies in Germany, one of the first official steps is to contact the appropriate consulate or embassy. They will advise you of the options for burial (locally or in another country) and can also provide the names of morticians experienced in preparing the body for transport home, if desired. You will probably also require a consular report of death, which may be necessary for probate in your home country. A consulate cannot issue this document until it receives an official death certificate (*Sterbeurkunde*) issued by the appropriate Registry of Births, Marriages and Deaths (Standesamt). You may also wish to request an International Death Certificate from the Standesamt, which are issued in several languages.

One important point to note is that a German death certificate (*Sterbekunde*) doesn't state the cause of death, without which you can encounter difficulty in settling insurance claims back home. To avoid this problem, the next-of-kin should obtain a 'cause of death' certificate (*Leichenschauschein*), which is normally issued only when the death occurred in suspicious circumstances. The cause of death certificate should be issued by the same doctor as the death certificate.

13.

INSURANCE

The German government and German law provide for various obligatory state and employer insurance schemes. These include health, pensions, unemployment, work accident and long-term care insurance – referred to as the five 'pillars' of the social security system, which was the world's first, established in 1883. Most working people and their families (over 80 per cent of the population) receive health treatment under the German social security system, although there's an option to take out private health insurance under certain circumstances. Social security also extends generous protection to students, the retired and trainees.

There are a few occasions in Germany where private insurance for individuals is compulsory. The most common is third party car insurance (see page 225). Some landlords require tenants to have third party liability insurance (i.e. to protect the landlord's interests) as a condition of the lease, and if you finance the purchase of a home, you will probably be required to have life insurance to protect your lender. If you lease a car or buy one on credit, the lender will insist that you have comprehensive car insurance (*Vollkasko*) until the loan has been paid off.

Forms of voluntary insurance include supplementary pensions, some forms of private health insurance, household insurance, certain third party liability, and travel, car breakdown and life insurance. For information about car and breakdown insurance, see pages 238 and 241 respectively.

In all matters regarding insurance, you're responsible for ensuring that you and your family are legally insured in Germany. It's unnecessary to spend half your income insuring yourself against every eventuality from the common cold to being sued for your last cent, but it's important to insure against any event that could precipitate a major financial disaster, such as a serious accident or your house burning down.

As with anything connected with finance, it's important to shop around when buying insurance. **Just collecting a few brochures from insurance agents or making a few phone calls could save you a lot of money.** Regrettably, however, you cannot insure yourself against being uninsured or sue your insurance agent for giving you bad advice!

If you wish to make a claim against an insurance policy, you may be required to report an incident to your insurer within strictly prescribed time limits or in the exact manner and level of detail outlined in your contract or policy documents. Filing a claim may also require you to provide a list of receipts for articles damaged or destroyed, police reports or photographs of damage. Obtain legal advice for anything other than a minor claim. **German law is likely to differ from that in your home country or your previous country of residence, so you should never assume that it's the same.**

You should ensure that your family has full health insurance during the interval between leaving your last country of residence and obtaining health insurance in Germany. One way is to take out a holiday and travel insurance policy (see page 298). However, it's usually better to extend your present health insurance than to take out a new policy (most policies can be extended to provide international cover for a few months), particularly if you have an existing health problem that may not be covered by a new policy. If you're coming to live in Germany without working, you will be required to prove that you have adequate medical insurance with cover that's at least equal to the German statutory programme before you will be granted a residence permit. Expatriate health insurance is provided by a number of international insurers and special group plans are available through some expatriate organisations and associations. See also **Supplementary Health Insurance** on page 295.

INSURANCE COMPANIES & AGENTS

Insurance is one of Germany's major businesses and there are numerous companies to choose from, many providing a broad range of insurance services, while some specialise in certain fields only. The major insurance companies have offices or agencies throughout Germany. Some of the larger, better-known companies are Allianz, AXA and Zürich, but there are plenty of others. In most cities and towns you can find a number of independent insurance agents and brokers (*Versicherungsmakler* or *Mehrfachagent*), who represent a number of insurance companies and allow you to compare policies from different companies. There are also a number of insurance consultants (*Versicherungsberater*), who will (for a fee) advise you on the insurance you require, in addition to finding you the best policies and rates. Some consultants, however, represent particular insurance companies and accept commission from them, so their advice may be biased and you should find an independent insurance consultant if you want impartial advice.

Many banks have insurance subsidiaries (for example, Deutsche Herold is the insurance branch of Deutsche Bank) and include an analysis of your insurance cover as part of their financial advice and investment services. Quelle, the big department store and mail-order company, provides its own insurance policies, including holiday, travel, car and life insurance, as do several other department stores and hypermarkets. Telephone-based insurance companies have appeared in recent years and usually offer competitive premiums, although there may be disadvantages to dealing with them; for example, it may be more difficult to obtain information or a decision regarding a claim over the telephone than face to face. In addition, you can find numerous insurance companies on the Internet (e.g. the very useful 🖥 www.verischerungsvergleich.de), many of which offer do-it-yourself price estimates and the facility to sign up online.

Since mid-1994, the European insurance market has theoretically been opened up to permit insurers to offer cross-border policies. This means that, if you're coming from another EU country, you may be able to retain many of your insurance policies from that country (particularly life insurance and supplementary pension policies). Check with your insurance company before you leave to see if they will cover you in Germany and to determine whether cover is adequate or can be adapted to meet German requirements.

INSURANCE CONTRACTS

Read all insurance contracts before signing them. If you cannot get an English translation and you don't understand everything, ask a friend or colleague to translate it or take legal advice. Like insurance companies everywhere, some German companies will do almost anything to avoid honouring claims and will use any available legal loophole. It therefore pays to deal only with reputable companies (not that this provides a guarantee). Terms and cover can be difficult to compare, as insurers can now offer a whole range of excesses (deductibles), co-payments, and special conditions and exclusions on what used to be standard policies.

Always check the notice period required to cancel (*kündigen*) a policy. In Germany, insurance policies, like most forms of contract, are automatically extended for a further period (usually a year) unless cancelled in writing at least three months before their expiry date. Some types of policy may run for two or more years before they can be legally cancelled. You can cancel an insurance policy before the term has expired only if the premium is increased by more than 20 per cent, or if the terms or value of the policy are considerably changed by circumstances beyond your control (such as when an insured object is damaged or destroyed). Unless you formally cancel a policy, you must pay the following year's premium, even if you no longer require it. You won't receive a reminder of cancellation dates and, by the time you're notified that the premium is due, your cancellation date will be long past!

Most forms of insurance are paid via a single annual lump-sum premium and, if you want to make payments on a bi-annual, quarterly or monthly basis (assuming this is possible), you will have to pay much more. Most insurers require a bank transfer authorisation allowing them simply to deduct premiums from your bank account at the appointed times. If you don't pay, you can be sued for the whole premium, the credit collection agency's fees and interest.

The good news is that the insurance premiums you pay for the most common forms of insurance can be deducted from taxable income on your income tax declaration. This applies to life insurance, private health insurance, long-term care insurance, accident insurance and most forms of liability insurance. Social security contributions are automatically deducted from taxable income.

SOCIAL SECURITY

Germany has a comprehensive social security system for all employees, covering health care (plus sickness and maternity), injuries and illnesses at work, old age (pensions), disability and death, unemployment and, since 1995, long-term care insurance. The labour and social services budget comprises the largest item in the federal government's budget, and a large portion of spending has been directed toward bringing social services and pensions in the eastern part of Germany up to a level comparable with that in western Germany.

Social security programmes in Germany also include a range of benefits and services available to those on low incomes, such as rent assistance, and food and clothing allowances. There is somewhat less stigma attached to accepting benefits from the government than in some other countries; in fact Germans are justifiably proud of their ability to take much of their social support network for granted.

Social security cost-cutting measures have been (cautiously) introduced in recent years by politicians who, while anxious to limit increases in contributions (primarily for employers), are well aware that they must maintain benefit levels if they wish to remain in power.

Employees' social security contributions are automatically deducted from their income by their employers, whereas the self-employed must pay their own contributions. Benefits aren't taxed.

The new Federal Ministry for Health and Social Security (Bundesministerium für Gesundheit und Soziale Sicherung) maintains a website (🖳 www.bmgs.bund.de) containing information on social security and other programmes in German and a number of other languages, including English, although this and other government websites are being reorganised in line with changes to ministerial responsibilities. An excellent booklet in English called *Social Security at a Glance*, which provides a thorough overview of the German social security system, is available from the ministry's publications department at Rochusstrasse 1, D-53123 Bonn. The order number is A998.

Eligibility

All employees and self-employed people in Germany are automatically enrolled in the state social security system, which also covers their immediate family members, i.e. spouse and children, as well as other dependent family members in the household. Students, trainees and apprentices are covered under special rules if they don't come under their parents' cover. Those drawing wage replacement benefits (unemployment, disability or old age pensions) are also covered, although they don't make any contributions. Your employer will provide you with a social security certificate that serves to verify your enrolment, which is necessary to claim certain benefits.

Social security agreements exist between Germany and over 30 other countries, including all EU nations and the US, whereby expatriates may remain under their home country's social security scheme for a limited period. For example, EU nationals transferred to Germany by an employer in their home country can continue to pay social security abroad for a year (forms E101 and E111 are required), which can be extended for another year in unforeseen circumstances (when forms E102 and E106 are needed). Americans should be aware that the US social security agreement with Germany covers pensions only, and that medical and some survivor benefits under the US Social Security programme (particularly Medicare) aren't payable to those living outside the US.

If you or your spouse work in Germany but remain insured under the social security legislation of another EU country, you will be able to claim social security benefits from that country. If you must claim benefits in Germany and have paid contributions in another EU country, those contributions are usually taken into account when calculating your qualification for benefits. There's a mutual agreement between EU countries whereby contributions made in any EU country count as contributions in your home country when calculating benefits. Contact your country's social security administration for information. In Britain information is provided in a booklet, *Your Social Security, Health Care and Pension Rights in the European Union* (reference number SA29), although in June 2003 only the 1998 edition was available. This can be obtained from the Department of Work & Pensions, (Formerly DSS), Centre for Non-Residents, Benton Park Road, Long Benton, Newcastle-upon-Tyne, NE98 1ZZ, or downloaded via the Internet (🖳 www.dwp.gov.uk – from the section covering social security agreements with other countries); the downloadable version is entitled *Your Social Security Insurance, Health Care and Benefits Rights in the EEA*.

Contributions

With the exception of work accident insurance, which is paid entirely by employers, social security contributions are split 50-50 between the employer and employee and are calculated as a percentage of your gross income – in some cases only up to a certain salary level. In general, you should expect your social security contributions to come to around 42.3 per cent of your gross salary, of which you pay half or a little over 20 per cent of your salary. Normally, the employer's share of the contribution is simply added to your pay and then the full amount of the contribution is deducted. The self-employed must pay the whole 42.3 per cent themselves.

Health Insurance

Enrolment in the statutory health insurance scheme is mandatory for all employees earning less than a certain monthly salary, which in 2003 was €3,825 (i.e. €45,960 per year) in both western and eastern states. These limits are indexed for inflation each year.

Health insurance is provided by a network of 600 non-profit making companies working with the state to administer the national health programme (Gesetzliche Krankenkassen/GKV). The most popular include the Allgemeine Ortskrankenkasse (AOK), BEK, BKK, DAK and KKH. Until 1996, you were limited to particular statutory health insurance companies according to your profession or employer, but you're now free to choose from almost all state insurers. It pays to compare a number before making a decision because, although benefits are uniform across all insurers, costs vary significantly, the smaller companies (who are trying to boost their membership) usually being among the cheapest. Generally, however, the AOK is among the cheapest and has the largest number of offices nation-wide. Rates are determined according to your salary and cover all family members, irrespective of the number of children you have; in other words, a single person pays the same contribution as a married person with several children. On average, the cost of health insurance through the statutory programme is around 14.3 per cent of gross pay up to €3,450 per month, of which the employee pays half. This limit also increases with inflation. However, a decision made in August 2003 means that contributions will be reduced to 13 per cent by 2006.

Statutory health insurance benefits are extensive and cover dentistry as well as medical care and even some spa treatments, if recommended by a doctor. However, orthodontics are usually covered only for children up to the age of 18 (when recommended by a dentist) and there's limited cover for spectacles and contact lenses. There's also a provision for insurance to pay 70 per cent of your normal salary when you're absent from work due to illness, if your employer doesn't continue to pay you, although he's obliged to pay you for at least six weeks and will normally continue to pay you indefinitely if you have a doctor's certificate that you're unfit for work.

As the government tries to cut the cost of health care, co-payments (i.e. the portion of costs patients must pay) have been increasing for things prescriptions, hospital stays, travel costs and dental care. However, for most doctors' appointments you simply show your health insurance card and the doctor bills the insurance company directly. For more information see **Chapter 12**.

If your salary exceeds the level where state insurance is mandatory (currently €3,825 per month), you may choose to purchase private health insurance from profit-making companies instead of opting for one of the statutory plans (see **Supplementary Health Insurance** on page 295).

Long-Term Care Insurance

Long-term care insurance (*Pflegeversicherung*) is the most recent addition to Germany's extensive social security benefits. Cover is mandatory and linked to your health insurance plan. For those in a statutory health care plan, the contribution is 1.7 per cent of your gross salary (up to €3,450 per month), with half paid by your employer. In Saxony this figure is marginally different. If you're eligible for private health insurance, you can also shop around for long-term care cover, but you must prove to your health insurance provider that the cover you choose meets statutory requirements. The cost of private insurance obviously varies according to the benefits and options you choose. Whether public or private, the long-term care cover you select includes everyone in your family who doesn't have cover on their own behalf.

You're considered in need of long-term care if your health insurance company determines that you require frequent or substantial help with normal day-to-day activities on a long-term basis, i.e. for six months or longer. Benefits may be provided in the areas of personal hygiene, eating, mobility and housekeeping, with the goal of helping you regain the ability to perform these tasks on your own or with limited supervision. There are several levels of care and, wherever possible, home assistance is made available in preference to institutional care.

Under the statutory plan, benefits can be tailored to individual needs, varying from cash reimbursement for private services engaged directly to contracting services from a social service agency. It's possible to receive nursing care training for family members or other care-givers in your home to reduce or eliminate the need for outside services. You may also be eligible for allowances to make modifications to your home or car, when necessary. Long-term care benefits include holiday stand-ins for household helpers or caretakers, and legislation a few years ago extended social security cover free of charge or at reduced rates to family members who reduce their paid employment in order to care for someone at home.

Unemployment Insurance

Unemployment insurance (*Arbeitslosenversicherung*) is mandatory for all employees in Germany, the contribution for which amounts to 6.5 per cent of your gross monthly salary up to €5,100 in the west and €4,250 in the east, the employer paying half.

Unemployment benefit is paid when you're unemployed or on short time or when an employer is unable to pay your wages, e.g. he has gone bankrupt. Part-time employees are also entitled to unemployment benefit when wholly or partly unemployed.

In order to qualify for unemployment benefit, you must have worked (and paid contributions) for at least 12 months in the last three years. To register for unemployment benefit, you must go to the local employment office (*Arbeitsamt*) with personal identification, your tax card, social security certificate and any previously issued documents from the *Arbeitsamt*, such as your work permit or prior benefit claims. It's wise to register as soon as you become eligible (i.e. the day you become unemployed, provided you've made the required number of contributions), as benefit is paid only from the date you register; if you put off registering for a couple of weeks, you have no right to backdated benefit. If your employer has given you notice of your impending lay-off or termination, you can register for benefit up to two months in advance so that benefit take effect from the first day that you're unemployed. On the other hand, if it's your own fault that you're unemployed, e.g. you quit your job without good reason or were fired for good cause, the *Arbeitsamt* can impose a holding period (*Sperrzeit*) of up to 12 weeks before starting your benefit. Again, this applies from the date you register as unemployed, not from the date you quit or were fired.

The benefit paid depends on your previous salary and whether or not you have children in your care, as noted on your tax card. Unemployed people with no children receive around 60 per cent of their previous net pay, rising to 67 per cent for those with children. There's also a set maximum benefit according to the tax class you were in during the previous year (see **Tax Card** on page 318). Benefit payments are made once a month directly into your bank account. Social security cover for pension, health, long-term care and accident insurance are maintained while you're drawing unemployment benefit.

How long you can continue to draw benefit depends on how long you've been working (and paying into the system) and your age. After you've been working for a year, you have the right to six months' unemployment benefit, provided you meet all the other requirements. For those under 45, the maximum entitlement is 12 months' benefit and to qualify you must have been employed for at least 24 months in the last three years. This increases to a maximum of 32 months benefit for those over 57 with at least 64 months' previous employment.

After you've exhausted your unemployment benefit, you may be eligible for unemployment assistance (*Arbeitslosenhilfe*) if you have no other means of support and no other working household member to assist you financially. This form of assistance is theoretically limited to 53 per cent of your previous net salary and 57 per cent if you have children up to the following ceilings: in the western states, €409.29 per month for those with at least one child and €380.59 for the childless; in the eastern states €409.29 and €326.97 respectively. Unemployment assistance is available indefinitely.

During the time you're drawing unemployment benefit, you must report to the *Arbeitsamt* at least every three months or whenever they summon you to discuss a possible job opportunity or training to improve your employment prospects. Recent reforms by a government intent on reducing unemployment levels mean that officials have become much less relaxed about this. And it has become far more difficult to turn down work even though you might think it beneath you, unrelated to your area of expertise or inadequately paid. (No sacrifice is too great to improve a government's image – provided it's made by someone else!) You can also be required to attend classes or training programmes, all of which are provided free of charge.

Technically, you're required to check your letter box for information or requests from the *Arbeitsamt* or your job counsellor at least once a day while drawing unemployment benefit, although you're entitled to take up to three weeks' holiday while unemployed, provided you notify the office in advance. If you miss an appointment, fail to turn up at classes or training programmes, or fail to follow up on job leads, you can be fined or have your benefit stopped for a period of days or weeks. You may be required to produce proof of your job-hunting efforts and you must notify the office immediately if you find a job or move house or your personal situation changes in any other way, e.g. you get married or divorced, or find that you're expecting a baby. There are provisions for paying reduced benefit if you find part-time work while drawing unemployment benefit, but if you don't notify the *Arbeitsamt* and continue to draw your benefit while being paid for full or part-time work, you can be charged with fraud.

If you're a citizen of another EU country, you may be entitled to receive up to three months' unemployment benefit from Germany if you move to another EEA country to seek employment. To qualify, you must notify the *Arbeitsamt* of your move and register with the unemployment office in your new country within seven days of your arrival.

Work Accident Insurance

Industrial accident insurance pays all medical and rehabilitation costs associated with injuries or illness occurring on the job, or while on your way to or from work. In the event of your death from a job-related injury or illness, your survivors receive a funeral allowance and pension benefits.

This insurance also covers children in school, students attending university or vocational training, people who help at the scene of an accident, civil defence and emergency rescue workers, and blood and organ donors. The contribution is paid entirely by your employer, the actual amount being based on the employer's health and safety record over time. The employer is required to participate in various programmes to evaluate and improve health and safety conditions in the workplace as a condition of this insurance scheme. If you're self-employed and aren't required to have this type of insurance by law or under some other agreement, you can voluntarily obtain cover through the state system.

If you're unable to work as a result of an injury or illness covered by insurance, 80 per cent of your wages will be paid for up to 78 weeks after the six-week period covered by your employer (see **Sick Leave** on page 58). In the event of long-term or permanent disability, you can receive occupational assistance, retraining, and any necessary modifications to your car or home.

You must notify your employer immediately if you suffer an injury at work or on the way to or from work, or notify the educational establishment if the accident involves a child or student. The employer or school is responsible for filing a claim with their insurance provider. Statutory work accident insurance provides benefits irrespective of fault and exempts your employer from liability claims for work-related accidents or illnesses.

Pensions

'Pension insurance' (*Rentenversicherung*) is the German social security programme that covers old age, invalidity and death benefits for retirees, their families and survivors. All employees must make contributions to the state pension fund, as must trainees, disabled people employed by sheltered workshops, and those doing military or civilian service. Most self-employed people also pay into this plan, although there are some alternatives open to professions with their own social welfare plan (*Sozialkasse*). Artists and those involved in publishing may be exempt from contributions after five years provided their income doesn't exceed certain limits.

The state pension programme is easily the most expensive of the generous welfare plans in Germany and the one employers are most anxious to see reduced (at least their portion of the cost). The pensions system has come under considerable strain in the years since reunification, due both to high unemployment (particularly in the eastern region) and to the changing age structure of the German population as a whole. The Pension Reform Act of 1999 attempted to reduce payments and the automatic indexing of pensions for several categories of recipients, but a public outcry and subsequent legislation have deferred these benefit cuts more or less indefinitely. (A voluntary private supplementary pension scheme has been introduced since, which it is obviously hoped will relieve the state of some of its burden – see **Supplementary Pensions** on page 296.)

The pension insurance contribution is 19.5 per cent of gross salary up to a maximum of €5,100 per month (€61,200 annually) in the western states and €4,250 per month (€51,000 annually) in the east. The percentage was reduced from 20.3 per cent at the beginning of 1999. As usual, employers pay half the sum and employees half (through payroll deductions); the self-employed must pay the full amount themselves.

In order to claim an old age pension, you must have reached a fixed age and have contributed for a minimum period, usually five years. (Special conditions apply to those with occupational disabilities or work-related illnesses.) The normal retirement age (i.e. the age at which you can retire with a full pension) for men and women has been rising since 2000 and in 2004 will be 65 for both sexes, although a government commission has recently recommended that the age should be increased to 67 and that no one should be allowed to retire before 64! Under certain circumstances, women, miners and those on unemployment or disability programmes are eligible for retirement at 60 or 63 with full benefits, although these exceptions are gradually being phased out. A reduced pension for early retirement is available from the age of 60 or 63 (according to your circumstances) and there are special provisions for pensioners wishing to go on partial retirement so that they can continue to work part-time.

The pension scheme also provides pensions for surviving family members in the event of the death of an insured person, and partial pensions are available to compensate for reduced earning capacity in cases of long-term illness, injury or other forms of disability of an insured person.

The formula for determining the level of pension benefit is based on a fairly complicated points system, which takes into account your contributions (and therefore your salary level) and the length of time you've been covered. The total number of points earned is multiplied by a factor corresponding to the type of pension you're claiming (i.e. retirement, disability, survivor, partial, etc.) and your age. The resulting number of points is then multiplied by the current pension 'value', which is based on the monthly pension that an average wage earner would receive after paying contributions for a calendar year. The aim has traditionally been to keep pension levels at around 70 per cent of previous salary, although it's projected that this will reduce to around 67 percent by 2030. (Given the current financial situation, even this figure might be optimistic.) The pension in eastern Germany is currently around 87 percent of that in the west.

If you move to Germany after working in another EU country (or move to another EU country after working in Germany) your state pension contributions can be exported to Germany (or from Germany to another country). German state pensions are payable abroad, and most other countries will pay state pensions directly to their nationals resident in Germany. Non-EU nationals should check with their respective consulate, embassy or social security agency for details on claiming their home-based national pension while living in Germany (or any other country). Under the terms of the pension-only social security agreements between Germany and certain countries, including the US and Canada, pension contributions made in Germany may count towards pension qualification or value in your home country.

Your pension cover is continued while you're on unemployment or other forms of income-replacement benefit, the relevant agency paying contributions on your behalf. Mothers and fathers on parental leave are automatically insured during their time off work, without having to make contributions.

SUPPLEMENTARY HEALTH INSURANCE

If your salary exceeds the level where state insurance is mandatory (€3,825 per month), you may choose to purchase private health insurance instead of the statutory scheme (see **Health Insurance** above), although recent reforms have made this more difficult. You must notify your employer if you choose this option, in which case the monthly premiums will be deducted from your salary and remitted directly to your insurance company by your employer. Private health insurance provides much more extensive cover than the state scheme, including the option of private or semi-private hospital rooms, 'alternative therapies' such as acupuncture and herbal treatments, eye examinations, glasses and contact lenses, cosmetic surgery and other treatment that isn't usually available under the state plan.

You will also have a greater choice of medical practitioners with a private scheme, as some doctors restrict their practices to privately insured patients only (some because it's more profitable, others because the maximum number of GPs allowed to register in a particular administrative area with the *Krankenkassen* has already been reached and they have no option).

However, premiums for this cover can be considerably higher than for state cover, especially if you opt for cover that eliminates most co-payments. Note also that many employers limit their contribution to half the maximum statutory rate, so that the extra employer cost as well as your own share of the contributions are payable by you if you decide to go private.

Private insurers can refuse to cover 'pre-existing conditions', so this may not be a practical option if you or a family member has existing or recurring health problems.

Another important point to bear in mind when considering private health insurance is that, once you've opted out of the state health insurance

system, you cannot go back unless your salary falls below the level where you're entitled to choose. Normally, you must make a decision on which health insurance *Kasse* you want to use within your first three months in a new job; if you aren't sure, it's best to sign up with one of the state insurers, as you can always go private later. At the end of each year there's an open enrolment period, when employees who are eligible for private health insurance can choose this option or change insurance companies.

SUPPLEMENTARY PENSIONS

Germans have traditionally placed considerable faith in the national pension scheme and supplementary private pensions were previously considered something of a luxury. However, with the cost of reunification and legislative moves to limit or even reduce state pension benefits, private pension insurance is slowly becoming more popular. If you already have private pension insurance in another country, it may not be necessary (or, in some circumstances, wise) to buy a supplementary pension policy in Germany, particularly if you will be moving on after a few years.

Technically, a private pension (*private Rentenversicherung*) in Germany is a form of life insurance investment, where you purchase an insurance contract for a set amount and a set term, usually 25 to 30 years. All policies for private pensions must run for at least 12 years to avoid being taxed as regular investments. At the end of the policy term, the accumulated benefits are paid to the insured person either as a monthly pension or in a lump sum. Where a private pension policy differs from a regular life insurance contract (see page 300) is in the manner in which proceeds are taxed after the death of the policyholder. When the pensioner dies, the remaining sum in the fund (or the face value of the policy if the policy hasn't yet matured) is paid to his heirs. While the pension payments made to the insured are tax-free, payments made to heirs after the death of the insured may be subject to tax (either inheritance tax or income tax, depending on the circumstances), whereas the proceeds of a life insurance policy are tax-free in all cases.

Because of the dramatic impact the low birth-rate is having and will increasingly have on the financing of the state pensions system, the government has recently introduced the state-assisted private supplementary pension. It's restricted almost entirely to those in the state insurance plan and is designed to soften the blow of future cuts in the state system on those who have been unable to take out a private supplementary pension and to prevent too wide a chasm emerging between the rich and the less-well-off. The system, which involves the government making 'bonus' payments into private pension schemes, should be fully in place by

2008. It's unlikely to affect the pension decisions of foreigners living for short periods in Germany.

HOUSEHOLD INSURANCE

As few Germans and even fewer foreigners buy their homes, buildings insurance isn't usually a concern, but household contents insurance (*Hausratversicherung*) is essential for most people. Contents insurance normally covers your property in the event of damage by fire, burglary, vandalism, storms and water and usually replaces damaged items at their current value, including furniture, appliances, clothing and books, as well as jewellery up to certain limits. It also covers you for a limited amount of cash. **It's important to make sure that your property is insured for its full value, or claims can be reduced by the proportion by which your property is under-insured.** For example, if it's determined that your insured property is worth €50,000 but you have it insured for only €40,000, a claim will be reduced by 20 per cent.

If you have possessions with a high value, it may be necessary to take out a separate policy or extension to cover them. These may include jewellery, antiques or financial documents (share certificates or bonds), where the value exceeds standard policy limits.

Contents insurance may also include provision for refunding hotel or rent and transport costs if your home is rendered uninhabitable for a period by fire, vandalism or another form of insured damage.

As always, it's important to read and understand all the terms of a household insurance policy. Storm damage, for example, is normally covered only when winds reach at least Force 8. You may also be required to show that you've done your best to minimise certain kinds of damage, e.g. by securing your possessions and home while you're absent, and some policies replace stolen articles only when there's evidence of forced entry. You may be able to obtain cover for 'mysterious disappearance' at an additional cost, but you should read the terms and conditions carefully.

Many household policies cover only items kept in your home and may not include garages, exterior storage areas or other off-site property unless specifically mentioned. It isn't uncommon to purchase a separate bicycle policy (*Fahrradversicherung*) or to add such cover to your regular household insurance, particularly if you use your bicycle for day-to-day transport or have a particularly expensive model. This insurance covers the theft of your bicycle under most circumstances where your regular household policy won't, although you must lock your bicycle whenever you aren't using it and store it in a locked area or bicycle shed when at home. Should it be stolen while in use, the theft must occur between the hours of 6am and 10pm for cover to be effective (apparently German insurance companies try to discourage late-night bicycle riding).

If you have an au pair or other non-family member living with you, you should check whether their possessions will be covered in a fire or other disaster. Non-related household members may need their own insurance cover for belongings, or your policy may require you to notify the insurer when you have a long-term house guest or other live-in arrangements.

THIRD PARTY & LEGAL INSURANCE

It's customary in Germany to have third party liability insurance (*Privathaftpflichtversicherung*). To take an everyday example, if your soap slips out of your hand while you're taking a shower, jumps out of the window and your neighbour slips on it and breaks his neck, he (or his widow) will sue you for €1 million (at least). With third party liability insurance, you can shower in blissful security. If you're renting accommodation, your landlord may insist on seeing proof that you have this sort of cover so that he's adequately protected.

Third party liability insurance covers all members of your family and includes damage done or caused by your children and pets (for example, if your dog or child bites someone). However, where damage is due to severe negligence on your part, benefits may be reduced or even denied. Many policies specifically exclude cover for claims resulting from certain dangerous sports or hobbies (sky-diving, power-boating or mountaineering, for example) or if you regularly keep explosive or inflammable material in or near your home.

Legal insurance pays for consultations with a lawyer and associated costs if you should require legal assistance or be taken to court. You can even obtain special forms of legal insurance, e.g. for your employment, for traffic accidents or for your apartment or house lease. Legal insurance doesn't cover legal fees for most non-adversarial situations, such as inheritance planning, patenting inventions or starting your own business; as always, you need to read a policy carefully to ensure that you understand the extent of cover and how to file a claim.

Third party liability insurance usually costs around €200 per year; legal insurance (*Rechtsschutzversicherung*) costs around €70 per year if purchased separately but only around €30 if added to a third party liability policy.

HOLIDAY & TRAVEL INSURANCE

Holiday and travel insurance is available from a variety of sources, including insurance companies, banks and travel agencies, and can be purchased at airports and railway stations in Germany. Before taking out travel insurance, you should carefully consider the level of cover you require and compare policies. Most policies cover you for loss of deposit or holiday cancellation, missed flight, departure delay at both the start and end of a holiday (a common occurrence), delayed and lost baggage and belongings, medical expenses (up to €3 million) and accidents (including evacuation home if necessary), loss or theft of money, personal liability (e.g. €3 million), legal expenses, holiday curtailment, and a tour operator going bust. Travel policies may also cover medical evacuation or repatriation of family members who fall ill or are injured while on holiday.

Under statutory German health insurance, you're covered for medical emergencies throughout Europe, although when travelling further afield you will need additional insurance.

If you travel frequently, you may find it more economical to have a permanent annual travel policy with world-wide cover that includes health insurance than to purchase a travel insurance policy for each trip abroad. These 'full-time' policies are available from insurance companies that specialise in travel policies, and some expatriate organisations offer attractively priced policies to members.

The Germans are renowned travellers and favour package holidays booked through local travel agents. As a result, a number of consumer protections are written into German law regarding full or partial refunds for holidays spoiled by overbooking, incomplete facilities, inflated advertising claims, etc., and you can often obtain a refund (in cash, possibly including compensation for the fact that you've wasted a holiday period) for such situations simply by asserting your rights (see **Consumer Associations** on page 394). For travel plans that go awry for other reasons, there are specific forms of travel insurance available:

- Travel agents will generally offer you a travel cancellation policy (*Reiserücktrittsversicherung*), which will refund your holiday fees in full or in part if you need to cancel or cut short your trip due to serious illness or the death of a family member.

- Also available is separate baggage insurance (*Reisegepäckversicherung*), which covers damage to or loss of your bags while you're on holiday.

- If you're going to be renting a car abroad, it's possible to purchase a so-called 'Majorca policy', which will bring the cover on a foreign rental car up to German levels (see **Car Insurance** on page 238). A 'Majorca policy' is particularly recommended for travel in southern European countries, where mandatory car insurance is considered wholly inadequate by Germans (hence the name). Before taking out such a policy, however, you should check your existing car insurance policy, as some German insurers include this cover in their standard policies.

LIFE INSURANCE

Although there may be worse things in life than death, your dependants may rate your death without life insurance (*Lebensversicherung*) high on their list. You can take out a life insurance or endowment policy with numerous German or foreign insurance companies. If you already have a life insurance policy in your home country, it may be easier to maintain it, particularly if you're likely to be moving on after a few years in Germany.

German policies are usually for life assurance and not insurance. (An assurance policy covers an eventuality that's certain to occur, e.g. your death, so a life assurance policy remains valid until the day you die, whereas a life insurance policy covers an eventuality that may happen but isn't a certainty, e.g. that you should die in a car accident).

Most Germans consider life insurance a form of long-term investment or saving scheme for old age; when you consider the generous orphan, widow and survivor benefits most families are entitled to under social security insurance, this attitude makes sense. The most common sort of life insurance is called capital life insurance (*Kapitallebensversicherung*), which works much like an investment. You pay premiums for a certain number of years (a minimum of 12) and at the end of the agreed term receive the capital accrued, either as a lump sum or over a period as an annuity. Insurance companies promise differing rates of return over the term of the policy and it's important to evaluate not only the rate you're being promised, but the company's performance over the last five or ten years. If the insured person dies before the end of the policy, the proceeds are paid to his beneficiaries. In most cases, the annual premiums on a life insurance policy are tax deductible and the proceeds are exempt from taxes whether paid to the insured or to his survivors. If a policy is cashed before 12 years have expired, these tax benefits don't apply and proceeds are treated like those from any other form of investment or speculation.

Another kind of life insurance available is *Risikolebensversicherung* (also called *Versicherung auf den Todesfall*), which works like a term life assurance policy: if you die during the term of the policy, your designated beneficiary receives the value of the policy tax-free. There's no accumulation of capital, however, and if you cancel the policy or reach the end of the term alive, your cover ends with no return of the premiums paid over the years. If you borrow money, for example, to build or purchase a house or to establish a business, the lender may require you to purchase this type of life insurance to secure the unpaid balance of the loan in the event of your premature death.

It's wise to leave a copy of all insurance policies with your will and with your lawyer. If you don't have a lawyer, keep a copy in a safe deposit box. A life insurance policy must usually be sent to the insurance company upon the death of the insured, with a copy of the death certificate.

14.

FINANCE

One of the surprising things about the Germans to some foreigners is that they don't usually pay bills with cheques or credit cards, although this is changing quite rapidly in some areas. Many prefer to pay in cash and it isn't uncommon to find shops, restaurants and even some small hotels that don't accept credit cards. (However, most such establishments will happily point you to the nearest cash machine so that you can use your credit card to draw out the cash to pay your bill!) Compared with many other western countries, particularly Britain and the US, Germany a credit oriented economy on the everyday level. However, don't be fooled into thinking that this means the Germans are old-fashioned in their attitude towards money and avoid borrowing. The country has a highly efficient and dynamic banking system, which is one of the most advanced in the world.

When you arrive in Germany to take up residence or employment, ensure that you have sufficient cash, travellers' cheques, luncheon vouchers, coffee machine tokens, gold sovereigns and diamonds to last at least until your first pay day, which may be some time after your arrival. During this period you may also find an international credit card useful.

GERMAN CURRENCY

The euro (€) is now the official currency of Germany (along with Austria, Belgium, Finland, France, Greece, the Republic of Ireland Italy, Luxembourg, the Netherlands, Portugal and Spain) following the Deutschmark's final bow into history on July 1st 2002. In April 2003, the euro reversed its decline against the dollar and pound (the Germans initially dubbed it the *teuro* – a pun on *teuer*, the German word for 'expensive') and is now worth more than at its launch. The euro exchange rates (*Wechselkurs*) against most major international currencies are listed in banks and daily newspapers, as well as on numerous financial websites (e.g. ⌨ http://cnnfn.com/markets/currencies).

As in most euro-zone countries, locals still talk largely in old currency – marks or Deutschmarks (DM) – and are likely to continue doing so for several years, so it's worth noting that two marks are roughly equivalent to one euro (officially €1 = 1.95583DM).

The euro (*Euro* in both singular and plural) is divided into 100 cents (*Cent* in both singular and plural). Coins are minted in 1, 2, 5, 10, 20 and 50 cents and 1 and 2 euro denominations. The coins all have a common European face, with a map of the European Union (EU) and the stars of the European flag. The obverse is different for each member country (designs on German coins include the Brandenburg Gate, an oak-leaf garland and an eagle – the state symbol), although all euro coins can be used in all euro-zone countries – in theory, as minute differences in weight can cause problems with cash machines, e.g. at motorway tolls.

Euro banknotes are printed in 5, 10, 20, 50, 100, 200 and 500 euro denominations. The design of the notes was subject to considerable debate and contention, and the winning design depicts 'symbolic' representations of Europe's architectural heritage. None of the images on any of the notes is supposed to be an actual building, bridge or arch, although there have been numerous claims in the press and elsewhere that the structures shown are actually landmarks in certain countries, including Germany.

When dealing with the euro, beware of counterfeit banknotes, some of which are made with sophisticated colour laser copiers. Genuine banknotes contain a number of anti-counterfeit devices, including watermarks, a metallic reflection strip and special inks and printing techniques, which change the colours you see depending on the angle from which you view the notes.

The euro symbol (€) is generally available on most computer keyboards and calculators unless you're using pre-1997 (or so) equipment or software. Financial software in most of Europe can be easily upgraded to make use of the symbol if it isn't already incorporated into the current release, and the Microsoft website (🖳 www.microsoft.com) has keyboard and operating system updates available for downloading.

IMPORTING & EXPORTING MONEY

Germany has no currency restrictions and you may bring in or take out as much money as you wish in any currency, although you're obliged to report to the Bundesbank any movements of cash into or out of the country exceeding €12,500.

When transferring or sending money to (or from) Germany, you should be aware of the alternatives, which include the following:

- **Bank Draft** – A bank draft (*Bankscheck*) should be sent by registered post. However, in the (albeit unlikely) event that it's lost or stolen, it's impossible to stop payment and you must wait six months before a new draft can be issued. Bank drafts aren't treated as cash in Germany and must be cleared, as with personal cheques.

- **Bank Transfer** – A normal bank transfer (*zwischenbankliche Überweisung*) should take three to seven days, but in reality can take much longer and an international bank transfer between non-affiliated banks can take weeks! Although German banks are among the most efficient in the world, it isn't unusual for transfers to and from Germany to get 'stuck' in the pipeline, which allows the German bank to use your money for a period interest free.

Americans might like to investigate the Paypal system (see 🖳 www.paypal.com or the German version 🖳 www.paypal.de), which, although designed to facilitate international payments for goods bought on the internet, provides the cheapest means of making international dollar-euro transfers in general, although it's principally attractive for minor transactions, in which the exchange costs would otherwise be high in proportion to the sum transferred.

- **SWIFT Transfer** – One of the safest and fastest methods of transferring money is via the Society of Worldwide Interbank Financial Telecommunications (SWIFT) system. A SWIFT transfer should be completed in a few hours, funds being available within 24 hours, although even SWIFT transfers can take five working days, especially from small branches that are unused to dealing with foreign transfers. Australian and UK members of the SWIFT system are listed on the Society's website (🖳 www.swift.com). The cost of transfers varies considerably – not only commission and exchange rates, but also transfer charges – but is usually between around €30 and €50. Britons should note that one of the cheapest ways to transfer money to France is via the Co-Operative Bank's TIPANET service, which costs just £8 for telephone transfers of up to £5,000.

- **Currency Dealer** – It may be quicker to use a specialist currency dealer (e.g. Currencies For Less in the UK, ☎ 020-7228 7667, 🖳 www.currencies4less.com) to carry out the transfer for you, and you may get a better exchange rate than from a bank.

Some banks add a service charge to transactions originating outside Germany, irrespective of the currencies involved and despite the advent of the euro. The European Commission has registered this fact and similar developments elsewhere with distaste, and as a result introduced EU-regulation No 2560/2001, which states that from 1 July 2003 the charge for an international payment in euros anywhere in the EU should be the same as if it were a domestic payment in the country in which it is made. This means that all such payments in euros within the EU should now be free of charge for private Postbank customers.

Always check charges and exchange rates in advance and agree them with your bank (you may be able to negotiate a lower charge or a better exchange rate). Shop around a number of banks and compare fees. Banks are often willing to negotiate on fees and exchange rates when you're transferring a large amount of money. Some foreign banks levy a flat-fee for electronic transfers, irrespective of the amount. British banks charge between £10 and £45 for transfers taking from one to five days or longer.

When you have money transferred to a bank in Germany, make sure that you give the account holder's name, the account number, the branch number and the bank code. If money is 'lost' while being transferred to or from an German bank account, it can take weeks to locate it.

If you plan to send a large amount of money to Italy or abroad for a business transaction such as buying property, you should ensure that you receive the commercial rate of exchange rather than the tourist rate.

If you routinely transfer large sums of money between currencies, you should investigate Fidelity Money Funds, which operate free of conversion charges and at wholesale rates of exchange.

There are many companies specialising in foreign exchange, particularly large sums of money, such as Currencies Direct (☎ UK 020-7813 0332, 🖳 www.currenciesdirect.com), Halewood (☎ UK 01753-859159, 🖳 www. hifx.co.uk) and Moneycorp (☎UK 020-7808 0500, 🖳 www.moneycorp.com).

Obtaining Cash

There are various methods of obtaining smaller amounts of money for everyday use. These include the following:

● **Bureaux De Change** – Most banks in major cities have foreign exchange windows, where you can buy and sell foreign currencies, buy and cash travellers' cheques, and obtain a cash advance on credit and charge cards. Banks tend to offer the best exchange rates and the post office the lowest charges (a flat rate of €6.50 per transaction, irrespective of the amount).

There are many private exchange bureaux at airports, main railway stations and major cities with longer business hours than banks, particularly at weekends. Most offer competitive exchange rates and low or no commission (but always check). They're easier to deal with than banks and, if you're changing a lot of money, you can usually negotiate a better exchange rate. Foreign currency can also be purchased from foreign currency dispensing machines at certain branches of major German banks, e.g. in shopping centres and at airports, while the most popular foreign currencies (e.g. US$, sterling and Swiss francs) can be changed into euros via currency machines at airports and major railway stations. **However, airport bureaux de change and change machines usually offer the worst exchange rates and charge the highest fees (e.g. handling charges).** Many German hotels and shops accept and exchange foreign currency, but almost always at a less favourable rate than banks. Never use unofficial money changers, who are likely to short change you.

- **Cards** – If you need instant cash, you can draw on debit, credit or charge cards (but there's usually a daily limit). Many foreigners living in Germany (particularly retirees) keep the bulk of their money in a foreign account (perhaps in an offshore bank) and draw on it with a cash or credit card. This is an ideal solution for holidaymakers and holiday homeowners (although homeowners will still need a German bank account to pay their bills). Exchange rates are better when obtaining cash with a credit or debit card as you're given the wholesale rate, although there's a 1.5 per cent charge on cash advances and ATM transactions in foreign currencies. Some ATMs may reject foreign cards – if this happens try again and if necessary try another ATM.

- **Eurogiro** – Giro postcheques (Eurogiros) issued by European post offices can be cashed (with a postcheque guarantee card) at main post offices in Germany. The maximum value per cheque depends on the country where issued, e.g. €250 if issued in the UK. There's a standard charge for each cheque of €3.80 plus 0.7 per cent of the amount. You can also send money to Germany via the Girobank Eurogiro system from post offices in 15 Europe and the US to some German banks.

- **Telegraphic Transfer** – One of the quickest (it takes around ten minutes) and safest methods of transferring cash is via a telegraphic transfer, e.g. Moneygram (☎ UK 0800-666 3947, 💻 www.moneygram.com) or Western Union (☎ UK 0800-833833, 💻 www.westernunion.com), but it's also one of the most expensive, e.g. commission of 7 to 10 per cent of the amount sent! Western Union transfers can be picked up from a post office in Germany (and 100 other countries) just 15 minutes after being paid into an office abroad. Money can be sent via American Express offices by Amex cardholders.

- **Travellers' Cheques** – If you're visiting Germany, it's safer to carry travellers' cheques (*Reisescheck*) than cash. It's also advantageous, as all banks give a higher exchange rate for travellers' cheques than for banknotes. You can buy euro travellers' cheques, which can be used anywhere in Europe. Travellers' cheques aren't as easy to cash in Germany as in some other countries, e.g. the US, and they're especially difficult to change in rural areas. They aren't usually accepted as cash by businesses, except perhaps in hotels, restaurants and shops in major cities, which usually offer a poor exchange rate. You can buy travellers' cheques from any German bank, usually for a fee of 1 per cent of the face value.

  Fees and rates vary considerably when cashing travellers' cheques in Germany. Among the cheapest is the post office, which charges €6.50 per cheque. Buying large denomination cheques saves on per-cheque exchange charges. American Express and Thomas Cook offices don't charge for cashing their own cheques. Banks usually offer a better exchange rate for travellers' cheques than for banknotes.

Always keep a separate record of cheque numbers and note where and when they were cashed. American Express provides a free, three-hour replacement service for lost or stolen travellers' cheques at any of their offices world-wide, provided you know the serial numbers of the lost cheques. Without the serial numbers, replacement can take three days or longer. Most companies provide toll-free numbers for reporting lost or stolen travellers' cheques in Germany.

One thing to bear in mind when travelling anywhere is not to rely on one source of funds only.

Since the advent of the euro, there has been demand for foreign exchange facilities in Germany, but you can still buy foreign currency, even in very small towns. However, it often pays to check in advance that they have the one you require.

As well as *bureaux de change*, most main railway stations have offices with extended opening hours where you can buy and cash travellers' cheques, cash postcheques, and obtain a cash advance on credit cards. When these offices are closed, most larger railway stations and airports have bank ATM machines (as do most bank branches), where you can withdraw cash in euros using a cash or credit card.

Happily you can donate any spare change weighing down your pockets to a variety of worthy causes when you pass through most airports in Germany and in much of the rest of Europe.

BANKS

There are three broad categories of bank in Germany: private commercial banks, public savings banks (*Sparkassen*) and credit co-operatives. The differences between the three types of bank relate principally to their legal forms and business structures rather than to the services they offer, and most banking institutions offer a full range of banking, investment and insurance services; many banks also provide advice regarding property rental and purchase and personal financial planning. It isn't unusual to find banks selling travel packages or tickets to local concerts and other events.

Private commercial banks include the so-called big three German banks: Deutsche Bank, Commerzbank and Dresdner Bank, often described as 'universal banks'. The private banking sector also includes almost 200 regional banks (e.g. Bayerische Vereinsbank, BfG Bank, and Berliner Bank), the Postbank (see page 132) and numerous branches of over 300 foreign banks (including Barclays and Citibank).

Public savings banks include the 600 or so local *Sparkassen* that are independently operated by town, district and municipal authorities, and linked to one another via regional and central giro institutions.

Co-operative credit associations, once limited to members of specific trades or associations, have long ago evolved into full service banks mostly operating under the names of *Volksbank* or *Raiffeisenbank*.

The banking industry in Germany is one of the most dynamic sectors of the economy. Twenty-four hour telephone banking has been available for many years and even the smallest banks now offer most services via the Internet and even direct computer link as well as via fax.

Opening Hours

Normal bank opening hours are from 8 or 9am until 4.30pm or sometimes as late as 6pm, with no closure over the lunch period in cities and large towns. The main offices of many banks tend to keep similar hours to the local shops and may even open on Saturdays, at least for some counter services. Most banks in Germany have automatic teller machines (ATMs) and statement machines available 24 hours a day in a secure lobby or vestibule area, so that customers can withdraw cash, make deposits and check statements at their convenience.

Opening An Account

One of your first things to do on arrival in Germany should be to open a bank account. Simply go to the bank of your choice and tell them you're living or working in Germany and wish to open an account. You will normally be asked to provide standard identification and it may be useful to be able to offer a letter of reference from your bank in your home country or from a German employer, although this isn't usually necessary.

If you prefer to open an Internet-based account, you must generally complete a form on the bank's website, after which you will receive an account information pack by post, although once you've opened an account you can perform most transactions online.

The almost universal method used to pay bills is by direct bank transfer (see page 312) and cheques are rarely used. However, in order to be able to make a direct bank transfer, you must have a giro account (*Girokonto*), which can be opened at any bank, including Postbank (see page 132). A *Postgirokonto* is among the cheapest bank accounts and, provided you deposit at least €1,000 per month or are under 26 (28 if you're a student), you're eligible for a *Giro Plus* account, for which there's no maintenance fee. If you don't fulfil either of these conditions, the monthly fee for a standard account is €5.90.

After opening an account, don't forget to give the details (account number and bank identification number – *Bankleitzahl* or *BLZ*) to your employer if you wish to be paid, as your salary usually goes directly into your bank account. Some companies have a preferential arrangement with a particular bank, which may result in lower bank charges for employees. Your monthly salary statement will be sent to your home address or given to you at work. Most banks allow giro account holders to overdraw their accounts (see **Overdrafts & Loans** on page 315).

You can usually make arrangements with your bank to send statements to you as often as you like, e.g. monthly, weekly or even daily if you want to keep a really close track of your money. However, some banks have discontinued this service, as an increasing number of customers use the Internet to check their accounts. There is, of course, a charge for the traditional statement service and the more frequently you wish to have a statement, the more expensive it is (most people receive monthly statements). However, most banks provide a separate machine in their lobby or alongside an ATM that permits you to print a bank statement whenever you want one, free of charge. You simply insert your bank card into the machine (at a branch of your bank), enter your PIN and a statement is printed detailing all transactions on your account since the last time you requested a statement.

Your statement will often be the only notification you receive from the bank about the charges they've deducted, so you should check it carefully. At the end of the year, your statement will include the annual totals required for tax and other reports. If you lose your copy of a bank statement, you must ask your bank for a duplicate, for which you will be charged a fee. If you use a bank's online banking services, be sure to print the statements you need periodically, and don't forget to make a copy of files if you download your banking information.

German banks issue multi-purpose bank cards (see **Cash & Debit Cards** below), which also act as cheque guarantee cards – usually up to around €200. Don't keep your bankcard and cheque book in the same place; if you lose both your card and cheques at the same time, or they're stolen and cheques cashed, you may find that you're liable for the amounts debited from your account due to negligence. You're largely responsible for loss, improper use or forgery, and for mistakes due to missing or unclear designation of the currency denomination. Bank staff can be lax when checking signatures or identification.

When writing figures in Germany (or anywhere in continental Europe), you should cross the down stroke of the number 7 in order to avoid confusion with the number 1, which is often written with a leading upstroke and resembles a seven to many non-Europeans (and Britons). Americans should note that Germans (like other Europeans) write the date with the day first followed by the month and year. For example, 1.9.04 is 1st September 2004 and not 9th January 2004. The conventional US form 9/1/04, with the month first and slashes between the digits, must never be used!

Direct Bank Transfers

The usual and most common method of making payments within Germany is a direct bank transfer. There are two basic kinds of bank transfer, depending on whether you're instructing the bank to transfer money from your account to another account (*Überweisungsauftrag*) or are authorising the bank to allow a third party (e.g. a utility company) take the money from your account (*Lastschriftverfahren*).

Überweisungsauftrag: The *Überweisungsauftrag* consists of a three-part form. You enter your name and account number and the identification number of your bank, and the name of the person or company you want to pay and their bank account and bank identification number. (This information must be printed on all bills and invoices sent to you for payment.) There's a space where you can enter the reason for the payment (whatever you put here will be printed on your bank statement) and another for the amount you want to transfer. You sign the form and keep one copy (the *Beleg für Auftraggeber*), giving the other two copies to your bank. You can either take or post the *Überweisungsauftrag* to your bank (most people post a number of forms at regular intervals).

Payment is generally made within one to two business days of the bank's receipt of the payment order.

Often when you receive a bill in the post, it will include an *Überweisungsauftrag* form with the company's bank details and the amount already completed. You simply insert your bank details and sign the form before giving or sending it to your bank (don't send it back to the company!).

An *Überweisungsauftrag* form doesn't include the date – either the date you submit the form to the bank or the date you want payment to be made – so you may wish to mark the date on your copy for reference. It's also wise to keep your copies of *Überweisungsaufträge* you've submitted to the bank in the same place as your bank statements, so you can check that payments have been made.

Lastschriftverfahren: Instead of directing your bank to pay a creditor, a *Lastschrift* is an authorisation permitting a creditor to debit a specified sum from your account, usually on a specific date (*Lastschriftverfahren* is the term for this process). While either an *Überweisungsauftrag* or a *Lastschrift* can be used to make a single payment, *Lastschriften* are often used to settle recurring expenses, such as rent, utility charges, car insurance premiums, magazine subscriptions and other regular payments made monthly, quarterly or annually.

Standing Orders: To arrange for a regular debit from your account (*Dauerauftrag*) – either a *Überweisungsauftrag* or a *Lastschriftverfahren* – contact your bank with the relevant payment information, including the bank account number of the person or company you want to pay. (Note that there's no distinction between a standing order and a direct debit, as there is in the UK, for example.) If you have an Internet or other electronic bank account, you can usually establish, change and cancel single or standing order payments over the Internet or by fax or phone. Make sure that you keep copies of all transactions you authorise, plus the associated contracts or bills containing the bank account details and amounts. Your bank is responsible for correcting any errors made when transferring funds to or from your account, but corrections can be made much more quickly if you can produce documentation to back up your claim.

Savings Accounts

You can open a savings account (*Sparkonto*) with commercial, co-operative and savings banks. Your employer may also offer a form of tax protected savings account at your own or another local bank. Most financial institutions offer a variety of savings and deposit accounts, with varying interest rates and minimum deposits, depending on the type of account and bank. In most cases the first €1,601 (€3,202 for a married couple) in savings account interest is exempt from taxes, and there are additional tax advantages for savings accounts established to buy a home. With deposit accounts (term deposits) you must be prepared to tie up your money for a period of 1 to 12 months. The longer the term, the higher the return.

You receive a pass book (*Sparbuch*) for a savings account, where all deposits and withdrawals are recorded. If you take part in an employer-sponsored savings plan, you must take your pass book to the bank every few months to have the balance updated.

Cash & Debit Cards

German banks issue customers with a bank card which enables them to obtain cash from ATMs and obtain statements from a bank's statement machine. The bank card functions not only as a guarantee card but also as a debit card, and it can be used to make purchases (such as petrol) from outlets displaying the relevant service sign, where goods up to the a certain weekly value can be paid for by card (€1,500 per week in the case of the Postbank card, for example, the sign to look for being 'Maestro'). You're also issued with a personal identification number (PIN). **Make a note of your PIN immediately and keep it in a secure place, as the ink on the form on which it's printed is designed to fade in a fairly short time.** Although you may make deposits without a PIN, you need it to make withdrawals. If you lose your bank card, notify your bank as soon as possible, as it can be used to withdraw cash and make purchases.

If you're banking with the Postbank (see page 132) or one of the associated Cash Group of banks (which includes the Commerzbank, Deutsche Bank, Dresdner Bank and the Hypo Vereinsbank), cash withdrawals are free at any of these banks. A withdrawal from the ATMs of other banks costs a standardised €3.80. There is a maximum of €500 a day for Postbank Giro account withdrawals from any source.

The latest innovation is the 'money card' (*Geldkarte*), which can be used at outlets displaying a 'GELDKARTE' sign. Cards are issued by your bank and can be 'charged' with up to €200 from your account.

CREDIT & CHARGE CARDS

Credit and charge cards are referred to collectively as credit cards; in fact, most of them operate like charge cards in that payments for purchases are due when billed and cannot be paid over a period of several months or years. It's sometimes possible to make deferred payments on travel costs (mostly air fares and hotel bills) charged to your card, but only over a few months (normally two or three months maximum).

Although they've been slow to gain acceptance, many Germans still preferring to pay for purchases in cash or with a debit card, there has been a marked increase in their popularity in the last decade, particularly due to their usefulness in shopping via the Internet or abroad. The most common cards are Visa and MasterCard, which are available from most banks. American Express, Diners Club and Barclaycard are also popular.

While credit cards in Germany can cost you as little as €12 per year if you're a student, most other people must pay between €20 and €80 per year. Top-of-the-range cards (i.e. those with the greatest pose-value), such as the American Express Centurion card, can set you back €400 annually. Some cards include travel or other forms of insurance as part of the annual fee or as an add-on feature; others provide free travel and accident life insurance when travel costs are paid for with the card.

Most credit cards allow you to withdraw cash from ATMs which are part of their network, although there's usually a hefty charge per transaction. In the case of the Postbank, which belongs to the Cash Group, for example, this is 2 per cent of the amount withdrawn and a minimum of €5. Before obtaining a credit or charge card, compare the costs and benefits.

As part of the sign-up process, you're required to indicate the bank account you wish to use to pay your monthly balance, and the contract includes a standing order payment to permit the card company to debit payments automatically from your account. You will receive a statement of your monthly charges around ten days before the date that the amount due is debited from your account, so you have an opportunity to review the statement and dispute any incorrect payments or charges. Like most other forms of contract in Germany, a credit card requires you to give formal written notification at least three months before its expiration date if you wish to cancel it and avoid paying the following year's fee.

If you maintain a bank account abroad, it's wise to retain your foreign credit cards. One of the advantages of using a credit card issued abroad is that your bill is usually rendered or your account debited up to six weeks later, therefore giving you interest-free credit – except when cards are used to obtain cash, when interest starts immediately. You may, however, find it more convenient and cheaper to be billed in euros than in a foreign currency, when you must wait for the bill from outside Germany and payments may vary due to exchange rate fluctuations.

If you lose a bank or credit card, report it immediately to the issuing office. You can insure against losing credit cards or you may be able to pay a fee to the card company, relieving you of any liability.

Even if you don't like plastic money and shun any form of credit, credit cards have their uses, e.g.no deposits on hire cars and no pre-paying hotel and other bills. Cards also provide greater safety and security than cash, as well as convenience and flexibility. They are particularly useful when travelling abroad and you must have some form of credit card if you wish to make purchases over the Internet (which often save you money).

OVERDRAFTS & LOANS

Most banks allow giro account holders to overdraw their accounts by a specific sum as part of their general account terms. You may find that you're advanced round sums (e.g. €100 for an overdraft of up to that amount) and will be charged interest on the amount advanced at the current overdraft rate until the overdraft is repaid; it therefore doesn't pay to go overdrawn for a few euros only!

All German banks provide loans, although they aren't as free with their money as banks in many other European countries, particularly regarding business loans to foreigners. Loans are subject to your income and the amount of debt you already have. In Germany, the old maxim still applies: the best way to qualify for a loan is to convince a bank that you don't really need one!

It pays to shop around for a loan, as interest rates vary considerably according to the bank, the amount, the purpose and the period of the loan. Generally, loans of up to a year are considered short-term credit, loans for one to four years are medium-term, and anything longer than four years is long-term. Interest rates in August 2003 ranged from around 9 per cent (for a 12-month loan) to around 10 per cent (for a six-year loan), although cheaper loans could be arranged via the Internet (e.g. around 7.5 per cent interest). German bankers are highly risk-averse and tend to prefer making loans where there's adequate collateral or where the borrower is also making a major investment from savings or other personal resources.

If you're making a major purchase, such as a car or an expensive household appliance, you may find that the vendor or manufacturer offers financing through a bank set up expressly for this purpose. These 'banks' are captive finance companies and don't offer any other banking services except for consumer credit for purchases of goods sold by their parent company. The deals they offer are usually quite competitive, but nevertheless it's worth shopping around and comparing interest rates and terms.

Borrowing from private loan companies, as advertised in newspapers, is expensive (i.e. interest rates are high). Use them only as a last resort, when all the other means have been exhausted. Even then, as a foreigner, you may find that the term of your loan is limited to the expiration date of your residence or work permit, or that you're required to repay the loan in full if you move abroad. In general, the more desperate your financial situation, the more suspicious you should be of anyone willing to lend you money.

Mortgages

Mortgages (home loans) are available from all major German banks, but the lending criteria are rather different from what you may be used to, particularly if you're from Britain or the US. Banks and other mortgage institutions base their loans on the value they assign to a property (the *Beleihungswert*) rather than to its actual purchase price and are permitted to lend only 60 per cent of this value as a principal mortgage, although you may be able to negotiate a higher *Beleihungswert*. If necessary, a homebuyer must secure a second mortgage (at less favourable terms) for the remaining amount. It isn't uncommon for German employers (particularly family-owned companies in the *Mittelstand*) to lend money directly to employees making home purchases, or even to co-sign or otherwise support a second mortgage through the employer's bank. While Germans often turn to their employers for mortgage loans in this manner, most British and American multinational companies have company policies specifically forbidding the practice, although their German branch offices may ignore this.

Mortgage loans in Germany can be at either a fixed or a variable interest rate and most lenders require that all mortgages are repaid before normal retirement age. (Add to this typical deposits of 20 to 50 per cent and another 4 to 10 per cent of the purchase price in fees, taxes and transfer costs, and it's easy to see why most people in Germany prefer to rent their homes rather than buy. See also **Chapter 5**.)

If you take out a mortgage, the lender may require you to purchase term life insurance (*Risikolebensversicherung*) to secure the unpaid balance of the loan in the event of your premature death (see page 300).

INCOME TAX

Income tax (*Einkommensteuer*) in Germany is the government's main source of revenue, providing around 35 per cent of the total budget, followed by value added tax (VAT), which brings in some 22 per cent. It's often contended that German income tax rates are high compared with the rest of Europe, but this was never entirely true and is now less true than it was, given recent tax reforms. The top rate is currently 47 per cent and will be down to 42 per cent by 2005, when the basic rate will be 15 per cent. This is unlikely to still the clamour for more radical tax cuts from those who see these as the magic wand that will solve Germany's economic problems, so any subsequent rate changes will almost certainly be in the downward direction, although the German government faces the same dilemma as those of many other countries in wanting neither add to the tax burden of businesses nor to cut spending on welfare programmes or benefits.

As in many other countries, employees' income tax (*Lohnsteuer* – literally 'salary tax') is deducted at source by their employers, i.e. pay as you earn (PAYE). The system used in Germany is extremely efficient and the amounts deducted usually cover your tax obligation almost to the cent, at least for those with no income other than from their regular employment. If you have no other source of income and no further credits or other adjustments to make for income tax purposes, you don't even need to file an income tax return. Most employees, however, end up having to file a return, if only to claim a refund or to declare and pay taxes on other sources of income.

The German tax system is somewhat complicated, above all if you don't have a good command of the language. There are usually changes to allowances or deductions each year and it can be difficult to keep up to date with the evolving tax laws. Unless your tax affairs are simple, it's prudent to employ a tax adviser (*Steuerberater*) to complete your tax return and ensure that you're correctly assessed. If you're self-employed or in business, finding a good one can mean the difference between success and failure, and his fee is tax-deductible!

If you decide to do it yourself, many books, websites, magazines and computer programs are available to help you understand and save taxes, prepare your tax returns and calculate your final tax bill. You must however understand German well (and possibly have a good business or legal dictionary handy!) to complete your tax return. Note that the information below applies only to personal income tax and not to companies. **There are ruinous fines and possible imprisonment for those caught evading tax.**

Liability

Your liability for German taxes depends on where you're domiciled, which is usually the country you regard as your permanent home and where you live most of the year. A foreigner working in Germany who has taken up residence there is considered to have his tax domicile in Germany. A person can be resident in more than one country at a time but can only be domiciled in one country. There are special tax rules that apply to people living in one country and working in another (known as 'border hoppers' – *Grenzenspringer*), but in general these people pay taxes in the country in which they live.

German residents are taxed on their world-wide income, subject to certain treaty exceptions, while non-residents are taxed only on income arising in Germany. Most countries exempt their citizens from paying income tax if they're living outside their home country for a certain period. Germany has an extensive network of double taxation treaties in order to ensure that income that has already been taxed in one treaty country isn't taxed again in another.

Americans should be aware that the US is the only country that taxes its non-resident citizens on income earned abroad and requires a tax return to be filed even if most or all of your income is exempt from taxation. US citizens can obtain information on tax filing requirements from an American embassy or consulate or via the Internet (🖥 www.irs.ustreas.gov).

Note that unmarried couples aren't treated (for tax purposes) in the same way as married couples, the latter enjoying certain tax advantages.

If you're in doubt about your tax liability in your home country, contact your nearest embassy or consulate in Germany.

Tax Card

Shortly after you register (*anmelden*) at your local *Stadtverwaltung* (see **Registration** on page 85), you will receive a tax card (*Lohnsteuerkarte*) based on the information you provided on registration. You should check the information printed on your tax card carefully, including your name, address, date of birth, church tax category (see page 86), and the number of children for whom you're claiming child credit or allowances. The tax card will show your taxpayer identification number, which you should quote on all correspondence with the tax authorities, and your assigned tax class (*Steuerklasse* – abbreviated to *StKl*), which determines how much your employer must deduct from your pay for income tax.

If you're single, you will probably be assigned to *StKl I*. (Single for tax purposes includes divorced, widowed and married people who are legally separated and living apart from their spouses.) *StKl II* is for single people drawing certain types of assistance, which entitles them to special income tax reductions. Married people are assigned to a tax class according to whether their spouse is employed or not: *StKl III* is for a married person considered to be the primary breadwinner for the family. If a husband and wife are both employed full-time, both spouses will normally be assigned to *StKl IV*. *StKl V* is reserved for married people who need or wish to have extra taxes deducted from their pay each month to make up for the fact that their husband or wife is already assigned to *StKl III*.

You should give your tax card to your employer as soon as you receive it, as it serves as the basis upon which taxes are deducted from your pay. At the end of the year, your employer returns your tax card with a statement showing your income for the year and the social security payments and taxes deducted and paid on your behalf.

If any changes must be made to your tax card, you should contact your local town hall immediately to have any corrections made, both on the card and in your file.

Taxable Income

The following seven types of income are subject to income tax under German law and you must report all income related to these categories, irrespective of the source:

1. Farming and forestry;
2. Trade or business;
3. Independent services (i.e. self-employment);
4. Employment;
5. Capital investment;
6. Rents and leases;
7. Other income.

Category 7 is strictly defined to include annuities, maintenance payments (alimony) and similar legally mandated payments between spouses or partners, and other types of income specifically named in the tax law. The good news is that, if you receive payments that aren't defined in law as coming under one of the seven categories, they're tax-free! One of these is lottery winnings, which aren't subject to income tax in Germany. (Americans, however, are expected to pay income tax to their own government if they win the German lotto while resident in Germany!)

As mentioned above, your employer is responsible for reporting and paying the appropriate income tax on your employment income. Income from employment includes not only your salary, but also such things as overseas and cost of living allowances, profit sharing plans and bonuses, storage and relocation allowances, language lessons provided for a spouse, personal company car, payments in kind (such as free accommodation or meals), home leave or holiday (paid for by your employer), and children's education expenses. Your employer is required to value these benefits and services and include them on your pay slip each month when calculating the taxes to be deducted from your salary. They should also be included in the amounts reported for the year on your tax card.

Allowances

The tax payments your employer makes for you take into account certain standard allowances against income. The allowances listed below applied to 2003 income (most allowances are indexed annually). Social security contributions are automatically deducted from taxable income.

- The cost of getting to and from your place of work, based on a flat rate per kilometre (currently €0.30);

- A deduction for general employee expenses (*Arbeitnehmerpauschalbetrag*) of €1,044. You can deduct more (up to certain limits) if you have receipts to justify the larger amount.

- Most insurance premiums, including life insurance, private health insurance, long-term care insurance, accident insurance and most forms of liability insurance up to a total of €3,068 for a single person or €6,136 for a couple;

- Contributions (*Spenden*) to charitable, religious or scientific research organisations, generally up to 5 per cent but in a few instances up to 10 per cent of your income;

- Costs incurred for 'extraordinary burdens' (*aussergewöhnliche Belastungen*) such as caring for a handicapped family member, hiring household help and private vocational training for a child;

- Training or continuing education in order to change or enhance your career (under certain circumstances and subject to limits);

- The first €1,601 of income from interest on investments or savings (€3,202 for a married couple filing jointly).

There are many other allowances, which usually change annually depending on specific government programmes. Any that aren't allowed for by your employer can be claimed on your annual tax return (see page 322).

Tax Calculation

The tax year in Germany is the same as the calendar year, from 1st January to 31st December. Families and married couples are usually taxed as a single entity; however, married couples can elect to file separate returns if they wish to claim individual tax credits and allowances.

Children under the age of 18 are included on their parents' (or a parent's) tax return. Children over the age of 18 can be included on their parents' tax return if they're enrolled in school or a vocational training programme. Earnings for the school year from part-time jobs or training schemes must be declared on the family's tax return, although they aren't generally subject to income tax.

The tax payable is calculated according to your taxable income minus allowances. Income up to the base threshold level (*Grundfreibetrag*) isn't taxed (or, officially, is taxed at a 0 per cent rate). In 2003 this level was €7,426. (It's due to rise to €7,664 by 2005.) Above the threshold level, income is taxed progressively at between 17 and 47 per cent as shown below on a sliding scale rather than in 'steps' as in most other countries, which means that you must wade through reams of income tax tables (*Einkommensteuer Tabellen*) to find out how much tax you owe.

In 2003, the tax burden for single taxpayers (or a couple filing separately) was as shown below.

Taxable Income (€)	Tax Rate (%)
Up to 7,426	0
7,426 – 12,755	17 – 24.97
12,755 – 52,292	24.97 – 47
Over 52,292	47

Married taxpayers (but not unmarried partners) filing jointly pay taxes based on so-called 'splitting tables' (*Splitting-Tabelle*), whereby their combined income is taxed at the rate that applies to half the total; for example, if a couple earns €100,000, they will pay tax on this amount but at the rate normally applied to an income of €50,000.

It's planned that the top rate of tax will be reduced to 42 per cent and the basic rate to 15 per cent by the year 2005.

Credits

Once you've calculated your tax due, you can claim a tax credit (*Kinderfreibetrag*) for each dependent child of €1,824 per parent (or €3,648 for parents filing jointly). Divorced parents with joint-custody arrangements are generally entitled to half a credit each per child, provided the child lives in Germany. It's possible to claim a credit for a child living outside Germany if you're legally obliged to support the child, e.g. under a divorce or separation agreement, or some other form of child support decree.

Surcharges

Those who declare themselves affiliated to certain religions must pay a church tax, which is levied at 8 or 9 per cent of the amount of income tax due (see page 86). There's also a solidarity surcharge, imposed in 1995 to help finance the reunification of the former East and West German states, which is currently levied at 5.5 per cent of your income tax due; although the government claims to intend to reduce it further (it was originally 7.5 per cent of tax), there's currently no sign of this happening.

Income Tax Returns

Some time in January, your employer will return your tax card to you, with the sections related to earnings, allowances, credits and payments completed for the year just ended. Normally you will also receive a set of tax forms and instructions from the local tax authorities (*Finanzamt*), but if you don't you can pick up copies from your town hall or the *Finanzamt* itself. Some post offices and banks keep copies of the most common tax forms.

Self-employed people, business owners and other non-employees must file a tax return if their income from all sources exceeds the threshold filing limit (see **Tax Calculation** above). Employees who have had income tax deducted from their wages and who have no other source of income aren't required to file a return unless they need to claim a tax adjustment. Most employees can normally dredge up a few extra allowances, however, and generally claim at least a small refund of taxes deducted.

Tax returns should be filed on or before 31st May of the year following the tax year; for example, the return for the year 2003 should be filed by 31st May 2004. The tax office is authorised to grant extensions and normally does so on request, up to the end of the year following the tax year, which is the absolute deadline for filing (i.e. 31st December 2004 for the 2003 tax return). If you haven't filed a return by this time, you lose any claim you may have had to a tax refund. To request an extension, you normally need only include a letter with your return, stating the reason you couldn't file by the 31st May deadline. Acceptable reasons include being busy with work, travel or family concerns. However, the tax inspector can impose a penalty of up to 10 per cent of the taxes due, so it's wise to file your return on time if there's any possibility that you will owe additional tax. (Needless to say, the tax authorities won't pay you interest if you're late claiming a refund!) If you haven't filed your return by the 31st May deadline, it's usually wise to have a tax adviser file it for you (the tax adviser's fee is deductible on your next tax return).

German tax returns can be complicated, particularly if you aren't familiar with the language and the specialist terms used on the forms. You must declare your income and document your rights to the various allowances and credits. The forms don't help you to calculate the amount of tax you must pay, although you can buy books and computer programmes that include the appropriate tax tables along with instructions on estimating your final bill. You must include your tax card with the return, so be sure to take a copy of your card, as well as a copy of your return and any additional documents included.

A general income tax form includes basic personal information such as your taxpayer identification number, name, address, occupation, spouse's name and his or her occupation. Most of this information will already be printed on the form if you received it by post from the *Finanzamt*. The tax authorities need your bank account number and the bank identification number (*BLZ*) for the account which you wish to use to pay your taxes or to receive any refund due. If you haven't received an identification number by the time you file your form, leave that space blank and the tax office will assign you a number and send it to you with your bill or statement.

You will also need other forms (*Anlage*) according to your situation. These may include:

- N – to report employment income;
- VL – to report capital investments (this form is usually provided by the investment institution);
- KSO – to report income from other investments (interest or dividends, annuities, mutual funds or any other income not otherwise reported);
- GSE – to report income and expenses from businesses you own or from self-employment;
- V – to report income and expenses from the rental and lease of property;
- FW – to claim certain benefits related to home ownership;
- AUS – to report foreign source income and tax paid;
- Kinder – to identify the children for whom you're claiming credits;
- K – to claim child credits (yes, these are separate forms!);
- U – to report maintenance payments (alimony) or other support payments between separated or divorced partners;
- *Eigenheimzulage* – to claim tax benefits from the purchase or improvement of a residence.

Tax Bills

Within a few weeks of filing your tax return, the tax office will send you a tax assessment (*Steuerbescheid*). If a refund is due, they will advise you of the amount, which will be transferred automatically to the bank account you listed on your return. If you owe money, you will be informed of the amount that will be debited from your bank account to settle your tax liability.

If you feel that your taxes haven't been correctly calculated, you have one month after receipt of the tax assessment to make a formal protest (*Einspruch*). To make a protest, you must have a specific complaint about the calculation and be able to show where the calculation is in error and the amount. The protest must be submitted in writing and you should either follow an established model or have a tax adviser prepare the letter for you in order to ensure that you follow the correct procedure.

VALUE ADDED TAX

Value added tax (VAT) is called either *Mehrwertsteuer* (*MwSt*) or *Umsatzsteuer* (*USt*) in Germany (and is usually the difference between a fair price and too expensive!). The two terms are used more or less interchangeably, although the legally correct term in Germany is *Umsatzsteuer*. Literally, it's a use tax rather than a sales tax, as it's levied on all goods and services used in Germany, irrespective of where they were purchased. If you buy goods by mail-order from outside the EU, you may be charged VAT by the post office when they're delivered, although on small purchases (under around €50 declared value) they often don't bother to collect the tax.

Most prices in Germany are quoted inclusive of tax (*einschliesslich Mehrwertsteuer/Umsatzsteuer*), although they're sometimes quoted exclusive of tax (*ohne Mehrwertsteuer/Umsatzsteuer*).

Germany has only two rates of VAT: the standard rate of 16 per cent, which applies to most goods and services, and a reduced 7 per cent rate that applies to certain food products and 'necessary' social services. The only services exempted from VAT are those that are taxed in some other way, such as certain forms of life insurance that are actually investments.

There's no threshold for registering for VAT; if you're engaged in any 'economic activity' to earn a living rather than just as a sideline, you're required to register with the local tax office (*Finanzamt*) and charge VAT to your clients, even if you're barely scraping a living. This obviously adds to the bureaucracy of setting up as a self-employed person in Germany. However, 'small' businesses (*Kleinunternehmen*) must charge VAT to their customers but don't have to remit it to the tax office (but also don't have the benefit of deducting any VAT they've paid). A small business for VAT purposes is one which had a turnover of less than €16,620 in the previous year (VAT is included in this figure) and which expects its turnover to be no more than €50,000 (including VAT) in the current year. All other businesses must include VAT at the appropriate rate on all their invoices, bills and receipts. If it's more advantageous for you, you can voluntarily contract into the system, even if your turnover is low.

Every month (or, in some cases, three months) you pay the VAT that you've charged your customers to the tax office, after deducting any VAT that you've paid to your own suppliers.

It's the declared aim of the EU eventually to have just one universal rate of VAT for the whole community, although this will take some time to accomplish, particularly as only Denmark has just a single rate on everything at present, the UK and Republic of Ireland have single rates but no tax on food, and other countries have at least two widely differing rates.

CAPITAL GAINS TAX

Capital gains from the sale of non-business assets (e.g. a second home) are generally exempt from tax unless they're considered to be speculative. In the case of property, a sale is considered to be speculative if it takes place within ten years of purchase. Gains from the sale of a substantial share (i.e. more than 10 per cent) in a company are also taxable. Capital gains tax rates are the same as those for personal income (see page 321).

INHERITANCE & GIFT TAX

As in most other western countries, dying doesn't free you (or rather your inheritors) entirely from the clutches of the taxman. Germany imposes both inheritance tax (*Erbschaftssteuer*) and gift tax (*Schenkungssteuer*) on its inhabitants, although in Germany it's the inheritor or the recipient of the gift (the beneficiary) who's responsible for filing a return and paying taxes, rather than the deceased (difficult!) or the donor.

Inheritance tax (called estate tax or death duty in some countries) is levied on the transfer of property from the deceased to his or her heirs. The amount of tax due depends on the value of the property inherited and the relationship between the deceased and the beneficiary. Gift tax is levied in much the same way on property that's granted or donated to another person before the owner's death.

A surviving spouse has a tax-free allowance of €307,000, while children and stepchildren are given an allowance of €205,000 and grandchildren or parents have a €51,200 allowance. Most other blood relatives (brothers and sisters, nieces and nephews) can claim only a €10,300 tax-free allowance, and all other beneficiaries receive an exemption of just €5,200. There are strict rules and regulations regarding how property (both land and buildings) is valued, based on rental values and the use of the property at the date of death or a gift. Buildings that produce rental income are considered particularly valuable assets at tax time.

Beneficiaries are grouped into three tax categories (*Steuerklasse*) according to their relationship to the donor. Category I includes the spouse and children; category II parents, siblings and other blood relatives; and category III more distant relatives or unrelated beneficiaries. The following tax rates apply to the amount of a gift or inheritance after the tax-free allowance has been deducted:

Value of Taxable Bequest (€)	Tax Payable (%)		
	Category I	Category II	Category III
Up to 52,000	7	12	17
52,000 – 256,000	11	17	23
256,000 – 512000	15	22	29
512,000 – 5,113,000	19	27	35
5,113,000 – 12,183,000	23	32	41
12,183,000 – 25,565,000	27	37	47
Over 25,565,000	30	40	50

Using the above table, the tax on a bequest of €1 million would be €131,670 for a spouse (€1 million - 307,000 = 693,000 x 19 per cent), €151,050 for a child (€1 million - 205,000 = 795,000 x 19 per cent), €256,176 for a parent (€1 million - €51,200 = 948,200 x 27 per cent) and €348,180 for a unrelated person (€1 million - 5,200 = 994,800 x 35 per cent). It's possible to purchase life insurance to cover the inheritance tax your heirs will have to pay.

If you inherit property in Germany from abroad, you should consult a notary (*Notar*) or lawyer who's familiar with international tax law and treaties, or contact the *Finanzamt* directly before claiming your inheritance. Under tax treaties, the German *Finanzamt* usually recognises taxes already paid on an estate overseas, but it's important to know what documents you require to verify this when repatriating an inheritance from abroad.

WILLS

It's an unfortunate fact of life that you're unable to take your hard-earned assets with you when you take your final bow (or come back and reclaim them in a later life). All adults should make a will (*Testament*) irrespective of how large or small their assets. The disposal of your estate depends on your country of domicile and, particularly if you own property (land or buildings), may also depend on where the property is located.

Under German law, you can indicate your final wishes regarding distribution of property and assets by drawing up a will. There are several kinds of valid wills in Germany, but as with all official documents there are strict forms and rules to follow when writing a will. It's therefore wise to consult a lawyer or notary (*Notar*) to ensure that you leave your final instructions in a legally valid form. If you choose a notarial will (*notarielles Testament*), you can tell the notary how you wish to distribute your property and he will draw up the legal documents for your signature. It's also possible to write your last wishes yourself and give them (sealed or not) to a notary, who will register the existence of your will and hold it until you pass on. The notary's fee is based on the value of your estate, irrespective of whether he actually writes up the document or just registers the existence of your sealed last testament.

You can also prepare a holographic will (*eigenhändiges Testament*), provided you follow the form and regulations carefully. A holographic will is simply one written in longhand, and in many countries (including Germany and France) it's a cheap way of making a will without using a notary or lawyer. The only catch is that someone has to know where it is after you've gone. If you decide to write a holographic will, it's important that you hand-write the entire text of the will and sign the document legibly at the end, indicating the exact date and place (i.e. town) of signature. No witnesses are required; in fact, this type of will shouldn't be witnessed at all or it will complicate matters.

It's possible for married couples to prepare a joint will, of which there are several variations, each with its own legal requirements and restrictions. A *Berliner Testament*, for example, must be hand-written by one of the spouses and signed by both in order to be valid.

It's possible to have two or more wills – one covering your property in Germany and others for property owned abroad – although it's important to ensure that they don't contradict each other, or none of them may be valid! It may be wise to have a German will that simply refers to another will in your home country or elsewhere. If you own property abroad, most legal experts advise you to have a separate will that's valid in the country where the property is located.

German law doesn't allow you to leave your property to anyone or anything you choose and you aren't permitted to disinherit entirely certain relatives, namely your direct descendants (children, grandchildren), your parents (if you have no children) and your surviving spouse. These privileged family members can claim their share of up to half the value of your final estate if they discover that you've left them out of your will. They have up to three years after your death to assert their rights and can even recover any gifts made in the ten years before your death. It's important to consider this requirement when drawing up your will, so as to avoid leaving your heirs squabbling over what's left when you're gone – unless that's your intention! Under German law, your heirs will inherit not only your property, but also any debts. However, if you die leaving more debts than assets, your heirs can choose to reject the bequest altogether, thereby avoiding all tax and debt issues.

If you don't have a will (i.e. die intestate), your estate will be divided among your heirs according to German inheritance law. Simply put, this means that your closest category of living family members will receive your property (and debts) to share among themselves. The exact rules depend on your marital status, the degree of relationship to surviving family members and any property sharing agreements or conventions that apply between you and your spouse (often based on the property laws at the date and place you were married).

Keep a copy of your will(s) in a safe place and another copy with your lawyer or the executor of your estate. Don't leave them in a bank safe deposit box, which in the event of your death is sealed for a period under German law. You should keep information regarding bank accounts and insurance policies with your will – but don't forget to tell someone where they are!

German inheritance law is a complicated subject and it's important to obtain professional legal advice when writing or altering your will.

COST OF LIVING

No doubt you would like to know how far your euros will stretch and how much money (if any) you will have left after paying your bills. First the good news: Germany has long been famous for having one of the highest standards of living in Europe. Wages are well above average (particularly in technical and engineering disciplines), inflation was 1.2 per cent in the 12 months to April 2003, which is historically around average, and the euro now looks like becoming a stronger and more stable currency reminiscent of the old Deutschmark.

The bad news is that Germany has a high cost of living and high taxes, and the cost of many goods and services is higher than in most of the rest of Europe (housing is among the most expensive in the world). Fuel costs are also high, due primarily to heavy taxes, although in many urban areas it's possible (and often even desirable) to get by without owning a car at all. Your food bill will almost certainly be higher than in your home country or previous country of residence; German food prices can be almost double those in the US, for example, and up to 50 per cent higher than in southern Europe.

Shopping around for 'luxury' items such as hi-fi equipment, electronic goods, computers and photographic equipment at discount centres and bargain stores (see **Chapter 17**) can result in considerable savings. It's also possible to save money by shopping for wine and other products in France or neighbouring countries or shopping overseas (e.g. in the US) by mail-order and via the Internet. Even in the most expensive cities, the cost of living needn't be astronomical and, if you shop wisely, compare prices and services before buying and don't live too extravagantly, you may be pleasantly surprised at how little you can live on.

Like all averages, an average cost of living encompasses a multitude of actual situations, determined by individual circumstances and lifestyles. There are also big differences in prices (and above all rents) between the major cities and more rural areas. For example, there's a considerable difference property rental rates between western and eastern Germany, and rents in cities such as Berlin and Munich can easily cost double or treble the figures shown below.

A particularly detailed survey into precise living costs, the *Einkommens und Verbrauchsstichproben* (*EVS*) is carried out every five years, the last from which statistics are available being 1998. If these are updated for inflation, the monthly expenditure for an average household will be as follows:

Item	Cost (€)
Food & drink	300
Clothes & shoes	125
Rent	500
Heating & utilities	100
Property maintenance	60
Leisure	370
Transport	300
Health	75
Household appliances & interior decor	150
Education	10
Newspapers & magazines	60
Other goods & services	100
Total	2,150

In interpreting these figures you should bear in mind that only a quarter of households in Germany include children and that over 34 per cent are single-person households. Monthly costs for middle-class families with children would be considerably higher.

15.

LEISURE

The Germans spend all their time sitting in beer gardens wearing *Gamsbart* hats and *Lederhosen*, drinking beer from huge Steins, eating radishes and sauerkraut, listening to an oompah band, and getting up only to dance polkas. This, at least, is the impression Hollywood and the Bavarian Tourist Office seem determined to peddle as far as German entertainment is concerned. The reality, however, is far more colourful and interesting, and leisure pursuits in Germany are as varied as in any country. It offers a huge variety of entertainment, sports (see **Chapter 16**) and pastimes and is blessed with a wealth of natural beauty - many tourists come to Germany to participate in outdoor sports, e.g. skiing and hiking, for which the country is famous. Germany is blessed with a wealth of fascinating historic cities and towns, and is particularly famous for its 'high' culture – theatre, concerts and opera – which rates among the best in Europe.

Many regions within Germany are accessible on a day trip due to an excellent transport infrastructure – except on those end-of-school days when everybody seems to want to go on holiday, when you will find over-crowded trains, over-run airports and the famously-fast autobahns converted into the biggest car park on the planet. Of all the nations in the world, the Germans seem to have the most developed herd instinct, and it sometimes appears that they will all decide to do exactly the same thing at the same moment. (Thankfully though, the different states stagger their annual school holidays now.)

Leisure information is available from the German National Tourist Office (GNTO), and local tourist and information offices, many of which have a ticket agency, and a wealth of city and regional entertainment papers such as Klappe, Main City and Fritz. Other information sources include local newspapers and radio programmes, and posters on those curious announcement pillars known as *Litfasssaülen*. Regional TV stations also provide the latest entertainment news via their teletext services, including details of local concerts, plays and musicals, art shows, sports events, flea markets and much more. Tourist information can also be obtained from a plethora of excellent travel books, including the Insight Guide Germany, *Lonely Planet Germany*, *Michelin Green Guide Germany* and the *Rough Guide to Germany* (see **Appendix B** for a list).

TOURIST OFFICES

Most German cities have a tourist office or, at the very least, an information office, often located at the town hall, many of which also provide a hotel reservation and ticket service. They're usually open during normal business hours from Mondays to Saturdays and also on Sundays in cities and areas where tourism is a major industry. The German National Tourist Office/GNTO (Deutsche Zentrale für Tourismus, Beethovenstr. 69, D-60325

Frankfurt, (☎ 069-9746 4287, 💻 www.germany-tourism.de) has offices in many countries including Australia, Austria, Belgium, Brazil, Canada, the Czech Republic, Denmark, Finland, France, Hong Kong, Hungary, Israel, Italy, Japan, South Korea, Mexico, the Netherlands, Norway, Poland, Russia, South Africa, Spain, Sweden, Switzerland, the UK and the US (see **Appendix A** for addresses). No matter what information you require, the GNTO will either be able to answer your question or give you an address or telephone number of someone who can. Local tourist and information offices are listed in guide books.

A wealth of information is also available from a multitude of websites, including 💻 www.germany-info.org, 💻 www. hotelstravel.com, 💻 www. travel24.com, 💻 www.donnerwetter.de for the weather situation and most cities also have their own websites (e.g. 💻 www.berlin.de and 💻 www. munichfound.com).

HOTELS

German hotels are generally spotless and efficient, and the standard of accommodation is invariably excellent, although the service may lack the eager friendliness one often finds in other countries. Don't expect the courtesies to go any further than a quick smile and an occasional *Guten Tag* in most hotels. You can expect to find every type of accommodation in Germany, including cosy rooms in private homes (look for *Zimmer frei* or *Fremdenzimmer* signs in windows), holiday rooms on farms, simple pensions up to superb five-star luxury hotels. Generally, the smaller the place, the friendlier the service – pensions are often particularly cosy (*gemütlich*) and homely places to stay.

Room rates usually include continental breakfast (basically coffee and rolls), while in some larger establishments a buffet-style cooked breakfast is offered for an extra charge. Hotels with restaurants offer half-board (breakfast and dinner) or full board (breakfast, lunch, dinner) at favourable rates. A *Hotel Garni* provides breakfast and beverages, but no other meals, while a *Gasthof* is a unique German institution roughly equivalent to a traditional English inn (a bar/restaurant with rooms). Further down the scale are pensions, guest houses, private rooms (bed and breakfast) and youth hostels (see page 336). A Pension is an official designation used for less formal (and slightly cheaper) establishments than hotels, which are called guesthouses (*Gästehäuse*) in some regions such as Bavaria. Rates vary from €30 to €50 per night for a single room (€50 to €70 for a double) in budget, pension and bed and breakfast accommodation, to over €350 per night at a top class hotel.

Hotels tend to be expensive in Germany and sometimes the price charged for a room has less to do with its quality or decor than with the amount of local competition (or lack of it). In some popular places, such as Frankfurt, even small pensions charge five-star rates during the popular trade fairs, and it's common for them to raise their prices steadily as the better establishments fill up. If you turn up in a city during a festival or international trade fair, you're likely to find yourself in poor quality, expensive accommodation on the outskirts of town, so make hotel reservations well in advance for popular events. An exception is the Etap Hotels chain which aims at the visitor on a budget and offers accommodation from €25 a night in pretty central locations. On the other hand, if you don't require easy access to public transport, you may wish to choose a hotel away from the bigger cities and the Autobahn, where rates are generally more affordable.

For those interested in history or architecture, many castles have been converted into hotels. Information is available in a GNTO brochure entitled *Castles, Royal Palaces and Stately Homes in Germany*. Bear in mind that the upkeep of such old buildings is expensive and therefore it isn't cheap to live as the aristocracy did in olden days – so be prepared to pay dearly for the privilege. At the other end of the scale, the lowest room rates are found in establishments run by the Friends of Nature Association (NaturFreunde Deutschlands e.V. Warschauer Straße 58a D-10243 Berlin, (☎ 030-2977 3260 ⌨ www.naturfreunde.de), which are similar to youth hostels, although targeted more at older people. There are some 500 of them in Germany, but some also exist elsewhere. Most are located in the countryside close to towns and provide accommodation in single and double rooms and/or small dormitories.

Germany has for a few years now been a member of Motorbike Hotels International, (Ignaz-Reder-Str. 3, D-97638 Mellrichstadt/Rhön, (☎ 097-7681 800, ⌨ www.motor-bike-hotels.com, ✉ info@motor-bike-hotels.com), the European network of hotels offering special services for those travelling by motorbike. Hotels are located in popular motorcycling areas and offer free maps plus safe parking areas, washing and maintenance facilities, boot polishing equipment, and heated drying rooms for wet gear. All hotel managers and many staff members are themselves active motorcycle riders. First-time guests receive a 'biker's pass' which provides each tenth night free.

Most tourist guides contain a wealth of information about accommodation and there are also a number of specialised hotel publications in English and German, including the *Michelin Red Hotel and Restaurant Guide Germany* and *Hotels Deutschland 2003* published by the Hotel Verband Deutschland.

Local tourist offices provide a wealth of information about accommodation at all price levels in their area and are happy to assist travellers in finding rooms and board in their towns. They also provide information for people with particular needs, such as children-friendly surroundings, kosher kitchens, disabled people or those travelling with pets. They may also have lists of bed and breakfast (B&Bs) establishments and rooms to let in private homes. Tourist offices that provide a room-finding service (*Zimmervermittlung*) may make reservations free of charge, while others charge a booking fee of from €2 to €5.

SELF-CATERING ACCOMMODATION

All tourist areas have self-catering accommodation (*Ferienwohnumgen*) and furnished apartments (*Ferienappartements*) available for short-term lease, which can be rented through agencies or in some cases directly from owners. While they all look good in the catalogues, the quality can vary hugely, and a high rental is no guarantee of quality. Most are spotlessly clean but they're furnished to variable standards and apart from basic furniture may contain little else. Some provide a few simple food items, soap and toilet tissue, but don't count on it. If you don't bring your own bed linen and towels, you may be charged an additional fee for laundry services. If you plan to arrive on a Sunday, bear in mind that shops will be closed, so bring any necessities with you. Generally you're required to do your own daily cleaning, unless an apartment is part of a larger hotel complex where chambermaids are provided. However, you will be charged an additional cleaning fee at the time of your departure, so you shouldn't be too meticulous about the cleaning!

Apartments are normally leased on a weekly basis, from Saturday to Saturday, and you will be required to vacate the premises before noon on the last day or face an army of cleaning ladies ready to remove you with the dustbins. The best way to find a holiday apartment is to write to the tourist office of the town where you wish to stay, who will send you a list of available properties and prices, sometimes with a map of the town showing the apartments' location. Prices vary considerably depending on the season, quality, size and location (e.g. closeness to amenities such as ski-lifts or scenic landmarks), and therefore it isn't possible to provide standard rates. The rental agreement is likely to include a deposit (payable in advance) and should specify any extra costs. In some areas there's an additional 'spa tax' (*Kurtaxe*) of up to a few euros per day, which is designed to help maintain the local spas and isn't included in room rates. If you're planning to stay in a town whose name starts with 'Bad' you will almost certainly have to pay this tax, which is also included in each item you consume at restaurants or cafes in spa towns.

The Verband der Mitwohnzentralen, Schulterblatt 112, D-20357 Hamburg, Germany (☎ 040-4313 5730) is an umbrella association for over 40 accommodation-finding services and can refer you to members in major cities throughout Germany.

CARAVANNING & CAMPING

Germany has over 2,000 official campsites and camping other than at official sites is frowned upon, although generally tolerated provided you have the permission of the landowner (camping on communally-owned land is illegal). It's also legal to stay one night in a caravan or mobile home at any public parking space. Campsites are graded from 'good' to 'excellent' depending on their facilities, which range from basic washing and toilet facilities and perhaps a shop, to luxury open-air 'hotels' with a wide range of amenities. These may include electricity hook-ups, hot showers, sauna, washing machines, supermarket, lock-up storage for valuables and a wide choice of sports facilities, which usually include a swimming pool (outdoor and/or indoor) and tennis courts. Sites may also have facilities for golf or crazy golf, volleyball, cycling, table-tennis, canoeing, fishing and boating. Many sites are situated in popular hiking and climbing areas. Large campsites usually have a restaurant and a bar.

Prices are based on facilities and location, with rates ranging from around €3 to €12 per person, per night plus around €3 to €8 per tent, with extra fees for cars and caravans. Most campsites are full between June and September and you should arrive early in the afternoon if you haven't made a booking. Some camping areas are open only during the summer season, while others remain open all year round. A free list of caravan and camping grounds can be obtained from the German National Tourist Offices and comprehensive guides are published by the German Camping Club (DDC, Mandlstr. 28, D-80802 Munich, ☎ 089-3801 420, 🖳 www.camping-club.de, ✉ info@camping-club.de), the ADAC motoring organisation (ADAC Reiseführer Camping) and the Aral petrol company (Aral Campingführer).

Caravans and mobile homes can be hired from various companies throughout Germany, but it's important to check that they're insured for self-drive rentals and licensed accordingly. Rented vehicles and those used for commercial purposes must conform to higher safety standards than those for private use and are subject to different insurance regulations.

YOUTH HOSTELS

For those travelling on a tight budget, the best way to stretch your financial resources is by staying at youth hostels (*Jugendherbergen*). Germany has the most extensive network of hostels in the world, with 579 throughout the country. Rates depend on the quality of the accommodation offered. Over 60 per cent of hostels fall into category four which is the highest one. These top of the range hostels can charge up to €22, but the average price is €15 and category one accommodation costs only €9. Seniors pay €3 more and the prices for double rooms vary from hostel to hostel. All prices now pleasantly include sheets as well as breakfast. Otherwise meals cost around €4. **Note that few hostels here have self-catering facilities**. If you're not a member of the International Youth Hostel Association (IYHA) you can buy 'welcome stamps' for one night for €3.10 or a booklet of six stamps for €15.50. Obviously, if you are a member then you won't need these.

Naturally there are some drawbacks, such as some hostels having only two large dormitories (one for men and one for women), and some hostel wardens strictly enforcing all rules, including some they make up as they go along! **Priority is given to those aged under 27 and 'wrinklies' over 27 are only supposed to get a place if a hostel isn't fully booked by 6pm unless they have a reservation.** In Bavaria, those aged over 26 aren't admitted to youth hostels unless accompanied by 'children' aged under 26.

Reservations are only held until 6pm, unless the warden is informed that you will be arriving late, with 10pm being the latest check-in time. All hostels have a curfew when the front door is locked, which may be as early as 10pm in rural areas, although it can be midnight or even 2am in large cities. The check-out time is usually 9am. The length of a stay at a youth hostel is limited to a maximum of three days, although this is only enforced when new arrivals would otherwise be prevented from getting a bed.

With the exception of a few private hostels, all hostels in Germany are operated by the German Youth Hostel Association (Deutsches Jugendherbergswerk/DJH, Haupverband, Bad Meinberger Strasse 1, 32760 Detmold ☎ 05231-993655, 🖳 www.jugendherberge.de) and indicated by a DJH sign. The DJH publish an annual *Handbuch der Jugendherbergen in Deutschland* listing all youth hostels in Germany with descriptions, facilities, photographs, travel instructions and rates. **Although most hostels are open throughout the year, some are closed in winter and a number even close every other weekend.**

FESTIVALS

Every German town, no matter how large or small, has an annual festival. Most people are familiar with Munich's *Oktoberfest* and some may even have heard of the *Cannstätter Wiesen* or the *Bad Dürkheim Weinfest*. There are many hundreds more, which although smaller, still possess that light-hearted, 'carousel-and-candy-floss' atmosphere. The larger festivals are invariably to celebrate the local beer and/or wine and you must usually pay a deposit on a beer mug at beer festivals or buy your own glass at wine festivals - the organisers have learnt from long experience that many glasses don't survive the evening or are taken home as souvenirs. **The number one rule on these occasions is never to drink and drive** but to use public transport, added to which the local police may be ill-humoured at having to work while everybody else is having fun, and generally take the alcohol laws even more seriously than usual.

There's also the so-called 'fifth season' in the Rhineland, otherwise known as *Fasching* (pronounced 'Fashing'). Don't assume that this is just fun and games – it's taken very seriously, particularly in Dusseldorf, Cologne, Mainz and Wiesbaden, where hundreds of people dedicate their free time to two or three annual events, particularly the big get-together or the Rose Monday parade. Once you get into the spirit of it you may wish to join a *Fasching* club, where you will discover that what looks like lots of fun to the visitor is actually considerable hard work and quite expensive. In fact, it's so costly that only millionaires can afford to accept the title of *Fasching* prince in the major locations. In Cologne it's estimated that the prince must spend around €60,000 just for the confectionery thrown from the parade's floats – a stiff bill for just 'three crazy days'.

There's a growing trend for medieval festivals, which are held in many parts of the country, particularly in the Angelbachtal and at Münzenberg Castle (near Butzbach) in spring or summer. An increasing number of people are drawn to this rather bizarre activity, which requires participants to make their own clothes, weapons and armour. Some of the groups involved, such the Society for Creative Anachronisms, take their hobby so seriously that they can hardly talk about anything else. Medieval festivals offer arts and crafts exhibits, jousting knights, jesters, wandering minstrels, an outdoor theatre, and plenty of hearty food and drink. **The castles are usually situated on hilltops, so you should be prepared for plenty of walking.**

THEME PARKS

Germany boasts a number of theme parks, including the top-rated Phantasialand (☎ 02232-36204) located in Brühl, near Cologne. This park has around 20 exhilarating rides and seven different shows, including some with animals. Free admission is provided for anyone visiting the park on their birthday (proof in the form of a passport or ID card is required). The newest addition to Germany's theme parks is Warner Brothers' Movie World (situated at Bottrop, north of Essen), a must for all Bugs Bunny fans, where you can experience a car chase or dive into the Bermuda Triangle. Holiday Park (Hassloch, between Mannheim and Karlsruhe) offers magic shows, a cypress garden and a water-ski performance, while Europa Park in the Black Forest (Rust, near the city of Freiburg) is set in an old castle park with a French quarter, an Italian section, a Russian corner and a Dutch village.

You should plan to spend at least a full day at any of these theme parks. All have plenty of parking, although coach trips are also offered by tour companies throughout Germany, usually on Saturdays or Sundays.

MUSEUMS

The diversity and range of museums in Germany is unequalled in any other European country, where it's said that every town with over 10,000 inhabitants has at least two museums (Berlin itself has over 100!). While most relate to the history of the local area (*Heimatmuseum*), others are world-renowned, such as the Deutsches Museum (science and technology) in Munich, the Pergamon Museum in Berlin and the Gutenberg Museum in Mainz. State museums aren't always where you may expect to find them, for example, you may expect the Hessian state museum to be located either in Frankfurt (Hessen's largest city) or Wiesbaden (the capital of Hessen), while it's actually located in Darmstadt, which was the capital until 1918. Admission charges vary considerably, from around €2 to €6, with some museums offering free admission, particularly those operated by a local authority or university. In most major cities, public transport tickets also provide admission to museums. Many museums close on Mondays (in eastern states many close on two days a week) and public holidays.

One of the most remarkable museums is the Technik Museum in Sinsheim, where you can hire some of the vehicles on display and take them for a 'spin' – from a 1930s racing car to a second world war tank - though prices and insurance aren't exactly cheap. In addition to its more traditional museums, Germany also has many interesting open-air museums and attractions, including the slate mines (*Schieferbergwerk Besuchergrube*) in Bundenbach/Hunsrück and the silver mines (*Reiche Zeche*) in Freiberg. If you're interested in architecture and 17th century half-timbered buildings in particular, head for New Anspach (near Frankfurt) to see the open-air museum (*Freilicht Museum*) at Hessen Park.

One of the strangest museums has to be the Crime Museum (*Kriminal Museum*) in Rothenburg o.d.T., open from April to October. The hair-raising displays include chastity belts, neck violins, human cages, a witch's chair, and even the dreaded Iron Maiden. The exhibits, covering some 2,000m^2 (over 21,000ft^2), span seven centuries, with information provided in English as well as German. (✉ info@kriminalmuseum.rothenburg.de). There's also a humorous side to some German museums and anybody who thinks the Germans have no sense of humour need only visit the Karl Valentin Museum in Munich, where a bowl of water is labelled 'a splendid snow sculpture, until brought inside'. Other unusual museums around Germany include the Bee Museum (located in Weimar), the Chair Museum (Rabenau), the Chocolate Museum (Cologne), the Toy Soldiers and Tin Figures Museum (in Kulmbach) and of course the peerless Chamber Pot Museum in Munich.

GARDENS, PARKS & ZOOS

Many of Germany's botanical and zoological gardens are world famous such as the Ottobrunn Zoo in Munich and Frankfurt's Palmengarten. Almost every city has a zoo, sometimes called a *Vivarium* or *Tiergarten*. All charge an admission fee. In addition to general botanical gardens there are also so-called 'teaching trails' (*Lehrpfade*) in some locations, designed to educate people about the local flora and agriculture. Admission is usually free unless the services of a guide are required. Garden lovers may also be interested in the German Federal Garden Show, held in a different city each year. A list of botanical gardens and zoos can be obtained from the GNTO and information can also be found in most good guide books.

Many regions have areas designated as national parks or nature reserves, indicated by a *Naturschutzgebiet* triangular white sign with a green border. There are no admission fees, but the strictly enforced rules include no camping, no fires, no picking flowers, no disturbing the animals and no dogs running free, while in some reserves visitors are restricted to marked paths.

CINEMAS

Cinema flourishes in Germany, which has a long tradition of film-making, although the majority of films shown nowadays are American imports (dubbed into German). There are numerous cinemas (*Kinos*) in German cities, mostly multi-screen with four to six screens (but they can go up to 16 or more) and most towns have at least one. Most cinemas show films only in German, although in most large cities there's at least one 'art-house' or 'alternative' cinema (*Kommunales Kino* or *Programmkino*) showing original-language versions, indicated by 'OF' (*Originalfassung*) or 'OV' (*Originalversion*). A foreign film with German subtitles is indicated by 'OmU' (*Original mit Untertiteln*) after the title. There may also be a cinema in some cities showing only English-language films. There are strict age restrictions for many films, which are shown by the word *ab* (from) followed by a number and the letter *J.* (short for *Jahren*, meaning 'years'), as follows:

Rating	Restriction
ab 6 J.	6 years and over
ab 12 J.	12 and over
ab 16 J.	16 and over
ab 18 J.	18 and over

Films suitable for all are classified *o. ALTB. (ohne Altersbegrenzung)*. It isn't unusual for cashiers or ticket collectors to ask to see some form of identification if a person looks younger than the age limit and anyone who cannot prove his age is refused admission. Tickets are usually quite expensive, e.g. up to €8 to €15 for a Saturday night showing of a first release, although discounts of up to 50 per cent are generally offered on one day a week (*Kinotag*). Most cinemas accept telephone reservations and you can often buy tickets at box offices in advance. In most cities you can obtain information about programmes by calling a local hotline (numbers can be obtained from tourist offices). Some towns, e.g. Berlin and Munich, stage annual international film festivals, during which participating cinemas are open 24 hours a day. See also **Video & DVD** on page 162.

THEATRE, OPERA & BALLET

High quality theatre, opera and ballet performances are staged in all major cities, many by resident companies, which receive generous government subsidies (including over 400 theatre companies). This doesn't, however, mean that tickets are cheaper than in other European countries – indeed, the opposite may be true. In many cities it's possible to buy a subscription, which includes a seat at each production during a season. Although expensive, this can be good value if you're able to attend every show or can split the cost with a friend. Tickets for popular theatre, opera and ballet at the most famous venues are in high demand and must be ordered well in advance. If you're planning to attend the annual Wagner festival in Bayreuth or the Passion Play held every ten years in Oberammergau, you will need to book literally years in advance. Political and satirical *Kabarett* entertainment featuring monologues and short sketches is common in larger cities, particularly Berlin, where the film Cabaret was set.

Top British musicals like those of Andrew Lloyd-Webber are performed in German in some cities and have been extremely popular, so much so that an entire tourist industry has sprung up around them. Tour companies offer overnight or weekend package deals, which include transport, hotel accommodation and tickets to shows. These all-inclusive deals usually represent excellent value for money, often costing little more than the price of a pair of tickets alone if you buy them from the box office.

Theatre performances are generally in German except for occasional international workshops, tours by American or British companies, or community theatres such as the English Theatre in Frankfurt (Kaiserstrasse 52, ☎ 069-2423 1620, 🖳 www.english-theatre.org). The Morale, Welfare and Recreation (MWR) division of the US military also sponsors English-language performances at its bases in Darmstadt, Hanau, Heidelberg, Giessen and Wiesbaden, which are open to the general public.

CONCERTS

Germany has a long tradition of classical music and opera (the birthplace of many of the world's greatest composers) and between the 16th and 19th centuries the country's musical dominance was virtually unrivalled. Germans love classical music and opera, and have long produced some of the best orchestras and opera singers in the world. Every major city has its own symphony orchestra and operatic company, many performing at the highest level. Classical concerts, music festivals and solo performances are regularly held throughout the country. Germany boasts not only some of the world's best concert houses, but two of its finest orchestras: the Berlin Symphony Orchestra (*Berliner Sinfonie*) and the Bavarian State Orchestra (Munich). Although the *Berliner* and Bavarian perform almost nightly during the season, it doesn't mean that obtaining a ticket is an easy task and most concerts are sold out well in advance. If you wish to attend a concert you should book your tickets as far in advance as possible.

Special performances are staged at the various Amerika Haus centres, such as those at Frankfurt and Leipzig, where performers are often Americans touring Europe who stage a free performance at the Amerika Haus. There are also many free classical and choral performances in parks and churches, some sponsored by local tourist boards. Look for notices in local newspapers and magazines and for posters in cities.

Many German cities such as Essen, Berlin, Frankfurt, Hamburg and Munich are venues on the world tours of major popular artists and bands, some of which stage concerts in all five cities, while others take in only one or two. Tickets are available from record stores, local information offices and ticket agencies. In spring and summer, huge outdoor rock concerts are staged in major cities, attracting tens of thousands of fans. The price of tickets for pop music concerts is generally high and in the case of superstars and top bands can be prohibitive. Don't, however, neglect the wealth of excellent home-grown talent; although virtually unknown abroad, Germany has a thriving club scene where everything from blues and jazz to folk and rock can be enjoyed nightly.

SOCIAL CLUBS

Club life has a special place in German culture and most Germans belong to a number of clubs or associations, including sports clubs. Many social functions are organised by clubs, including municipal services such as fire-fighting which are performed by volunteer associations in small towns. There are many social clubs and expatriate organisations in Germany catering for both foreigners and Germans, including Ambassador clubs,

American Women's and Men's Clubs, Anglo-French clubs, Business Clubs, International Men's and Women's clubs, Kiwani Clubs, Lion and Lioness Clubs and Rotary Clubs.

Expatriates from many countries have their own clubs in major cities, a list of which is often maintained by embassies and consulates (see page 87) in Germany. Many local clubs organise activities and pastimes such as chess, bridge, art, music, sports activities and sports trips, theatre, cinema and visits to local attractions. Joining a local club is one of the easiest ways to meet people and make friends. If you want to integrate into your local community or German society in general, one of the best ways is to join a local German club. Ask at the local town hall or library for information.

DISCOS & NIGHT-LIFE

Night-life varies considerably depending on the town or region. In some small towns you may be fortunate to find a bar with music or a discotheque, while in major cities such as Berlin, Hamburg and Munich, you will be spoilt for choice and can party round the clock. The major cities offer a wide choice of entertainment, including jazz clubs, cabarets, discos, sex shows, music clubs, trendy bars, night-clubs and music halls. The liveliest places are the music clubs, which are infinitely variable and ever-changing with a wide choice of music from jazz to rock and funk to folk. The most popular clubs change constantly and are listed in newspapers and entertainment magazines. For those with less tolerant eardrums, establishments such as *Tanz-Club*, *Tanz-Café*, or *Jazz-Club* may be more suitable.

Some places, whose fame is usually spread by word of mouth, have special programmes, such as the 16th century house in Zell/Moselle where internationally renowned groups used to drop in for a gig. Berlin and Hamburg are famous for providing opportunities for new groups and acts (it wasn't only the Beatles who made their name here). One place worthy of a special mention is the Tiger Club in Frankfurt, a successful combination of night-club, circus and variety show. **Be warned, however, that many establishments have very smoky atmospheres.**

Discos are very much part of youth culture in Germany, where the usual fare includes pounding techno music (Germany is its spiritual home) played at very high volume. Many discos are usually selective about who they will admit (unless business is slow), especially those with a fashionable 'reputation' such as the P1 in Munich. Here you have to be either rich and/or famous, or conform to a rigid (often outrageous) dress code to get past the doorman. Discos generally don't admit people under 18 after midnight and may ask them to leave (even if accompanied by adults) after that time. Places that cater only to teenagers aren't allowed to serve alcohol (although beer isn't reckoned to be an acoholic drink in Bavaria!). Youth discos open as early as 7pm and generally close at midnight, while those targeted at adults often don't get going until midnight and go on until dawn or later, although most close between 1 and 3am. The admission fee to clubs is usually from €4 to €10, although it can sometimes be as much as €20, which may include a 'free' drink or two, or there may be a minimum drink purchase. **Some clubs offer free entry, but drinks can be very expensive.**

Germany is one of the world's more tolerant countries as far as gay people are concerned and most cities have thriving gay scenes. For listings of gay men's clubs consult *Männer*, a bi-monthly magazine or contact the Bundesverband Homosexulität (Boxenhagenerstrasse 76–78, 10245 Berlin), while lesbian establishments are listed in *GAIA's Guide* and the monthly magazine, *UKZ-Unsere Zeitung*.

CASINOS & GAMBLING

The casino (*Spielbank*) and spa combination is a centuries old tradition in Germany, where resorts such as Baden-Baden (established 1810), Bad Homburg and Wiesbaden have achieved huge popularity among the jet-set, not to mention world-wide fame and notoriety in popular fiction and film. Most states have at least one licensed casino (many situated in spa towns), mainly because the bulk of casino earnings goes to the state in the form of taxes and licence fees. The casino crowd is much changed from the elite crowd that used to frequent Baden-Baden and Wiesbaden in the 19th century. Nowadays you can expect to find punters in casual dress and even wearing T-shirts and shorts during the afternoon. However, most casinos insist on formal attire in the evening or at the very least a collar and tie for men and a dress for women. All the usual casino games are offered, including roulette, blackjack, poker and craps, plus a wide variety of slot machines. Most casinos have a high maximum stake and if Lady Luck is with you, 'breaking the bank' is still a (remote) possibility. There's a nominal entrance fee of around €5 and you must show your passport or identity card.

In stark contrast, most gambling outside casinos is illegal. Among the few exceptions are the state and national lotteries, and slot machines limited to a small maximum pay-out per game. Sadly, the latter seem to be among the most addictive form of gambling in the world and no matter what initiatives are taken by the authorities (short of outlawing them), they're responsible for an increasingly large number of compulsive gamblers. State lotteries donate around half their profits to charities or community programmes (e.g. *Aktion Sorgenkind*, which funds programmes for mentally and physically disabled children) and pay out the other half in winnings.

The only other legal way to gamble in Germany is on horse races, where bets are accepted at courses and through the (government-controlled) national lottery outlets. Horse racing includes both trotting (the most popular form) and flat racing, with most medium and large cities having at least one racetrack.

BARS & PUBS

There's at least one bar (*Bierlokal*) or inn (*Gasthof*) in every town and most villages in Germany, although they can occasionally be rather seedy establishments. If you're looking for a place with a bit more class you should seek out a *Gaststätte* (also called a *Kneipe* in some regions), which may open as early as 10am and close well after midnight – they must usually close by 2am, although *Kneipen* in Berlin must close for only one hour in every 24 hours for cleaning (and most are to be avoided)! While some are purely drinking establishments, others offer a variety of fairly basic, traditional dishes.

Irish-style pubs offering Guinness and other Irish beers are also common throughout Germany and even have a humorous publication devoted to them. These establishments have almost a cult following and often offer live music. German bartenders rarely demand payment after every drink, but note each drink on your beer mat, with the possible exception of popular tourist haunts and Irish and other 'foreign' pubs. Darts can be played at many British and Irish pubs in Germany.

Southern Germany has a wealth of traditional beer halls known variously as a *Brauereikeller*, *Brauerei* or *Bierkeller*, where drinking is often accompanied by a brass band and food (and possibly dancing if you can still stand). In many Bavarian beer gardens you're permitted to bring your own food and you're usually required to pay a deposit on your glass. As you will quickly learn, drinking toasts are almost mandatory in Germany and include *Prost*, *Prosit* and *Zum Wohl* (similar to the British 'Cheers!').

The main draught beer served in a bar or pub varies depending on the region, and broadly speaking will be *Pils* (Pilsen style), Export, *Weizenbier* (wheat beer, mostly in Bavaria), *Berliner Weissbier* or *Kölsch* (Cologne style). Most bars have only one kind of beer on draught, but usually have a variety of bottled beers. In Bavaria, there are also some special beers served only at certain times of the year such as Christmas. One such beer is *Starkbier* (strong beer), which is strong enough to be classified as a spirit in most other countries, and which is frozen to remove a large proportion of the water, therefore increasing the alcohol content to as much as 25 per cent. Needless to say, it should be drunk with caution. If you're a real beer fan, you may wish to visit the Brewery Museum in Cologne or, better still, a brewery (most of which offer private tours, including free tastings).

Bars also serve a variety of other drinks, including soft drinks, wine, spirits, champagne or German sparkling wine (*Sekt*) and the usual assortment of cocktails, although the prices for these can be very expensive.

The wine list varies depending on the particular bar and region, with local wines usually predominating. Most bars close on one day of the week (*Ruhetag*), which is noted on a sign on the door. **If you're a non-smoker, don't expect to find a non-smoking section in a German bar.**

When in Frankfurt you can hop aboard the Apple Wine Express, a vintage tram that winds through the city streets on weekends and public holidays. Apple wine (cider) is a Frankfurt tradition and the celebrated drink is produced only in a limited number of centuries-old, family-run establishments. Apple wine (called *Ebbelwei* in the local dialect), served in a blue-and-grey pottery jug called a *Bembel*, is made from a mixture of apples, water, sugar and yeast, and the cloudy, alcohol-rich result can make your head hurt for days if you drink too much. Apple wine pubs (*Apfelweinwirtschaft*) can be found throughout the old district of Sachsenhausen in Frankfurt, where customers sit outdoors at long wooden tables and toast each other with their apple wine glasses (known as a *Schobbeglas*). Those in the know order cheese in vinaigrette as an accompaniment. In wine-growing areas there are also wine bars (*Weinstuben*) and cellars (*Weinkeller*), although these are rare in German cities outside the wine regions.

You will usually find at least one local newspaper and perhaps also a regional one in bars for customers to read. Card playing is permitted (although not if it involves gambling) as well as chess and draughts/checkers (boards are provided in many places). A popular card game is *Skat*, a three-player, 32-card game, which is an institution in Germany, where *Skat* clubs abound. In most establishments there's a table reserved for regular customers called the *Stammtisch* – the locals may be upset if an outsider dares sit there, which particularly applies in Bavaria where foreigners include everybody but locals.

Bear in mind that drink-driving laws are strict in Germany, where just a couple of drinks can put you over the legal limit (see **Drinking & Driving** on page 257). If you're over the limit when breathalysed, you will be fined and will also easily lose your licence. If you have an accident while intoxicated, you will be required to pay for at least part of the damage and a judge may rule that the accident could have been avoided had you been sober – in which case you will be viewed as the guilty party, even if someone runs into the back of your car! See **Alcohol** on page 380.

CAFES

Cafes don't usually serve many alcoholic beverages, although you may get a glass of sparkling wine and perhaps a choice of two or three beers. What you will find is a good selection of coffees, including iced versions, and teas. An establishment offering a wide range of fine cakes and pastries may be called a *Cafékonditorei*, while one specialising in ice cream, an *Eiscafé*. Usually you must go to the counter to choose your cake or pastry, which will then be served with the rest of your order. Snacks are available and usually include salads, home-made soups and simple toasted sandwiches, although you shouldn't expect much beyond this.

Cafes can be quite elegant places, often enjoyed as a Sunday outing. They're an institution throughout Germany and aren't simply a place to grab a cup of coffee or a bite to eat, but are meeting places, shelters, sun lounges, somewhere to make friends, talk, write, do business, study, read a newspaper or just watch the world go by. Some cafes have a piano player or other entertainment and most (like bars) provide free newspapers for customers and possibly also a few magazines. Germans spend a lot of time in cafes, perhaps nursing a single drink, and nobody will usually rush you to finish, unless it's the height of the tourist season and people are waiting for tables. Cafes generally close one day a week.

RESTAURANTS

The only field in which full, multicultural integration has been achieved in Germany is in its restaurants. No matter what cuisine you fancy, whether it's, Chinese, Greek, Indian, Italian, Japanese, Spanish, Thai, Turkish, Yugoslavian or Vietnamese, you should be able to find it somewhere in the major cities. The quality varies widely, ranging from Michelin-starred fare to fast food at its worst. Prices are comparable with other central European countries and the service is generally good (and seldom provided by Germans). With the proliferation of ethnic restaurants, it has become increasingly difficult to find places offering traditional German cuisine. They do exist, however, and are well worth seeking out. Sausage (*Wurst*) is the most popular dish in Germany, of which there are a huge variety (some 1,500) made from beef, pork, veal or a combination of these. *Wurst* is usually accompanied by steamy *Sauerkraut* (fermented cabbage cooked with apple, sometimes – in the cheaper varieties – with wine added to speed up the fermentation process), hot or cold potato salad, or dumplings.

Germany isn't noted for its food, although it boasts a number of regional specialities and isn't exactly a gastronomic wasteland. There are many books on German regional cuisine. In Bavaria a popular dish is leg of pork stuffed with red bell pepper, assorted minced meats and breadcrumbs, Berlin has its *Berliner Leber* (veal liver cooked with apples and onions) and a Bremen speciality is chicken casserole simmered in cream, cognac and white wine. Frankfurt has its *Rippchen mit Kraut* (thick, salted pork chops, boiled in water, cooked with juniper berries and served with sauerkraut), Mecklenburg offers breast fillets of duck with carrots and apples (flavoured with butter, pepper, sugar and marjoram), while a Hamburg speciality is

Hamburger *Aalsuppe* (eel soup, with plums and vegetables). Saarland is noted for its rabbit cooked in red wine and garlic, Schwabia for its sliced veal with cream sauce, served with noodles flavoured with juniper berries, while Thuringia is famous for its sauerkraut rice and sausage slices with onions, apple wine and paprika.

Germany isn't exactly Shangri-la for vegetarians, but meat-free alternatives can be found. Among the best bets are Chinese restaurants (order a 'Buddhaplatter' - simply vegetables over rice) or Indian restaurants (where many rice dishes are served without meat and vegetable curry is a favourite). Salad bars can be found at cafeterias in department stores and also at fancy hotels offering over-priced Sunday brunches. In fact, there's usually at least one meat-free dish on the menu at any German restaurant, although the quality is variable and most options are often heavy on potatoes. True vegetarian restaurants are few and far between, although they do exist. If you don't have a restaurant guide, you can ask at a health food shop (*Reformhaus*) whether there are any vegetarian restaurants in the area. If you eat fish, you can get fish salads and sandwiches at the Nordsee fast food chain, although fresh fish isn't a regular item on the average German menu.

Restaurants are required to display their menu and price list outside the main entrance, so that you can see what's on offer and the price (which includes tax and service) before entering. You can buy a filling meal from around €10 at ethnic restaurants and from set menus (*Tagesmenü*), although for a good meal with wine you should be prepared to pay at least €20 per head. **You must find your own seat and there's highly unlikely to be a no-smoking zone.** In a busy restaurant, it's common for strangers to share tables and you shouldn't be surprised if someone asks to join you at your table. **Many restaurants allow dogs and it's common for customers to bring their dogs with them.**

A menu is called a *Karte* or *Speisekarte*, while in German a *Menü* offers set meals only (such as the *Tagesmenü*). Wine lists (*Weinkarten*) range from a few local house wines to the best French vintages at astronomical prices, and a good restaurant will usually offer a wide selection of wines from around the world. Water isn't provided unless you ask for it and generally only bottled water will be available (and charged to your bill). Bread is included only if stated on the menu and if you request it as an extra it will also be added to your bill. Don't be surprised if you're presented with the bill (*Rechnung*) half way through the meal, as this is common practice when staff are changing shifts, when the waiter (addressed as *Herr Ober* or *Fräulein*) must balance his account. Tipping (*Trinkgeld*) isn't a big thing in Germany and you don't need to feel uncomfortable if you haven't got any change or just a few small coins; tips aren't the waiters' wages, but are considered a 'thank you' for a job well done.

Many restaurants have a separate room that's provided free of charge for social functions, provided the participants book in advance and order plenty of drinks or food. Most restaurants close one day a week (*Ruhetag*), which is shown by a sign on the door. The best restaurant guides for Germany include the *Michelin Red Hotel and Restaurant Guide: Germany* and the *Aral Restaurant Führer*.

LIBRARIES

Most towns have a public library and those that don't are usually served by a mobile library (*Bibliothek auf Rädern*) which also accepts special orders from catalogues. Library opening times vary considerably and can be anywhere between 8am and 10pm Mondays to Fridays, and 8am to noon on Saturdays. Many smaller libraries open on only one or two days a week and are closed throughout the school holidays, while major libraries open six (or even seven) days a week. Most libraries offer CDs and videos in addition to books. Generally there's a membership fee of €3 to €10 (costs are climbing fast) for those wishing to borrow books and you must show proof of residence to obtain a library card. In addition to public libraries, most school and university libraries are open to the general public.

German libraries usually have a selection of books in foreign languages, including English, French, Italian and Spanish. In some areas such as Leipzig and Frankfurt, the Amerika Haus service (a branch of the United States Information Service or USIS) provides an extensive English-language library complete with a reference section. Unfortunately, due to recent budget cuts, Amerika Haus locations are increasingly closing their doors.

FOREST HUTS & RECREATIONAL AREAS

Most towns own a recreation area and/or a forest hut, which can be hired for a nominal fee for private parties and social functions. The actual fee depends on the amenities and services provided with the hut, which may include running water, toilets, electricity, basic appliances, and possibly beer mugs, glasses, cookery utensils and cutlery. Forest grill huts are excellent for those planning to throw a big party. You can build a log fire to keep warm and add to the atmosphere, you don't have to worry about spilled food and drinks on your carpet, and you can pump up the volume as loud as your speakers (or eardrums) will stand. Anything short of burning down the hut is acceptable, but the bad news is that you must clean up the mess the next day or pay for someone to do it. Some companies also specialise in catering for these outdoor parties, which although it adds considerably to the cost, reduces the risk of someone burning themselves trying to cook a steak after their second bottle of wine. Bear in mind that you must book months in advance, as almost everybody in town will want to organise an event there sometime, be it a birthday party or an office function.

EVENING CLASSES

A relatively inexpensive way to learn German or another language in Germany is at the people's high school (*Volkshochschule*), which originated in the early 20th century as popular education institutions for the masses. They were sponsored by left-wing political parties, including the Social Democrats, and are similar in many ways to the WEA (Workers' Education Authority) in the UK. The schools target was to meet the early trade unions' demands to 'work eight hours, learn eight hours and sleep eight hours'. Nowadays they're government-run. The modern *Volkshochschule* (*VHS*) offers courses ranging from basic basket-weaving to offshore sailing, with just about every imaginable subject in between. They run one-day seminars on topics such as tenants' rights, weekend courses on how to repair your bicycle and standard term or semester-based programmes. The most popular courses are foreign languages, but psychology, computers, health and 'new age' subjects are also widely available, some of which may have waiting lists. Course fees seldom exceed €200 for a full term, plus the cost of books and other course materials.

Each *VHS* publishes a course catalogue, many running to hundreds of pages, which are usually distributed free via bookshops and municipal buildings, although in some places you may be required to pay a nominal fee. Enrolment couldn't be simpler – you simply complete a postcard and post it. Prospective students can visit a *VHS* without an appointment during enrolment periods and receive free guidance and counselling. Some *VHS* courses offer an official certificate – such as German proficiency examinations or a high school diploma – while others are just for fun.

Private schools are less popular in Germany, probably because most Germans don't think that the quality of instruction matches the generally high fees. Those that exist mostly survive thanks to government contracts and the courses they organise for companies such as international banks.

16.

SPORTS

Germany was largely responsible for developing sport towards its present role in modern society, with the introduction of gymnastics into schools during the Napoleonic wars as a means of pre-military training and the development of a physical culture (*Körperkulur*) in the 19th century. In modern times, few regimes have exploited sport as a means of gaining international prestige as much as those of the Nazis and communist East Germany. Although not as successful as the East Germany of pre-unification days, which was a (drug-fuelled) superpower in world sports, particularly in athletics and swimming, the united Germany remains a force to be reckoned with. The most widely practised sports include football, tennis, gymnastics and shooting, while athletics, handball, table-tennis, horse riding, skiing and swimming are also popular. Hiking, cycling, hockey (including ice), basketball, squash, motor sports, water sports and aerial sports have many dedicated practitioners and followers.

Responsibility for sport is shared between the federal authorities, states and municipalities, the latter being responsible for providing sports facilities. Most towns have a public municipal sports and leisure centre with a host of sports facilities, including a fitness centre. Facilities are excellent in the western states, although not so good in the eastern states where sport was formerly an elitist pursuit. Participation in some sports is expensive, although costs can be reduced through the purchase of season tickets, annual membership or by joining a club.

The Germans are sports-crazy, whether as participants or spectators, and their enthusiasm is second to none (a number of TV stations are devoted solely to sports). Almost every sport is organised and performed somewhere in Germany, where there are well over 85,000 sports clubs (*Sportsvereine*) affiliated to the German Sports Federation (Deutscher Sportbund/DSB), which has 19 regional federations and numerous associated sports groups. Around one-third of all Germans (over 25 million) are members of a sporting club, while a further ten million people enjoy sports activities outside formal clubs. Unlike in many other countries, such as the UK and the US, German schools and universities don't compete against each other in inter-school/college sports competitions, and the main nurseries for professional sports in Germany are amateur competitions.

The DSB sponsors physical fitness programmes such as the long-running *Trim dich* (literally 'trim your weight') campaign, – jogging paths and work-out areas abound throughout the country to assist in this aim. Likewise, 'sport for everybody' (*Sport für Jedermann*) has encouraged millions of Germans to abandon their TVs and take up active sports. The DSB awards bronze, silver and gold medals (around 750,000 annually) to qualifying amateur sportsmen and women, who receive the German sports badge (*Deutsche Sportabzeichen*).

Various publications are available from tourist offices promoting special sports events and listing local sports venues. Most states and cities publish comprehensive booklets listing local sports organisations, facilities and classes. The addresses of national and state sports associations in Germany can be obtained from the Deutscher Sportbund, who also publish a yearbook of sports (*Jahrbuch des Sports*). Their address is DSB, Otto Fleck-Schneise, 12, D-60528 Frankfurt (☎ 060-6700, 🖥 www. dsb.de, ✉ dsb-info@dsb.de), but the yearbook, which costs €19, and contains a full 626 pages, is obtainable from the Schors-Verlags-Gesellschaft, Postfach 65522 Niedernhausen, ☎ 06127-8029. Postage isn't included.

AERIAL SPORTS

Germany has many areas that are ideal for aerial sports, particularly gliding, hang-gliding, paragliding and hot-air ballooning. The Alps are a favourite spot due to the updraughts and the low density of air traffic (apart from all the gliders, hang-gliders and balloons!). Hang-gliding is popular in Germany, which has many schools, as is paragliding (*Gleitschirm*), which entails jumping off steep mountain slopes with a parachute. Participants must have the proper equipment and complete an approved course of instruction, after which (if they survive) they receive a proficiency certificate and are permitted to go solo. Ballooning has a small but dedicated band of followers. Participation is generally limited to the wealthy due to the high cost of balloons. A flight in a balloon is a marvellous experience, particularly over the Alps. There is, however, no guarantee of distance or duration, and trips are dependent on wind conditions and the skill of your pilot.

Light aircraft and gliders (sailplanes) can be hired with or without an instructor (provided you have a pilot's licence) from most small airfields in Germany, where there are also many gliding clubs. Free-fall parachuting (sky-diving) flights can be made from most private airfields, although it's an expensive sport with training and equipment running to many thousands of euros. Information about aerial sports is available from the German Aero Club (Deutsche Aero Club, Bundesgeschaeftsstelle, Hermann-Blenk-Str. 28, 38108 Braunschweig (☎ 0531-235400, 🖥 www.daec.de).

Before taking up the above sports, you're advised to make sure that you have adequate health, accident and life insurance and that your affairs are in order. Why not try fishing instead?

CYCLING

Cycling is popular in Germany, not only as a means of transport or a serious sport, but also as a relaxing pastime for the whole family. The country has over 170 long-distance cycling tracks totalling over 40,000km (25,000mi), forestry tracks (*Forstwege*), city cycling trails and special tourist routes. Special itineraries are planned by the Allgemeiner Deutscher Fahrrad-Club/ADFC (see below) throughout Germany. Cycling maps (*Radwanderführer*) are published by Kompass. Cycle racing has a huge following and races are organised at every level, including mountain-bike races. Germany has a good record in international racing, particularly track racing, and the world's premier cycle race, the Tour de France, was won by a German, Jan Ullrich, in 1997, the first German winner in the event's history.

As required by law, German motorists generally give cyclists a wide berth when overtaking, but cycling in some major cities can be still dangerous. There are many cyclists in cities like that of Muenster. Cyclists must use cycle lanes where provided and mustn't cycle in bus lanes or on footpaths. If you cycle in cities, you should wear reflective clothing, protective head gear, a smog mask and a crucifix. **You must also take care not to get your wheels stuck in tram or railway lines.**

It isn't necessary to wear expensive sports clothing when cycling, although a light crash helmet is advisable, particularly for children. Head injuries are the main cause of death in cycling accidents, most of which don't involve accidents with cars, but are a result of colliding with fixed objects or falls. Always buy a quality helmet that has been approved and subjected to rigorous testing. Take particular care on busy roads and don't allow your children onto public roads until they're experienced riders. **Bikes must be roadworthy and be fitted with a horn or bell and front and rear lights.** They should also be fitted with an anti-theft device such as a steel cable lock (the only police-approved bike lock), although they're still not thief-proof. If your bicycle is stolen you should report it to the local police – but don't expect them to find it! Some insurance companies cover bicycle theft.

You can hire a bike from railway stations participating in the Call-A-Bike scheme operated by *Deutsche Bahn*. At present these are Frankfurt, Berlin and Munich but the plan is to extend coverage. The bikes are scattered around the cities and when you want one you hire it by making a phone call. You return it by locking it to a stand or traffic sign when you've finished with it so that someone else can come along and repeat the procedure. You're billed every month once you've registered, and charges are from €0.04 a minute. Full details are on their website at ⌨ www.bahn.de. For other bike hire, look in the yellow pages under *Fahrradverleih*. **You must usually leave a deposit of around €30.** You can also transport your bike on German trains by purchasing a bicycle ticket (*Fahrradkarte*) for €8 on long-distance trains which allow bikes or €6 if you have a *Bahncard*. On local/regional trains it costs €3. **Don't forget to**

take drinks, first-aid kit, tool kit and a puncture repair outfit when on a long cycling trip.

There are a number of cycling organisations in Germany, including the Allgemeiner Deutscher Fahrrad-Club (ADFC), Bundesgeschäftsstelle, Postfach 10 77 47, D-28077 Bremen (☎ 0421-346290, 💻 www.adfc.de), who publish a free brochure, *Discovering Germany by Bicycle*, and the Bund Deutscher Radfahrer, Otto-Fleck-Schneise 4, D-60528 Frankfurt (☎ 069-9678 000, 💻 www.bdr-online.org.de).

FISHING

Fishing is very popular in Germany, which has an abundance of well-stocked waters. However, there are no public fishing waters in Germany (apart from sea fishing), as all waters belong to the state, private individuals or fishing clubs, and you must buy a licence and pay the owner of a stream, river pond or lake a fee. A daily permit (*Tages Karte*) can be purchased from between around €5 and €20 for most waters, although some of the most famous and productive locations can cost as much as €60 or more per day! A general permit (€10 to €15) valid for one year is also required and is available from local tourist offices for visitors or town halls for residents. A non-resident can obtain a temporary licence to fish in Germany, e.g. a three-month licence for Bavaria costs around €30. Deep sea fishing is also possible in the North Sea and Baltic off Germany's northern coast, where boats can be hired from many ports. German residents must compete months of instruction on fish habitat, biology, regulations and general knowledge before they can become licensed anglers (you receive a certification card or *Prufunzeugnis*). Visitors aren't required to take a test.

The main sport fish are trout (rainbow, brown, brook), grayling and carp. Fishing for brown trout and grayling is popular in the mountain streams in the south, where Bavaria offers the best opportunities for fly-fishing. The trout season usually runs from 1st May to the end of October, although in some waters the dates are based on when the fish begin to spawn. There are strict regulations regarding the season, minimum size of catch and the number of fish that can be caught. For more information contact the Federation of German Sport Anglers (Verband der Deutscher Sportfischer, Siemensstr. 11-13, D-63071 Offenbach, (☎ 069-855006, 💻 www.vdsf.de). Panna Verlag (Josef-Bauer Str. 6, D-90584 Allersberg, ☎ 09176-90431) publish a pamphlet (in German) and map showing over 400 fishing locations throughout Germany called *Wo Angeln Extra*, and the Landesfischerei-verband Bayern (Pechdellerstr. 16, D-81545 Munich, ☎ 089-6427260, ✉ lfvbayern@t-online.de) publishes a fishing guide for Bavaria entitled *Angelführer Bayern*. Angling competitions are organised in many areas.

FOOTBALL

Football or soccer (*Fussball*) is Germany's unofficial national sport, with literally thousands of amateur football clubs, and it's one of the most successful nations in the world at both club and international level. Germany has won the World Cup three times, in 1954, 1974 and 1990 (only Brazil has won it more times) and was the runner-up in 1966, 1982, 1986 and 2002; it has also won the European Championships three times in 1972, 1980 and 1996. In 2000, Germany won the right to host the World Cup in 2006.

The national team is going through a transition phase and, that like certain other nations, is suffering from the large number of foreign players in its domestic league, which hinders the progress of home-grown talent. Many top German players also play abroad, mostly in Italy, but increasingly in the UK, which has also affected the performance of top club teams in European competition, although German football clubs have a long and distinguished record here. Though not quite as rabid as Italian or Spanish fans, German fans are as dedicated as their counterparts in most other countries.

The federal football league (*Bundesliga*) is Germany's premier competition, comprising 18 teams, among which the top dogs in recent years have included Bayern Munich, Borussia Dortmund, Bayer Leverkusen, Hamburg SV, Werder Bremen, FC Köln, FC Kaiserslauten and VfB Stuttgart. Bayern Munich (who play at the Olympic stadium in Munich) is Germany's most successful club side, but the current champions are Borussia Dortmund. If you want to discover more or find details of forthcoming games, go to the *Bundesliga* website (🖳 www.bundesliga.de).

The football season runs from September to December and February to June (there's a mid-winter break from Christmas to mid-February), with most matches played on Saturday afternoons (although they're also played on Fridays and Sundays) and attended by an average of around 25,000 spectators per match. German cup (DFB) matches are usually played during the week, as are European competition matches. Tickets can usually be purchased at grounds on the day of matches or from ticket offices, and cost from around €15 for standing places (*Stehplätze*) and from €20 for seats. Tickets for big matches and internationals cost at least €50.

Almost every village or town has a football club, and there are local leagues throughout Germany. For local details and more information about the game as a whole, contact the Deutscher Fussball-Bund, Otto-Fleck-Schneise 6, D-60528 Frankfurt (☎ 069-67880, 🖳 www.dfb.de).

GOLF

Although an expensive and elitist sport in Germany, golf has enjoyed increasing popularity in the last decade, boosted by the success of Bernhard

Langer, who has been in the top ranks of world golf for some twenty years. The country now boasts over 500 clubs with over 300,000 members, an increase of well over 70 per cent during the last decade. However, most are private clubs with long waiting lists for membership and there are very few public golf courses in Germany. Club information is available on the Internet (🖳 www.golfeurope.com/euro_clubs/germany.htm). Most clubs admit non-members with a handicap card for a green fee of around €25 a round during the week and €50 at weekends and on public holidays. The German Open golf tournament is held annually in August in Dusseldorf and the Golf Word Championship was held in Germany (Berlin) in 2000 for the first time. For more information contact the German Golf Federation (Deutscher Golf-Verband, Viktoriastr. 16, D-65189 Wiesbaden, ☎ 0611-990200, 🖳 www.golf.de).

HEALTH CLUBS

There are gymnasiums and health and fitness clubs in most towns in Germany. 'Working out' is becoming increasingly popular and many companies provide health and leisure centres or pay for corporate membership for staff. In addition to many private clubs, most public sports centres have tonnes of expensive bone-jarring, muscle-wrenching apparatus. If you aren't fit, you shouldn't over-exert yourself, as this can result in serious sports injuries. A good gymnasium or health club will ensure this doesn't happen and will carry out a physical assessment, including a blood pressure test, fat distribution measurements and heart rate checks.

To join a club, you must usually pay an initial fee which ranges from €100 to €400, depending on the type of membership chosen, and then a monthly fee of from €50 to €100. Normally, the higher the initial sum paid, the lower your monthly fee. You can reduce the fee by opting to use the facilities only during off-peak times, for example, during the mornings or before 5pm. In addition to superbly equipped gymnasiums, most clubs offer aerobics and keep-fit classes, a sauna and/or Jacuzzi, a swimming pool, and some also have tennis, squash and badminton courts (for which an additional fee is payable, depending on your membership). Other facilities may include a resident physiotherapist, a beauty salon (offering massage and aromatherapy) or spa area, and child care (usually from one year of age). Clubs allow you to buy a daily card (from around 20 to €40) or take a 'sniff' (*Schnupper*) day to assess whether you want to join. Clubs usually provide a free trial and assessment and produce personal training programmes for members.

Many top class hotels have health clubs and swimming pools that are usually open to the general public, although access to facilities may be restricted only to residents at certain times.

HIKING

Germans, of all ages, are keen hikers. Although the main hiking season is from around May to September, hiking isn't just a summer sport and most winter sports resorts keep trails open for walkers throughout the winter. Germany is a great hiking (*Wandern*) country with over 100,000km (62,000mi) of marked hiking and mountain-walking tracks administered by regional hiking clubs (*Wandervereine*) and mountaineering groups. It has a national network of paths with routes which vary in their degree of difficulty, although most are fairly easy. Hikes take in romantic forests, beautiful landscapes, or tranquil lakes, and most pass through picturesque villages where there's usually somewhere you can make an overnight stop.

Germany has some of the most beautiful hiking country in Europe, although the terrain isn't usually as rugged as in some other countries such as France or Spain. The most popular hiking areas are Bavaria and the Schwarzwald (Black Forest - the world's most famous forest, although it isn't black or even a dark shade of green!), stretching from the resort town of Baden-Baden to the Swiss border. Other popular hiking areas include the Erzgebirge, the Thuringian Forest, the Harz Mountains, the Sauerland, the Rhön, the Fichtelgebirge and the Swabian mountains. A social and organised hike of up to 42km (26mi) is called a *Volksmarsch* and attracts huge numbers of participants who usually receive a commemoration (certificate, pin or medal) for completing it.

Those who are keen on Alpine walking should contact the German Alpine Association (Deutsche Alpenverein, Vohn-Kahr-Str. 2-4, D-80997 Munich (☎ 089-14030, 🖳 www.alpenverein.de), which maintains some 50 mountain huts and around 15,000km (over 9,000mi) of Alpine paths. It can provide courses in mountaineering and touring suggestions for both summer and winter routes, while a number of mountaineering schools offer courses ranging from basic techniques for beginners to advanced mountaineering. Those who feel up to it may wish to try the challenging 60km (37mi) 'Allgäu high-level' route between Oberstdorf and the Oberjoch in the Alps, staying overnight in forest huts. Mountain walking shouldn't be confused with hiking as it's generally done at much higher altitudes and in more difficult terrain. It can be dangerous for the untrained and should be approached with much the same degree of caution and preparation as mountaineering. Free hiking maps are available from tourist offices, although the best hiking maps (*Wanderkarten*) are the *Wanderführer* series published by Kompass. For more information contact the Federation of German Mountain and Hiking Clubs (Verband Deutscher Gebirgs-und Wandervereine, Wilhelmshöher Allee 157-159, D-34121 Kassel, (🖳 www. dt.wanderverband.de), the German People's Sports Federation (Deutscher Volkssportverband e.V, Fabrikstr. 8, D-845503 Altötting, (☎ 08671-

8071/96310) or the Federation of German Ski and Mountain Guides (Verband Deutscher Ski und Bergführer, Untersbergstrasse 34, 83451 Piding (☎ 08651-71221, 💻 www.bergfuehrer-verband.de)

Safety

The following notes may help you survive a stroll in the mountains:

- If you're going to take up hiking seriously, a good pair of walking shoes or boots is mandatory (available from most local shoe and sports shops). Always wear proper walking shoes or boots where the terrain is rough. Unfortunately walking boots are usually uncomfortable or hurt your feet after a few hours. Wearing two pairs of socks can help prevent blisters. Break in a new pair of boots on some gentle hikes before setting out on a marathon hike around Germany.

- Don't over-exert yourself, particularly at high altitudes where the air is thinner. Mountain sickness usually occurs only above 4,000m/13,000ft, but can also happen at lower altitudes. A few words of warning for those who aren't particularly fit; take it easy and set a slow pace. It's easy to over-exert yourself and underestimate the duration or degree of difficulty of a hike. Start slowly and build up to those weekend marathons. If you're unfit, use chair-lifts and cable-cars to get to high altitudes.

- Don't attempt a major hike alone as it's too dangerous. Notify someone about your route, destination and estimated time of return. Check the conditions along your route and the times of any public transport connections (set out early to avoid missing the last cable-car or bus). Take into account the time required for both ascents and descents. If you're unable to return by the time expected, let somebody know. If you realise that you're unable to reach your destination, for example, due to tiredness or bad weather, turn back in good time or take a shorter route. If you get caught in a heavy storm, descend as quickly as possible or seek protection, e.g. in a mountain hut.

- Check the weather forecast, usually obtainable from the local tourist office. Generally the higher the altitude, the more unpredictable the weather, even for local meteorologists.

- Hiking, even in lowland areas, can be dangerous, so don't take any unnecessary risks. There are enough natural hazards, including bad weather, rockfalls, avalanches, rough terrain, snow and ice, and wet grass, without adding to them.

- Don't walk on closed tracks at any time (they're sign-posted). This is particularly important in the spring when there may be the danger of avalanches or rockfalls. If you're in doubt about a particular route, ask in advance at the local tourist office. Beware of anything that is signposted as being dangerous (*Gefahr/Lebensgefahr*) – as you can be sure it is!

- Wear loose fitting clothes and not, for example, tight jeans, which can become uncomfortable when you get warmed up. Shorts are excellent in hot weather and lightweight cotton trousers are comfortable unless it's cold. You can wear your shorts underneath your trousers and remove your trousers when you've warmed up.

- Take a warm pullover, gloves (in winter) and a raincoat. Mountain weather can change suddenly and even in summer it's sometimes cold at high altitudes. A first-aid kit (for cuts and grazes), compass, identification, maps, small torch and a Swiss army knife may also come in handy. A pair of binoculars are handy for spotting wildlife. Take a rucksack to carry all your survival rations. A 35 to 40-litre rucksack is best for day trips or a 65-litre rucksack for longer hikes.

- Take sun protection, for example, a hat, sunglasses, and sun and barrier cream, as you will burn more easily at high altitude due to the thinner air. Use a total sun block cream on your lips, nose and eyelids, and take a scarf or handkerchief to protect your neck from the sun. You may also need to protect yourself against ticks and mosquitoes in some areas.

- Take a water bottle. This is much appreciated when you discover that the restaurant that was just around the corner is still miles away because you took the wrong turn.

- Beware of wild animals that appear ill or unnaturally friendly as they may have rabies.

- Don't take young children on difficult hikes unless you enjoy carrying them. Impress upon children the importance of not wandering off on their own. If you lose anyone, particularly children, seek help as soon as possible and before nightfall. It's advisable to equip children with a loud whistle and some warm clothing, in case they get lost.

- Hikers should observe the 'rules' of the countryside:
  - Take care not to damage trees, flowers and bushes.
  - Leave animals in peace (dogs mustn't be allowed to disturb farm animals).
  - Be careful with fire and never start one in a forbidden area.
  - Watch where you walk and keep to the paths.
  - Don't litter the countryside.
  - Think of others.
  - Close all gates after use.

RACKET SPORTS

Tennis is the second most popular sport in Germany (after football) and the German Tennis Association (Deutsche Tennis Bund) has over two million members and the largest club network of any country, with over 10,000 tennis clubs, some 50,000 outdoor courts and more than 4,000 indoor courts. Tennis has really flourished in Germany in the last few decades thanks to the success of stars such as Boris Becker, Steffi Graf, Michael Stich (all grand slam event winners) and Anke Huber. Prior to the success of Becker and Graf, tennis was previously something of an upper class sport, although it's now played by people from all backgrounds.

Many towns have public courts (although they aren't as common as in many other countries) where you don't need to be a member of a club and anyone can just book a court. Most courts are clay or astroturf (artificial grass) and hard (asphalt) or grass courts are rare in Germany. When playing on an indoor court you must wear shoes with non-marking soles – if you don't have any, they can usually be purchased or hired. Court fees vary from €15 to €30 per hour, depending on the season, day of the week and the time of day (they're usually cheaper before 5pm on weekdays), indoor courts being more expensive than outdoor courts. Local courts and clubs are listed in the yellow pages under *Tenniscenter* and *Sportanlagen*.

Germany stages a number of professional tournaments annually, among them the German Open in Hamburg (May), the BMW Tennis Open in Munich (April/May) and the Mercedes Cup in Stuttgart in July. Germany also has a Federal Tennis League in which top German and foreign tennis players compete. For more information, contact the German Tennis Federation (Deutscher Tennis Bund, Hallerstr. 89, D-20149 Hamburg, (☎ 040-411780, 💻 www.dtb-tennis.de, ✉ dtb@dtb-tennis.de)

Squash and badminton are popular in Germany, although the country has yet to make any big waves in either sport. This could have something to do with the cost of playing: squash courts can be hired for between €15 and €30 for 45 minutes, while badminton courts cost between €20 and €30 per hour. Court costs for both sports vary with the day of the week and the time of day, courts generally being cheaper before 5pm.

SKIING

Skiing is a very popular sport in Germany, where millions of people ski regularly, although the majority head over the border to neighbouring countries. Germany doesn't have many very large ski centres and most are small, long-established resorts with older lift systems. The larger resorts often offer passes taking in a number of nearby ski centres (although they're rarely linked by ski-lifts), including some over the border in Austria. German resorts are noted for their traditional architecture and the country doesn't go in for the purpose-built affairs, such as are common in France. Most resorts offer good *après-ski* and many have excellent public sports facilities, including indoor swimming pools. The skiing season runs from the middle of December to the end of March, although at higher altitudes such as the Zugspitze (up to 2,830m/8,490ft) glacier near Garmisch, you can often ski from November until the middle of May. Although it isn't quite in the same league as Austria, France and Switzerland, Germany has had considerable success in World Cup events and championships over the years.

The Alps of southern Bavaria are Germany's main winter sports region, where Garmisch-Partenkirchen (720-2,966m/2,362-9,730ft) and Oberstdorf (700-2,224m/ 2,296-7,296ft) are the top resorts, both regular venues on the World Cup Downhill circuit. Other Alpine resorts, suitable mainly for beginners and moderate skiers, include Bayrischzell, Berchtesgaden, Mittenwald and Schliersee. In addition to the Alps, you can also ski in the Allgäu, Bavarian Alps, Black Forest (Swarzwald), Erzgebirge, Fichtelgebirge, Harz, Rhön, Sauerland (a cross-country paradise), Swabian mountains and the Thuringian Forest, although many resorts have just a few downhill (*Alpin*) runs or offer only cross-country (Langlauf) skiing. Among the most popular resorts outside the Alps are the Black Forest resorts of Furtwangen, Schonach, Todtmoos and Todtnau. The upper Harz (Hochharz) is also noted for its excellent cross-country skiing and ski hikes.

The price of ski-lift passes is around average for Europe, as shown below:

Pass	Price (€)	
	Child	Adult
1 Day	11 – 13.50	14 – 28.50
2 Day	22 – 26.50	28 – 56.50

Family passes (2 adults/2 children) are available from around €65 for one day.

Passes that combine areas are much better value than those for individual resorts and cost around one-third more. Special off-season or 'white week' (*Weisse Woche*) rates, are offered by most winter resorts for cross-country and downhill holidays, which include bed and breakfast or half board plus ski lessons. Equipment (skis, poles and boots) can be hired from around €15 per day.

The Garmisch-Partenkirchen ski pass is valid for 28 lifts and provides access to 55km (34mi) of ski terrain, including the world famous ski runs of Kandahar and Olympia (both of which have snow-making equipment).

In winter 2003 a one-day pass cost €27 for an adult (€21.50 for youths aged 16 or 17 and €17.50 for children aged 5 to 15), and a half day pass, after or before noon, €19.50 (youths €16 and children €13). A slightly cheaper pass is available after 1.15pm. A seven-day 'happy ski card', for the area around the Zugspitze, costs €156 for adults (€144 for youths and €94 for children). There are also various family discounts, special passes and season passes.

The ADAC motoring organisation (see page 261) provides a recorded 'snow conditions' telephone service (☎ 089-7676 2556) for most regions. For further information, contact the German Skiing Federation (Deutscher Skiverband, Hubertusstr. 1, D-82152 Munich-Plannegg (☎ 089-857902, 🖳 www.ski-online.de).

SWIMMING

Swimming is very popular in Germany, where an estimated two-thirds of the population swim regularly. There are outdoor (*Freibad*) and/or heated indoor (*Hallenbad*) swimming pools in most German towns and resorts, many open year-round. However, admission fees have been increased and the opening hours of many pools reduced in recent years. Swimming hats may be required at some pools and when necessary are usually sold at reception. Germans are keen on nude bathing and many pools have special days from nude bathers and it's also permitted on certain beaches, shown by an *FKK* (*Freiekörperkultur*) sign. There are indoor sea-water pools in coastal areas and many lakes also have swimming areas which are off-limits to other water-sport enthusiasts. Swimming in rivers, particularly the larger ones, isn't recommended and in some cases is prohibited (Baden Verboten), either due to shipping, pollution or dangerous waters.

You can find a list of public swimming pools in your local area under *Freizeit-, Hallen- und Freibäder* in the journal section of your yellow pages (*Gelbe Seiten*). Most swimming pools and clubs organise swimming lessons for all levels and run life saving courses. Children can join a swimming team at a local pool that competes against other teams (the clubs are called *Schwimmvereine*). For more information, contact your local swimming club (*Schwimmverband*). The former East Germany excelled in international swimming competitions and a new generation of swimmers is now emerging to rival the international supremacy of Australia and the US.

There are a number of large indoor swimming centres and aquatic and water parks in Germany where the facilities may include hot-water pools, sulphur baths, thermal whirlpools, connecting indoor and outdoor pools, wave machines, huge water slides, solariums and saunas (many mixed sex). The entrance fee is high, e.g. €15 to €30 usually for a limited period, although they make a pleasant change from the local pool for a special day out. Spas (see page 274) throughout Germany have thermal or mineral-water indoor pools where day visitors can swim or relax in the water.

For further information, contact the German Swimming Association (Deutscher Schwimmverband, Korbacherstr. 93, D-34132 Kassel, (☎ 0561-940830, ▣ www.dsv.de).

WATER SPORTS

All water sports, including sailing, windsurfing, waterskiing, rowing, canoeing and sub-aquatic sports are popular in Germany, which has a good record in world and Olympic competitions, particularly rowing and sailing. Boats and equipment can be hired on most lakes and at coastal resorts, where instruction is available for most disciplines. Windsurfing is particularly popular on Bavarian lakes, although it has had to be restricted due to collisions with swimmers, and rowing and canoeing is possible on most lakes and rivers in the country. **Wetsuits are recommended for windsurfing, waterskiing and subaquatic sports, even during the summer.** A licence is required for a boat with an output of more than 3.6kW (around 5 horsepower). Be sure to observe all warning signs on lakes and rivers!

The North Sea and Baltic coasts are a Mecca for sailors together with numerous lakes such as the Bodensee, Chiemsee, Müritz, Schweriner See and Starberger See. The most popular rivers include the Danube, Elbe, Main, Neckar, Oder, Rhine, Saale and Weser. Lake sailing is popular, particularly on the Chiemsee in Bavaria and on the Bodensee (Lake Constance). There are some 200 sailing schools on the North Sea and Baltic coasts alone, where Kiel and Rostock are the main sailing centres. For information contact the appropriate organisation:

- **German Canoeing Federation** (Deutsche Kanu-Verband, Bertaallee 8, D-47055 Duisberg, ☎ 0203-997590, ▣ www.kanu.de).
- **German Rowing Federation** (Deutscher Ruderverband, Maschstr. 20, D-30169 Hanover, (☎ 0511-980940, ▣ www.ruderverband.org).
- **German Motor Yacht Federation** (Deutscher Motoryachtverband, Vinckeufer 14, D-47119 Duisberg, (☎ 0203-9975 960, ▣ www.dmyv.de).
- **German Sailing Federation** (Deutscher Seglerverband, Gründgensstr. 18, D-22309 Hamburg, (☎ 040-6320 090, ▣ www.dsv.org).
- **German Waterskiing Federation** (Deutscher Wasserskiverband, Gründgenstr. 18, D-22309 Hamburg (☎ 040-6399 8732, ▣ www.dwsv.de).
- **German Windsurfing Association** (VSWS, Fasserstr. 30, D-82363 Weilheim, Oberbayern).

OTHER SPORTS & ACTIVITIES

The following is a selection of other popular sports in Germany:

Athletics

A very popular sport in Germany. The country has excellent facilities and an excellent record in international competitions. Germany stages three Grand Prix athletics meetings in early September in Berlin, Cologne and Koblenz. Most German towns and villages have local athletics clubs and organise local competitions and sports days.

Ballet & Jazz Ballet

Dance, training and exercise classes are provided in many towns throughout Germany and are also organised by gymnasiums.

Basketball

A popular sport in Germany, where the top teams participate in the European Clubs Championship. Professional basketball has a strong following, including both domestic and American (NBA) games.

Billiards & Snooker

Many hotels, bars and sports clubs have billiard or snooker tables and there are a few billiards clubs in the larger towns. English-style snooker isn't played in public clubs in Germany.

Boxing

Boxing is not really that popular, although Germany has produced a number of world champions over the years, and performs well at the amateur level. Finding a boxing club or gymnasium is easier in major towns and cities.

Bungee Jumping

If your idea of fun is jumping out of a cable car or a hot-air balloon with an elastic rope attached to your body to prevent you merging with the landscape, then bungee jumping may be just what you're looking for.

Fencing

A sport that has lost a lot of its popularity since the invention of the gun, although a hard core of enthusiastic fencers are holding out in a small number of clubs. Germany has traditionally been very strong in international fencing competitions.

Frisbee

Believe it or not, throwing plastic discs around has actually developed into a competitive 'sport', with national and local league and cup competitions.

Gymnastics

An extremely popular sport in Germany, where gymnastic clubs abound in all areas, even in small towns and villages.

Handball

Another very popular sport in Germany, which is one of the world's top countries. Played indoors on a pitch similar to a five-a-side football pitch, handball players pass the ball around by hand and attempt to throw it into a small goal.

Hockey

Hockey (also called land hockey to prevent confusion with ice hockey) is another popular sport in Germany, which has enjoyed considerable success in world and Olympic competitions. Equally popular among both sexes.

Horse Racing

A popular enough sport in Germany, where the premier race is the German Derby held in Hamburg in late June, while the spring and autumn meetings at Iffezheim (near Baden-Baden) are also fashionable occasions. Trotting is also popular.

Horse Riding

Germany is one of the world's leading equestrian nations, and there's a long tradition of horsemanship. This is usually expressed in competitive sporting terms in the show jumping arena where Germans are always at the top of the rankings or thereabouts. Horse riding for fun is popular but expensive. There are numerous riding schools and equestrian centres (*Reiterhöfe*) in Germany, although some insist on minimum riding proficiency before allowing novices to go on treks. Some resorts organise cross-country riding holidays and information about riding excursions (costing around €20 per hour) can be obtained from tourist offices. The leading equestrian events are held in Aachen and Hamburg in June, while famous dressage displays take place in September and October in Celle.

Martial Arts

Unarmed combat such as Kung Fu, Judo and Karate are taught and practised in most towns.

Motor Sports

Motor racing, particularly Formula 1, is extremely popular, where every kid's idol is Michael Schumacher (whose brother Ralf is also a top driver) who drives for the Italian Ferrari team. The German Grand Prix is normally held in August at Hockenheim (near Heidelberg). In addition the Belgian Grand Prix just the merest hop across the border at Spa-Francorchamps is usually a pretty German dominated event spectator-wise too.

Rollerskating, Rollerblading, Skateboarding & BMX

Rinks and specially designed circuits are provided in many towns for skateboarding and BMX cycles (acrobatics on a bicycle). Children can start at around age seven, but participants of all ages should be protected against falls with crash helmets and elbow and knee pads. It's difficult to hire equipment as it's too easily stolen, although BMX bikes can usually be hired. Rollerskating rinks are available in many areas, sometimes using local sports and leisure centres. Skates can be hired and coaching is usually available. Many centres organise roller-discos for teenagers. In-line skating is inevitably popular too. Many cities organise rollerblade nights, when a few streets are closed to traffic from 8pm so that kids can skate in safety. Keen rollerskaters and rollerbladers often play roller hockey.

Running

Competitive running has a strong following in Germany and jogging is also a popular fitness pursuit in the major cities, where jogging trails take in local gardens and parks.

Shooting

Shooting ranges abound in Germany, where most towns and villages have a local shooting federation that organises local competitions. Rifle clubs (*Schützenvereine*) have a long tradition, including ceremonies and uniforms, and an enthusiastic social side. Crossbow shooting is also popular in Germany. Germans shoot wild animals, although hunting with dogs isn't practised, and there are few restrictions as to what may be shot. Those wishing to shoot animals must take both a theory and a practical examination, preceded by a course lasting at least six months.

Ten-Pin Bowling

There are ten-pin bowling centres in all major German cities and towns, as well as 9-pin skittles (*Kegeln*). *Kegeln* uses smaller balls with no finger-holes, just a large opening for your hand, and is performed on a long, narrow bowling lane (*Kegelbahn*). It's a lot of fun and usually connected to a restaurant. Reservations are a must – look in yellow pages under *Kegelbahnen* and *Kegelbahnenrestaurant*.

Trampolining

A popular sport and there are a large number of clubs (both junior and senior) throughout Germany, where courses are organised for all ages.

Weightlifting

There are weightlifting clubs in most large towns in Germany, many using the facilities of a local sports or leisure centres or a health and fitness club.

Miscellaneous Sports

Many foreign sports and pastimes have a group of expatriate fanatics in Germany, including cricket, American football (NFL exhibition games draw huge crowds), baseball, *boccia*, *boules*, croquet, polo, rounders, rugby football and softball. For more information enquire at community and tourist offices, embassies and consulates (see **Appendix A**).

17.

SHOPPING

Germany offers a wide choice of shopping, ranging from ultra-sophisticated specialist shops and world-renowned department stores to the charm of local farmers' markets and festivals featuring regional specialities. As with so many aspects of German life, commerce is subject to a plethora of rules, regulations and legal constraints, which influence when, where and how you can shop. On the other hand, the abundance of regulations also affords considerable protection to consumers and in general you will find that goods are of uniformly high quality, if rather expensive compared with many other countries, particularly the US. However, Germans are expert bargain hunters, particularly in the south of the country, where the Schwabians claim to be European penny-pinching champions.

Much of the regulation of retailing stems from German labour laws designed to protect shop employees from exploitation. Shop opening hours are strictly controlled (see below) and staff can only be required to perform the job they were hired to do. Even Germans joke about the surly customer service you can encounter in much of Germany, although standards are improving.

All prices advertised or quoted to individuals include value added tax (*Umsatzsteuer/USt* or *Mehrwertsteuer/MwSt*) and are the total price you pay.

Most shops accept exchanges or offer refunds unless they have an advertised policy to the contrary (in which case you should shop elsewhere!), but they usually require you to produce your receipt and, in some cases, the original packaging. However, as part of Germany's environmental legislation, all shops are required by law to take back the packaging from the goods they sell, so you should check that that the goods are in order as far as possible before leaving the shop. Some shops have recycling bins in their car parks or near entrances for cartons and other packing material. If you have goods delivered to your home, you can ask the delivery people to take the packaging material away with them.

The Germans are only sluggishly warming to credit cards, despite the fact that most issued in Germany are linked directly to a bank account and function more like debit cards. The situation is changing quite rapidly, but you will still probably find some shops that won't accept credit cards.

Bargain Shopping

There's minimal bargaining over prices in most stores, although some shops may offer discounts to members of the local sports club or other social or civic associations. Prices aren't directly controlled, but retailers cannot easily change prices once posted, and most smaller stores adhere to the manufacturer's recommended retail price. A shopkeeper may reduce prices on a single line of products in order to sell off remaining stock, but such price reductions are limited to a small proportion of the total goods available, and generally apply only where the product was a one-time purchase that won't be re-ordered.

Major sales are limited to two two-week periods per year; one at the end of the winter season (*Winterschlussverkauf*) and the other at the end of the summer season (*Sommerschlussverkauf*). The exact dates are set by regional authorities and vary slightly between states, but in general the *Winterschlussverkauf* starts at the end of January and the *Sommerschlussverkauf* at the end of July. Price cuts during these official sale periods are generous and it's an excellent time to stock up on seasonal merchandise, e.g. skiing and winter clothes in the end-of-winter sales, and swimming and holiday wear at the end of the summer. As quite often in Germany, practice isn't as stringent as theory, however, and despite the precision of the regulations sales can start earlier than advertised.

Goods purchased during the end-of-season sales generally aren't returnable, so you should shop carefully at sale times.

Due to the high overall level of prices, there's an active market in Germany for secondhand goods, especially furniture (including complete kitchens) and appliances. Secondhand clothing and appliance stores can be found in almost every town with over 5,000 inhabitants and are listed in the local phone book and newspapers. Local newspapers contain classified advertisements for household goods, and several weekly publications devoted solely to such advertisements are sold at news stands.

Many towns run an annual flea market (*Flohmarkt*), where the locals can set up a stall (for a small fee, payable to the town) to sell off used household and other items (they're a good source of toys and children's clothing).

Expatriate clubs are a good source of secondhand goods, which are either advertised in newsletters nor sold at annual or bi-annual flea markets. Most cities in Germany are home to at least one (or usually more) British or American clubs with a high enough turnover of members each year to ensure a healthy exchange of used goods at reasonable prices.

Another place to purchase used clothing and books is the shops of British charity Oxfam, which has been steadily expanding in Germany after opening its first shop in Frankfurt in 1995 and now also has shops in Berlin, Bonn, Cologne, Mainz and Wiesbaden. Oxfam shops provide an ideal way to clear out your spare clothing, books, records, CDs and other small items, but most don't have sufficient space for larger objects.

Stiftung Warentest: Stiftung Warentest is a respected, independent and non-profit-making foundation which compares and tests products and services (rather like Which? and the Consumers' Association in the UK). Some 1,700 products (from grapefruit juice to hig-fi equipment) are tested each year as well as services related to investment, health, tourism, and transport. Companies whose products receive good or very good ratings indicate this in their advertising.

OPENING HOURS

Shopping hours are still strictly controlled under federal labour law. The 'liberalisation' of shopping hours in 1996 meant that shops were allowed to remain open on weekdays from 6am until 8pm, and until 4pm on Saturdays; recent legislation has extended permissible Saturday opening hours to 8pm. However, these are the maximum permitted opening hours, and most shops other than bakeries and some news stands don't open for business until 9am. Bakeries can also open for a few hours on Sunday mornings to sell fresh bread and rolls, but otherwise there's no Sunday trading. Smaller shops, particularly those in towns and villages, often close for an hour or so at lunchtime to allow employees to go home for their main meal of the day.

The only retail outlets that are exempt from normal shopping hours are those at airports and railway stations and petrol stations. Frankfurt airport, in particular, has an extensive underground shopping area which includes a grocery store open all day Sunday and late evenings during the rest of the week. Prices in airport shops are high, as you would expect, but most shops accept credit cards for almost any purchase. Petrol stations, particularly those on or near motorways, often run a convenience shop, where you can find most 'essentials' (at inflated prices).

SHOPPING CENTRES & MARKETS

Germany has a variety of indoor shopping centres, located mostly in the larger towns and cities, and there's a wide range of shops and services in the underground passageways of most major underground and railway stations (e.g. in Frankfurt or Munich). The Germans haven't gone in for building vast indoor shopping malls on the outskirts of cities and towns, as are common in France and the US, although there are small clusters of large stores (usually hypermarkets and discount stores) in industrial and commercial estates on the periphery of many towns. These developments have a down-to-earth practical air but offer free parking, which is rarely to be found in towns.

Most German towns have a shopping street closed to traffic except for early morning delivery hours (*Fussgängerzone*). In most cases, it's in the centre of town and well served by public transport. Parking in the centre of most cities and towns is expensive and difficult, particularly on Saturdays and during sales periods or the pre-Christmas shopping season.

Most towns and all cities have regular open-air markets throughout the year. Most popular is the farmers' or food market, which is usually a weekly event at least (in Freiburg, for example, there's an open-air market six days a week in the Münsterplatz). These open-air markets aren't to be missed, particularly for regional and seasonal specialities such as white asparagus (*Spargel*) – available only in the spring – and the various types of wild mushroom (*Pilz*) – an autumn speciality. Other treats you will find in open-air markets include locally produced honey (*Honig*), sausages (*Wurst*) and hams (*Schinken*), along with a wide variety of fresh fruit and vegetables. Market vendors set up at around 6 or 7am and shut up shop in the early afternoon.

In the run-up to Christmas, many towns hold *Adventmarkts* or *Christkindlmarkts*, well-stocked with local craft items, traditional Christmas ornaments and plenty of *Lebkuchen* (a form of gingerbread), *Stollen* (iced fruit loaf), *Spekulatius* or *Spekulatus* (an almond-flavoured biscuit) and other Christmas foods, including *Glühwein* (hot, spiced and sweetened red wine) to keep your Christmas shopping spirits up!

Other outdoor markets include flea markets (*Trödelmärkte*) and wine, crafts and other festivals organised by local authorities. Keep an eye out for posters around town announcing these events or ask at your local town hall or tourist office.

DEPARTMENT & CHAIN STORES

Germany has no shortage of excellent department stores, both indigenous and foreign, but after a long period of stability this sector has become the scene of mergers and takeovers in recent years. Kaufhof has partnered Horten, Karstadt has joined up with Hertie, and Kaufhalle has been bought by the Italian La Staedo group. These are fine stores, but Germany's flagship store is KaDeWe in Berlin, the largest department store on the European continent and perhaps best known for its remarkable food department, where shoppers can sample exotic delicacies at the many gourmet counters and wash them down with champagne. In most large cities, there are foreign department stores such as H&M and C&A, while east Berlin even boasts a Galeries Lafayette in its new KuDamm shopping district.

Department stores offer a dizzying variety of high quality merchandise, with all well-known brands represented as well as usually a range of good value own-brand items. Practically all department stores accept major credit cards, which isn't always the case in other shops. At some stores (e.g. those of the Hertie/Karstadt group) you can apply for a preferred customer card, which provides a 3 per cent discount on all purchases after a qualifying period.

The department store chains of Hertie/Karstadt and Kaufhof have excellent food markets, typically on the ground floor or at basement level. Their gourmet offerings are superb and they often specialise in international foodstuffs as well. Here you can usually find fresh, good quality, pre-packaged foods, which is helpful if your German is at a basic level and you're looking for something recognisable to cook for dinner.

Chain stores are popular throughout Germany, including US-style speciality chains, most notably Toys 'R' Us. There's at least one large hardware and DIY chain store (e.g. OBI) on the edge of most towns, and there are also a number of discount electronics chains where you can buy TVs, appliances and stereo equipment at competitive prices.

SUPERMARKETS & FOOD SHOPPING

Most towns in Germany have one or more supermarkets offering a full range of food and drinks and some small household items. Among the major chains are Tengelmann, Edeka, Rewe, Metro and Wertkauf (recently taken over by WalMart). HL is a well-known smaller chain. There are many smaller international supermarkets, particularly Italian and Turkish, which can be good for vegetables and unusual items.

When the American merchandising giant WalMart purchased the German chains Wertkauf and Interspar in 1997, it started by renovating all its newly acquired stores and introducing a wider range of brands than were found in most German chains, including many American imports. However, when it tried to implement the American customs of 'bagging' customer purchases and valet parking, Germans protested. WalMart also massively underestimated the competitiveness of chains such as Aldi and has recently been forced to close two shops.

The large discount chains include PennyMarkt, Lidl and Aldi, where some amazing bargains can be found, although the selection can be relatively limited. Note that these discount shops can become very crowded and you may have to wait a long time at the checkout.

Supermarkets sell primarily food items. Germany also has a wide range of hypermarkets, which are shops with over 2,500m² (27,000ft²) of floor space, selling electronic goods, household appliances, books, clothing and hardware as well as food, and are usually found on the outskirts of major towns and cities. The main hypermarket chains are Allkauf, E-center, Globus, Real and Wallmart.

Although some of the brand names may be unfamiliar, most products are similar to those found in supermarkets in other countries and can meet most of your daily requirements.

Germany boasts a fine range of *Wurst* (which translates as 'sausage' but also includes cold cuts, salamis and processed meats) and cheeses. You may also be surprised at the variety of bread, rolls and buns on offer in even the smallest grocery shop. The Germans make bread out of almost every form of grain – maize, wheat, rye, barley, etc. – the best and most delicious of being heavy textured and thinly sliced. Foreign products, such as those dear to British tastes, aren't generally available, although stilton and peanut butter can be found in some shops.

The quality of fruit and vegetables varies from shop to shop. Some supermarket chains pride themselves on the quality (categorised from I to III) and freshness of their produce, while in others the indifferent quality is matched only by the unattractive displays. Some stores stock only lower quality category II and III produce, as shown on labels. **Many fruit and vegetables are treated with fungicides and must be thoroughly washed before eating.** Shops in rural areas often buy fruit and vegetables from local farmers, which is generally fresher and of better quality than that available in towns and cities and may even be cheaper. It helps to find out when your local shops receive fresh deliveries and time your shopping trips accordingly. In general, Mondays are the worst days if you're looking for fresh produce or baked goods, and Saturday mornings are also to be avoided if possible, as this is the busiest time in most shops.

Eggs aren't generally washed or polished, giving them a more 'rustic' appearance than you may be used to. However, the fact that an egg doesn't shine doesn't mean that it's any less wholesome. For those opposed to battery farming, free-range eggs are available (marked *Bodenhaltung*). Milk is sold in three varieties: full-cream milk (*Vollmilch*), low fat/skimmed (*Fettarme Milch*) and heat-treated (*H Milch*). H Milch doesn't need refrigeration until it's opened, as it has been sterilised. If you plan to do any baking, note that the quality of flour is indicated by the 'type number' on the packaging: the less refined, the higher the number, e.g. cake flour carries the number 405, while wholemeal flour is in the 1600 range. Freshly ground coffee can be bought at most supermarkets.

Supermarkets also sell beer, soft drinks and mineral water by the crate, which usually represents excellent value for money. Due to the (many) ecological and recycling laws, drinks are sold only in glass bottles. You must pay a deposit (*Pfand*) on both the bottles and the crate, which is refunded when you return the empties to the store. Most supermarkets have a separate bottle return station where you return your bottles and receive a credit slip to redeem at the checkout. Some shops are equipped with machines that do this automatically; you simply place the bottles on a turntable, press a button when they've all been inserted and the machine issues a receipt.

The 50 cents deposit on tin cans introduced in January 2003 means that you must bring them back to the shop where you bought them, along with your till receipt to reclaim your money. The system isn't very practicable from the retailer's point of view and coordination between retailers has been poor. The upshot has been that several shops (particularly the Aldi and Lidl chains) have reduced tinned goods to a minimum. (An aluminium recycling plant at Rheinfelden has closed as a result.) In reaction to this, the government is introducing a centralised scheme for dealing with tin can deposits, which should be operative by October 1st 2003, but by then most people will probably have realised they don't really need to buy tinned goods anyway.

Many people arrange to have drinks delivered to their homes rather than struggle home with heavy crates from the supermarket (although you will be amazed at how many crates some people manage to transport by bicycle!) Deliveries are often made by the local brewery representative or you can ask your neighbours who makes deliveries (also check your letter box for leaflets). •

Most supermarkets in Germany don't provide free carrier bags or pack your purchases at the checkout. You can usually buy plastic carrier bags for €0.10 to €0.30, but it's more economical (and ecological) to bring your own bags. At most supermarkets, a €1 coin (or similar size token) is required to unlock a trolley from a rack and is returned when you replace the trolley.

Service in some supermarkets and hypermarkets can be particularly brusque. Don't expect cashiers to wish you *Guten Tag* or even to smile, and don't be surprised to find full pallets of merchandise left in the middle of an aisle blocking access to shelves in some discount stores, where staff are at a premium. If you buy anything from the produce section, you're usually expected to weigh and label it yourself; don't make the mistake of arriving at the checkout without weighing your fruit or vegetables (a cardinal sin).

When shopping for food, don't overlook the smaller specialist food shops, which include butchers', bakers' and greengrocers'. Fishmongers' are few and far between, except in coastal areas and cities with large foreign populations, and cheesemongers' can be found mainly in upmarket areas.

ALCOHOL

Drinking is a popular pastime in Germany, despite strict drink-driving laws (see page 257) and growing concerns over alcoholism. Beer is the number one tipple, although its popularity seems to be past its peak – in 1986, the average German consumed 153 litres compared with 125 litres in 2002 – but a possible shortage of beer, as was threatened a few years ago, can still bring the country to the brink of collective nervous breakdown. Wine drinking has grown in popularity over the last few decades, over 26 litres now being consumed per person per annum (the statistic includes the whole population, so the average adult drinks considerably more than this). Spirits are drunk in moderation, the most popular being Schnapps, which is also deemed to be the major cause of alcoholism!

Beer

Almost a third of the world's breweries – some 1,270 at the last count – are situated in Germany, producing over 5,000 different varieties of beer. Beer is brewed everywhere and styles differ considerably from area to area. Some of Germany's best brews are associated with monasteries, most notably the Kloster Weltenburg on the Danube, famous for its strong, chocolate-dark ales. *Roggenbier*, also from Bavaria, is brewed by the princes of Thurn and Taxis in the medieval city of Regensburg, using rye instead of barley; malted and effervescent, it's almost a meal in itself. Another Bavarian beer enjoying growing success in world markets is *Weizenbier* (wheat beer), also known as *Weissbier* (white beer), which is brewed using wheat and barley malts. Tangy, fruity and full, it's best drunk slightly chilled. From eastern Germany there's *Schwarzbier* (black beer), brewed using burnt barley malt, with a stout-like consistency and a toasted flavour. The speciality of Cologne is *Kölsch*, a light, dry pale brew with virtually no effervescence, typically served in small fluted glasses. Some people find that it lacks flavour compared with the nutty beers of southern Germany, but it's easier to drink and seems to bloat less.

Alt (old) beers are popular around Dusseldorf. The term doesn't mean that the beer has been 'aged', but that it's brewed according to traditional, top-fermenting methods. *Alt* beers are dark in colour and can taste hops-bitter or malt-sweet, depending on the recipe. *Bock* beers, in contrast, which are particularly associated with Munich, are bottom-fermented and quite strong. They can be either dark or light. *Pilsner* (or *Pils*) beer is the most widely brewed (and drunk) in Germany and has become famous in other parts of the world. Strictly speaking, the term describes a brewing method, first practised in the Bohemian town of Pilsen in 1842, rather than a type of beer. The main ingredients of a *Pilsner* beer are pale malt, soft water, bottom-fermenting yeast and extremely aromatic hops. Most *Pils* is a pale golden colour, although you will occasionally come across a darker version, which has been brewed with dark malt.

German beer has a well-deserved reputation for quality and flavour, which is due, at least in part, to the *Reinheitsgebot* (purity law) promulgated by the Duke of Bavaria in 1516. Brewing throughout Germany is still regulated by this decree, according to which beer made and marketed anywhere in the country may contain only grain malt, hops, yeast, water and, in some cases, sugar. Only natural ingredients are allowed, with preservatives and other additives strictly forbidden. The Germans successfully used the purity law to bar the import of almost all foreign-made beers until they were taken to the European Court of Justice by other EU members for unfairly restricting trade. A 1987 decision by the court forced Germany to accept foreign beers that didn't meet the purity criteria, although they haven't made much of a dent in the market, as Germans aren't generally willing to buy them.

Further information about German beer can be found on the brewing industry's website (⌨ www.bier.de – available in English).

Wine

The reputation of German wine has suffered in recent decades, although any visitor will soon discover that Germany offers much more than the sickly-sweet *Liebfraumilch* so popular in Britain during the 1970s and 1980s. The German wine trade is currently reverting to older traditions and aiming for better quality wine of all types. The 2002 vintage, which enjoyed ideal weather conditions in most of the wine-producing regions, is one for which expectations are high.

Germany has 13 official wine-producing regions, all of which are located along rivers or around lakes: Ahr, Baden, Franken, Hessische Bergstrasse, Mittelrhein, Mosel-Saar-Ruwer, Nahe, Pfalz, Rheingau, Rheinhessen, Saale-Unstrut, Saxony and Württemberg. These regions are loosely grouped into areas, of which the principal two are the Rhine (whose wine is sold in tall, brown bottles) and Moselle (tall green bottles). Around 87 per cent of the country's vineyards are planted with white grape varieties, with just 13 per cent red. (A tiny amount of rosé wine is produced in the Ahr valley, but all of it is drunk locally.)

German wine is, by law, divided into two main categories, the lower of which is *Tafelwein* (table wine). Better quality wine is labelled *Qualitätswein*, which is roughly equivalent to the French *Appellation Contrôlée* and should signify a wine which is at least drinkable. *Qualitätswein* is further divided into *Qualitätswein eines bestimmten Anbaugebietes* (usually abbreviated to *Qualitätswein b.A.* or just *QbA*) and the best quality, *Qualitätswein mit Prädikat* (*QmP*), which literally means 'quality wine with a description'. *QmP* wines have six grades or 'attributes' corresponding to the ripeness (sugar content) of the grapes they were made from. These are, in ascending order of ripeness (but not necessarily sweetness), as follows:

- *Kabinett* – fine, usually light wines, made from fully ripened grapes. The lightest of the *Prädikat* wines, they're excellent with food or on their own.

- *Spätlese* – wines of superior quality made from grapes harvested after the normal harvest. *Spätlese* wines are more intense in flavour and concentration, but not necessarily sweet. They're good with richer, more flavourful foods or on their own.

- *Auslese* – wines are made from selected, very ripe grapes. They're intense in bouquet and taste, and usually, but not always, sweet.

- *Beerenauslese* – Harvested from selected overripe berries, these are rich, sweet dessert wines, which can also be enjoyed by themselves.

- *Eiswein* – wines of *Beerenauslese* intensity, made from grapes harvested and pressed while frozen (hence the name 'ice wine'). The flavour is unique, with a remarkable concentration of fruity acidity and sweetness.

- *Trockenbeerenauslese* (*TBA*) – wines made from grapes which are overripe and dried almost to raisins. *TBAs* are rich, sweet, luscious, honey-like wines.

QmP wines, which are made entirely with natural ingredients, include the finest Germany has to offer. However, it should be noted that wine made from riper grapes isn't necessarily of better quality, simply one which is likely to be sweeter and/or stronger.

When buying, look for *'Erzeugerabfüllung'* or the new, more strictly defined *'Gutsabfüllung'* on the label, which indicate a wine bottled by the producer or estate. Wines without these words are likely to be blended varieties. The grape type should also be indicated on the label; if it isn't, the wine will be inferior, probably a blend of *Müller Thurgau* or worse. Legally, a wine needs to contain only 85 per cent of the declared grape variety. The classic German grape variety is *Riesling*, but some others can also be good, such as *Ruländer* (*Pinot Gris*) and the new varieties of *Kerner* and *Scheurebe*.

Alcohol levels tend to be low in German wines. Dry *Auslesen* generally have the highest alcohol levels, up to 15 per cent in some cases, while *Kabinetts* and even *TBAs* can come in at under 8 per cent. If a wine's sweetness isn't indicated on the label, it's likely to be slightly to extremely sweet, in rough proportion with the ripeness level. If you want a dry wine, look for one labelled *'trocken'* (dry) or *'halbtrocken'* (semi-dry). Wines up to *Auslese* level may be produced in a dry style.

Most wines of the *QbA* and *Kabinett* grades are ready to drink when marketed and are at their best when young; they should be kept for no more than five years. *Spätlese* may also be consumed young, but the wine is likely to be enjoyable up to ten years after bottling. The 'higher grades' (*Auslese* and above) are usually longer-lived, generally reaching their peak when seven to ten years old, and with good storage can remain at their best for many years longer. Wines from the Rheingau often take longer to reach their potential, while other Rhine wines – from Rheinhessen, Pfalz and Nahe – tend to mature faster. The wines of the Mosel-Saar-Ruwer are the most delicate, and the lesser grades from this region should definitely be drunk sooner rather than later. If you decide to buy wine for ageing, it's best to try a bottle before purchasing a case, and it's also wise to sample stored wines from time to time, so that they don't go past their best without your noticing.

A good source of information about German wine is the German Wine Institute (Deutsches Weininstitut, Postfach 1660, D-55116 Mainz, ☎ 06131-28290, 🖳 www.deutscheweine.de), which has branches in the UK (German Wine Information Service UK, Phipps PR, 33 Long Acre, Covent Garden, London WC2E 9LA (☎ 020-7759 7405, ✉ german.wine@phippspr.co.uk) and the US (German Wine Information Bureau, 245 Park Avenue, 39th

Floor, New York, NY 10167 (☎ 212-792 4134, ✉ info@germanwineusa.org). Both provide a range of useful publications, including *Balance of Flavours – German Wine and Food Pairing Guide*. Wine buffs may also wish to visit the comprehensive German winegrowers' website (🖳 www.germanwine.de), which covers everything anyone but a PhD student in viticulture could ever want to know about German wine and wine-making.

Schnapps

Schnapps (*Schnaps*) is served mainly as an aperitif or a digestive, although it's also sometimes drunk with a glass of beer – what Americans and Britons would call a chaser. Either way, it's normally served neat, at room temperature, in a one-shot glass called a *Kleine-kleine* ('small small'). Many regional brands exist, although they all look and taste much the same. Most are fruit-based, popular varieties, including apples (*Apfelschnaps*), pears (*Birnenschnaps*), plums (*Pflaumenschnaps* or, in Bavaria, *Zwetschgengeist*) and wheat (*Kornschnaps*). Others contain a high proportion of roots and herbs (arnica, angelica, bloodwort, etc.) and all have a high alcohol content (from 25 to 60 per cent) and should be consumed with caution. The extravagant health claims sometimes made for schnapps – that it cures everything from indigestion to infertility – should be taken with a large pinch of *Salz*!

CLOTHES

In general, Germans aren't known as flashy dressers and people of all ages, male and female, dress roughly as people in Britain and North America, perhaps a little more conservatively. One major factor in this is, of course, the climate. The winter months in most parts of Germany are cold and damp, and winter clothing, including warm gloves, hats, boots and waterproofs, is essential. Lightweight clothes are suitable for the summer, which rarely becomes uncomfortably hot.

Germans, it must be said, can be intolerant when it comes to unusual clothing. In some parts of the country, if you wear an unconventional outfit, such as a kilt or sari, you're likely to become an object of curiosity or even derision. Therefore, if you don't wish to stand out from the crowd you should observe how your German friends and neighbours dress and copy their style (it isn't, however, mandatory to wear *Lederhosen*). In some rural areas, Germans are still expected to wear their 'Sunday best' on Sundays, while in the cities attitudes are far more relaxed and more 'radical' clothing is acceptable. For everyday wear, jeans and T-shirts are as popular in Germany as anywhere else and are perfectly acceptable for most leisure activities. At more expensive restaurants, men are usually expected to wear a jacket and tie in the evening, and many German women are highly fashion-conscious and wear stylish outfits to restaurants and the theatre, particularly in the larger cities.

Although conservative, the dress code for business is less rigid than it once was, and is similar to that of North America and most northern European countries. Top management dresses more conservatively than those lower down the chain, and western Germans are generally more style-conscious than those from the east of the country. For men, a well-made jacket (preferably dark) with contrasting trousers is acceptable, but a dark, muted business suit is the best choice in most situations, and a tasteful tie is essential. For women, conservatively tailored suits and dresses are appropriate, and tight or revealing clothing should be avoided.

Clothing in Germany is fashionable and generally of very good quality, but tends to be expensive. All styles can be found in the major cities, but continental sizes may differ from those in other countries such as the UK and the US (see **Appendix D**). Britons and Americans may also have difficulty in finding shoes that fit, as German feet tend to be wider and shorter. Shops selling Italian and Swiss footwear provide a wider range of sizes, although at higher prices.

German cities and larger towns have department stores offering extensive ranges of clothing and sportswear (see **Department & Chain Stores** on page 377), and clothing can be bought at specialist stores such as C&A, Hennes & Mauritz, and Peek & Cloppenburg. Peek & Cloppenburg, or P&C as it's known, is the place to go for stylish but conservative apparel. It stocks good quality brands, and prices are usually reasonable. Hennes & Mauritz, a Swedish chain, can be found throughout Germany and targets the young and trendy on a budget. C&A is also widespread, appealing to budget customers with more conservative preferences.

Winter sportswear is a best buy in Germany, where locally made garments are world class. Leatherwear is also a speciality, although the styling may not appeal to foreigners. The most interesting German traditional dress is that of Bavaria, where Munich is the place to shop. Much of what's sold here is aimed at the children's market, although a good range of adult wear is also available. However, it's difficult to find a good leather jacket for less than €250. Bavaria is also the place to buy hunting gear.

NEWSPAPERS, MAGAZINES & BOOKS

Newsagents and book shops are plentiful throughout Germany, and most supermarkets, hypermarkets and department stores sell a selection of books and magazines. There are no true national newspapers in Germany, other than the *Bild Zeitung* (generally known as *Das Bild*), a tabloid published by the Springer concern with a very low-brow image.

The leading serious conservative newspapers in Germany are the *Frankfurter Allgemeine Zeitung*, generally referred to as the *FAZ*, and *Die Welt* (along with its sister publication *Die Welt am Sonntag*). Their counterparts on the centre-left are the *Süddeutsche Zeitung* (*SZ*) and the *Frankfurter Rundschau* (*FR*). These are available in national editions throughout the country, although the *FR* includes a local news section in its Frankfurt edition; the same applies to the Munich edition of the *SZ*.

There are also numerous excellent regional newspapers, including the *Berliner Zeitung, Stuttgarter Zeitung* and *Westfaelische Nachrichten*. The newspapers with national scope tend to have fewer advertisements and fewer photographs, while regional newspapers (not surprisingly) provide more local information, including advertisements, cinema and theatre listings, and news of civic events. Regional or local newspapers are generally much easier to read than the *FAZ*, particularly if you're just learning German. Many city and town newspapers distribute a free weekly edition containing selected articles and local shop and classified advertising through letterboxes and to apartment block foyers.

For decades, the major weekly news magazines in Germany were *Der Spiegel* and *Stern*. *Der Spiegel* is known for hard news and thorough analysis of issues and events, while *Stern* is a larger format magazine with more pictures and a far softer news content that includes celebrity interviews and features. In the last decade, *Focus* has emerged as a competitor to its more established rivals. Modelled on the American-style news weeklies (*Newsweek* and *Time*), *Focus* combines hard news with more photographs, graphs and graphics than *Spiegel*, and has gained readers for that reason, although *Der Spiegel* remains one of the world's leading news magazines.

Many newspaper kiosks, even in small cities, sell major European English-language newspapers and magazines, including the *International Herald Tribune*, the *Financial Times Deutschland* and the London *Times*, as well as *Time*, *Newsweek* and several British and American magazines. Many are printed in Germany, with the content sent electronically from the originating country to German printers. There are international news kiosks in city centres and at major railway stations and airports offering a much wider range of foreign newspapers and magazines. Expect to pay a premium for English-language publications, particularly those that are available on the date of publication. In smaller towns, the issues on sale may be anything from a day to a week late, depending on the publication.

If you prefer to subscribe to your favourite publications, you must usually pay an overseas or airmail delivery charge in addition to the usual subscription price. In the case of US publications, this charge can amount to more than the subscription cost. Where an additional delivery charge isn't added, you will usually receive your publication in a slimmed 'international' edition. *American Time, Newsweek* and *Business Week*, for example, are all available only in international editions in Germany.

German publication subscriptions work somewhat differently from those in other countries. The subscription price for most magazines is slightly higher than the news-stand price. Most subscriptions are for a year and are automatically renewed unless written notice is given at least three months before the expiry date. Miss the notification date by a day and your bank account will be automatically debited for an additional year!

Most book shops in Germany, even those in fairly small towns, offer at least a small selection of English-language books. In major cities, large book shops such as H. Hugendubel have well-stocked English-language sections, and most book shops selling technical or computer books stock a range of English-language titles. Prices for imports, as always, tend to be high, but competition from foreign mail-order and Internet booksellers is starting to reduce prices a little. The leading Internet bookseller is Amazon, which has German (🖳 http://amazon.de), British (🖳 www.amazon.co.uk) and American (🖳 www.amazon.com) websites. The German branch provides books in both German and English, with prices considerably below those charged by most shops. Delivery costs from the German branch are significantly lower than from Amazon in the UK or US, and your books should arrive much sooner. Using the German or UK site has the added advantage of avoiding VAT and duty charges (see page 393).

Anyone who loves books and enjoys reading in any language should visit the Frankfurt Book Fair (*Buchmesse*) at least once. This is the world's premier publishing industry fair held annually in Frankfurt in early October. Except at the times given below, you will need some form of 'professional' credentials to gain access, such as a business card with a title suggesting that you work in publishing, printing or book selling in any capacity. On Friday afternoon, Saturday, Sunday and Monday morning, the fair is open to the public for a fee (€9 for one of these days or €25 for the whole period). Once inside, you will find all the latest titles in more languages than you knew existed, with publishers presenting their newest titles and authors, while all around deals are being done for foreign language and printing rights. For the bibliophile, the *Buchmesse* provides an opportunity to preview titles that aren't yet available in the shops.

FURNITURE & FURNISHINGS

Germans take great pride in their homes and furniture. The lounge or living room usually contains a large cupboard or sideboard called a *Wohnschrank*, made of solid wood and very heavy, which is used to store dishes and dinner services for entertaining, wine glasses, table linens, and perhaps a bottle of sherry or dessert wine. It also frequently serves as a home for the

TV, video recorder and music centre. Even if you arrive in Germany with your own furniture, you may eventually decide to indulge in a *Wohnschrank*. If you're planning to take one home with you, consider first whether it will fit through the doorways!

Wohnschränke and other items of furniture are available in a wide variety of styles, quality and price ranges. German tastes range from traditional, massive wood-and-upholstered pieces to high-tech glass and stainless steel, often in bold colours and avant-garde designs. Furniture prices in specialist shops tend to be high, but the quality and design are usually impeccable. In many large cities you can find a branch of the upmarket chain Roche Bobois as well as several local quality furniture stores. If you're looking for serviceable furniture at more reasonable prices, there's a full range of do-it-yourself and discount furniture retailers.

IKEA, the Swedish furniture manufacturer, has outlets throughout Germany where you can buy stylish, modern Scandinavian furniture at reasonable prices for home assembly. IKEA stores have free crèches and a restaurant, in case your shopping expedition takes longer than planned. There are also a number of German furniture chains and individual retailers who offer discount prices on a wide range of furniture and household goods.

If you're in the market for custom-made furniture, the town to visit is Kelkheim in south-eastern Germany, known as the *Möbelstadt* (furniture town), where craftsmen have been employed for centuries creating fine furniture. Local manufacturers sponsor an annual furniture exhibition (*Möbelausstellung*) in the autumn at which local manufacturers proudly display their wares.

Most large items of furniture must be ordered, as shops don't keep them in stock, and some, such as upholstered chairs, will need to be made to order, even at discount stores. Delivery takes from 4 to 12 weeks in most cases, unless you're buying a display item, in which case the shop will usually deliver within a week. Shops normally require a deposit when you order and expect you to pay the balance to the delivery people by cheque or in cash; therefore, if you plan to pay by credit card, you must pay the full amount in advance.

Carpets and curtains can be purchased at specialist shops, general furniture shops and department stores. Note, however, that many apartments and houses have metal blinds on the windows, and the fashion is to have net curtains. There are many oriental carpet stores, some of which seem to offer a 'this-week-only' deal or a 'going-out-of-business' (*Ausverkauf*) sale continually, despite strict laws forbidding this.

If you're bringing a bed from the UK or North America, you will need to bring bed linen (*Bettwäsche*) with you, as standard German bed linen (e.g. pillow cases, duvet covers and fitted sheets) is unlikely to fit; if you come without a bed, don't bother to bring sheets and blankets as they won't fit

German mattresses. The Germans use duvets and huge soft feather pillows typically measuring 80cm x 80cm (31in x 31in). Bed linen sets contain duvet covers and pillowcases and you must also buy a fitted sheet (*Spantuch*) to cover the mattress. Most fitted sheets will cover mattresses ranging from 90 x 180cm (36in x 72in) to 100 x 200cm (39in x 78in), but check before buying.

Kitchens

One of the first surprises to hit many newcomers to Germany is the discovery that many rented apartments and houses don't include kitchen appliances or even cupboards and a sink unit. If you ask beforehand, it's sometimes possible to purchase the kitchen from the outgoing tenant, saving considerable effort on your part (as well as on the part of the departing tenant).

Most furniture shops and nearly all DIY stores offer kitchens and kitchen appliances in a wide range of styles, colours and various degrees of do-it-yourself installation. IKEA offers attractive, good quality products at keen prices. The good news is that cupboards, cabinets and appliances come in standard sizes and can be taken with you and fitted as required if you move to another apartment or house. If you don't fancy doing the installation yourself, most furniture and kitchen stores will do it for you (it may even be included in the price), including contacting a licensed plumber and electrician to connect appliances as required by law. Those that don't do installation will recommend a local tradesman who can do the work for you.

HOUSEHOLD GOODS

Germany boasts a number of high quality manufacturers of household electrical appliances, including AEG, Bosch, Braun and Siemens. German products tend to be a bit more expensive than some of their lesser-known competitors, but German consumers expect reliable and well-designed products, and the appliances you buy in Germany will last you a long (long) time. Before buying, however, check the efficiency rating, which is shown on all new appliances, to see how expensive an appliance will be to run; it may be worth buying a slightly more expensive model if you will save on electricity in the long run.

Unless you're coming from a country with a 110/115V electricity supply, it's usually worthwhile bringing small household appliances to Germany, as all that's required is a change of plug. The mains voltage is 240/250V at 50 cycles per second. If you're coming from a country with a 110/115V electricity supply, you will need transformers for any appliances you bring. You should also note that appliances which rely on 60 cycle power to run a clock or other timing device won't operate correctly, even with a transformer.

For Americans, who cannot understand how Germans function with those 'tiny' refrigerators, there's some good news: large American-style refrigerators (some even with ice and cold water distribution in the door or automatic ice making facilities) are coming into vogue in Europe and models conforming to the German electrical system can be purchased locally. However, they aren't among the most economical when it comes to running costs, and running water pipes to the refrigerator isn't an easy or cheap task. You may also have trouble fitting them into a standard German kitchen.

For information about televisions and videos, see **Chapter 8**.

LAUNDRY & DRY CLEANING

All towns and shopping centres have dry cleaners (*chemische Reinigung*), most of which also do minor clothes repairs, invisible mending, alterations and dyeing. However, 'express cleaning' may mean a few days rather than hours, even where dry cleaning is done on the premises. You usually pay in advance and charges are quite high, particularly for leather clothes. Note that, unless you purchase special insurance for your garments, the dry cleaner's liability for damage is limited to 15 times the cost of the cleaning. If you have expensive or particularly fragile items, be sure to mention this and enquire about insurance.

There are relatively few self-service launderettes in Germany, other than in larger cities. Most German families either have their own washing machines or, if they live in an apartment block, have access to communal washing and drying rooms (most apartments have some form of drying room or area). The preferred method of drying clothes in Germany is to hang them in the fresh air outdoors, either on a clothes line or using a folding drying rack on a balcony or terrace.

Ironing services (*Bügelei*) are available in many areas for a nominal charge if you don't want to do the ironing yourself. Look for signs in windows or announcements on shop notice boards, as this is a popular way for housewives to earn extra money in many small towns.

HOME SHOPPING

Shopping by post has long been popular in Germany and, given the stringent regulations and efficient postal system, is a safe and convenient way to buy many items. Mail-order is dominated by three vast companies: Neckermann, Otto-Versand and Quelle, all long-established and well-respected. You will see advertisements for these companies in many popular magazines and are likely to find promotional leaflets in your letterbox. All three have established a reputation for their own brands, particularly for household appliances and electronic equipment, and are known for providing quality products at considerably lower prices than those in shops, which are backed with ironclad guarantees and warranties.

Neckermann, Otto-Versand and Quelle also have stores in most German cities and maintain agencies in smaller cities and towns where customers can consult catalogues and place orders. Many smaller items are delivered within 24 hours and even larger appliances and furniture are usually delivered quicker than by local stores, e.g. in a matter of days rather than weeks. All three companies provide a 24-hour ordering service, seven days a week via the Internet (⌨ www.neckermann.de, www.otto.de and www.quelle.de). In 2003, Quelle added cars to their catalogue – certain Ford, Nissan, Smart and Volkswagen models, which they claim to offer at up to 22 per cent below list prices.

You will receive numerous other leaflets and brochures in your letterbox offering a variety of products for sale by mail-order, particularly at Christmas time. Bear in mind, however, that once you've ordered from one mail-order service, you will receive promotional material from many more.

As with mail-order shopping in any part of the world, you should be wary of offers that sound too good to be true, as they usually are. Many mail-order companies, particularly those selling magazine, record and book subscriptions, offer attractive gifts or premiums at reduced prices to entice customers to subscribe to their services. Very often the price you pay for the 'gift' is higher than the comparable item in a local shop or the real price is buried in the membership or cancellation fees.

Many major shops abroad publish catalogues and will send goods anywhere in the world, e.g. Fortnum & Masons and Harrods in the UK. Many provide account facilities or payment can be made by credit card. Although some mail-order companies won't send goods abroad, there's nothing to stop you obtaining catalogues from friends or relatives and ordering through them. Buying goods by mail-order from the US can result in huge savings, even after postage, VAT and import duty, although you should check exactly what charges will apply (see **Duty & VAT** on page 393).

If possible, always pay by credit card when buying by mail-order or over the Internet, as the credit card company is jointly liable with the supplier. Note, however, that some card companies claim that the law doesn't cover overseas purchases, although many issuers will consider claims up to the value of the goods purchased (and they could also be liable in law for consequential loss). See also **Shopping Abroad** below.

Internet Shopping

With Internet shopping the world is literally your oyster and savings can be made on a range of goods, particularly items like books, CDs and software which lend themselves to the concept, or services such as insurance, pensions and mortgages. Savings can also be made on holidays and travel. Small high-price, high-tech items (e.g. cameras, watches, and portable and hand-held computers) can sometimes be purchased cheaper elsewhere in Europe or in the US, with delivery by courier within as little as three days.

The E-Bay site is as popular in Germany as elsewhere, and some other sites which are useful starting points are 🖳 www.mall-usa.com, www.bizweb.com, www.UKshopping.com, and www.all-internet.com.

SHOPPING ABROAD

Shopping abroad can be a pleasant day out (or a nightmare) and can also save you money. Germany's neighbours include Austria, Belgium, the Czech Republic, Denmark, France (popular for food and wine), Luxembourg, the Netherlands, Poland and Switzerland. Don't forget your passports or identity cards, car papers, dog's vaccination papers and foreign currency where relevant. When visiting countries that are signatories to the Schengen agreement (see page 82) there are no border controls, and you won't need to change currency if you're shopping in France, Belgium, Luxembourg, Austria or the Netherlands. Most shops in border towns in other countries gladly accept euros (because they offer a poor exchange rate!). It may pay you to use a credit card when shopping in non-euro countries, when you usually receive a better exchange rate (and can delay payment). You're also offered a certain amount of security if goods are found to be faulty.

When buying goods abroad, ensure that you're dealing with a bona fide company and that the goods will work in Germany. When you buy expensive goods abroad, always have them insured for their full value.

Since the 1st January 1993, there have been no cross-border shopping restrictions within the EU for goods purchased duty and tax paid, provided goods are for personal consumption or use and not for resale. Although there are no restrictions, there are 'indicative levels' for certain items, above which goods may be classified as commercial quantities. For example, people entering Germany aged 17 or over may import the following amounts of alcohol and tobacco without question:

- 10 litres of spirits (over 22° proof);
- 20 litres of fortified wine (under 22° proof);
- 90 litres of wine (or 120 x 0.75 litre bottles or ten cases), of which a maximum of 60 litres may be sparkling wine;
- 110 litres of beer;
- 800 cigarettes, 400 cigarillos, 200 cigars and 1 kg of smoking tobacco.

There's no limit on perfume or toilet water. If you exceed the above amounts, you may need to convince the customs authorities that you aren't planning to sell the goods. There are huge fines for anyone who sells duty-paid alcohol and tobacco, which is classed as smuggling.

Never attempt to import illegal goods and don't agree to bring a parcel into Germany or deliver a parcel in another country without knowing exactly what it contains. A popular trick is to ask someone to post a parcel in Germany or to leave it at a railway station or restaurant. **THE PARCEL USUALLY CONTAINS DRUGS!**

Duty & VAT

When buying goods overseas, take into account whether you will be liable for duty and VAT. There's no duty or tax on goods purchased within the EU or on goods from most other countries worth below around €50, depending on the shipping method. If you make purchases from a mail-order catalogue company or Internet vendor outside the EU, you may receive a separate bill for VAT and/or customs duty, depending on the declared value of your shipment and the method of shipping. Parcels shipped from outside Europe by express mail services are more likely to be charged VAT, irrespective of their declared value is, due to the customs clearing methods used by shippers. Where charges are due, the postman will collect them when he delivers the parcel or leave a collection notice in your letterbox instructing you to collect the parcel and pay the charges due at the local post office.

Duty-Free Allowances

Duty-free shopping within the EU ended on 30th June 1999, although it's still available when travelling to and from non-EU countries (such as the Czech Republic, Poland and Switzerland). For each journey outside the EU, travellers aged 17 or over are entitled to import duty-free:

- two litres of still table wine;
- one litre of alcohol over 22° volume or 38.8 per cent proof (e.g. spirits) **OR** two litres not over 22° volume (e.g. fortified or sparkling wines);
- 200 cigarettes **OR** 100 cigarillos **OR** 50 cigars **OR** 250g of tobacco;
- 60cc/ml (50gr or 2fl oz) of perfume;
- 250cc/ml (8fl oz) of toilet water;
- other goods (including gifts, souvenirs, beer and cider) to the value of €175.

Duty-free allowances apply on both outward and return journeys, even if both are made on the same day, and the combined total (i.e. double the above limits) can be imported into Germany. Since 1993, duty-free sales have been 'vendor-controlled', meaning that vendors are responsible for ensuring that the amount of duty-free goods sold to individuals doesn't exceed their entitlement. Duty-free goods purchased on board ships and ferries are noted on boarding cards, which must be presented with each purchase.

RECEIPTS

When shopping in Germany, make sure that you receive a receipt (*Quittung*) and retain it until you've left the store or reached home. This isn't only in case you need to return or exchange goods, which may be impossible without the receipt, but also to verify that you've paid if an automatic alarm sounds as you're leaving a shop or any other questions arise. When you buy a large object that cannot easily be wrapped, a sticker should be attached to it as evidence of purchase.

It's wise to keep receipts and records of all major purchases made while resident in Germany, particularly if your stay is for only a short period. This may save you both time and money when you leave Germany and are required to declare your belongings in your new country of residence.

CONSUMER ASSOCIATIONS

There are strict laws in Germany regarding the rights of consumers, as well as those of employees and shopkeepers. Germans are usually well versed in the regulations that most affect them and, in the case of a dispute with a merchant, often all that's necessary is to quote the relevant law or regulation in order to receive satisfaction. On the other hand, if the law establishes a limit on the merchant's liability or responsibility, you're unlikely to sway him with any form of logic.

If you have a complaint against a retailer or manufacturer that you're unable to resolve with them, your first stop should be the local consumer association advice bureau (*Verbraucherzentrale*) to determine your legal position and rights. *Verbraucherzentrale* are found throughout Germany and, while privately owned and operated, are funded by the federal government and the states. For a list of your local *Verbraucherzentrale* check the *Verbraucherzentralen* website (🖥 www.verbraucher.de) or contact the umbrella organisation, Verbraucherzentrale Bundesverband e.V., Markgrafenstrasse 66, 10969 Berlin.

18.

ODDS & ENDS

This chapter contains miscellaneous information that may be of interest to anyone living or working in Germany, arranged in alphabetical order of subject from citizenship to tipping and toilets.

CITIZENSHIP

There are three ways to become a citizen of Germany: you can be born a citizen, you can be naturalised (*Einbürgerung*) or you can exercise the so-called 'right of return' available to ethnic Germans living in Eastern Europe. Germans take the issue of citizenship and nationality very seriously, and for years Germany's citizenship laws were strictly based on the principle of *jus sanguinis* ('rights of blood' or nationality by inheritance rather than place of birth). Until 1975, a child born in Germany had to have a German father in order to claim German nationality and a German woman married to a foreigner could not transmit her nationality to her children. This changed in 1975, when the law was revised to permit either parent to transmit German nationality to their offspring.

A child born in Germany today is automatically granted German citizenship if either of the parents is a German citizen. In 2000, a major change was made to the law to grant citizenship to children born to foreign couples in Germany, provided one of the parents had lived legally in Germany for at least eight years at the date of a child's birth. A child can hold dual nationality (i.e. German and the nationality of his parents or a parent) only until the age of 23, by which time he must decide on one or the other. However, a child who 'inherits' dual nationality by having one German parent and one foreign parent who each transmit their nationality to the child, doesn't need to make this choice and can remain a dual national, even as an adult.

To obtain German citizenship by naturalisation, you must have resided legally in Germany for eight years. You must be able to show that you've not been convicted of a major crime and can support yourself and your family without resort to public assistance (though naturalisation won't limit your eligibility for future assistance). Applicants for German citizenship must also demonstrate their proficiency in the German language and declare their allegiance to the German Constitution (*Grundgesetz*). The language test is very much practical rather than literary.

You will be expected to give up your previous citizenship. Much of the debate over changing the citizenship law in 2000 was related to this sensitive 'sticking point', and there are still many Germans who feel the new law went too far. Germans don't believe that a person can properly honour an allegiance to two different nations and Germans who move abroad and take on a new citizenship are expected to give up their German nationality – unless they can demonstrate close personal or property ties in

Germany. There are a few exceptions to the ban on dual nationality, including recognised political refugees, elderly individuals who would suffer 'unreasonable hardship' (such as the loss of their foreign pension rights), and cases where the other country imposes high fees or other unreasonably harsh conditions on anyone renouncing their citizenship. This provision specifically mentions economic losses or the curtailment of property rights, and is intended to address the issue of many Turkish residents of Germany who can lose their rights of inheritance in Turkey on taking German nationality.

A few countries refuse to accept the renunciation of nationality from a native-born citizen and it's possible you could receive your old passport back in the post. US citizens will find that even a formal renunciation of citizenship may not exempt them from their US tax obligations and it could result in their being denied entry to the US, even for just a visit. In any event, considering renunciation of your prior nationality is a grave step, which could have serious and life-long consequences. If you're considering taking German nationality, make sure that you check with your country's embassy first so that you understand exactly what rights you may or may not be giving up along with your passport.

CLIMATE

Overall, Germany's climate is moderate, with warm summers and cool winters but few real extremes in temperature. Now and then it experiences a particularly hot spell in summer or a vicious cold snap in winter, but these phenomena are usually short-lived. In winter it can seem as if the country is almost upside down, with temperatures in the north averaging several degrees warmer than those in the south (which is more mountainous). Summers are damp and warm, and while many Germans like to spend their summer holidays on the beaches in the north of the country, the weather there is hardly as balmy as you will find on the *Côte d'Azur* or in Majorca – both much more highly favoured spots for most Germans! It's unusual to find air-conditioning anywhere in Germany and for the most part it isn't really needed.

The Alps are a major influence on the climate in the southern region, where winters are long and cold. Snowfall can be almost constant at higher altitudes in the Bavarian Alps, where annual rainfall can be as high as 200cm (79in). For the rest of the country, annual rainfall of 60 to 80cm (24 to 31in) is normal, with summer the main 'rainy season'. Ice and freezing rain are more frequent hazards in winter than heavy snows. In the north, storms sweeping across the Arctic Circle, referred to as Icelandic lows, bring strong winds and gales to the coastal regions. Due to the counter-clockwise circulation, however, the winds are moderated by the warm Gulf Stream, and winter temperatures along the North Sea coast average a degree or two above freezing. Centres of high pressure to the east of Germany can bring periods of cold, bright days in winter.

When a low pressure system crosses the central part of Germany, conditions are ripe for the *Föhn*, a warm dry wind from the south. Due to the changes in atmospheric pressure that create the *Föhn*, don't be surprised if you come down with a headache when the wind is from the south! Germany isn't normally subject to catastrophic weather conditions such as tornadoes, hurricanes or cyclones. However, in spring there's always a danger of flooding, even in some of the minor river valleys, if heavy rains combine with melting snow from the mountains.

Average daily maximum/minimum temperatures in Celsius and Fahrenheit (in brackets) for selected cities are show below:

Location	Spring	Summer	Autumn	Winter
Berlin	13/4 (55/39)	23/14 (73/57)	13/6 (55/43)	3/-3 (37/27)
Frankfurt	16/6 (61/43)	24/14 (75/57)	14/7 (57/45)	4/-1 (39/30)
Hamburg	13/3 (55/37)	22/13 (72/55)	13/6 (55/43)	3/-2 (39/28)
Leipzig	14/4 (57/39)	24/13 (75/55)	14/6 (57/43)	3/-3 (37/27)
Munich	14/3 (57/37)	23/13 (73/55)	13/4 (55/39)	2/-5 (36/23)

The German weather forecast is available via the TV teletext service and in all daily newspapers and also includes the pollen count (*Pollenbericht*) from March to July.

A quick way to make a rough conversion from Centigrade to Fahrenheit is to multiply by two and add 30 (see also **Appendix D**).

CRIME

Compared with some other western countries, Germany has historically had a low crime rate and, although a sharp increase occurred in the years following reunification, later figures showed a levelling out, with a fall in youth crime due to demographic changes. Instances of fraud, bribery and corruption (so-called white collar crime), however, increased significantly over this period and became a preoccupation of the authorities.

The latest statistics paint a mixed picture. Total recorded crime increased by 2.3 per cent in 2002 but fell in eastern Germany by 1.8 per cent. Although the number of cases has declined, theft remains by far the most common (over 47.5 per cent) of all reported crime, followed by vandalism and fraud. Vehicle thefts reduced by 6.4 per cent. However, crimes of violence and of a sexual nature, both increased.

Due to its central location Germany is at the crossroads of Europe, not only for trade but also for such organised crime, Berlin often serving as its centre of operations. Drugs are a major concern for law enforcement officials and the country is both a market for illegal narcotics and a transit point for the distribution of marijuana, heroin and cocaine to Scandinavia and Britain. Other activities associated with organised crime include car theft (particularly luxury models), counterfeiting, arms smuggling, prostitution and gambling. German tabloid newspapers and TV documentaries feature periodic *exposés* of white slavery rings, which are said to lure women to Germany with promises of office work or au pair positions, while actually selling them into prostitution. While such stories are sometimes sensationalised for the viewing audience, it pays to be aware that offers of easy employment, free from the usual immigration formalities, are unlikely to be legitimate.

During the 1970s and early 1980s, Germany developed something of a reputation as a centre for terrorist activity, mostly connected with radical left-wing groups such as the Baader Meinhof Gang and Red Army Faction (*Rote Armee Faktion*), which carried out attacks on government and business targets. By 1992, the left-wing groups had sworn off violence in pursuit of their goals, but the right-wing fringe had taken their place in the headlines with equally violent attacks against refugees and asylum seekers.

While racist violence is still a problem in Germany, there's no reason for undue anxiety or paranoia about ordinary crime. Basic common sense and being 'street wise' should help you avoid most sources of trouble. There are pickpockets in major cities and tourist centres, so don't walk around with your wallet or purse on display, and never keep your wallet in your back trouser pocket. Muggings and armed robbery are, fortunately, still rare in most of Germany, and you can safely walk almost anywhere, day or night. Larger cities, especially Berlin, have their seedy areas, which you should avoid (particularly after dark) – you can ask any policeman, taxi driver or local person which districts to avoid. Remember to lock your car and put any valuables in the boot or out of sight, particularly when parking overnight in a public place (see **Car Crime** on page 258).

In cities, most apartments are equipped with sturdy locks and spy-holes, as well as a telephone entry system so that you can identify visitors before admitting them to the building. In contrast, in rural areas there are still villages and small towns where people don't lock their homes and cars, although these are fast disappearing.

GEOGRAPHY

Germany is the second-largest country in western Europe after France, covering an area of almost 357,000km² (140,000mi²) and stretching 840km

(520mi) from north to south and 620km (385mi) east to west. Germany shares borders with nine countries: Poland and the Czech Republic to the east, Switzerland and Austria to the south, France, Luxembourg, Belgium and the Netherlands to the west, and Denmark to the north. Land boundaries total 3,621km (2,250mi), while the coastline (which is entirely in the north bordering the North and Baltic Seas) extends for 2,389km (1,484mi).

Germany's geography has played a major role in much of its history and contributed greatly to the standing of the country within Europe. Located in the centre of the continent and sharing borders with so many other countries, Germany has long been a link between eastern and western Europe. The nation state of Germany has existed only since 1871, when Bismarck created the German Empire following the defeat of France. Prior to that, there were numerous small kingdoms, duchies, principalities and city states, some of which are reflected in the names and borders of the modern states (*Länder*). Although Germany is one of the few modern European states without overseas territories, parts of many of its neighbouring states have been German at one time or another.

Geographically, there are three major regions in Germany. In the south, the terrain is mountainous, with the Bavarian Alps and the foothills of the Swiss Alpine mountain range. The Central German Uplands consist of forested black mountains and intermediate plateaux, which are part of the same formation as the Massif Central in France and continue east into Poland. The north of the country is part of the North European Lowlands, made up of marshes and mud flats extending to the coast and into Denmark. The country generally 'slopes' from south to north, starting with the Zugspitze, the highest point in the Bavarian Alps (2,962m/9,718ft), and dropping to sea level along the two sea coasts in the north. Germany is criss-crossed by many rivers, including the massive and spectacular Rhine, which forms part of its border with France.

A map of Germany showing the 16 states and state capitals is included in **Appendix E**.

GOVERNMENT

As its official name indicates, Germany is a federal republic. The current form of government was established in 1949, after it became clear to the occupying forces in the western part of Germany (the Americans, British and French) that the Soviet Union wasn't going to reach an agreement with them on the future of Germany. Administrative structures had already been re-established at state level (the *Länder*) under the occupying forces, so these existing legislatures were charged with selecting delegates to the council which would become the German Parliament. The Parliamentary Council drafted a constitution, called the 'basic law' (*Grundgesetz*), which was then approved by the individual states. The first national elections to the Parliament were held in August 1949.

Ten states comprised the former West Germany: Bavaria, Baden-Württemburg, Hesse, Lower Saxony, North-Rhine Westphalia, Rheinland-Palatinate, Saarland, Schleswig-Holstein, and the cities of Hamburg and Bremen. West Berlin was accorded a special non-voting status as an 11th state, as it has always been considered the 'real' capital city of Germany, even while Bonn was established as the 'temporary' capital and seat of government. With reunification, the five eastern states were added: Brandenburg, Mecklenburg-Western Pomerania, Saxony, Saxony-Anhalt and Thuringia.

Most governmental authority is vested in the states, each of which has its own constitution, parliament, judiciary, cabinet of ministers and even a Minister-President (although not every citizen knows who he is). With reunification in 1990, the German government could finally realise the long-held dream of re-establishing Berlin as its capital city. The move from Bonn to Berlin got under way in 1999, but several government agencies still remain there to placate the locals, many of whom opposed the change.

Parliament

The German legislature is a parliamentary system, consisting of two houses called the *Bundesrat* and the *Bundestag* (there's no word in German for both legislative bodies together). The *Bundesrat* is the upper house of parliament, made up of delegates selected by the state governments to represent the interests of the individual states. Each state has from three to six representatives in the *Bundesrat*, depending on the population of the state; they have the right of veto over legislation passed by the lower house (*Bundestag*), and they must approve certain types of legislation affecting the states.

Members of the *Bundestag* are elected by voters using a two-vote system combining proportional representation for political parties with the direct election of candidates within districts. Each voter has two votes in a parliamentary election. One is cast for individual candidates running within the legislative district, the winner gaining a seat in the *Bundestag*. The second vote is cast for a political party and all its state representatives (*Landesliste*), and the total number of seats each party receives in the *Bundestag* is determined by the result of this second vote.

In theory, there are two seats for each voting district in Germany, making a total of 656. However, if the results of the party vote differ from those of the individual elections, additional seats may be added to reflect the proper proportional outcome; for example, in the 1994 elections it was necessary to add 16 seats.

The *Bundestag* makes and changes federal laws, makes constitutional amendments, debates government policy, approves the federal budget and ratifies treaties dealing with Germany's external interests. It's the *Bundestag* that elects the prime minister, called the chancellor (*Kanzler*).

Chancellor & President

The chancellor is the head of government and is responsible for setting the policy guidelines within which the federal ministers run their departments. The government is accountable to the *Bundestag* for its actions but (yet another demonstration of the German devotion to order and stability) the *Bundestag* can only unseat the chancellor in a vote of no-confidence if they've elected a new chancellor at the same time by an absolute majority. The *Bundestag* cannot unseat individual ministers.

There's also a federal president, who's the official head of state of Germany, charged with responsibility for appointing and dismissing federal ministers, judges, civil servants and officers of the armed forces. The post, however, is largely ceremonial, although recent presidents have wielded considerable influence over public opinion.

Political Parties

There are six major political parties represented in the *Bundestag*: the Christian Democratic Party (CDU), founded in 1945 by Konrad Adenauer; the Social Democratic Party (SPD), which has its roots in the working class movements of the late 19th century; the Christian Social Union (CSU); the Free Democratic Party (FDP); the Alliance 90/Greens (usually referred to simply as the Green Party); and the Party of Democratic Socialism (PDS).

The CSU is primarily a Bavarian party and reflects the strong Catholic influence within the Bavarian state government. On the national level, the CSU is aligned with the larger CDU, which has broad support in the business and agriculture sectors. Four of the six post-war chancellors have been Christian Democrats, although the campaign-funding scandal which broke in 2000 has partly undermined public confidence in the party.

The CDU is the party of Helmut Kohl, post-war Germany's longest-serving chancellor and once seen as the father of reunification.

Alliance 90 was predominantly an East German environmental party, which allied with the western Greens in 1993. The Greens have been an important partner in the coalition that first put SPD Chancellor Gerhard Schröder at the head of the government in 1999 and ensured that he stayed there at the last election.

The PDS has its roots in the former state party of the German Democratic Republic and currently represents mostly east German voters, although it's working to expand its appeal in the west.

The FPD is a right-wing 'liberal' party, which tends to represent the interests of independent professionals and the owners and managers or small and medium size businesses. Although small, it's politically important, as it often holds the balance of power.

There are a number of smaller parties active in the states, although none has been able to amass the 5 per cent vote needed for representation in the *Bundestag*.

German law permits the free establishment of political parties but requires parties to conform to democratic principles in their structure and to publicly account for the sources of their funding. Before it can nominate candidates, a new party must have a written constitution and a platform. Any party that seeks to impair or abolish the free democratic order or to endanger the existence of the Federal Republic of Germany can be banned. So far, the federal courts have banned two national parties, both in the 1950s, one a far right-wing group and the other the Communist Party of Germany.

Of course, there's no longer a Nazi party in Germany and all literature, symbols, salutes and uniforms of the old National Socialist German Workers Party are banned, and there are heavy fines and jail terms for their use or display. Small groups of neo-Nazis have surfaced from time to time, particularly since reunification, and there's a fear that their numbers may be on the increase. So far, however, these splinter groups have been closely monitored and, in a number of cases, banned by courts in the states before they could organise on a national level.

States

The federal government derives its authority from the states, rather than the other way around. The states are responsible for legislation, government and the administration of justice, whereas the federal government is responsible for matters of national importance, such as defence and foreign policy.

Elections

German citizens are eligible to vote at the age of 18, provided they've lived in Germany for at least the three months before the election date. Those living abroad can vote by absentee ballot for ten years after leaving Germany. Citizens of the EU resident in Germany may participate in local elections and can vote and stand for election as representatives to the European Parliament.

LEGAL SYSTEM

The German legal system is based on the civil codes enacted by the *Bundestag* (see above). The national constitution is called the 'basic law' (*Grundgesetz*) and spells out in minute detail the division of powers between the individual states (*Länder*) and the national federation.

At times it seems that there are laws and regulations for literally everything, and many Germans jokingly explain the legal system with the phrase 'anything not expressly permitted is prohibited' (as opposed to the French system where 'anything not expressly prohibited is permitted'). However, the Germans seem to find security and stability (*Ordnung*) in having laws or regulations to cover almost every conceivable situation.

Most book shops stock inexpensive editions of the various civil codes, popular legal reference books (*Ratgeber*) and analyses of laws and regulations by subject. A surprising number of Germans are able to quote chapter and verse from miscellaneous regulations limiting rent increases, governing work rules and regarding consumer rights.

Judges and prosecutors are appointed by the state and enjoy a status similar to that of a career civil servant. At federal level, judges are chosen by panels composed of the relevant federal ministry, the appropriate state ministries and deputies from the *Bundestag*. The court system is decentralised, and within each state there's a variety of specialised administrative, criminal and civil courts.

In a German court, it's a judge (or a panel of judges) who asks the questions and tries to determine the facts of the case. The prosecutor or defence counsel is permitted to ask questions or cross-examine defendants or witnesses, but this is rarely done (courtroom practice is considerably less dramatic than in the US). The judge determines the facts of the matter and then rules according to the law that applies. There are strict laws limiting publicity, both before and during a trial, so it's rare to see or read details about an ongoing case on TV or in the newspapers.

An unfavourable decision can be appealed against in a superior court, but only on points of law, not on the facts of the case. There are five federal courts that handle appeals in their respective areas of jurisdiction: the Federal Court of Justice (civil and criminal cases) in Karlsruhe; the Federal Administrative Court in Berlin; the Federal Financial Court in Munich; the Federal Labour Court in Kassel; and the Federal Social Court, also in Kassel. The Federal Constitutional Court deals solely with matters involving basic law, federal/state disputes and legislation on appeal from lower courts or the states. This 'supreme' court also rules on the constitutionality of political parties and on charges against the federal president. A decision in a superior court overrules a lower court's decision, but only for the facts and circumstances of that particular case, as German law doesn't recognise the notion of precedence, where a decision in one case is used as a model for future cases.

In Germany, a person is presumed innocent until proven guilty under the law and has the right to legal counsel. The judge will appoint a defence lawyer in cases where the accused is unable to pay for one, particularly in complicated cases or where a defendant is believed to be unable to defend himself. An accused person can only be imprisoned pending trial (i.e. on remand) where there's strong evidence that he committed a crime and a judge issues a written arrest warrant.

MARRIAGE & DIVORCE

As in many other western countries, marriage in Germany is becoming less popular. Many couples prefer to live together without becoming married and the average age at which people marry for the first time is increasing (it's currently over 28 for women and 31 for men). A majority of weddings in western Germany are celebrated in church but only a small percentage of those in the east. In Germany, the civil wedding ceremony at the registrar's office (*Standesamt*) is the important one. A church wedding, which is optional, can take place only after the civil ceremony. Most friends and family members will, however, expect a big party to celebrate the wedding, irrespective of where the formalities take place.

To get married in Germany, you must apply at the registrar's office in the town where one or other of the partners is resident. If neither partner is resident in Germany, you can contact one of the central registrar offices, which can grant permission to any office within their district to perform a wedding for non-residents. There are four regional registrars: in Munich (for Bavaria), Baden-Baden (south-west Germany), Hamburg (northern Germany) and Berlin (eastern Germany).

The local registrar will tell you what documents to provide, but in all cases you will need identification (national identification card or passport), documentation establishing your residence and marital status, and the names of your parents and their marital status at the time of your birth. For most Germans, this means obtaining a form from the local *Einwohnermeldeamt* (to establish their own residence and marital status), and providing an official extract from their parents' *Familienbuch*, which provides the necessary family history details.

Many registrars also require a medical certificate, which involves primarily the standard blood tests. Foreigners planning to marry in Germany must provide a certified copy of their birth certificate, showing their parents' names and their marital status at the date of birth. If the prospective bride or groom are widowed or divorced, they will be asked to provide the appropriate certificates or decrees proving their status. All documents that aren't in German must be translated by a certified translator. Foreigners must also provide a so-called 'Certificate of No Impediment' from their home country. This is issued by the national authorities of the foreigner's home country and states that under the law of that country there's no reason why the person cannot get married. A number of countries (including the US) don't issue such certificates, in which case you must to apply to the President of the Higher Regional Court (*Oberlandesgericht*) for an exemption. The local registrar can draw up a request for this, so that you don't need to go to court. If you want the titles of any qualifications to be mentioned in the wedding documents and announcements, you may also be advised to provide certificates of any diplomas or academic designations.

All this paperwork must be submitted to the registrar around four to six weeks before a wedding is planned. Germany no longer requires 'publication of the banns' – the practice of posting notice of an impending marriage on the *Rathaus* notice board for a week or two in case anyone wants to oppose your marriage or convince you to back out. Foreign nationals may be required to notify their embassy or consulate of their marriage.

Marriage in Germany is legally considered to be the same as any other contract or legal obligation, so both partners must be of legal age (i.e. 18) to get married. It's possible for a minor to marry at 16 with the permission of his parents, but only if the other partner is of legal age.

Some industry labour contracts may provide for an extra day of paid holiday for the bride and groom, and sometimes even for the parents of the happy couple.

Upon marriage, most couples take the traditional route and use the husband's last name as both their married names, but a married woman can keep her own name if she wishes. Either the husband or wife or both can use a double-name (*Doppelname*), by adding the wife's maiden name to that of the husband. On the birth of their first child, however, a couple must choose a family name (*Familienname*), which will be the surname for that child and other children born within their marriage.

Unless they opt for a marital contract (*Ehevertrag*), a couple will be covered by a form of community property (*Zugewinngemeinschaft*), under which each partner is separately responsible for their own property and debts, except for the expenditure necessary to maintain the common household. In the case of a divorce, the household property and debts acquired during the marriage are split between the partners fairly evenly. However, it's possible to maintain complete separation of each partner's assets and debts by executing a marital contract, either before or during the marriage, which must be drawn up by a notary or lawyer.

Marriage of a non-German citizen to a German citizen doesn't confer any preferential rights on the foreigner when it comes to taking German citizenship (see **Citizenship** on page 398).

Divorce

You can be divorced under German law when either spouse is a German citizen or when two non-German spouses are resident in Germany. German law has largely abandoned the need for one spouse to accuse the other of some wrongdoing. The first step in getting divorced is generally that of establishing a separation (*Trennung*) between the partners, which involves not only the segregation of financial affairs but also the physical separation of the household. (It isn't always necessary for one of the partners to move out and it's possible to establish a separation with both spouses still living under the same roof.) Unless there are extraordinary circumstances, the couple won't be eligible for divorce until after at least a year's formal separation. If both parties are agreed to the divorce at that time, a court reviews the division of property and rules on any child support claims, after which the divorce becomes final. Where one of the partners isn't willing to go through with the divorce, the court will intervene to determine the state of the marriage and rule whether or not to finalise.

After three years' separation, a divorce will be granted automatically unless there are grave extenuating circumstances (such as serious illness or mental problems of one of the partners).

MILITARY SERVICE

Since 1994, German troops been permitted to participate in various military operations under UN auspices with the approval of the *Bundestag* and currently have peace-keeping forces in Afghanistan.

Defence spending is a sensitive political issue given Germany's recent history and relatively high tax levels, consuming as it does around 10 per cent of the federal budget. There's constant pressure (particularly from the Green Party, who are coalition partners) to reduce it, but in the aftermath of the US-Iraq war, the government is considering revising Germany's basic military concept from that of national territorial defence, using heavy armoured formations, to one of readiness to intervene anywhere in the world to defend the country's interests, with much lighter, more mobile forces.

Germany's armed forces (*Bundeswehr*) consist of around 340,000 military personnel: 233,000 in the army, 77,000 in the air force and 27,000 in the navy. Young men are subject to conscription between the ages of 18 and 25, although this can be postponed in cases of family or job-related hardship, the basic obligation being ten months' service. An alternative is to do 13 months' non-military service, usually in a hospital or other health care facility.

Military service is generally considered excellent preparation for the working world, and many young men display their service records proudly on their CVs when looking for their first job. Women aren't subject to the draft, although there are around 3,500 serving in various medical support roles in the military. German law strictly limits them to non-combat duty.

Soldiers in the German military can join a soldiers' union, although they aren't permitted to go on strike. They even have a parliamentary ombudsman (*Wehrbeauftragter des Deutschen Bundestages*) to whom they can take their complaints without having to go through other channels.

PETS

If you plan to take a pet (*Haustier*) to Germany, it's important to check the latest regulations. Make sure that you have the correct papers, not only for Germany, but for all the countries you will pass through to reach Germany. Careful consideration must be given before exporting a pet from a country with strict quarantine regulations. If you must return, even after just a few days in Germany, your pet may have to go into quarantine, which, apart from being expensive, is distressing for both pets and owners.

Britain has particularly strict quarantine laws, which were originally introduced to avoid importing rabies from continental Europe. However, on 28th March 2000, Britain introduced a pilot Pet Travel Scheme (PETS), which replaced quarantine for qualifying cats and dogs and now includes rabbits, mice, rates, guinea pigs and ferrets. Under the scheme, pets must be micro-chipped (they have a micro-chip inserted in their neck), vaccinated against rabies, undergo a blood test and be issued with a health certificate ('passport'). **The PETS certificate isn't issued until six months after all the above have been carried out.**

The scheme is restricted to animals imported from rabies-free countries and countries where rabies is under control; initially this was 24 European countries (the 15 EU countries plus Andorra, Gibraltar, Iceland, Liechtenstein, Monaco, Norway, San Marino, Switzerland and the Vatican), but 15 islands have since been added to the list as well as Canada and the US, and other countries are expected to be included. However, the current quarantine law remains in place for pets coming from Eastern Europe, Africa, Asia and South America.

The new regulations cost pet owners around £200 (for a microchip, rabies vaccination and blood test), plus some £60 per year for annual booster vaccinations and approximately £20 for a border check. Shop around and compare fees from a number of veterinary surgeons. To qualify, pets must travel by sea via Dover or Portsmouth, by train via the Channel Tunnel or via Heathrow airport (only certain carriers are licensed to carry animals, one of which is Lufthansa). Before doing anything, check the current regulations Department for Environment, Food and Rural Affairs (DEFRA) in London. Their UK helpline (☎ 0870-241 1710) is manned between 8.30am and 5pm (UK time). Further information can be obtained from the DEFRA website and via email (🖳 www.defra.gov.uk/animalh/quarantine/index.htm and ✉ helpline@defra.gsi.gov.uk).

You can take up to three dogs or cats into Germany when you're in transit or moving there. (A female cat or a bitch with a litter of kittens or puppies under the age of three months counts as a single animal.) You must have a vaccination certificate for each animal, showing that it was vaccinated against rabies within the last 12 months and at least 30 days before your arrival in Germany. The certificate must be issued by a licensed veterinary surgeon or state veterinary agency and indicate the address of the issuer clearly as part of the seal or stamp.

Dogs (see also below) and cats from Britain and Ireland are admitted into Germany without vaccination, providing they have identification papers and are free from contagious diseases, but they must be vaccinated against rabies immediately on arrival at their destination. It's usually much easier to have your pet vaccinated by your vet before you leave. You can import up to three pet rabbits or hares; reptiles, aquarium fish, hamsters and guinea pigs aren't subject to import restrictions.

Up to three parrots or parakeets can be imported into Germany, provided they have a health certificate issued no more than ten days before their departure. All other birds require a special import permit from the highest veterinary authority of the state (*Land*) where you enter Germany. You should also contact the veterinary authority if you're planning to import an animal that hasn't been mentioned above. The German consulate can provide you with a list of the veterinary authorities for each state, who can usually provide bi-lingual forms for your vet to use for vaccination or health certification.

Dogs & Cats

If you own a dog which belongs to what could possibly be deemed a dangerous breed, you must check with the authorities whether you're allowed to bring it into Germany. The government has passed legislation analogous to the British Dangerous Dogs Act, and for similar reasons, which prevents the import into Germany or the breeding there of certain types of dog. The states also have varying regulations on the subject. German diplomatic missions can provide detailed information if you think these restrictions might affect you.

Dogs must be licensed in Germany, which involves having a rabies certificate. Dog licences vary from town to town, e.g. between €70 and €100 a year for one dog, the fee for a second dog often being double that of the first.

Dogs are considered a potential nuisance in Germany, with their tendency to make noise and foul the pavements. Dog owners are expected to take the time and trouble to train their dogs, keep them on a lead in public areas and (most importantly) pick up any mess they make. A well-trained dog, however, is usually welcomed everywhere, and it shouldn't surprise you to find a dog quietly dozing under a table in a cafe or restaurant while its owner is enjoying a meal or a beer. Shops which don't permit dogs usually post a polite message asking your dog to wait for you outside (evidently most German dogs can read) and sometimes providing rings on the wall for you to attach your pooch to in case it's tempted to disobey.

Cats needn't be licensed in Germany, although if they roam free it's wise to keep them up to date with the recommended vaccinations, particularly rabies. An outdoor cat should also have a collar and identification tag so that the local animal shelter (*Tierheim*) can contact you if your pet is lost.

POLICE

Police (*Polizei*) forces in Germany are organised and maintained by each state and include several specialist services. The *Schutzpolizei* are responsible for general law and order, traffic control, patrolling of streets, and much of the on-site investigation of crimes and accidents. The *Kriminalpolizei* get involved in serious crimes and investigations involving murder, robbery, organised crime and terrorism. The *Bereitschaftspolizei* are a national unit formed from state ranks, who are controlled jointly by the states and the federal government. They provide security in the event of natural disasters or catastrophic accidents. They also assist at demonstrations, sporting events and other large gatherings where crowd control is of particular concern, major traffic control operations and large-scale police actions.

The police in Germany wear green uniforms and police cars are green and white and marked prominently with the word *Polizei*. Police vehicles may range from small Opels to Porsches. It isn't unusual for a police car to sport a powerful loudspeaker system, which is used to tell you exactly where and how to pull over and stop when you've been driving too fast or have committed some other offence. If you start to turn the wrong way into a one-way street you may hear what sounds like a voice from on high barking out a command in German to 'Halt!' It's rather unnerving the first time it happens, but it can save you from a nasty accident. All German police are armed (so be polite to them).

In general, Germans have a lot of respect for their police, as they represent the law and help maintain order, which is so important in German society. Most of the time, your dealings with any member of the police force will be formal, precise and strictly according to the rules and regulations, as prescribed by law. German police don't have a particularly 'warm and friendly' image, but they also aren't normally considered brutal, prone to abusing their powers or corrupt. You should **never** try to bribe a police officer or offer money or anything else to 'forget' a transgression if you've been stopped, which is a particularly serious offence.

POPULATION

The population of Germany is some 82.3 million, with an average population density of 230 inhabitants (*Einwohner*) per km^2 (900 per mi^2), one of the highest in Europe. However, population density varies enormously from region to region. The highest average density is in the industrial belt of North Rhine-Westphalia (528 per km^2) and the lowest is in Mecklenburg-Western Pomerania (77 per km^2) in the east. The 12 largest cities in Germany account for almost 15 per cent of the population, Munich (third-largest with 1.2 million) being the country's the most densely populated city with over 3,800 inhabitants per km^2. The largest city in Germany, not surprisingly, is Berlin, with nearly 3.5 million *Einwohner* and a density of just under 3,800 per km^2. Other major cities are Hamburg (1.7 million), Cologne (963,000) and Frankfurt (644,000). In the east, the largest cities are Dresden and Leipzig, with populations of 477,000 and 490,000 respectively, although Leipzig's high population density makes it much more crowded than Dresden.

Since reunification, many easterners (*Ossies*) have relocated to the west in search of jobs and the rumoured good life, with only limited movement to the east by westerners (*Wessies*). The population in the east in 2000 was around half a million less than in 1991, while the west was home to around 3 million more people. Most of the 2.2 per cent overall growth in population in the 1990s is attributed to the influx of foreigners. In fact, not counting recent immigrants, the population of Germany is declining.

Average life expectancy in Germany is 80.6 for women and 74.4 for men, and increasing. Meanwhile, the death rate is declining along with the birth rate. Over two-thirds of households in Germany comprise just one or two people and the number of households with three or more is falling fast.

There are currently around 7.5 million foreigners officially living in Germany or some 9 per cent of the population, plus an estimated half a million who aren't registered as residents. In the 1960s and 1970s, the Federal Republic recruited large numbers of foreign workers, euphemistically called 'guest workers' (*Gastarbeiter*) and mostly from Mediterranean countries, in response to labour shortages. Many guest workers stayed on as long-term residents, so that by the end of 1994 there were over 2 million foreigners employed in western Germany, the largest national groups being (in diminishing order) those from Turkey, the states of the former Yugoslavia, Greece and Italy. The now defunct German Democratic Republic recruited a number of Vietnamese workers, several thousand of whom now live and work in what was formerly East Germany. At the end of 1997, immigrants from Thailand and China made up the fastest-growing segment of the foreign population. According to official statements, half the foreigners in Germany have lived there for over 20 years, while a third of them have lived in the country longer than 30 years. Until recently it was extremely difficult even for long-time residents of Germany to obtain German nationality (see **Citizenship** on page 398).

Negative attitudes towards foreigners in Germany attract considerable attention abroad from time to time, but immigrants' experiences vary widely and many are highly positive. In general, foreigners from the EU are accepted and well tolerated throughout Germany, although a small segment of the population still harbours visceral attitudes that can only be described as racist, mostly directed toward the Greek and sometimes even Italian immigrant groups. Americans (who are known as *Amis* or *Amies*) have hitherto had no problems, but whether this will change in the wake of the Iraq war remains to be seen. Attitudes towards some other non-Europeans (and Turks) can be hostile, although it must be emphasised that this is on the popular rather than official level.

Germany has justly prided itself on having some of the most liberal and open policies on political asylum in Europe. When the former Yugoslavia disintegrated, for example, it was Germany which still took in far more refugees and asylum seekers than most of its neighbours, despite already having enormous financial commitments with the reunification of the two German states. However, in recent years popular pressure has led to the tightening of asylum legislation and the German government has attempted to meet the needs of those it considers legitimate refugees, without encouraging permanent settlement in the country.

RELIGION

Some 70 per cent of the population are Christian, split fairly evenly between the Roman Catholic and Protestant faiths. The remaining 30 per cent of the population includes some 3 million Moslems, around 82,000 Jews and those claiming to have no religion at all, at least as far as church tax registration is concerned (see page 86). While there's no official state religion, recognised churches receive funding from the state in exchange for operating a variety of public services, such as hospitals, nursing homes, day care centres and workshops for the handicapped. Because of the relatively recent arrival of Islam in Germany, the state hasn't got around to officially recognising the Moslem faith and mosques receive no public funds, although Moslems are exempt from church tax.

Freedom of religion and a ban on discrimination based on religious observance are incorporated into the German constitution and rigorously enforced. Religion is taught as a separate subject in state schools, where children attend religious education classes according to their faith, although parents can choose to have their children exempted from these classes. The northern part of Germany is primarily Protestant, while the southern states (particularly Baden-Württemburg and Bavaria) are predominantly Catholic. Bavaria, in particular, takes its Catholicism seriously, in both political and educational matters, and the southern states observe additional public holidays, thanks to the influence of the Catholic Church (see **Public Holidays** on page 57).

The Jewish community in Germany tends to be Orthodox, with little remaining of the Conservative or Reform branches of the religion more common before the war. Berlin, Frankfurt and Munich have the largest Jewish communities, and there are smaller communities in at least 80 other towns throughout Germany. The government of Germany has established a special relationship with the state of Israel and considers itself under a moral obligation to accept and welcome Jewish immigrants from Eastern Europe.

Adherents of Scientology should note that the practice is strongly discouraged in Germany and they're likely to encounter official hostility.

SOCIAL CUSTOMS

All countries have their social customs and Germany is no exception. As a foreigner you will probably be excused if you accidentally insult your host, but you may not be invited again, so it's better to know what constitutes acceptable and unacceptable behaviour in advance. A few German social customs are described below.

- When you're introduced to a German, you should address him or her as Mr (*Herr*) or Mrs (*Frau*) followed by his or her family name and shake hands without gloves (unless it's 20 degrees below freezing). When saying goodbye, it's customary to shake hands again. Note that *Frau* is used nowadays for most women over the age of 18, whether or not they're married (although waitresses are always referred to as *Fräulein*, whatever their age).

- When you're introduced to someone, always use the formal form of address (*Sie*). Don't use the familiar form (*Du/Ihr*) or call people by their Christian names until invited to do so. If you've previously been on formal terms with someone, there's quite a bit of ceremony attached to the decision to change to the familiar form of address (*duzen*, as opposed to *siezen*) often involving going out for a beer (and sometimes three or four!) to celebrate.

- It's customary to say good day (*Guten Tag*) or good morning (*Guten Morgen*) on entering a small shop or arriving at your place of work, and to say goodbye on leaving. The Germans are well known for their 'wish' greetings among friends or close associates. Rather than saying simply good-bye (*auf Wiedersehen*), it's considered more sociable to wish someone a good evening, a good weekend, even a good meal! At lunchtime in many offices and other workplaces, you will hear people saying *Mahlzeit* to each other; this literally means 'mealtime' but is code for 'have a good lunch'. On leaving work in the evening, the usual term is *Feierabend* (literally, 'quitting time' or 'evening off'), and on Fridays people wish one another a *schönes Wochenende* (literally 'beautiful weekend'). If someone is leaving on holiday, you should wish them *schönen Urlaub* or *gute Reise* if you know they're off on a trip. You will also hear *Viel Spass* ('have fun') and even *Kommen Sie gut Heim/nach Hause* ('have a safe trip home'). The all-purpose response *gleichfalls* (same to you) is usually appropriate.

- When you're dining with another person, whether they're a family member or a complete stranger, you shouldn't begin to eat until you've wished the him *guten Appetit*.

- Don't arrive late for an invitation and don't overstay your welcome. The Germans are extremely punctual and will invite you for exactly the time they expect you to arrive. If the invitation states a finishing time, you will be expected to make your move for the door at the appropriate hour.

- If you're invited to someone's home, it's usual to take along a small present of flowers, a plant or chocolates. If you take flowers, there must be an odd number, and you should unwrap them before handing them to the hostess. Flowers can be tricky, as there are specific meanings attached to certain kinds of flowers, and these may differ considerably from what you're used to. To Germans, who take these things seriously, carnations mean bad luck, chrysanthemums are for cemeteries and roses signify love. For newcomers, a potted plant or a box of chocolates could be a safer bet.

- Always close inside doors behind you when visiting someone's home. The Germans keep all inside doors closed when rooms aren't in use, including toilets and bathrooms. You should also get into the habit of turning off lights as you leave a room.

- Always identify yourself before asking to speak to someone on the telephone and don't telephone at meal times or after 9pm unless you're sure they're night people (or foreigners). Incidentally, goodbye on the telephone is *Auf Wiederhören*.

- If you're planning a party, it's polite to notify your neighbours so that they don't call the police and complain about the noise. Some people will advise you always to invite your neighbours, and in some areas there's an unofficial policy of not calling the police the first time someone throws a noisy party, provided the neighbours have been invited. If you're the one who calls to complain, you could find yourself the neighbourhood pariah – at least for a few weeks afterwards.

● It's considered bad luck to wish someone a happy birthday (or happy anniversary of any kind) before the actual date. Stay up late and wait until just after midnight or catch them the next day if you must, but don't celebrate the day before or give them an early present!

● If you live in an apartment with a communal clothes line (outdoors or indoors), check whether each apartment has a scheduled day and time for using it. There's certainly no quicker way to alienate yourself than to use communal facilities out of turn. If you hang your laundry out to dry on your balcony or anywhere that's visible to the public, check whether there are any local by-laws against drying clothes on Sundays or public holidays, which are most common in small towns in the south of Germany.

TIME DIFFERENCE

Like most of the continent of Europe, Germany is on Central European Time (CET), which is Greenwich Mean Time (GMT) plus one hour in winter. The Germans change from winter to summer time and vice versa at the same time as the rest of central Europe (i.e. on the last Sundays in March and October). Time changes are announced in local newspapers and on radio and TV, and take place at 2 and 3am respectively.

The time in selected major cities when it's noon (in winter) in Germany is shown below:

LONDON	JO'BURG	SYDNEY	AUCKLAND	LOS ANGELES	NEW YORK
11am	1pm	10pm	Midnight	3am	3am

Times (e.g. in timetables) are usually written using the 24-hour clock, when 10am is written as 1000 *Uhr* and 10pm as 2200 *Uhr*. Midday is 12 *Uhr* and midnight is 24 *Uhr* or *Null Uhr*. The 24-hour clock is also often used in speech; for example, 7pm (*sieben Uhr abends*) may be referred to as *neunzehn Uhr* (1900). Be careful if people say they'll meet you at 'half eight' (*halb acht*), because in German this is 7.30, not 8.30, and they won't be happy if you turn up an hour late. Similarly *Viertel acht* ('quarter eight') is 7.15 (a quarter of the way to 8 o'clock), unless clearly stated as 'quarter to' (*Viertel vor*) or 'quarter past' (*Viertel nach*) the hour.

TIPPING

Most restaurants and hotels include a 12 to 15 per cent service charge in their prices, so leaving a tip (*Trinkgeld*) is optional. Normally, if you want to show your appreciation for the service, you round up the price you're quoted to the next whole euro, permitting staff to keep the change (literally). Rounding up to the nearest five or ten euros is a way of indicating that you found the service exceptionally good, and of course is always appreciated. If you're out with a group of people, each person (or couple) is normally expected to settle his own part of the bill. Obviously, if every member of a large party rounds up his portion of the bill, the waiter will have been suitably rewarded for his efforts.

Although tipping is optional in most other situations, it's traditional to leave a couple of euros for the maid when you check out of a hotel room. Taxi drivers normally receive around 10 per cent of the fare, a tour guide a few euros at the end of a tour, and at the hairdresser you should leave a couple of extra euros for the shampoo girls (often trainees or apprentices). Porters, toilet attendants and cloakroom personnel often advertise their charges, so it's open to question whether a tip is necessary.

TOILETS

Public toilets (*Toiletten*) in Germany can be in exasperatingly short supply. When you are in a town and need one, your best bets are large department stores, cafes and restaurants or the foyers of large hotels. On the motorway, rest areas (*Raststätten*) with public toilets are clearly marked (*Toiletten*), although cleanliness varies. A bathroom is a *Badezimmer*, although this term is never used for a toilet. Public toilets are usually labelled *Herren/Männer* (gentlemen/men) and *Damen/Frauen* (ladies/women) or simply *H* and *D*.

Pay toilets are normal in Germany, particularly in railway stations and many department stores, although urinals are sometimes free. The fee ranges from 10 to 50 cents, usually collected by means of a coin-operated lock, so be sure you always have some change with you. Some toilets have a sign indicating the charges for various 'services' such as using a urinal or WC and washing your hands with hot water Some toilets have an attendant, whom it's usual to give a 'tip' on your way out.

The traditional German-style toilet may come as a bit of a surprise to unsuspecting newcomers. For some reason, the main part of the toilet bowl is rather shallow, forming a sort of platform. When you flush, the water flow from the tank (often concealed in the wall) pushes anything on this platform to the front of the bowl, where it's carried away down the disposal pipe. Some claim that this unique design caters to the German obsession with monitoring their health.

19.

THE GERMANS

Who are the Germans? What are they really like? Let us take a candid and prejudiced look at the German people, tongue firmly in cheek, and hope they forgive my flippancy or that they don't read this bit (which is why it's hidden away at the back of the book).

The typical German is a green, a businessman, proud, bureaucratic, subservient, militaristic, punctual, competitive, a unionist, chauvinistic, private, a sun worshipper, angst-ridden, loud, unsympathetic, organised, perfect, overweight, superior, honest, industrious, hygienic, a workaholic, taciturn, healthy, tidy, frugal, selfish, well-educated, insecure, rigid, arrogant, affluent, Conservative, authoritarian, formal, malleable, responsible, self-critical, a pacifist, stoical, materialistic, ambitious, intolerant, unromantic, reliable, conscientious, obstinate, efficient, enterprising, humourless, unloved, obedient, liberal, stolid, orderly, insensitive, xenophobic, meticulous, inventive, prejudiced, conventional, intelligent, virtuous, egotistical, dependable, law-abiding, a good footballer and infuriatingly Teutonic!

You may have noticed that the above list contains 'a few' contradictions, which is hardly surprising, as there's no such thing as a typical German. Modern Germany is a patchwork of former feudal states with enclaves and cities reflecting the tribalism and eccentricities of the old dukedoms and principalities. Germans are first and foremost inhabitants of a particular city (Berliners, Dresdeners, Frankfurters, Hamburgers, Müncheners, etc.) followed by Bavarians, Friesians, Hessians, Prussians, Saxons, Swabians or whatever. They're Europeans third and Germans a distant fourth – and only then among foreigners and because it says it on their passports.

There's long been a north-south divide, the more conservative northerners dismissing the less inhibited southerners as lazy and soft, while the southerners reciprocate with taunts of 'dour' and 'dull'. There's a less tangible divide between the solid Saxons in the east and the cosmopolitan Rhinelanders in the west, although this been sharpened by the reunification of the inhabitants of the former West Germany (*Wessies*) and of East Germany (*Ossies*). To the *Ossies*, west Germans are seen as arrogant colonisers, while east Germans are viewed by *Wessies* as lazy socialists, more than happy to live off state handouts. However, while it's true that not all Germans are stereotypes (some are almost indistinguishable from 'normal' people), I refuse to allow a few eccentrics to spoil my arguments . . .

Although not always the xenophobes they're painted, Germans don't exactly like foreigners (particular those living in their country) but respect most English-speakers as equals, including (some) Americans, Australians, British – all of whom are English to Germans – Canadians, Irish and New Zealanders. They also have a grudging regard for Austrians, French, Dutch, Scandinavians and Swiss (most of whom are more 'Germanic' than the Germans). They tolerate the people of other countries in the European

Union (because they have to and they like to holiday in the sun) but are generally prejudiced against southern or eastern Europeans, not to mention non-Europeans.

Unlike many other countries with a large foreign population, Germany isn't an ethnic melting pot but a jumble of splinter groups living entirely separate lives with their own neighbourhoods, shops, restaurants, clubs and newspapers. The Germans' attitude to foreigners is typified by their name for foreign workers, euphemistically called 'guest workers' (*Gastarbeiter*), whom they previously imported in vast numbers to do all the dirty, menial jobs that Germans didn't want. However, millions of foreigners, particularly Greeks, Italians, Spaniards, Turks and former Yugoslavians (plus Vietnamese in eastern Germany), failed to follow the 'rules' and return home after their usefulness expired, and many 'guest' families are now into their third generation. Very few people immigrate in the true sense of the word, making a permanent home in Germany, changing their names to Fritz or Frieda and taking up citizenship (which is still not that easy).

Germany is also a magnet for the homeless and dispossessed, and it has attracted huge numbers of refugees and asylum seekers in the last few decades, which it initially welcomed with open arms. However, since reunification in 1990 relations have been more strained and there have been a number of violent incidents involving refugees and foreign workers, some of whom have died at the hands of neo-Nazi, extremist skinheads. Today's refugees and *Gastarbeiter* serve a useful purpose as a convenient scapegoat for Germany's ills, whether it's unemployment, crime, pollution, housing shortages or social problems. Nevertheless, Germany has an ageing population and a low birth-rate, which makes immigration essential if they're to maintain their high standard of living.

Germans pride themselves on their lack of class-consciousness and apart from some with aristocratic names (beginning *von*) and a few who still live in castles, Germans generally consider themselves to be middle or working class. However, Germany is far from being a classless society and status is as important there as it is anywhere else, although it's invariably based on money rather than birthright. Germany generally has no class or 'old school tie' barriers to success (unlike the UK and France) and almost anyone, however humble his origins, can fight his way to the top of the heap – although ethnic barriers aren't so easy to overcome.

There's no truth in the rumour that laughter is forbidden (*Lachen ist Verboten*) in Germany, although you may sometimes wonder whether there's a tax on humour. To Germans, humour is something to be taken very seriously – they don't even laugh when you tell them they have no sense of humour! Germans have no sense of irony or sarcasm, rarely make jokes about other people and never laugh at themselves, although the misfortune of others is a source of much pleasure – called *Schadenfreude*. It's also what everyone else in the world feels when the Germans lose at football! Of course, not all Germans lack a sense of humour, although foreigners are unlikely to understand their complex 'jokes' and locals who appreciate a good jest have usually been corrupted by working too long with frivolous foreigners! Life is taken seriously in Germany and, if foreigners followed their example, perhaps they too would be rich.

It's difficult to become close friends with Germans – even for other Germans – and Germans from other parts of Germany living in small towns and villages can remain 'outsiders' for decades! You may even be unaware that you have German neighbours, except when they complain. They won't welcome you when you move into a new house or apartment and, if you can speak German, it's up to you to invite them round for a drink and introduce yourself. Only close friends or relatives call on each other unannounced (when Germans entertain a stranger everything must be spotless and in perfect *Ordnung*).

In business the Germans are even more formal. After many years, colleagues may still address each other as Herr Schmidt or Frau Müller, using the formal *Sie* form of address. Germans aren't usually so strict with foreigners and, if you speak with them in English, you may find yourself on first name terms after a relatively short period. It's rumoured that they're less formal and relaxed – even friendly – when entertaining guests in their own homes, although you're unlikely to receive an invitation.

Germans are very law-abiding (except when it comes to speed limits) and follow all rules and regulations to the letter. Anyone loitering in town at 3am is more likely to be waiting for a green light to cross the road than preparing to rob a bank. The Germans slavishly follow all rules and regulations and delight in pointing out others' transgressions. In Germany, there are rules for everything – which, no matter how trivial, certainly aren't made to be broken. If you use an IN door to exit or park a few centimetres over a line, it will invariably be brought to your attention by an upstanding German citizen. It's often said that in Germany everything that isn't illegal is forbidden (*verboten*), while everything else is compulsory.

On the surface, Germans appear to be reasonably healthy, if a 'little' overweight, but in reality they all suffer from something, even if it's 'only' stress brought on by worrying about their non-existent health problems. Fortunately, Germany has a lot of spas, which are a cure all for everything from *Kreislaufstörung* (a euphemism for a variety of ailments) to the common cold. However, there's no cure for the national epidemic of anxiety (*Angst*), which permeates all facets of their lives. The Germans worry about everything from their diet to their bank balance, their appearance to their sex lives, their careers to what their friends and neighbours really think of them. Their *Angst* extends far beyond their immediate lives and they worry incessantly about the environment, their country's image and place in the world, the national football team, whether the nuclear power station down the road will explode and kill them all, and whether the euro will create hyperinflation (*Euroangst*) and lead to the end of the world. This leads to another unique German complaint, *Weltschmerz* (literally 'world pain'), which roughly translates as weariness of life or a pessimistic outlook.

Germany isn't exactly noted for its food and there's no such thing, really, as German cuisine. German food consists mostly of sausages (*Wurst*), pork, dumplings, potatoes, cabbage, *sauerkraut*, black bread and cake, washed down with numerous steins of beer. Not for Germans some prissy *nouvelle cuisine*; they want simple, hearty peasant food and plenty of it. One thing Germans never worry about is starving. Germans are among the world's most committed carnivores and vegetarians are thin on the ground. Surprisingly, considering their diet, Germans are often particular about what they eat and are careful to avoid anything remotely connected with a health scare.

The Germans also know a thing or two about drinking and are among the world's most prolific consumers of alcohol, particularly beer, although you will rarely see a legless German unless it's at a *Bierfest* (and even then it's likely to be a foreigner). They produce a vast variety of beers, all of which are made to the standards and natural ingredients laid down in the 16th century (impure foreign beer is labelled to warn consumers that it's 'unclean'). In stark contrast to their excellent beer, most of Germany's wine leaves much to be desired, although there are a few notable exceptions.

The Germans are car-fanatics and second only to Americans in their worship of all things automotive (provided they're made in Germany), and they have a passionate and enduring love affair with their cars, which are more important than their homes, spouses and children. Many people are loath to forsake their cars under any circumstances and would rather endure a ten-hour traffic jam that resort to public transport. When they aren't stuck in traffic jams, it's mandatory for Germans to drive everywhere at over 200kph. Germany is renowned for its excellent motorway network, which was originally conceived by Hitler as a convenient and fast way of invading the neighbours.

In Germany, you are what you drive: Mercedes are for doctors, politicians and captains of industry (and football managers), Porsches are for flashy media types, pop stars and football players, while BMWs and Audis are for middle managers, engineers and hairdressers. The peasants drive Fords, Opels and Volkswagens, although those who are really beyond the pale drive foreign cars. However, even worse than a foreign car is a dirty car – anyone who doesn't pamper his car (usually a foreigner) doesn't deserve to own one!

In Germany your car says more about you than what you wear, where you live or even how much money you have, although there are always a few oddballs (like the former football star, Jürgen Klinsmann, who drives an old VW Beetle). A German car must be reliable and, if one should ever break down, it's likely to be blamed on the *Gastarbeiter* who built it.

Sport is a source of great national pride or shame, depending on whether the Germans are thrashing everybody in sight – usually the case – or unluckily losing narrowly to opponents who cheated, bribed the referee or caught the Germans on a bad day (Germans are never beaten by superior opponents). Sports stars are icons and national heroes, are feted wherever they go and are to be found on chat shows at all times of day and night expounding on a variety of topics, including (sometimes) sport.

The German attitude towards sex is open and up-front, and they delight in flaunting their (often gross) bodies at every opportunity. German newspapers, magazines and television are obsessed with sex and routinely carry out surveys of the nation's (and other nations') sexual habits, while late night TV is dominated by explicit sex. Germans are unembarrassed about discussing sex with strangers and will relate the most intimate details of their love lives at the drop of a pair of *Lederhosen*. Sex clubs, bars and shops abound in most towns, mixed nude bathing and saunas are commonplace, and Germans are enthusiastic naturists.

Germany isn't exactly a land of milk and honey for the dedicated career woman, who's considered something of an eccentric in the western states (in eastern Germany most women lost their jobs after reunification) and very few receive equal pay with their male colleagues or make it to the top of the heap. Although women theoretically have equal rights with men, in reality this often isn't the case, and they usually must be at least twice as qualified and three times as smart as men to compete on an equal footing. Until fairly recently, women didn't even have rights over their own bodies and until 1974 abortion was illegal (it was punishable by death in the 1930s). However, most women don't appear overly concerned about the status quo and many seem to actually enjoy their subservient role, provided they're treated as ladies. Most German men still believe that a woman's place is in the church or home, cooking or taking care of the children (*Kinder, Küche, Kirche*).

The Germans' seemingly permanent prosperity and stability was first jolted in the early 1990s by the recession and reunification, which has cost (and is still costing) the Germans far more than they bargained for. They're encumbered by myriad petty rules and regulations and beset by red tape at every turn. Among the biggest concerns facing the nation are unemployment and job security, asylum seekers and refugees, drug addiction and crime, intolerance, the environment, pensions, burgeoning social security costs, housing shortages, high taxation, corruption, increasing competition and high labour costs (not necessarily in that order). Germans can no longer afford to live in the past and many are fearful of what the future may hold.

To be fair, the Germans do have a few good things going for them. They're excellent footballers, master brewers, superb architects and designers, the world's best engineers, and their products are famous world-wide for their quality and reliability. The Germans are, however, slow to make changes, both individually and as a nation, although they're quick to embrace new technology, particularly when it will make them rich(er). Their society is a model of functionality and orderliness compared with most other countries, and they have a strong sense of community and social justice. Germany enjoys a high standard of living, low inflation, still relatively good industrial relations, and a very impressive economy (despite the pessimism and unemployment).

They have superb public services, excellent social security benefits (although the country can barely afford them), superb health services and hospitals (no waiting lists), efficient local government, exceptional working conditions and employee benefits, and a first-class transport system with magnificent motorways and among the world's fastest trains. They also have a rich cultural history and have produced many great artists, composers, poets, philosophers and writers, including such world-famous names as Bach, Beethoven, Brahms, Brecht, Duden, Dürer, Goethe, the Grimm brothers, Handel, Hegel, von Humbolt, Luther, Mann, Marx, Mendelssohn, Nietzsche, Schiller, Schubert, Schumann and Wagner, to name but a handful. Today, Germany remains at the forefront of the arts, particularly classical music, and has some of the world's foremost conductors, composers, musicians, orchestras, theatres, galleries and museums.

While doing battle with German bureaucracy is enough to discourage anybody, Germans are generally welcoming and, provided you're willing to meet them half way and learn their language, you will invariably be warmly received. Contrary to popular belief, Germans aren't baby-eating ogres and, although they can be difficult to get to know, when you do you invariably make friends for life. The mark of a great nation is that it rarely breeds indifference in foreigners – admiration, envy, hostility or even blind hatred, but seldom indifference! Love it or hate it, Germany is a unique, vibrant, civilised, bold, sophisticated and challenging country. Germans enjoy one of the world's best lifestyles and an enviable quality of life, and although foreign residents may criticise some aspects of life, most feel privileged to live in Germany and very few seriously consider leaving.

Auf Deutschland!
Long live Germany!

20.

MOVING HOUSE OR
LEAVING GERMANY

When moving house or leaving Germany, there are numerous things to be considered and a 'million' people to inform. The checklists contained in this chapter are intended to make the task easier and may even help prevent an ulcer or nervous breakdown – provided of course you don't leave everything to the last minute.

MOVING HOUSE WITHIN GERMANY

When you're moving house within Germany, you should consider the following points:

- You must usually give your landlord at least three months notice before vacating rented accommodation (refer to your contract). If you don't give your landlord sufficient notice or aren't resigning on one of the approved moving dates, you must find someone to take over the property (see page 102). Your resignation letter must be sent by registered post to reach your landlord by the last day of the month at the latest. This will also apply if you have a separate contract for a garage or other rented property, e.g. a holiday home, in Germany. Arrange a date with your landlord for the hand-over.

- Inform the following:
  - Your employer;
  - Your present Council a week before moving house and your new Council within a week of taking up residence (see **Registration** on page 85);
  - Your electricity, gas, telephone and water companies;
  - Your insurance companies (e.g. health, car, house contents and private liability); banks, post office, stockbroker and other financial institutions; credit card and hire purchase (credit) companies; lawyer; accountant and local businesses where you have accounts;
  - Your family doctor, dentist and other health practitioners. Health records should be transferred to your new doctor and dentist, if applicable;
  - Your family's schools. If applicable, arrange for schooling in your new community. Try to give a term's notice and obtain a copy of any relevant school reports or records from your children's current schools;
  - All regular correspondents, subscriptions, social and sports clubs, professional and trade journals, and friends and relatives. Give or send them your new address and telephone number. Address cards are available free from post offices. Arrange to have your post redirected by the post office (see **Change of Address** on page 132);

- If you have a German driving licence or a German registered car, you must contact the *Führerscheinstelle* department at your local district administration office (Landratsamt) and the local motor vehicle branch (*Kfzzulassungsstelle*) in your new town;

- Your local consulate or embassy if you're registered with them (see page 87);
- Return any library books or anything borrowed;
- Re-register your dog with your new council (see page 410);
- Arrange removals or transport for your furniture and belongings;
- Arrange for a cleaning company and/or decorating company for your apartment, if necessary (see page 103);
- If applicable, ensure the return of the deposit from your landlord;
- Cancel the newspapers;
- Ask yourself (again): 'Is it really worth all this trouble?'

LEAVING GERMANY

Before leaving Germany for an indefinite period, the following items should be considered *in addition* to those listed above under **Moving House Within Germany**:

- Give notice to your employer, if applicable.
- Check that your own and your family's passports are valid.
- Check whether there are any special entry requirements for your country of destination by contacting the local embassy or consulate in Germany, e.g. visas, permits or inoculations. An exit permit or visa isn't required to leave Germany.
- You may qualify for a rebate on your income tax (see page 317) and pension insurance. Your employer and council will assist you with these. Tax rebates are normally paid automatically.
- Your private company pension contributions may be repaid in full. Before your pension fund will repay your funds, you must provide a statement from your council stating that you've de-registered and are leaving Germany.
- Arrange to sell anything you aren't taking with you (e.g. house, car and furniture) and to ship your belongings. Find out the exact procedure for shipping your belongings to your country of destination (see page 112).

Check with the local embassy or consulate of the country to which you're moving. Special forms may need to be completed before arrival. If you've been living in Germany for less than a year, you're required to re-export all imported personal effects, including furniture and vehicles (if you sell them, you should pay duty).

- If you have a German registered car that you plan to take with you, you must import and re-register it in your new country of residence within a limited time.

- Pets may require special inoculations or may need to go into quarantine for a period (see page 410).

- Contact Deutsche Telekom to cancel your contract and pay the final bill when it arrives (see page 139).

- Arrange health, travel and other insurance (see **Chapter 13**).

- Depending on your destination, you may wish to arrange health and dental check-ups before leaving Germany. Obtain a copy of your health and dental records and a statement from your health insurance company stating your present level of cover.

- Terminate any German loan, lease or hire purchase (credit) contracts and pay all outstanding bills (allow plenty of time as some companies are slow to respond).

- Check whether you're entitled to a rebate on your road tax, car and other insurance. Obtain a letter from your German motor insurance company stating your no-claims bonus.

- Sell or let your house, apartment or other property (see **Chapter 5**).

- Check whether you need an international driving licence or a translation of your German or foreign driving licence for your country of destination (see page 234).

- Give friends and business associates in Germany an address and telephone number where you can be contacted.

- If you will be travelling or living abroad for an extended period, you may wish to give someone 'powers of attorney' over your financial affairs in Germany so that they can act on your behalf in your absence. This can be for a fixed period or open-ended and can be limited to a specific purpose only. **You should, however, take legal advice before doing this.**

- Buy a copy of Living and Working in ******** before leaving Germany. If we haven't written it yet, drop us a line and we'll get started on it straight away!

*Gute Reise!/*Have a good journey!

APPENDICES

Appendix a: Useful Addresses

Embassies & Consulates

Foreign Embassies In Berlin

The following list includes the major embassies and consulates in the capital Berlin (telephone code 030). Many countries also have consulates in other cities (listed in the yellow pages under *Konsulate*).

Afghanistan: Wilhelmstrasse 65, 10117 Berlin (☎ 229 2612).

Albania: Friedrichstrasse 231, 10969 Berlin (☎ 259 3050).

Algeria: Görschstrasse 45/46, 13187 Berlin (☎ 4809 8724/26).

Angola: Wallstrasse 58, 10179 Berlin (☎ 240 8970).

Argentina: Dorotheenstrasse 89, 10117 Berlin (☎ 226 6890).

Armenia: Hillmannstrasse 5, 13467 Berlin (☎ 405 0910).

Australia: Friedrichstrasse 200, 10117 Berlin (☎ 880 0880).

Azerbaijan: Axel-Springer-Strasse 54, 10117 Berlin (☎ 206 2946).

Bahrain: Potsdamerplatz 11, 10785 Berlin (☎ 2589 4040).

Bangladesh: Dovestrasse 1, 10587 Berlin (☎ 398 9750).

Belarus: Am Treptower Park 32, 12435 Berlin (☎ 536 3590).

Belgium: Jägerstrasse 52-53, 10117 Berlin (☎ 206420).

Bolivia: Wichmannstrasse 6, 10787 Berlin (☎ 263 9150).

Bosnia-Herzegovina: Ibsenstrasse 14, 10439 Berlin (☎ 814 1210).

Brazil: Wallstrasse 57, 10179 Berlin (☎ 726280).

Brunei Darussalam: Kronenstrasse 55–58, 10117 Berlin (☎ 206 0760).

Bulgaria: Mauerstrasse 11, 10117 Berlin (☎ 201 0922).

Burkina Faso: Karolingerplatz 10/11, 14052 Berlin (☎ 3010 5990).

Burundi: Berlinerstrasse 36, 10715 Berlin (☎ 8639 9028).

Cambodia: Benjamin-Vogelsdorff-Strasse 2, 13187 Berlin (☎ 4863 7901).

Canada: Friedrichstrasse 95, 10117 Berlin (☎ 203120).

Cape Verde: Dorotheenstrasse 43, 10117 Berlin (☎ 2045 0955).

Chile: Mohrenstrasse 42, 10117 Berlin (☎ 726 2035).

China: Märkisches Ufer 54, 10179 Berlin (☎ 275880).

Columbia: Kurfürstenstrasse 84, 10787 Berlin (☎ 263 9610).

Costa Rica: Dessauerstrasse 28/29, 10963 Berlin (☎ 2639 8990)

Croatia: Ahornstrasse 4, 10787 Berlin (☎ 2362 8951).

Cuba: Stavangerstrasse 20, 10439 Berlin (☎ 9161 1810).

Cyprus: Wallstrasse 27, 10179 Berlin (☎ 2759 1270).

Czech Republic: Wilhelmstrasse 44, 10117 Berlin (☎ 226380).

Denmark: Rauchstrasse 1, 10787 Berlin (☎ 5050 2000).

Dominican Republic: Dessauerstrasse 28/29, 10963 Berlin (☎ 2575 7760).

Ecuador: Kaiser-Friedrich-Strasse 90, 10585 Berlin (☎ 238 6295).

Egypt: Stauffenbergstrasse 6/7, Berlin 10785 (☎ 477 5470).

El Salvador: Joachim-Karnatz-Allee 47, 10557 Berlin (☎ 206 4660).

Eritrea: Stavangerstrasse 18, 10439 Berlin (☎ 446 7460).

Estonia: Hildebrandstrasse 5, 10785 Berlin (☎ 2546 0600).

Ethiopia: Boothstrasse 20, Berlin 12207 (☎ 772060).

Finland: Rauchstrasse 1, 10787 Berlin (☎ 505030).

France: Pariser Platz 5, 10117 Berlin (☎ 5900 39000).

Gabon: Hohensteinerstrasse 16, 104197 Berlin (☎ 8973 3440).

Gambia: Kurfürstendamm 103, 10711 Berlin (☎ 8968 9801).

Georgia: Heinrich-Mann-Strasse 32, 13156 Berlin (☎ 484 9070).

Ghana: Stavangerstrasse 19, 10439 Berlin (☎ 447 9052).

Great Britain: Wilhelmstrasse 70, 10117 Berlin (☎ 204570).

Greece: Jägerstrasse 54/55, 10117 Berlin (☎ 206260).

Guatemala: Joachim-Karnatz-Allee 45-47, 10557 Berlin (☎ 206 4363).

Haiti: Meinekestrasse 5, 10719 Berlin (☎ 8855 4134).

Honduras: Cuxhavenerstrasse 14, 10555 Berlin (☎ 39749710/11).

Hungary: Unter den Linden 76, 10117 Berlin (☎ 203100).

Iceland: Rauchstrasse 1, 10787 Berlin (☎ 5050 4000).

India: Tiergartenstrasse 16/17, 10785 Berlin (☎ 2579 8213).

Indonesia: Lehrterstrasse 16-17, 10557 Berlin (☎ 478070).

Iran: Podbielskiallee 67, 14195 Berlin (☎ 843530).

Iraq: Remeisterstrasse 20, 14169 Berlin (☎ 814880).

Ireland: Friedrichstrasse 200, 10117 Berlin (☎ 220720).

Israel: Auguste-Viktoria-Strasse 74–76, 14193 Berlin (☎ 8904 5500).

Italy: Dessauerstrasse 28/29, 10963 Berlin (☎ 254400).

Jamaica: Schmargendorferstrasse. 32, 12159 Berlin (☎ 859 9450).

Japan: Hiroshimastrasse 6, 10785 Berlin (☎ 210940).

Jordan: Heerstrasse 201, 13595 Berlin (☎ 369 9600).

Kazakhstan: Nordendstrasse 14/15, 13156 Berlin (☎ 470070).

Kenya: Markgrafenstrasse 63, 10969 Berlin (☎ 259 2660).

Kirghizstan: Otto-Suhr-Allee 146, 10585 Berlin (☎ 3478 1337).

Korea (North): Glinkastrasse 5–7, 10117 Berlin (☎ 229 3189).

Korea (South): Schöneberger Ufer 89–91, 10785 Berlin (☎ 260650).

Kuwait: Griegstrasse 5–7, 14193 Berlin (☎ 897 3000).

Laos: Bismarckallee 2a, 14193 Berlin (☎8906 0647).

Latvia: Reinerzstrasse 40/41, 14193 Berlin (☎ 8260 0222).

Lebanon: Berlinerstrasse 127, 13187 Berlin (☎ 474 9860).

Lesotho: Dessauerstrasse 28/29, 10963 Berlin (☎ 257 5720).

Liberia: Pücklerstrasse 8, 14195 Berlin (☎ 8410 9007).

Libya: Schützenstrasse 15–17, 10117 Berlin (☎ 200 5960).

Liechtenstein: Mohrenstrasse 42, 10117 Berlin (☎ 2018 7187).

Lithuania: Charitestrasse 9, 10117 Berlin (☎ 8906 8110).

Luxembourg: Klingelhöferstrasse 7, 10785 Berlin (☎ 263 9570).

Macedonia: Königsallee 2, 14193 Berlin (☎ 890 6950).

Malawi: Westfälischestrasse 86, 10709 Berlin (☎ 8049 5308).

Malaysia: Klingelhöferstrasse 6, 10785 Berlin (☎ 885 7490).

Mali: Kurfürstendamm 72, 10709 Berlin (☎ 319 9883).

Malta: Klingelhöferstrasse 7, 10785 Berlin (☎ 263 9110).

Mauritania: Kommandantenstrasse 80, 10117 Berlin (☎ 206 5883).

Mauritius: Kurfürstenstrasse 84, 10787 Berlin (☎ 2639 3610).

Mexico: Klingelhöferstrasse 3, 10785 Berlin (☎ 269 3230).

Moldova: Gotlandstrasse 16, 10439 Berlin (☎ 4465 2969/70).

Monaco: Klingelhöferstrasse 7, 10785 Berlin (☎ 263 9033).

Mongolia: Dietzgenstrasse 31, 13156 Berlin (☎ 474 8060).

Morocco: Niederwallstrasse 39, 10117 Berlin (☎ 206 1240).

Mozambique: Stromstrasse 47, 10551 Berlin (☎ 3987 6500/1/2).

Myanmar (Burma): Zimmerstrasse 56, 10117 Berlin (☎ 2061 5710).

Namibia: Wichmannstrasse 5, 10787 Berlin (☎ 2540 9510 19).

Nepal: Guerickestrasse 27, 10587 Berlin (☎ 3435 9920).

Netherlands: Friedrichstrasse 95, 10117 Berlin (☎ 209560).

New Zealand: Friedrichstrasse 60, 10117 Berlin (☎ 206210).

Nicaragua: Joachim-Karnatz-Allee 45, 10557 Berlin (☎ 206 4380).

Nigeria: Platanenstrasse 98a, 13156 Berlin (☎ 477 2300/01).

Norway: Rauchstrasse 1, 10787 Berlin (☎ 505050).

Pakistan: Schaperstrasse 29, 10719 Berlin (☎ 212440).

Panama: Joachim-Karnatz-Allee 45, 10557 Berlin (☎ 2260 5811).

Paraguay: Hardenbergstrasse 12, 10623 Berlin (☎ 3180 2725).

Peru: Mohrenstrasse 42-44, 10117 Berlin (☎ 206 4103).

Philippines: Uhlandstrasse 97, 10715 Berlin (☎ 864 9500).

Poland: Lassenstrasse 19-21, 14193 Berlin (☎ 223130).

Portugal: Zimmerstrasse 56, 10117 Berlin (☎ 5900 63500).

Romania: Matterhornstrasse 79, 14129 Berlin (☎ 803 3018).

Russian Federation: Unter den Linden 63-65, 10117 Berlin (☎ 229 1110).

Saudi Arabia: Kurfürstendamm 63, 10707 Berlin (☎ 889250).

Senegal: Genthinerstrasse 11, 10785 Berlin (☎ 2308 6523).

Seychelles: Rauchstrasse 26, 10787 Berlin (☎ 3190 7660).

Singapore: Friedrichstrasse 200, 10117 Berlin (☎ 2263 4318).

Slovakia: Pariser Strasse 44, 10707 Berlin (☎ 889 2620).

Slovenia: Hausvogteiplatz 3/4, 10117 Berlin (☎ 206 1450).

South Africa: Friedrichstrasse 60, 10117 Berlin (☎ 220730).

Spain: Schöneberger Ufer 89–91, 10785 Berlin (☎ 254 0070).

Sri Lanka: Niklasstrasse 19, 14163 Berlin (☎ 8090 9743 49).

Sudan: Kurfürstendamm 151, 10709 Berlin (☎ 890 6980).

Swaziland: Neue Promenade 8, 10178 Berlin (☎ 2809 6250).

Sweden: Rauchstrasse 1, 10787 Berlin (☎ 505060).

Switzerland: Otto-von-Bismarck-Allee 4a, 10557 Berlin (☎ 390 4000).

Tajikistan: Otto-Suhr-Alllee 84, 10585 Berlin (☎ 347 9300).

Thailand: Lepsiusstrasse 64–66, 12163 Berlin (☎ 794810).

Tunisia: Lindenallee 16, 14050 Berlin (☎ 3082 0673).

Turkey: Rungestrasse 9, 10179 Berlin (☎ 275850).

Turkmenistan: Langobardenallee 14, 14052 Berlin (☎ 3010 24520).

Ukraine: Albrechtstrasse 26, 10117 Berlin (☎ 288 8710).

United Arab Emirates: Katharina-Heinroth-Ufer 1, 10787 Berlin (☎ 516516).

United States of America: Neustädtische Kirchstrasse 4–5, 10117 Berlin (☎ 238 5174).

Uruguay: Budapesterstrasse 39, 10787 Berlin (☎ 263 9016).

Uzbekistan: Perlebergerstrasse 62, 10559 Berlin (☎ 394 0980).

Vatican City: Apostolische Nuntiatur, Lilienthalstrasse 3a, 10965 Berlin (☎ 616240).

Venezuela: Schillstrasse 9–10, 10785 Berlin (☎ 832 2400).

Vietnam: Elsenstrasse 3, 12435 Berlin (☎ 5363 0108).

Yemen: Rheinbabenallee 18, 14199 Berlin (☎ 897 3050).

Yugoslavia (Serbia & Montenegro): Taubertstrasse 18, 14193 Berlin (☎ 895 7700).

Zambia: Axel-Springer-Strasse 54a, 10243 Berlin (☎ 2694 8706).

Zimbabwe: Kommandantenstrasse 80, 10117 Berlin (☎ 206 2263).

German Diplomatic Representation Abroad

The following is a list of German embassies, consulates or diplomatic missions in selected countries.

Australia: 119 Empire Circuit, Yarralumla, Canberra, ACT 2600 (☎ 02-6270 1911).

Canada: 1 Waverly Street, Ottawa, ON K2P (☎ 613-232 1101).

Ireland: 31 Trimleston Avenue, Bootersown, Blackrock, Co. Dublin (☎ 012-693011).

New Zealand: 90-92 Hobson Street, Thorndon, Wellington (☎ 04-473 6063).

South Africa: 180 Blackwood Street, Arcadia, Pretoria 0083 (☎ 012-427 8900).

United Kingdom: 23 Belgrave Square, London SW1X 8PZ (☎ 020-7824 1300).

USA: 4635 Reservoir Road, NW, Washington, DC-20007-1998 (☎ 202-298 4000, 🖳 www.germany-info.org).

Government Offices

The principal federal ministries (*Bundesministerien*) and other government services in Germany are as follows (BM is short for *Bundesministerium*):

Chancellery (Bundeskanzleramt), Schlossplatz 1, 10178 Berlin.

Foreign Office (Auswärtiges Amt), Werderscher Markt 1, 10117 Berlin (☎ 01888-1703).

Ministry for Consumer Protection, Food & Agriculture (BM für Verbraucherschutz, Ernährung und Landwirtschaft) Wilhelmstrasse 54, 10117 Berlin (☎ 03- 20060).

Ministry of Defence (BM der Verteidigung), Stauffenbergstrasse 18, 10785 Berlin (☎ 01888-2400).

Ministry of Economic Co-operation & Development (BM für Wirtschaftliche Zusammenarbeit und Entwicklung), Europahaus, Stresemannstrasse 94, 10963 Berlin (☎ 01888-5350)

Ministry for Economics & Labour (BM für Wirtschaft und Arbeit) Scharnhorststrasse 34-37, 10115 Berlin (☎ 01888-6150).

Ministry of Education & Research (BM für Bildung und Forschung), Hanoverschestrasse 28–30, 10115 Berlin (☎ 01888-570).

Ministry for the Environment, Nature Conservation & Nuclear Safety (BM für Umwelt, Naturschutz und Reaktorsicherheit), Alexanderplatz 6, 11055 Berlin (☎ 01888-3050).

Ministry for the Family, Senior Citizens, Women & Youth (BM für Familie, Senioren, Frauen und Jugend) Taubenstrasse 42/43, 10117 Berlin (☎ 03-206550).

Ministry of Finance (BM der Finanzen), Wilhelmstrasse 97, 10117 Berlin (☎ 03-22420).

Ministry for Health & Social Security (BM für Gesundheit und Soziale Sicherung) Wilhelmstrasse 49, 10117 Berlin, PA, 11017 Berlin (☎ 01888-440).

Ministry of the Interior (BM des Innern), Alt-Moabit 101 D, 10559 Berlin (☎ 01888-6810).

Ministry of Justice (BM der Justiz), Moehrenstrasse 37, 10117 Berlin (☎ 03-202570).

Ministry for Transport, Building & Housing (BM für Verkehr, Bau- und Wohnungswesen), Invalidenstrasse 44, 10115 Berlin (☎ 03-20080).

Parliament (Deutsche Bundestag), Platz der Republik 1, 11011 Berlin.

German National Tourist Offices

Amsterdam: Hoogoorddreef 76, Noord-Holland 1101, Netherlands (☎ 020-6978066/6911293, 🖥 www.duitsverkeersbureau.nl).

Beijing: c/o Delegate of German Industry and Commerce Beijing, Landmark Tower 2, #0811, 8 North Dongsanhuan Road, Chaoyang District, Beijing 100004, China (☎ 010-659 0092 62154, ✉ gntobj. xu@ahkbj.org.cn).

Beverly Hills: 8484 Wilshire Boulevard, Suite 440, Beverly Hills, CA 90211, USA (☎ 323-655 6085, ✉ gntolax@aol.com).

Brussels: Gulledelle 92 Val d'Or, 1200 Brussels, Belgium (☎ 02-245 9700, ✉ gntobru@d-z-t.com).

Chicago: Box 59594, Chicago, IL 60659-9594, USA (☎ 773-539 6303, ✉ gntoch@aol.com).

Copenhagen: Vesterbrogade 6 D III, 1620 Copenhagen, Denmark (☎ 033-436800, ✉ gntocph@d-z-t.com).

Frankfurt-am-Main: Beethovenstrasse 69, 60325 Frankfurt-am-Main (☎ 069-9746 4287, 🖥 www.germany-tourism.de).

Helsinki: c/o Deutsch-Finnische Handelskammer, PL 859, SF-00101 Helsinki, Finland (☎ 09-680 1774, ✉ dztinfo@dfhk.fi).

Hong Kong: German National Tourist Office, 3601 Tower One, Lippo Centre, 89 Queensway, Hong Kong (☎ 252 65481, ✉ info@ahk. org.hk).

London: Box 2695, London W1A 3TN, UK (☎ 020-7317 0908, ✉ gnto lon@d-z-t.com).

Madrid: San Agustin 2, Plaza de las Cortes, E-28014 Madrid, Spain (☎ 091-4293551/4295877, ✉ infoalemania@d-z-t.com).

Milan: CP 10009, I-20110 Milan, Italy (☎ 02-8474 4444, ✉ gntomil@d-z-t.com).

Moscow: c/o Lufthansa German Airlines, Olimpinski Prospekt 18/1, Moscow 129110, Russia (☎ 095-737 6408, ✉ dztmow@glasnet.ru).

New York: 122 East 42nd Street, New York, NY 10168-0072, USA (☎ 212-661 7200, 🖥 www.visits-to-germany.com).

Oslo: St Olavs Plassen, PB 6723, 0130 Oslo, Norway (☎ 022-853491, ✉ tyskrb@tyskrb.no).

Paris: 47 avenue de l'Opéra, 75002 Paris, France (☎ 01-40 20 07 46, ✉ gntopar@d-z-t.com).

Prague: c/o Travel Plus SRO, Na Prikope 24, Prague 11000, Czech Republic (☎ 02-2422 8417, ✉ info@dzt.cz).

São Paulo: Câmara de Comércio e Indústria Brasil-Alemanha, Rua Verbo Divino, 1488-3.andar, São Paulo, São Paulo 04719-904, Brazil (☎ 011-51812310).

Stockholm: Box 10147, 10055 Stockholm, Sweden (☎ 08-665 1881, ✉ DZT_STO@csi.com).

Sydney: c/o German Australian Chamber of Industry & Commerce, Box 1461, Sydney, NSW 2001, Australia (☎ 02-8296 0488, ✉ gnto@ germany.org.au).

Tel Aviv: Box 8082, 61080 Tel Aviv, Israel (☎ 03-514 2306, ✉ dzt@ netvision.net.il).

Tokyo: 7-5-56 Akasaka, Minato-ku, Tokyo 107-0052, Japan (☎ 03-3586 0380, ✉ gntotyo@d-z-t.com).

Toronto: 175 Bloor Street East, North Tower, Suite 604, Toronto, Ontario M4W 3R8, Canada (☎ 416-968 1570, ✉ gnto toronto@look.ca).

Warsaw: VIA POLSKA Sp. z.o.o., Uliza Krucza 46/lok. 122, Warszawa 00-509, Poland (☎ 022-622 9882, ✉ EB Marketing@bigfoot.de).

Zürich: Talstrasse 62, 8001 Zurich, Switzerland (☎ 01-213 2200/11, ✉ gntozrh@d-z-t.com).

Miscellaneous

Allgemeiner Deutscher Automobilclub (ADAC), Am Westpark 8, 81373 Munich (☎ 089-76760, 💻 www.adac.de).

American Chamber of Commerce, Rossmarkt 12, 60311 Frankfurt-am-Main (☎ 069-929 1040, 💻 www.amcham.de).

Association of German Chambers of Industry & Commerce (Deutscher Industrie-und Handelstag), Breitestrasse 29, 10178 Berlin (☎ 030-203080, 💻 www.diht.de).

British Chamber of Commerce in Germany, Severinstrasse 60, 50678 Cologne (☎ 0221-314458, 💻 www.bccg.de).

British Council, Hackescher Markt 1, 10178 Berlin (💻 www.british council.de).

British Trade Office, British Consulate-General, Yorckstrasse 19, Dusseldorf (☎ 021-94480, 💻 www.british-dgtip.de).

Central Placements Agency (ZAV), Villemomblerstrasse 76, 53123 Bonn (☎ 0228-7130, 💻 www.arbeitsamt.de/ZAV).

Federal Insurance Agency (Bundesversicherungsanstalt für Anges tellte), 10704 Berlin (☎ 030-8651, 💻 www.bfa.de).

German Academic Exchange Service (DAAD), 34 Belgrave Square, London SW1X 8BQ, UK (☎ 020-7235 1736, info@daad.org.uk) and 871 United Nations Plaza, New York, NY 10017, USA (☎ 212-758 3223, ✉ daadny@daad.org). The principal website is also available in English at 💻 www.daad.de. The HQ of the German Academic Exchange Service (Deutscher Akademischer Austauschdienst) is Kennedyallee 50, 53175 Bonn, or Postfach 20 04 04, 53134 Bonn for postal correspondence (☎ 0228-88207, 💻 www.daad.de).

German Arts Council (Deutscher Kulturrat e.V), Bundesges chäftsstelle, Chausseestrasse 103, 10115 Berlin (☎ 030-2472 8014, 💻 www.kulturrat.de).

German-British Chamber of Industry & Commerce, Mecklenburg House, 16 Buckingham Gate, London SW1E 6LB, UK (☎ 020-7976 4100, 💻 www.germanbritishchamber.co.uk).

German Federal Labour Office (Bundesanstalt für Arbeit), Regensburgerstrasse 104, 90478 Nuremberg (☎ 0911-1790, 💻 www.arbeitsamt.de).

German Sports Federation (Deutscher Sportbund), Otto Fleck-Schneise 12, 60528 Frankfurt-am-Main (💻 www.dsb.de).

Goethe Institut Inter Nationes, Helene-Weber-Allee 1, 80637 München, Postfach 19 04 19, 80604 Munich (☎ 089-159 2107, 💻 www.goethe.de).

Institute for Foreign Relations (Institut für Auslands-beziehungen e.V.), Charlottenplatz 17, 70173 Stuttgart (☎ 0711-222507, 💻 www.ifa.de).

National Association of German Business Consultants (Bundesverband Deutscher Unternehmensberater), Zitelmannstrasse 22, 53113 Bonn (☎ 0228-91607, 💻 www.bdu.de.).

National Chamber of Tax Consultants (Bundessteuerberaterkammer), Neue Promenade 4, 10178 Berlin (☎ 030-2400 8707, 💻 www.bstbk.de).

Major Property Exhibitions

Property Exhibitions are common in the UK and Ireland, and are popular with prospective property buyers who can get a good idea of what's available in a particular area and make contact with estate agents and developers. Below is a list of the main exhibition organisers in the UK and Ireland. Note that you may be charged a small admission fee.

Homes Overseas (☎ UK 020-7939 9852, 💻 www.blendoncommuni-cations.co.uk). Homes Overseas are the largest organisers of international property exhibitions and stage a number of exhibitions each year at a range of venues in both the UK and Ireland.

Incredible Homes (☎ UK 0800-652 2992, Spain 952-924 645, 💻 www. incredible-homes.com). Incredible Homes are based on the Costa del Sol and organise several large exhibitions a year in both the UK and Ireland.

International Property Show (☎ UK 01962-736712, 💻 www.inter-nationalpropertyshow.com). The International Property Show is held several times a year in London and Manchester.

Spain on Show (☎ UK 0500-780878, 🖥 www.spainonshow.com). Spain on Show organises several annual property exhibitions at venues around the UK.

Town & Country (☎ UK 0845-230 6000, 🖥 www.spanishproperty. uk.com). This large estate agency organises small Spanish property exhibitions at venues around the UK twice monthly.

World Class Homes (☎ UK 0800-731 4713, 🖥 www.worldclass homes.co.uk). Exhibitions organised by World Class Homes are held in small venues around the UK and mainly include only UK property developers.

World of Property (☎ UK 01323-726040, 🖥 www.outbound publishing. com). The *World of Property* magazine publishers (see **Appendix B**) organise three large property exhibitions a year, two in the south of the UK and one in the north.

APPENDIX B: FURTHER READING

The lists below are only a selection of the hundreds of books written about Germany. In addition to the (mostly) general guides listed, there are numerous guides covering individual regions and cities. The publication title is followed by the author's name and the publisher's name (in brackets). Some titles may be out of print but may still be obtainable from book shops and libraries. Books prefixed with an asterisk are recommended by the author.

General Tourist Guides

*AA Baedeker's Germany (AA Publishing)

AA Explorer Germany (AA Publishing)

*Berlin, Gordon McLachlan (Odyssey)

Berlitz Traveller's Guide Germany (Berlitz)

*The Best of Germany, Andre Gayot (Gault Millau)

*Birnbaum's Germany (Houghton Mifflin)

*The Blue Guide to Berlin and Eastern Germany, Anne Massey (A&C Black)

*The Blue Guide to Western Germany, James Bentley (A&C Black)

Fodor's Germany: East and West, Lawrence Cheek (Fodor's)

Fodor's UpClose Germany (Fodor's)

*Frommers Germany (Pocket Books)

Germany, Rodney Bold & Rachel Fielding (Cadogan)

Germany, Nicola Cunningham (Duncan Petersen)

Germany at its Best, Robert S. Kane (Passport)

*Insight Guide: Germany (APA Publications)

*Karen Brown's Charming Inns & Itineries, Karen Brown & Others (Karen Brown Guides)

*Let's Go Germany (MacMillan)

**Lonely Planet: Germany, Andrea Schulte-Peevers & Others (Lonely Planet)

*Michelin Green Guide to Germany, Fleur Speakman (Michelin)

*Michelin Red Hotel and Restaurant Guide: Germany (Michelin)

Off The Beaten Track, Germany, Janet Aldrighe & Others (Moorland Publishing)

On The Loose in Germany and Austria (Fodor's)

On the Road Germany, Adi Kraus (AA Publishing)

***The Penguin Guide to Germany** (Penguin)

***The Rough Guide to Berlin**, Jack Holland & John Gawthrop (Rough Guides)

***The Rough Guide to Germany**, Gordon McLachlan (Rough Guides)

Touring Germany, Adi Kraus (AA Publishing)

Visitor's Guide Germany (Moorland)

History & Politics

***A Concise History of Germany**, Mary Fulbrook (CUP)

***After the Wall**, Marc Fisher (Simon & Schuster)

The Federal Republic of Germany at 50, Peter H. Merkl (Macmillan)

The Federal Republic of Germany since 1949, Klaus Larres & Panikas Panayi (Longman)

The German Comedy, Peter Schneider (I. B. Tauris)

***Germany and the Germans**, John Ardagh (Penguin)

Germany and the Politics of Europe's Money, Karl Kaltenthaler (Duke University)

***Germany in the Twentieth Century**, David Childs (Batsford)

Germany Inc., Werner Meyer-Larsen (John Wiley)

Germany Profiled, Barry Turner (Macmillan)

Jews in Germany, Nachum T. Gidal (Konemann)

Modern Germany, Peter James (Routeledge)

***The New Germans**, Giles Radice (Michael Joseph)

The New Germany, Derek Lewis & John R. P. McKenzie (UEP)

***The New Germany: Land, People, Economy**, Aubrey Diem (Aljon Print-Craft)

Party Politics in New Germany, Geoffrey K. Roberts (Pinter)

Politics & Culture in Modern Germany, Gordon Craig (UWP)

Recasting East Germany, Chris Flockton & Eva Kolinsky (Frank Cass)

*The Rise and Fall of the Third Reich, William L. Shirer (Fawcett Crest)

*Understanding Contemporary Germany, Stuart P. Parkes (Routeledge)

Miscellaneous

*America in the Eyes of the Germans: An Essay on Anti-Americanism, Dan Diner & Alison Brown (Markus Wiener)

The Business Culture in Germany, Collin Randlesome (Butterworth Heinemann)

Business Germany: A Practical Guide to Understanding German Business Culture, Peggy Kenna (NTC Publishing)

Business Travel Guide to Germany (Mercury)

Culinary Voyage Through Germany, Hannelore Kohl (Abbeville)

Customs and Etiquette in Germany, Waltraud Coles & Uwe Koriek (Global Books)

Doing Business with Germany, Roderick Millar & Jonathan Reuvid (Kogan Page)

Education and Work in Great Britain, Germany and Italy, Annette Jobert & Others (Routledge)

Festival of World: Germany, Richard Lord (Heinemann)

A Flavour of Germany, Mike Hirst (Hodder)

The Garden Lover's Guide to Germany, Penelope Hobhouse (Princeton)

The German Way, Hyde Flippo (Passport)

Germany by Bike, Nadine Slavinski (Manasha Ridge)

Germany: in Pictures (Lerner Publishing)

*Germany's Romantic Road, Gordon McLachlan (Cicerone)

Germany Today: A Student's Dictionary, Charlie Jeffrey & Ruth Whittle (Arnold)

*The Germans, Gordon A. Craig (Meridian)

*The Germans, Norbert Elias (Columbia University)

The Germans: Portrait of a New Nation, Jeffrey Gedmin

*The Germans: When Lies Were Decreed As Truth . . . and a Nation Allowed Itself to be Deceived, Harry Conway (Shengold)

*The Germans: Who are they now?, Alan Watson (Mandarin)

Getting to Know Germany and German, Janine Armos (Barron's)

*The Good Beer Guide to Munich, Graham Lees (CAMRA)

The Gourmet's Companion: German Menu Guide and Translator, Bernard Rivkin (John Wiley)

The Green Guide to Germany, Fleur & Colin Speakman (Green Print)

How to Eat Out in Germany, Gabriele Horvath (Gremese)

How to Get a Job in Germany, Christine Hall (How to Books)

*Langenscheidt's Pocket Menu Reader Germany (Langenscheidt)

*A Little German Cookbook, Gertrude Philipine Mathes (Appletree)

*Living and Working in Berlin, Andrew Covey & Others (Geographical Association)

Simple Guide to Customs and Etiquette in Germany, Waltraud Coles (Global)

Steam and Rail in Germany, Paul Catchpole (P. Catchpole)

Step into Germany, Claire Boast (Heinemann)

*These Strange German Ways, Susan Stern (Atlantik-Brücke)

A Traveller's Wine Guide to Germany, Kerry Brady Stewart (Aurum)

*Understanding Cultural Differences: Germans, French and Americans, Edward Twitchell & Milred Reed Hall (Intercultural)

Universities in Germany, Werner Becker & Others (Prestel Verlag)

A Visit to Germany, Peter Roop (Hienemann)

*Walking in the Bavarian Alps, Grant Bourne & Sabine Kröner-Bourne (Cicerone)

*Walking in the Black Forest, Fleur & Colin Speakman (Cicerone)

*Wine Atlas of Germany, Hugh Johnson (Mitchell Beazley)

Women in 20th Century Germany: A Reader, Eva Kolinsky (MUP)

*Xenophobe's Guide to the Germans, Stefan Zeidenitz & Ben Barkov (Oval Books)

Appendix c: Useful Websites

German Websites

Berlin (🖳 www.berlin.de): the website of the German capital containing copious information about all aspects of life in the city.

Berlin Mietspiegel (🖳 www.stadtentwicklung.berlin.de/wohnen/mietspiegel): provides information on rents in Berlin.

Bund (🖳 www.bund.de): a portal which provides access to numerous official websites. If you want to find out anything about what the government does and what it wants you to do, this is a good place to start looking.

Campus (🖳 www.campus.de): information for foreigners thinking of studying in Germany.

Deutschebibliothek (🖳 www.ddb.de): website of the German National Library.

Deutschebildungsserver (🖳 www.deutschebildungsserver.de): everything about the world of German education.

Deutsche Welle (🖳 www.dw-world.de): website of the German equivalent of the BBC World Service.

Ebookers (🖳 www.ebookers.de): last minute travel and hotel bookings.

Film (🖳 www.film.de): the latest news from the world of the cinema in Germany and abroad.

Fireball/Paperball (🖳 www.paperball.fireball.de): search engine which covers the German press.

Flugplan (🖳 www.flugplan.de): flight timetables to just about everywhere.

Focus Money (🖳 www.focus-money.de): financial information website.

Frankfurter Allgemeine Zeitung (🖳 www.faz.de): the online version of Germany's premier broadsheet newspaper.

Frankfurter Rundschau (🖳 www.frankfurterrundschau.de): the online version of Germany's principal left-leaning liberal newspaper, the equivalent of the Guardian in Britain.

Germany Info (🖳 www.germany-info.org): comprehensive information about many aspects of Germany in English.

Kultur Portal Deutschland (💻 www.kulturportal-deutschland.de): a portal which provides access to an array of German cultural information.

Munich Mietspiegel (💻 www.pst.informatik.uni-muenchen.de/ personen/fruehwir/miet-demo.html): information on rents in Munich.

Privatschulberatung (💻 www.privatschulberatung.de): information about private schools in Germany.

Shopping24 (💻 www.shopping24.de): web shopping portal for everything from flights to flowers.

Sport (💻 www.sport.de): portal to comprehensive sports coverage but with the emphasis on football and Formula 1 motor racing.

The Voyage (💻 www.the-voyage.com): website which provides much information on German-British youth exchanges.

Weihnachten Info (💻 www.weihnachten-info.de): information on Germany's many Christmas markets.

Wohnen (💻 www.wohnen.de): lots of links related to accommodation.

Wowi (💻 www.wowi.de): this is a website intended for landlords and investors in rental property, but contains lots of interest to tenants, particularly clear and straightforward coverage of changes in the law in this area.

General Websites

Au Pair Forum (💻 www.aupair-forum.com): experiences of au pairs and tips for those thinking of becoming one.

Australia Shop (💻 www.australia.shop.com): Expatriate shopping for homesick Australians.

British Expatriates (💻 www.britishexpat.com and www.ukworld wide. com): Two sites designed to keep British expatriates in touch with events in and information about the UK.

Direct Moving (💻 www.directmoving.com): General expatriate information, tips and advice, and numerous links.

Escape Artist (💻 www.escapeartist.com): One of the most comprehensive expatriate sites, including resources, links and directories covering most expatriate destinations. You can also subscribe to the free monthly online expatriate magazine, Escape from America.

ExpatAccess (⌨ www.expataccess.com): Aimed at those planning to move abroad, with free moving guides.

ExpatBoards (⌨ www.expatboards.com): A comprehensive site for expatriates, with popular discussion boards and special areas for Britons and Americans.

Expat Exchange (⌨ www.expatexchange.com): Reportedly the largest online 'community' for English-speaking expatriates, including articles on relocation and a question and answer facility.

Expat Forum (⌨ www.expatforum.com): Provides cost of living comparisons as well as over 20 country-specific forums.

Expat Mums (⌨ www.expat-moms.com): Information for expatriate mothers.

Expat Network (⌨ www.expatnetwork.com): The UK's leading expatriate website, which is essentially an employment network for expatriates, although it also includes numerous support services and a monthly online magazine, Nexus.

Expat Shopping (⌨ www.expatshopping.com): Order your favourite foods from home.

Expat World (⌨ www.expatworld.net): Information for American and British expatriates, including a subscription newsletter.

Expatriate Experts (⌨ www.expatexpert.com): Run by expatriate expert Robin Pascoe, providing advice and support.

Global People (⌨ www.peoplegoingglobal.com): Includes country-specific information with a particular emphasis on social and political issues.

Living Abroad (⌨ www.livingabroad.com): Includes an extensive list of country profiles, which are available only on payment.

Outpost Information Centre (⌨ www.outpostexpat.nl): Contains extensive country-specific information and links operated by the Shell Petroleum Company for its expatriate workers, but available to everyone.

Real Post Reports (⌨ www.realpostreports.com): Includes relocation services, recommended reading lists and 'real-life' stories written by expatriates in cities throughout the world.

Save Wealth Travel (⌨ www.savewealth.com/travel/warnings): Travel information and warnings.

Trade Partners (⌨ www.tradepartners.gov.uk): A UK government-sponsored site providing trade and investment (and general) information about most countries, including the USA.

The Travel Doctor (⌨ www.tmvc.com.au/info10.html): Includes a country by country vaccination guide.

Travelfinder (⌨ www.travelfinder.com/twarn/travel_warnings.html): Travel information with warnings about danger areas.

World Health Organization (⌨ www.who.int): Health information.

The World Press (⌨ www.theworldpress.com): Links to media sites in practically every country in the world's media.

World Travel Guide (⌨ www.wtgonline.com): A general website for world travellers and expatriates.

Yankee Doodle (⌨ www.yankeedoodleiow.com): Import American products.

Websites for British Expatriates

British Expatriates (⌨ www.britishexpat.com and www.ukworld wide. com): These websites keep British expatriates in touch with events and information in the United Kingdom.

Trade Partners (⌨ www.tradepartners.gov.uk): A government-sponsored website whose main aim is to provide trade and investment information for most countries. Even if you aren't intending to do business, the information is comprehensive and up to date.

Websites for Women

Career Women (⌨ www.womenconnect.com): Contains career opportunities for women abroad plus a wealth of other useful information.

Expatriate Mothers (⌨ http://expatmoms.tripod.com): Help and advice on how to survive as a mother on relocation.

Spouse Abroad (⌨ www.expatspouse.com): Information about careers and working abroad. You need to register and subscribe.

Third Culture Kids (⌨ www.tckworld.com): Designed for expatriate children.

Women Abroad (💻 www.womanabroad.com): Advice on careers, expatriate skills and the family abroad. Opportunity to subscribe to a monthly magazine of the same name.

Worldwise Directory (💻 www.suzylamplugh.org/worldwise): Run by the Suzy Lamplugh charity for personal safety, the site provides practical information about a number of countries with special emphasis on safety, particularly for women.

APPENDIX D: WEIGHTS & MEASURES

Germany uses the metric system of measurement. Those who are more familiar with the imperial system of measurement will find the tables on the following pages useful. Some comparisons shown are only approximate, but are close enough for most everyday uses. In addition to the variety of measurement systems used, clothes sizes often vary considerably with the manufacturer (as we all know only too well). Try all clothes on before buying and don't be afraid to return something.

Women's Clothes

Continental	34 36 38 40 42 44 46 48 50 52
UK	8 10 12 14 16 18 20 22 24 26
USA	6 8 10 12 14 16 18 20 22 24

Pullovers

Pullovers	Women's	Men's
Continental	40 42 44 46 48 50	44 46 48 50 52 54
UK	34 36 38 40 42 44	34 36 38 40 42 44
USA	34 36 38 40 42 44	sm med lar xl

Men's Shirts

Continental	36 37 38 39 40 41 42 43 44 46
UK/USA	14 14 15 15 16 16 17 17 18 -

Men's Underwear

Continental	5	6	7	8	9	10
UK	34	36	38	40	42	44
USA	sm	med		lar	xl	

Note: sm = small, med = medium, lar = large, xl = extra large

Children's Clothes

Continental	92	104	116	128	140	152
UK	16/18	20/22	24/26	28/30	32/34	36/38
USA	2	4	6	8	10	12

Children's Shoes

Continental	18	19	20	21	22	23	24	25	26	27	28	29	30	31	32
UK/USA	2	3	4	4	5	6	7	7	8	9	10	11	11	12	13

Continental	33	34	35	36	37	38
UK/USA	1	2	2	3	4	5

Shoes (Women's and Men's)

Continental	35	36	37	37	38	39	40	41	42	42	43	44
UK	2	3	3	4	4	5	6	7	7	8	9	9
USA	4	5	5	6	6	7	8	9	9	10	10	11

Weight

Avoirdupois	Metric	Metric	Avoirdupois
1oz	28.35g	1g	0.035oz
1lb*	454g	100g	3.5oz
1cwt	50.8kg	250g	9oz
1 ton	1,016kg	500g	18oz
2,205lb	1 tonne	1kg	2.2lb

Length

British/US	Metric	Metric	British/US
1in	2.54cm	1cm	0.39in
1ft	30.48cm	1m	3ft 3.25in
1yd	91.44cm	1km	0.62mi
1mi	1.6km	8km	5mi

Capacity

Imperial	Metric	Metric	Imperial
1 UK pint	0.57 litre	1 litre	1.75 UK pints
1 US pint	0.47 litre	1 litre	2.13 US pints
1 UK gallon	4.54 litres	1 litre	0.22 UK gallon
1 US gallon	3.78 litres	1 litre	0.26 US gallon

Note: An American 'cup' = around 250ml or 0.25 litre.

Area

British/US	Metric	Metric	British/US
1 sq. in	0.45 sq. cm	1 sq. cm	0.15 sq. in
1 sq. ft	0.09 sq. m	1 sq. m	10.76 sq. ft
1 sq. yd	0.84 sq. m	1 sq. m	1.2 sq. yds
1 acre	0.4 hectares	1 hectare	2.47 acres
1 sq. mile	2.56 sq. km	1 sq. km	0.39 sq. mile

Temperature

°Celsius	°Fahrenheit	
0	32	(freezing point of water)
5	41	
10	50	
15	59	
20	68	
25	77	
30	86	
35	95	
40	104	
50	122	

Notes: The boiling point of water is 100°C / 212°F.

Normal body temperature (if you're alive and well) is 37°C / 98.4°F.

Temperature Conversion

Celsius to Fahrenheit: multiply by 9, divide by 5 and add 32. (For a quick and approximate conversion, double the Celsius temperature and add 30.)

Fahrenheit to Celsius: subtract 32, multiply by 5 and divide by 9. (For a quick and approximate conversion, subtract 30 from the Fahrenheit temperature and divide by 2.)

Oven Temperatures

Gas	Electric	
	°F	°C
-	225–250	110–120
1	275	140
2	300	150
3	325	160
4	350	180
5	375	190
6	400	200
7	425	220
8	450	230
9	475	240

Air Pressure

PSI	Bar
10	0.5
20	1.4
30	2
40	2.8

Power

Kilowatts	Horsepower	Horsepower	Kilowatts
1	1.34	1	0.75

Appendix E: MAP OF GERMANY

The map opposite shows the 16 German states and their capitals (indicated by black dots) and other major towns (white dots). Note that Berlin, Bremen and Hamburg are city states with their own 'state' governments. The states are listed below, with the German name in brackets where it differs from the English name.

Baden-Württemberg

Bavaria (Bayern)

Berlin

Brandenburg

Bremen

Hamburg

Hesse (Hessen)

Lower Saxony (Niedersachsen)

Mecklenburg-Western Pomerania (Mecklenburg-Vorpommern)

North-Rhine Westphalia (Nordrhein-Westfalen)

Rhineland-Palatinate (Rhineland-Pfalz)

Saarland

Saxony (Sachsen)

Saxony-Anhalt (Sachsen-Anhalt)

Schleswig-Holstein

Thuringia (Thüringen)

INDEX

D

E

N

O

P

Q

R

S

LIVING AND WORKING SERIES

Living and Working books are essential reading for anyone planning to spend time abroad, including holiday-home owners, retirees, visitors, business people, migrants, students and even extra-terrestrials! They're packed with important and useful information designed to help you **avoid costly mistakes and save both time and money.** Topics covered include how to:

- Find a job with a good salary & conditions
- Obtain a residence permit
- Avoid and overcome problems
- Find your dream home
- Get the best education for your family
- Make the best use of public transport
- Endure local motoring habits
- Obtain the best health treatment
- Stretch your money further
- Make the most of your leisure time
- Enjoy the local sporting life
- Find the best shopping bargains
- Insure yourself against most eventualities
- Use post office and telephone services
- Do numerous other things not listed above

Living and Working books are the most comprehensive and up-to-date source of practical information available about everyday life abroad. They aren't, however, boring text books, but interesting and entertaining guides written in a highly readable style.

Discover what it's *really* like to live and work abroad!

Order your copies today by phone, fax, mail or e-mail from: Survival Books, PO Box 146, Wetherby, West Yorks. LS23 6XZ, United Kingdom (☎/▤ +44 (0)1937-843523, ✉ orders@ survivalbooks.net, ▣ www.survivalbooks.net).

BUYING A HOME SERIES

Buying a Home books are essential reading for anyone planning to purchase property abroad and are designed to guide you through the jungle and make it a pleasant and enjoyable experience. Most importantly, they're packed with vital information to help you **avoid the sort of disasters that can turn your dream home into a nightmare!** Topics covered include:

- Avoiding problems
- Choosing the region
- Finding the right home and location
- Estate agents
- Finance, mortgages and taxes
- Home security
- Utilities, heating and air-conditioning
- Moving house and settling in
- Renting and letting
- Permits and visas
- Travelling and communications
- Health and insurance
- Renting a car and driving
- Retirement and starting a business
- And much, much more!

Buying a Home books are the most comprehensive and up-to-date source of information available about buying property abroad. Whether you want a detached house, townhouse or apartment, a holiday or a permanent home, these books will help make your dreams come true.

Save yourself time, trouble and money!

Order your copies today by phone, fax, mail or e-mail from: Survival Books, PO Box 146, Wetherby, West Yorks. LS23 6XZ, United Kingdom (☎/▤ +44 (0)1937-843523, ✉ orders@ survivalbooks.net, 🖳 www.survivalbooks.net).

ORDER FORM

ALIEN'S GUIDES / BEST PLACES / BUYING A HOME / DISASTERS / WINES

Qty.	Title	Price (incl. p&p)*			Total
		UK	**Europe**	**World**	
	The Alien's Guide to Britain	£5.95	£6.95	£8.45	
	The Alien's Guide to France	£5.95	£6.95	£8.45	
	The Best Places to Buy a Home in France	£13.95	£15.95	£19.45	
	The Best Places to Buy a Home in Spain	£13.45	£14.95	£16.95	
	Buying a Home Abroad	£13.45	£14.95	£16.95	
	Buying a Home in Britain	£11.45	£12.95	£14.95	
	Buying a Home in Florida	£13.45	£14.95	£16.95	
	Buying a Home in France	£13.45	£14.95	£16.95	
	Buying a Home in Greece & Cyprus	£13.45	£14.95	£16.95	
	Buying a Home in Ireland	£11.45	£12.95	£14.95	
	Buying a Home in Italy	£13.45	£14.95	£16.95	
	Buying a Home in Portugal	£13.45	£14.95	£16.95	
	Buying a Home in Spain	£13.45	£14.95	£16.95	
	How to Avoid Holiday & Travel Disasters	£13.45	£14.95	£16.95	
	Renovating & Maintaining Your French Home	Autumn 2003			
	Rioja and its Wines	£11.45	£12.95	£14.95	
	The Wines of Spain	£15.95	£18.45	£21.95	
				Total	

Order your copies today by phone, fax, mail or e-mail from: Survival Books, PO Box 146, Wetherby, West Yorks. LS23 6XZ, UK (☎/▤ +44 (0)1937-843523, ✉ orders@ survivalbooks.net, 💻 www.survivalbooks.net). If you aren't entirely satisfied, simply return them to us within 14 days for a full and unconditional refund.

Cheque enclosed/please charge my Amex/Delta/MasterCard/Switch/Visa* card

Card No. _ _ _ _   _ _ _ _   _ _ _ _   _ _ _ _

Expiry date _____   Issue number (Switch only) _____

Signature _____   Tel. No. _____

NAME _____

ADDRESS _____

_____

_____

* Delete as applicable (price includes postage – airmail for Europe/world).

ORDER FORM

LIVING & WORKING SERIES / RETIRING ABROAD

Qty.	Title	Price (incl. p&p)*			Total
		UK	Europe	World	
	Living & Working Abroad	£16.95	£18.95	£22.45	
	Living & Working in America	£14.95	£16.95	£20.45	
	Living & Working in Australia	£14.95	£16.95	£20.45	
	Living & Working in Britain	£14.95	£16.95	£20.45	
	Living & Working in Canada	£16.95	£18.95	£22.45	
	Living & Working in the Far East	Winter 2003			
	Living & Working in France	£14.95	£16.95	£20.45	
	Living & Working in Germany	£16.95	£18.95	£22.45	
	Living & Working in the Gulf States & Saudi Arabia	£16.95	£18.95	£22.45	
	Living & Working in Holland, Belgium & Luxembourg	£14.95	£16.95	£20.45	
	Living & Working in Ireland	£14.95	£16.95	£20.45	
	Living & Working in Italy	£16.95	£18.95	£22.45	
	Living & Working in London	£11.45	£12.95	£14.95	
	Living & Working in New Zealand	£14.95	£16.95	£20.45	
	Living & Working in Spain	£14.95	£16.95	£20.45	
	Living & Working in Switzerland	£14.95	£16.95	£20.45	
	Retiring Abroad	£14.95	£16.95	£20.45	
				Total	

Order your copies today by phone, fax, mail or e-mail from: Survival Books, PO Box 146, Wetherby, West Yorks. LS23 6XZ, UK (☎/▤ +44 (0)1937-843523, ✉ orders@ survivalbooks.net, 💻 www.survivalbooks.net). If you aren't entirely satisfied, simply return them to us within 14 days for a full and unconditional refund.

Cheque enclosed/please charge my Amex/Delta/MasterCard/Switch/Visa* card

Card No. __ __ __ __   __ __ __ __   __ __ __ __   __ __ __ __

Expiry date _____   Issue number (Switch only) _____

Signature _____   Tel. No. _____

NAME _____

ADDRESS _____

_____

_____

* Delete as applicable (price includes postage – airmail for Europe/world).

OTHER SURVIVAL BOOKS

Survival Books publishes a variety of books in addition to the *Living and Working* and *Buying a Home* series (see previous pages). These include:

The Alien's Guides: *The Alien's Guides to Britain* and *France* provide an 'alternative' look at life in these popular countries and will help you to avoid the most serious gaffes and to appreciate more fully the peculiarities (in both senses) of the British and French.

The Best Places to Buy a Home: *The Best Places to Buy a Home in France* and *Spain* are the most comprehensive and up-to-date sources of information available for anyone wanting to research the property market in France and Spain and will save you endless hours choosing the best place for your home.

How to Avoid Holiday and Travel Disasters: This book is essential reading for anyone planning a trip abroad and will help you to make the right decisions regarding every aspect of your travel arrangements and to avoid costly mistakes and the sort of disasters that can turn a trip into a nightmare.

Renovating & Maintaining Your French Home: New for 2003 is the ultimate guide to renovating and maintaining your dream home in France, including essential information, contacts and vocabulary and time and cost-saving tips.

Retiring Abroad: This is the most comprehensive and up-to-date source of practical information available about retiring to a foreign country and will help to smooth your path to successful retirement abroad and save you time, trouble and money.

Wine Guides: *Rioja and its Wines* and *The Wines of Spain* are required reading for lovers of fine wines and are the most comprehensive and up-to-date sources of information available on the wines of Spain and of its most famous wine-producing region.

Broaden your horizons with Survival Books!

Order your copies today by phone, fax, mail or e-mail from: Survival Books, PO Box 146, Wetherby, West Yorks. LS23 6XZ, United Kingdom (☎/▤ +44 (0)1937-843523, ✉ orders@ survivalbooks.net, ▱ www.survivalbooks.net).